THE TRIALS AND TRIUMPHS OF

LES
DAWSON

Louis Barfe

Atlantic Books
LONDON

First published in hardback and trade paperback in Great Britain in 2012 by
Atlantic Books, an imprint of Atlantic Books Ltd.

This paperback edition published in Great Britain in 2012 by Atlantic Books.

9 8 7 6 5 4 3 2 1

A CIP catalogue record for this book is available from the British Library.

ISBN: 978 184887 251 6

The Trials and Triumphs of Les Dawson

Louis Barfe was born in 1973 in Epsom, Surrey. He studied at Lancaster University. He has written for *Private Eye*, *The Oldie*, *New Statesman* and the *Independent on Sunday*. His books include *Where Have All the Good Times Gone: The Rise and Fall of the Record Industry* and *Turned Out Nice Again: The Story of British Light Entertainment*.

For Judy Godman, my mother-in-law

CONTENTS

LIST OF ILLUSTRATIONS

1. The Dawson family. Private Collection.
2. Thornton Street, Collyhurst. Courtesy of Manchester Libraries, Information and Archives, Manchester City Council.
3. Dawson the boxer. Mirrorpix.
4. Dawson in his Sunday best. Mirrorpix.
5. Dawson and Army pals. Private Collection.
6. Trooper Dawson. Private Collection.
7. Dawson and friends. Private Collection.
8. Les and Meg at the Hoover works dinner and dance. Private Collection.
9. Les and Meg sign the register. Private Collection.
10. The Dawson family. Private Collection.
11. Cissie Braithwaite and Ada Shufflebotham. Author's Collection.
12. *The Dawson Watch*. Author's Collection.
13. *Workers' Playtime* anniversary admission ticket. Author's Collection.
14. Dawson with Ruth Madoc and Su Pollard. Author's Collection.
15. Bill for the Grand Theatre, Blackpool. Author's Collection.
16. Les and Tracy's wedding. Mirrorpix.
17. Dawson with Charlotte. Mirrorpix.
18. Dawson in *The Les Dawson Show*. ©PA/Topham.
19. Dawson as Morton Stanley in *Demob*. Brian Moody/Scope Features.

INTRODUCTION

When Les Dawson died on 10 June 1993, it was one of the very few occasions where the great comedian's timing deserted him. Changes in television light entertainment had meant that he was finding it harder to get the quality and quantity of work that he was used to, and Dawson was wondering if his career was on the wane. His last series of *The Les Dawson Show* for the BBC had been in 1989, and *Blankety Blank*, the game show that he had made his own after Terry Wogan moved to a thrice-weekly chat show, had come to an end in 1990. Another game show, *Fast Friends*, had lived up to the first half of its title by lasting for only one series in 1991.

Perhaps surprisingly, though, for a man who mined laughs from a pit of pessimism, he acknowledged the silver lining of his professional cloud: that his declining fortunes as a performer would give him more time to write, one of his great passions. Also, drama directors were beginning to recognize his qualities as a straight actor. Dawson was more than just a gag machine, and undoubtedly would have used his considerable intelligence to continue his career of creativity one way or another, even if his days as a top-flight comic were numbered.

Which, of course, they weren't. Had Dawson survived even another decade, he would have undergone a renaissance similar to that of Bob Monkhouse – panel games, the Edinburgh Festival, younger comedians queuing up to drop his name as an influence. He shared one important quality with Monkhouse: a generosity of spirit, born from a lack of professional insecurity. Like Monkhouse, Dawson knew how good he was, and he also realized that if a show got a laugh, it reflected well on everyone involved. Morecambe and Wise had the same attitude. While many top-line performers look after number one to the exclusion of all else, and ensure that the pole they clambered up is well greased to prevent others joining them, Dawson always had time for everyone and didn't try to keep all of the best lines for himself. Had he lived, he would have been 80 in 2011, the proud father of four children, with the youngest still only in her late teens. It's impossible not to conclude that he went far, far too soon.

Although his shows are rarely repeated, there remains a surprisingly high level of awareness of his work, alongside an unsurprisingly immense reserve of public love and goodwill towards this great performer and indisputably genuine man. People barely old enough to remember his TV career refer to pulling 'a Les Dawson face'. Situations are still described as 'like something out of a Les Dawson monologue'. Standing only five feet six inches when alive, in the afterlife he casts a long, benign shadow over the nation.

Looking at Dawson's life, what becomes apparent are the contradictions. His carefulness with money was balanced by a great generosity when it came to giving his time. When at home with his family, he favoured tea by the gallon. Away from home, faced with the temptations of the touring life, he could drink anyone under the table. Even though he was always coming up with new comic ideas and material, he had a tendency to fall back on old standbys. Physically fearless and willing to do anything in pursuit of a laugh, he could be a coward when faced with confrontation in his professional life. In short, he was human, and that's why audiences loved him and continue to love him.

What follows is the story of a comedian who, perhaps more than any other, spoke for the phlegmatic, resigned, sarcastic, glorious British attitude to life.

CHAPTER 1

'Slumps don't bother me. I was a failure during the boom.'

In global terms, 2 February 1931 was just another average Monday in the Great Depression. Over in the US, the House of Representatives and the Senate were in deadlock over drought and unemployment relief. In Britain, a weavers' union deputation trekked to London to protest to Cabinet ministers about the 'more looms' system, whereby they were expected to work harder for less pay, while Winston Churchill used a speech in support of the Tory candidate in the East Toxteth by-election to denounce the Labour Government of the day, led by Ramsay MacDonald. There was some good news, though. On the sands of Ormond Beach, Daytona, Captain Malcolm Campbell pushed his car *Bluebird* to an unofficial speed of 240 mph, beating Sir Henry Segrave's world land speed record of 231.36 mph.[1] Meanwhile, there was derring-do closer to home when a film crew taking aerial footage of London had to make a casualty-free emergency landing in a Brixton garden.

While all this was going on, 203 miles north of Brixton, at 246 Thornton Street, Collyhurst, in the Blackley sub-district of Manchester North, a boy was born to Julia Dawson, formerly Nolan, and her brick-layer husband Leslie, after whom the child was named. The two-up, two-down house was home not only to the Dawsons, but also to Julia's parents, David and Ellen Nolan, and her brother, Tom. In other words, as a result of financial strictures, Leslie Dawson senior was forced to live with his in-laws. Leslie junior never had a middle initial and would never use a professional pseudonym, being proud to take his father's name to the top of the bill at the London Palladium. He would save the fancy stuff for the comic characters he would go on to play, among

1

them the myopic lecher Cosmo Smallpiece, a down-at-heel actor known variously as Quentin Sadsack and Rathbone Mole, drunken conjuror Zebediah Twine, and gurning housewife Ada Shufflebotham.

In later life, Dawson made light of the environment in which he grew up. 'Manchester in the thirties ... was a depressed decade and most of the people who lived in our area were decayed,' he wrote in 1983.[2] He wasn't exaggerating for comic effect. Writing about a nostalgic programme Dawson made in 1982, *Guardian* TV critic Nancy Banks-Smith observed that Dawson's Mancunian accent had rendered the place of his origin as 'Colliers', leading her to wonder if he had been 'perhaps lacking a home of his own – as W.C. Fields had, when a boy, lived in a hole in the ground'.[3] Collyhurst and the 'cramped room lit by sickly gas'[4] where Dawson entered the world were better than a hole in the ground, but it was a deeply deprived neighbourhood.

On the day that Dawson was born, the *Manchester Guardian*'s front page advertised a free lecture by the Reverend H. Allen Job, FRGS, FZS, at Platt Hall Branch Gallery and Museum on 'The Treasure Island of Tasmania', while the works of L.S. Lowry were on show at the Salon Gallery in Oxford Road. The adult Dawson would devour lectures and trips to art galleries, but the item of greatest interest to Collyhurst residents in February 1931 would have been the masthead advertisement for Wood Street Mission, asking for 'food, clothing and footwear' to pass on to 'needy children'.[5]

In the mid-thirties, Collyhurst was, according to *The Times*, 'the largest single area for slum clearance in any clearance area in the country'.[6] Today, there is still a thoroughfare called Thornton Street, but the back-to-backs of Dawson's youth have been replaced with tidy, low-rise eighties' housing. John Donnelly, one of Dawson's contemporaries, remembered the old Collyhurst as a place of 'thousands of shops with everything in – second-hand shops, home-made toffee shops – there used to be a barber's with a big gym at the back. He trained a lot of champions, you could have a haircut and watch them train'.[7] When neighbours died, everybody pitched in. 'They used to lay the bodies out, clean 'em up, tek the kids in and feed 'em,' Donnelly recalled, admitting that, despite the suffering, he 'enjoyed being a kid in Collyhurst'.

So did Dawson, who, when not revelling in his adult reminiscences of squalor and deprivation, tended to romanticize slightly the place and era of his birth. In 1985, looking disdainfully at 'cities that are dying for the want of a community more interested in people than possessions', he recalled a time when 'nobody locked their doors, old citizens never died for want of caring, no child ever lacked supervision. Every street was a commune. Each one had its amateur midwife, undertaker, judge and medical advisor … If two men fought, it was with fists and fair play, and all the policemen were beefy Sons of Erin, who corrected an offender with a judicial clout, not a charge sheet.'[8]

It's a lovely, evocative piece of writing, and Dawson had a point about materialism, with credit now accessible, however temporarily, to those who all too often can't afford the items they covet. But had anyone said to his childhood neighbours that they didn't know how lucky they were, they would likely have been given a robust response. In 1959, pioneering documentary maker Denis Mitchell recorded the sights and sounds of the back-to-backs in Liverpool and Manchester, as well as the thoughts of the residents, in his BBC Television film *Morning in the Streets*. One of the men interviewed by Mitchell declared 'Oh no, it's a better world than it was. I'm sure of that,' while one of the women provided greater detail:

> Oh, you've no idea how we lived. Fancy five of us in one bed. Five of us, and my mother used to be trying to cover us, and she'd have old coats on us, you know. And the night men would come and knock at the door, and if that man found three of us in that bed, my mother was brought to the court and fined five shillings. And you'd have to go out in the back yard in the shivering cold and sit in the lavatory until he went. The good old days? There were no good old days. We're cursed.[9]

The grinding poverty and lack of hope in the thirties led some to be seduced by far-right politics, and the large Jewish community in

Manchester made the city a potential target for fascists. In 1934, with support for his British Union of Fascists declining in the south of England, Sir Oswald Mosley, who had strong family links with the city, considered moving his political headquarters there. On 29 September of that year, Mosley addressed a thousand of his black-shirted supporters at a rally in Belle Vue Gardens; another seven hundred people also attended, many of them dead set on drowning him out with shouts of 'Down with the blackshirt thugs' and 'We want Mosley alive or dead'. Aided by amplification, Mosley was able to retort that his taunters were 'sweepings of the continental ghettoes, hired by Jewish financiers' and 'an alien gang imported from all corners of Britain by Jewish money to prevent Englishmen putting their case'.[10] Years later, Dawson claimed that Leslie senior was one of the working-class Mancunians who joined Mosley's blackshirts, but 'for one reason only: he needed a shirt no matter what the colour'.[11] It's a superb line, but it may be merely that, a line. If true, it's unlikely that the cash-strapped Dawson senior attended the rally, for, as *The Times* noted, Belle Vue Gardens was 'a pleasure resort to which admission was obtainable only on payment'.[12]

Employment in the building trade was hard physical work. Dawson remembered his father's 'calloused and angry red hands',[13] and Julia 'rubbing oil into his back because he was a hod-carrier ... He was in terrible pain with his back and I always remember that and the sense of despair'.[14] There was also precious little job security, with the work being mostly casual and requiring him to be peripatetic. When times were good, a builder could go from one site to the next without a break. In the slump, Leslie senior had to take whatever work he could when he wasn't needed on the sites, and some of his money-making schemes were of dubious legality, raising funds as 'a card sharp ... a back-street gambler, a billiard hall marker'.[15]

Living with Julia's family was only ever meant to be a temporary situation, but it was one that lasted several years. By the mid-thirties, a major programme of building work was underway in Thornton Street itself, with Corporation flats being erected, but by then Julia and both her Leslies were at last able to move. Their first home was a terraced house at 168 Moston Lane, Blackley, where they lived until the early years of the Second World War.[16] With Leslie senior serving overseas, Julia and young Leslie then moved to Lightbowne Road, New Moston. The family's final settling place was a smart semi-detached house at 21 Keston Avenue, Blackley, into which the Dawsons moved in 1945.

At some point in the late thirties, Julia became pregnant a second time, but the child died. From Dawson's different accounts of this tragic event it's unclear what exactly happened. In his autobiography, his younger brother, named Terry, is referred to as 'stillborn', but when recounting the incident to Anthony Clare in 1993, Dawson said 'I had a brother but he died, he died when he was very young'.[17] No new infant Dawsons appear on the Manchester North births register in that period, so the stillbirth is likely to be the true version.[18] Certainly that would fit with Dawson's recollection of 'people rushing in the house and, you know, holding my mother down and all the rest of the house in a turmoil ... Everybody was there to dance attendance on the pregnancy', suggesting that the aforementioned Collyhurst community spirit had as much to do with nosiness as caring.[19] There's little doubt that Cissie and Ada, the gossips who became a major part of Dawson's act forty years later, would have been in that room on that awful day.

On Dawson's mother's side the blood was Irish, and his grandmother was given to singing the rebel song 'The Wearing of the Green' when in her cups, as well as settling arguments with a flat iron secreted in her handbag. Her son, Tom Nolan, Julia's brother, might have been a street fighter, but old Mrs Nolan ruled the roost. Julia herself had, in her son's words, 'the dark beauty found only in a slum child'.[20] Unbelievable as it may seem, when considering his later physiognomy, the young Dawson took very much after his mother in looks. Beer, beef and boxing would turn the striking dark-eyed child into the rotund, gurning Les of adulthood.

One story of the Dawsons' poverty came up in Les's first appearance on *This Is Your Life* in 1971, concerning a trip to Morecambe with the

56th Manchester Scouts. Dawson had to get there by whatever means he could, as his friend Ken Cowx remembered: 'I was lucky enough to be treated to the train fare, but Les had to follow on an old bike ... Les and I, I think, had the distinction of being the hardest-up scouts in the troop, and that bike of his, where he got it from or how he made it, I don't know. I think it had tyres patched up with pieces of wellington boot.'[21] That week in Morecambe was, Dawson said, 'the only holiday the boy ever had'. With no spending money, he 'won the other scouts' respect by being able to get pennies out of machines by poking thin wire into the slots'.[22] The main pleasure of the excursion was, however, free, it being the first time the young Dawson had ever seen the sea.

The family's dire financial straits were made up for by kindness, decency and a great deal of affection from both parents, Julia in particular. She 'cried and laughed a lot ... and she cushioned me with love'.[23] Dawson remained unashamedly sentimental for the rest of his life, and while the impression left by the lack of financial security lasted to his death, so did the emotional security and stability of his youth. In a business where needy performers are the norm, Dawson never became one, having known real genuine need. 'He was very generous with praise,' recalls friend and scriptwriter David Nobbs. 'Not necessarily verbal praise, [but] just laughing at your jokes and not thinking "Wait a minute, I'm the man who makes the jokes around here." Les was uncontrollable with delight at the comedy of life. Les slapping his thigh when you topped him with a gag. That's the generosity.'[24]

Children from Collyhurst were never expected to amount to much, and Dawson recalled the 'limited scope' of the education he received at Moston Lane Infants' Elementary School.[25] The one glimmer of hope was the eleven-plus, with the prospect of a place at North Manchester High School for Boys on Chain Bar in Moston. Dawson failed the exam and spent his secondary school years at Moston Lane Elementary, where he did not distinguish himself academically or athletically. One event at Moston Lane, however, would become part of the Dawson mythology.

[T]here was one teacher who breathed life into the lessons ... tall, grey, spare man ... Bill Hetherington was at heart an actor ... he inspired and gave confidence. One day, Bill had me in front of the whole form and he took me to task about my maths and geography, two subjects about which even he could not enthuse me. I had been bent over and given six of the best, and it was hard for me not to sob openly with pain and humiliation. 'Before Dawson goes back to his seat, I'd like to say a word about his essay from yesterday' ... Bill began to read my essay ... 'A Winter's Day'.[26]

Dawson recalled that the essay began 'Mantles of white gentleness caress a sullen earth', suggesting that the florid tone and love of overegged prose that would later serve him so well comedically was in place from an early age. In Dawson's version, as Hetherington's reading went on, both Dawson and the rest of the class expected that ridicule and scorn would soon follow. Instead, Hetherington declared the essay 'superb' and stated that Dawson had 'the talent to be a fine writer'. As we shall see, Dawson wasn't averse to improving anecdotes, but almost always from a base of truth. So we can be reasonably sure that, even if the details were polished retrospectively, Dawson did receive a morsel of praise from an admired teacher, and cherished that praise to his dying day. And Dawson made another important discovery at Moston Lane: his writing talent was matched by his ability to make his classmates laugh. 'I was small and chubby, I could pull sidesplitting faces, and I had a gift for mimicry,' he recalled fifty years later. 'I made my entrance on the stage of existence.'[27]

Dawson took his cue from a combination of variety performers and film comedians. It has become tempting to view all of this old-school comedy as a barrage of rotten gags and worse catchphrases. The whole attitude was encapsulated brilliantly in the nineties by *The Fast Show*, with the character Arthur Atkinson, played by Paul Whitehouse. The unlovely Atkinson trotted out impenetrable nonsense; lines that sounded like jokes because of the speed and rhythm of their delivery, but which, on closer inspection, contained not a single atom of humour or sense. The quick-fire merchants undoubtedly existed. A listen to any of the surviving recordings of Tommy Handley's cross-talk-heavy forties radio series *ITMA* (*It's That Man Again*) will prove as much – while not as humourless as Atkinson's shtick, the rattling pace of the delivery accounts for around 90 per cent of the entertainment value. The settings of the Atkinson sketches and the character's nasal voice also bear a slight resemblance to the surviving footage of Max Miller on stage, but there the similarity ends – if anything, Atkinson was an unfunny version of the hilarious Miller.

The best of the variety comedians were, however, cleverer and more subtle than is usually acknowledged now, particularly the northern contingent, many of whom were gentle and eloquent, rather than relentless. Although known nationally to radio audiences, Robb Wilton was purest Lancashire, and a lover of words. Mike Craig, a respected comedy writer and later historian, called Wilton one of the 'phrase makers'. There's a particularly fine example of Wilton's phrase-making at the start of one of his best known sketches, where he plays a hapless, hopeless police constable:

> They don't give you much to work on. 'Description of man wanted. Dressed in brown suit, all except blue serge coat and trousers. Hair, just turning grey. May have turned, by the time *you* catch him. Believed to be lurking in some passage, between Yarmouth and Aberdeen.' Oh well, I mean, you can't work on a thing like that.[28]

The care taken in the choice of words only becomes obvious if you try to substitute alternatives. 'Lurking in some passage' is funnier than 'hiding in an alley'. Yarmouth and Aberdeen are not intrinsically funny place names, unlike, say, Kettering or Penge, but used in conjunction they work splendidly, as Great Yarmouth is 530 miles from Aberdeen. A brown suit with blue serge trousers isn't a brown suit, it's just a brown jacket. Also, the fact that the culprit is wearing blue serge raises the faint possibility that he stole his clothes from one of Wilton's constabulary colleagues. When asked by Michael Parkinson in 1974 about his influences, Dawson cited Robb Wilton without a second's hesitation, explaining that he reflected the experiences of privation shared by many in the north at the time:

> Humour in the north … was based on adversity more than anything else … and people like Robb Wilton and all the other great comics were steeped in this. There was a great warmth and depth. One of his lovely things was where he said 'Things were very bad. A friend of mine said, "Let's buy a greyhound and win a few bob at White City." So we bought a greyhound called Flash. I wouldn't say it was slow, but on its first race, the hare bit its leg. I said to this friend of mine, I said, "This is ridiculous, it's costing a fortune in fodder. Let's get rid of it." My pal said, "You're quite right, I'll tell you what we'll do, we'll throw it in the canal." "Oh," I said, "there's no need to do that. We'll just run away from it."' That's the sort of humour that transcends the so-called generation gap. It's a funny remark with a lot of heart in it.[29]

Another 'phrase-maker' was the notorious Wigan-born funnyman Frank Randle, a subversive soul who specialized in lecherous characters onstage and biting the hand that fed him offstage. Facing a ban from the Moss Empires circuit for using the word 'bastard' in his act, he claimed he was telling an over-enthusiastic audience to pipe down in Italian: 'Basta! Basta!'. Meanwhile, a disagreement over a bar bill caused Randle to smash every fitting in his dressing room at the Hulme Hippodrome. Randle claimed that nobody could drink £96 worth of alcohol in a week, and that the bar managers were trying to fleece him. The truth was that Randle probably could drink that much, even when £96 was a sizeable down-payment on a house. This was, after all, a man who slept with a crate of Guinness under his bed and a bottle opener on a string around his neck.

Randle had entered show business by accident; he was working out at an Accrington gym when a representative from an acrobatic troupe that had arrived at the local Hippodrome for the week came looking for someone to stand in for their indisposed 'catcher'. Having the required strength to catch flying performers, Randle took the job and found the stage life to his taste. However, despite being a robust man, he came to be best known for his decrepit grotesques, characters who were all stoop and libido, not least of which was a creation called 'the Old Hiker':

> Eighty-two and I'm as full of vim as a butcher's dog. I'm as lively as a cricket ... I attributes me excellent health to moderation, exercise and plenty of fresh air ... just look at these for a pair of legs. I tossed a sparrow for these and lost.[30]

Norman Evans was another performer who was regarded as a demigod in the north. Equally at home sat at a piano in an evening suit or in drag, his best-known characters included the pessimistic Auntie Doleful, bringing misery to all around her, and particularly those she visited in their sickbeds:

> You're not looking too well, are you? I brought some flowers. I thought if I was too late they'd come in handy, but I see you're still here. I tell you what, it's a very awkward bend at the top of t'stairs here to get a coffin down, isn't it? Scrape t'wallpaper a bit, won't they ... You want a drink of water? Yes, you're looking a lot worse than when I just come in.[31]

Auntie Doleful is less well remembered now than Evans's other great creation, the toothless gossip conducting a one-sided conversation over a garden wall. Evans was also a proficient pianist, a skill that he put to comic use with versions of the same tune played by musicians of varying ability, from a naughty schoolboy forced to take piano lessons to a stuffy, pompous church organist. Over thirty years later, Dawson would take elements of Wilton's, Randle's and Evans's styles and develop them in his own image. Evans's influence would be the most obvious, but Wilton made his presence felt in a more subtle manner. One of his comic tics was to place his little finger in his mouth to give himself a contemplative air. It was a bit of business that Dawson lapsed into many times on television, later on, when Wilton was far less well known than he had once been. Dawson knew that a proportion of his audience would appreciate the homage.

One other comedian who represented a less obvious, but no less important, influence on Dawson was Jimmy James, regarded in the profession as 'the comedian's comedian', the one they all admired and watched. Even performers who were not known for their modesty bowed down to the great Jimmy James, as his son James Casey explains:

> Tommy Trinder, who was the biggest thing in show business at the time, walked into the café where all of the pros used to go, for coffee, and said in a loud voice – well of course, everything with him was in a loud voice – he said, 'Have you seen Jimmy James? Have you been to the Palladium? Well, if you haven't, get there as soon as you can and learn what comedy timing is all about, because he is the master.'[32]

A teetotaller who did the best drunk act in the business, James had been born James Casey in Stockton-on-Tees in 1892. He had begun in variety aged 12, having run away from home to fulfil his ambition. In his early days, he worked as part of a singing group, but eventually switched to comedy, relying less on jokes than on incongruities and a bemused, laconic, deadpan delivery. Timing was important, but James's material was endlessly inventive and whimsical. Usually taking the stage to the strains of Liszt's *Liebestraum*, he was assisted, or rather hindered, by a buffoon in a hat and long coat going by the unlikely name of Hutton Conyers, and a stammering overgrown schoolboy in a deerstalker, who had been given the name of Bretton Woods.[33] James fielded Conyers' ludicrous claims and conspired with Woods to get rid of the lunatic interloper, to little avail. James's best-known routine concerned Conyers approaching James with the question 'Is it you that's putting it about that I'm barmy?', before proving himself to be so by claiming to have, variously, a giraffe, an elephant and two man-eating lions in a box stowed under his arm. James begins by thinking himself a beacon of sense and reason, but Conyers' relentless abuse of logic begins to make him wonder whether he's not a madman too. Woods makes some valiant attempts to rationalize the absurd situation, but gets only a withering response from James: 'I'll stop you going to those youth clubs'.

Slightly less well remembered, but no less funny, was the 'Chipster' routine, which became a favourite of young Les Dawson's. It begins with a complaint that the band is playing the wrong music for Woods (also known as Eli), who is now a pop singer. 'That was ballet,' James tells the musical director. 'He doesn't do the ballet now, not since he had the accident doing the *Nutcracker Suite*. That brought the tears to your eyes, didn't it?'[34] This was a staple of James's act, putting words into Eli's mouth, partly out of necessity, given Woods's genuine stammer. On walks Conyers, to whom James replies that he's not looking for any trouble, having given up a good job to put Eli on the stage:

JAMES: I was the head chipster at my uncle Joe's fried-fish shop. You're not talking to a mug. You're talking to the champion chipster of Europe. Eight years running, chipping champion ... Mind you, I used to cheat in the championships. I used to use King Edwards. You're not supposed to. Now you see, King Edward potatoes have got no eyes. They can't see the chopper coming down and you get more chips. Keep that to yourself ... You're not interested, are you? You don't care about anything. You don't care about the Government. Are they in or out? Was it you who put them in?

CONYERS: No.

JAMES: Are you sure?

CONYERS: Yes.

JAMES: It was somebody like you, then ... There's a knack in this chipping. I know I can tell you and you won't let it go any further. You get hold of the potato on the block and you get hold of the handle, and it's on-pull-chop, on-pull-chop. Only, get your fingers out quick, or you'll think you've got more chips than you've chopped. You can see them, bad chipsters, hundreds of them all over the country walking about ... You can always tell a bad chipster. He walks into a pub and says 'Four pints'. [*Holds up index finger and little finger*][35]

Other occupational hazards proliferate, most memorably chipper's wink and batterer's elbow. However, of all James's lines, Dawson was most enamoured of the revelation that a good chipster puts the potato on the block sideways. 'Your chips are shorter, but there's more of 'em,' ran the logic.[36] Another favourite was the price charged by Eli's mum when she took in lodgers to make ends meet: 'She charged them a pound all in, use of cruet.'[37]

James's flow of comic invention was not confined to working hours. Even when his chronic gambling addiction caught up with him and bankrupted him for the third time, he emerged from the courtroom and told the waiting press that this verdict meant he had won the Official Receiver outright. Then there was the day when he took advantage of the old music-hall rule that the first person to place their band parts on the stage each Monday morning could lay claim to a particular song. Appearing on the same bill as Petula Clark, he connived with the musical director to claim her latest hit as part of his act. 'He had her going with it for a whole afternoon,' Barry Cryer relates. 'He was wicked. They sang it terribly, and she's standing there: "They're doing my song". "Sorry, love, we're doing this. We close the act with it, it goes down very well," and she's standing there. Wicked.'[38] Jim Casey recalls another incident where an elaborate joke was woven solely for the benefit of a young television floor manager:

We'd been hanging about for a long time when this studio manager came up and said, 'Ah, Mr James, glad I've caught you. Now what exactly do you do?' I would have probably said 'underwater paper-tearing' or something, but he said, 'I'm glad you asked because Eli's been worried about it. I've told him not to worry. You know what you're doing, you fellows. Now, when we open on the trapezes in Chinese costumes, singing "By the blue lagoon she's waiting" in three-part harmony, it'll be all right because the camera doesn't have to move. But when we finish, with a bowl of goldfish in our teeth, spinning them, will it be wide enough for all of us? That's what he's been worrying about. I've told him that you've got it all worked out, you lads.' This fella just ran to the producer and then I was able to laugh. I said to my father, 'Three Chinese singing "By a blue lagoon she's waiting?"' He said, 'It's a great song. Don't you know it?' Where did that come from? Instead of coming back with one line, he created this wonderful picture of three Chinese hanging upside down spinning bowls of goldfish. That's what he always used to do. He was the greatest ad-libber I ever knew, in all my experience, but he didn't just ad-lib a line. What he did was he created a picture.[39]

A certain young Mancunian would later do the same, and also become a close friend of Jim Casey's.

In his formative years, Dawson was also, like most cinema-goers of his generation, looking to the other side of the Atlantic for inspiration and escapism. However, while most had Clark Gable and Betty Grable in their sights, Dawson was discovering a profound love of the great American comedian W.C. Fields. In later life, it didn't take much for Dawson to lapse into a pitch-perfect impersonation of his hero, but there would be other similarities. Both liked a drink. Both wrote a lot of their own material. Both loved wordplay and silly names: one of Fields's regular noms-de-plume was Mahatma Kane Jeeves, while, in *The Bank Dick*, he bestowed on a drunk and incapable film director character the glorious monicker of J. Pismo Clam.

Later on, in the fifties, when many young men were glued to the wireless each week for *The Goon Show*, Dawson was out playing the pubs and clubs of Manchester. He can't have been unaware of Spike Milligan's comedy revolution, but it didn't reach him in the same way as it would some of his generation. When he finally came to prominence, the mature Dawson's comedy remained more in the spirit of those film comics and earthy northern variety surrealists than much British comedy, providing a link back to a previous era.

Rationing seemed to have the least effect on those who were used to poverty and want. In some ways, it levelled the playing field and gave the less needy an idea of what it was like to go without. Julia made ends meet with various jobs, while Leslie senior was away serving with the Eighth Army. All through the war, the Hallé Orchestra played on, under various conductors including Malcolm Sargent and Sir Henry Wood, giving concerts at the Paramount cinema on Oxford

Street (which became the Odeon in April 1940) and the Opera House. Pubs did a brisk trade too, as Mancunians tried to keep calm and carry on. Money being short, some pleasures were still free, including books from the public library, a welcome resource for a lad who had taken away from his limited education the beginnings of a love of words and their application.

During the early part of the war, the city got away lightly in the various bombing raids, but with so much vital heavy industry based in the area, it was unsurprising that Manchester would take a hefty beating eventually. The worst damage came on the nights of 22 and 23 December 1940, an event that became known as 'the Manchester Blitz'. Among the casualties of those two nights were Manchester Cathedral, the Royal Exchange and the Free Trade Hall in the city centre, and numerous houses were also hit. Dawson later remembered telling his children 'about seeing corpses lying twisted in burning debris'.[40] As a result, for boys and girls of Dawson's vintage lucky enough to escape unscathed – Dawson having spent some time in Blackpool as an evacuee – there were bomb sites to explore, and other distractions, like 'hanging around on street corners, brawling, looking at girls as the sex drive meshed into gear; delivering newspapers in order to supplement the family income, and ... petty pilfering on the side'.[41]

The brawling did not come naturally to Dawson, despite his physique and the Nolans having a pugnacious streak. In an ideal world, he would have used his love of the English language to avoid violence, but it wasn't at all an ideal world, and eloquence was treated with suspicion. '[T]o talk about poetry in the area I was brought up in meant of course you were wearing nylon stockings and a blouse. You didn't talk about things like that ... you had to appear hard, you see,' he explained in 1993.[42] Declaring himself, unashamedly, to be a coward, he tried to avoid confrontation where possible. When it proved impossible, he took little pride in a successful outcome:

I remember fighting one kid who was at the top of the school and for a week I was physically sick; then, when we had a fight he hit me and a red

mist came down and I knocked and the next thing, he's on the floor ...
[T]hat horrified me that I could do that, you see.[43]

There was one notable benefit to having a reputation as a handy
fighter. It increased the chances of being left alone. Although outwardly sociable and full of cheer, Dawson liked to maintain a little
distance between himself and most others. He was self-contained
and self-sufficient, traits that remained until the end of his life. Many
would come to regard him as a friend, but very few outside his family
felt they ever truly got close to him. What Dawson called cowardice can
perhaps be interpreted more as self-preservation. With the extreme
poverty of his upbringing, he was a survivor. He could have walked
around Collyhurst foppishly with a slim volume of T.S. Eliot sticking
out of his pocket, but that would have invited trouble. The result was
that he could switch from being a sensitive, eloquent, deep-thinking
young man to one of the lads very easily. This adaptability was later at
the heart of his bathetic comedy.

Dawson never regarded his contemporaries as beneath him, but
he realized early on that he was cut from a different cloth. Almost
from birth, he took equal delight in the highbrow and the lowbrow.
Until 1946, radio's cultural treats could be found on the Home Service,
nestling between mainstream programmes like *ITMA, Happidrome*
and *Monday Night at Eight.* When the Forces Programme became
the entertainment-led Light Programme, and the opera and classical
side of radio got its own network – the BBC Third Programme – many
bemoaned the move and feared ghettoization, preferring a world
where the mass audience could chance upon great art. Moving it to
its own network meant they'd have to seek it out. Dawson's radio-
listening habits in these formative years are undocumented, but, as
an adult comic, his points of reference were equal parts Home, Light
and Third, with a sudden retuning from Third to Light having the
greatest comic effect.

In all Dawson's reminiscences of his youth, his mother is the
dominant figure. She, he believed, was responsible for his wit, being

'a great mimic' and 'full of good humour'.[44] His father's influence was diminished greatly by his absence during the Second World War. Until Leslie senior was called up, father and son had been close. The absence of paternal guidance was all too apparent to Dawson as an adult. Reflecting on his youth in 1985, he observed that 'we were a lost generation, the discipline wasn't there, either at home or at school'.[45] Compared to some of his associates, though, Dawson was an angel. One notorious urchin was 'always in trouble with authority [and] finished up doing many years in prison, as many of my contemporaries did'.[46] The delinquent in question came to Dawson's attention when he joined a boxing club, he says, 'to fight my innate cowardice'. The red mist descended again, Dawson flattened the hard man and achieved acceptance.

It was a boxing injury that gave Dawson the mobility of jaw that would serve him so well professionally, providing the basis for Ada Shufflebotham's gurn and Cosmo Smallpiece's leer, two of the characters that would feature most prominently in Dawson's later career. Dawson's experiences in the boxing ring also inspired some of his early writing. In an essay entitled 'My First Fight', featured in a 2004 television documentary about Dawson's diaries, the comedian recalled: 'Friends all around the ring – the lights shining brilliantly down ... We touch gloves – my heart pounds within me; my blood surges madly in my temples; my stomach trembles; thoughts run wildly through my head – will I lose? Will I win? Sweat, grunts, the thud of gloves against flesh and the quickening of one's breath. It is then the end – what is the verdict – I lose on points. Dejected, I leave the ring. My friends say "Hard luck" and so forth, but 'tis of no avail. I *have* lost.'[47] The style is a little overwrought, a cross between a newspaper report and a hard-boiled crime story, but it shows distinct promise in terms of pacing. In any case, it seems very unlikely that Dawson's opponent went home and wrote up the experience at all. No, Les was definitely different.

Looking at Dawson's self-assessments, the word 'cowardice' is a recurring theme. It's true that Dawson grew to hate confrontation. In later life, his colleagues noted a tendency to take the least satisfactory option in any dilemma if it was the one that guaranteed short-term peace. However, cowardice and pragmatism are two different things, and, in other ways, Dawson was anything but yellow. He was physically robust, and writers and directors knew that whatever they wanted him to do, he'd do it, as long as it was funny. 'I think Les was pretty fearless, generally,' says Andy Hamilton, who worked with Dawson at the start of his own long and distinguished comedy-writing career.[48]

By the time the VE Day celebrations got underway, Dawson had turned 14, and his education was at an end. It was time for him to go out to work. Had he been born ten years later, improved educational opportunities might have enabled him to capitalize on his wayward brightness rather more than he had, being undoubtedly intelligent, but lacking application. However, the Education Act of 1944 arrived too late to make any difference to his choices. With a father still awaiting demob and nothing on the curriculum to engage his interest, it made sense for Leslie junior to go out and bring some money into the house. When his father finally came back from service in North Africa, the returning hero was, to young Leslie's eyes, a diminished creature compared to the man who had left the family home years before. 'He was a taller man that went and a much younger man, a vibrant man,' Dawson recalled in 1993, adding that he thought 'This isn't the dad I had'. The adult Dawson realized that the child had been fooled by an illusion created by his own development. It was the same dad, 'but of course, I'd grown up'.[49] Indeed he had.

Dawson's first job was as a dogsbody in the drapery department at the Co-operative Wholesale Society's headquarters in Balloon Street, Manchester. It entailed 'dragging basketwork skips through winding labyrinths from one underground vault to another' for 21 shillings a week.[50] He regarded the job as 'soul-destroying', but Julia approved, for one simple reason. '[My] mother's idea of a successful life was security at all costs and the only thing that ever seemed secure to our very small and limited lives was the Co-op,' he told Anthony Clare in 1993.[51]

After the privation she had been through, her gratitude and caution were understandable and, given its high ethical standards, the Co-op was just about the best employer an unskilled worker could hope to have. The prospects were good for those who kept their heads down and did their jobs well. The young Les Dawson was not one of them. When he threatened to jack in his safe but back-breaking job, a compromise was reached with Julia, and it was agreed that he would seek alternative employment within the CWS. An apprentice electrician's job came up, and Dawson applied successfully. 'It was', he said years later, 'to prove a grave error of judgement: I was to that employ what the Pope is to brothel management.'[52] In adulthood, Dawson admitted that he couldn't 'look at a fuse without bursting into tears', such was his technical ineptitude.[53] Working on complicated installations in commercial premises, his lack of skill was, at best, a hindrance. At worst, it was a serious safety hazard. Somehow, though, he kept his job.

When he wasn't putting the lives of his colleagues in danger with his wiring skills, his meagre earnings went mostly into the tills of the pubs of Collyhurst, Blackley and Moston. Rochdale Road was a popular crawl for Dawson and chums, bounded by the Derby Arms at 500 Rochdale Road, known to all as 'the Bottom Derby', and the Derby Inn at number 935, referred to locally as 'the Top Derby', later taking the name officially. In between was the Milan, while just off Rochdale Road was what would later become Bernard Manning's Embassy Club.

There was also the matter of sex. He spent his late teens 'constantly trying' for it but largely failing.[54] He claimed that he was relieved of his virginity at the age of 17 on the vandalized back seat of a number 61 bus by, of all people, the conductress, 'a formidable matron of generous proportion'. His rather brutal experience with this 'uniformed harridan' left him feeling 'utterly dirty and disgusted'.[55]

Dawson's progression from boy to man was completed by his conscription into the army in the summer of 1949. He went to Catterick Camp in North Yorkshire for his basic training, and had his initial cockiness knocked out of him by a drill sergeant, the whole experience adding greatly to his understanding of self-preservation. 'I began to learn the art of surviving in a military jungle,' he recalled in his first volume of memoirs, *A Clown Too Many*. 'When my kit was stolen I went out and stole somebody else's. When any NCO appeared, I made myself look busy. I learnt never to volunteer for anything, and older hands taught me how to creep out of camp for a night's booze in Richmond.'[56] After the six-week training period, Dawson went to Dale Barracks near Chester to join the Queen's Bays (2nd Dragoon Guards) as a trooper. On 19 October 1949, during his short stay there before the Queen's Bays were posted to Bad Fallingbostel in Lower Saxony, West Germany, the Queen herself came as commander-in-chief to inspect her troops and unveil a new war memorial.

Out of necessity, Dawson picked up a smattering of conversational German in his National Service years. Something he didn't pick up at this time was venereal disease, although he claims to have had a narrow escape with a whore when interrupted by Military Police looking for soldiers fraternizing with the locals. Caught in the head-lights of their truck, he said he saw the sores on her body and ran. He reluctantly continued boxing through his army days, which, along with his sense of humour, doubtless helped his reputation with his fellow squaddies. There was something that made him a favourite of the officers too, and meant that they were willing to overlook his occa-sional transgressions against military discipline: Dawson could play the piano. His elementary education hadn't included tuition in any musical instrument, and Dawson only discovered his musical ability during his army service. One day, at a loose end, he sat at a mess piano and began to pick out tunes by ear. Soon he was proficient enough to entertain his associates. The talent came into its own on Cambrai Day, celebrated in tank regiments on 20 November each year to mark the Battle of Cambrai in 1917, the first time that tanks were used seriously in warfare. It was Cambrai Day 1950 when Dawson was hauled into the officers' mess at Fallingbostel and instructed to play drinking songs for the officers. His playing passed muster and 'from then on ... life became quite tolerable'.[57]

The limits of his tolerance were, however, tested by global events. When Dawson began his military service, the standard period of conscription was eighteen months. In June 1950, just as Dawson's intake was reaching the home straight and looking forward to demob, North Korea invaded South Korea, an action that resulted in intervention from UN forces, including the British. Three months later, Prime Minister Clement Attlee responded by extending the National Service period to two years. So, not only did Dawson have to endure six further months of military service, there was the realistic prospect of being sent to fight in a real war, with all of the risks that entailed. Hardly the ideal outcome for a self-confessed coward. Fortunately, the call never came, and Dawson merely spent a few extra months in Germany as a reluctant boxer but an enthusiastic mess-room entertainer, finally being demobbed in the summer of 1951. The regulated nature of military life appealed to some directionless young men, but not Dawson. 'The burden of regimentation was a manacle to my soul,' he observed in 1985, 'and I unshackled it with a burning relief.'[58]

He went back to his old job as a Co-op apprentice electrician, until his ineptitude finally caught up with him and he was sacked. Fortunately, menial work that paid just enough for a lad's beer was easy to come by, but Dawson was convinced that he was cut out for something different, something better. He just didn't quite know what. His diary entries for this interim period, some of which were featured in a 2004 television documentary about his early life, are not what might be expected from a failed Co-op apprentice. 'Long-haired, with a pronounced leaning towards philosophy, I find myself a complete rebel to conformity; a rebel against progress: in fact most everything. I am alone – utterly alone . . . I am determined to break away from this life – a life of absolute dreariness and try to rise from the mire.'[59]

Eventually, seizing on his old teacher's prediction, he decided to become a writer. From his childhood, he had been a voracious reader, developing a particularly great love of the novels of Nevil Shute, whose *Trustee from the Toolroom* he chose as his book on *Desert Island Discs* in 1978. Many years later, he gave his friend Bob Monkhouse some insight into his reading habits. 'I love to read Sherlock Holmes because Conan Doyle hated the character and put things in there so ridiculous', he told Monkhouse.[60] Unfortunately, the example he gave – Watson being unable to comprehend that a musician could also be a murderer, with Holmes pointing out that Moriarty was a virtuoso bassoonist – appeared not in any of Conan Doyle's original stories, but in the 1945 film *Pursuit to Algiers*.[61] When Alan Plater was asked to adapt Anthony Trollope's Barsetshire novels for television, he accepted, having not yet read them himself, but having had glowing reports from Dawson. 'I remembered Les saying they were good, so I said yes,' Plater was reported as saying in a 1989 *Observer* profile of the comedian, adding that 'I read the lot with Les's voice in the background.'[62]

The means by which Dawson aimed to become an author has become part of his mythology, repeated in books and on chat shows. In his own version, he went to live in Paris, and ended up paying his keep by working as a pianist in a brothel, playing only the Charlie Chaplin composition 'Limelight' from the film of the same name. He talks of surviving on 'dry bread and wine so cheap, it was probably fermented for a shilling a gallon',[63] and of growing an 'existentialist' beard. The length of his stay varies, but is always recounted as having lasted for months rather than weeks or days.

In fact, as C.P. Lee pointed out in the television documentary *Les Dawson's Lost Diaries*, the Parisian sojourn lasted a mere ten days, and was, from the outset, planned as a holiday, or, more accurately, a jolly boys' outing. Dawson claimed to have made the trip alone, but closer inspection of the diary entries reveals that Dawson went to Paris with friends from Manchester, named in his diary as Roy and Joe. Travelling on the midnight train to London on Monday 6 July 1953, they then caught another train to Newhaven for the Dieppe ferry, reaching Paris on Wednesday, 8 July. ' Paris at last!' cries Dawson's journal. 'The wines: the food: the women! Oh la! la! We go on the Eiffel Tower: boozing in cabarets to hot music – the life of a lord.'[64] The phrase 'hot music' recurs in Dawson's diary entries for the entire trip, as do references to 'lovely prostitute[s]', 'lovely whore[s]', 'hot carresses' [*sic*], and the lads' dwindling supply of money, as 'we gorge ourselves on steaks and wine'. It wasn't all bacchanalian, though. There are also enthusiastic references to museum and exhibition visits. In the official version of the story, the initial heady fun of being in Paris is replaced by a stark descent into extreme hardship. 'She is magnificent: if you have money,' Dawson observed.[65] As Dawson and pals were able to borrow money from their landlady, on a strict promise of paying her back once they'd returned to Manchester,[66] they experienced only the magnificence of the French capital, and the diary entries make it clear that they had a ball. The tales of poverty are merely Dawson extrapolating what probably would have happened had he stayed on any longer.

Dawson almost certainly did find himself playing piano in a Parisian brothel, but only for a couple of nights, and then unpaid. In the official version, he refers to an intoxicating affair with a black prostitute called Emerald, and as the diaries refer to a night spent 'play[ing] the piano in a nightclub again mauling the negress',[67] this element of the tale seems to be based in fact. From these kernels of truth grew a seductive and far from implausible fiction that outlived its creator. In a 1974 interview, Michael Parkinson seems to nail the inspiration for the expanded, embroidered brothel story, when he points out to Dawson that W.C. Fields also worked as a bordello pianist. From boyhood visits to the cinema right up to his death, Dawson venerated Bill Fields, and adopting the brothel story as his own seems likely to have been an act of homage. So, Les Dawson's great Paris story is, at best, only half-true. Far from being the profound philosophical interlude that he later claimed, it seems to have been business as usual, only in a foreign city. However, while the details were 'improved', both the real course of events and the mythical version show the deep impression left by Paris on the young man.

After this, Manchester seems to have been an anti-climax. Dawson refers to the 'dreary trip' home and 'how dead they [his regular run of pubs] seem'. Compared to Paris, Manchester may have felt dreary, but compared to the rest of the British Isles in those days of austerity and rationing, Manchester was a hive of fun. Indeed, although Dawson's contemporary reaction to his home city was one of disappointment, viewed from a distance of thirty years, he seemed more inclined to see the excitement. Writing in 1983, he mentioned the 'three hundred nightclubs ... within a seven-mile radius of Piccadilly' where 'for the price you would pay for a pint in an ordinary pub, you could see all the top stars of the day'.[68] Places like Dino's, the Northern Sporting Club, the Garden of Eden, the Stork Room, the Stage and Radio, the Square Wheel and Foo Foo La Mar's (which was owned by noted Mancunian drag artiste Frank 'Foo Foo' Lammar) were all bursting with vitality and entertainment, as Royston Mayoh, later a producer at ABC Television in Manchester, but then just a teenage show business fan, recalls:

> It was wonderful. The whole place was jumping with clubs. I'm living in Levenshulme now. Just behind me here, there's a big restaurant called Al Waali's. That was the Southern Sporting Club when I was a lad. The Yew Tree pub in Wythenshawe was the best pub in town with acts. The acts queued up at seven o'clock to go on, just rolling acts all night. Frank Tansey was the pub owner at the Yew Tree, and he notoriously went out every now and again: 'Will somebody buy some focking beer?' It was packed, wonderful.
>
> There was a Catholic club called Our Lady Queen of Sorrow. There's a wonderful story about Jimmy Tarbuck, there. He went on and halfway through his act, everybody stood up and went down on their knees. He thought 'What the hell's going on?' and the priest was there, because the priest always did the prayer at nine o'clock. Right in the middle of his act.
>
> The clubs were electric. There was Mr Smith's in Manchester, the Cabaret Club, Wilton's, the Ponderosa in Chorlton. There were thousands of them. I used to go out every night, not drinking, just walking from club to club, because I'd hear 'The Delmonts are on at such and such'. A wonderful duo. 'Oh Christ, you've just missed ...' A trapeze artist in a pub.[69]

Having learned to play the piano during his National Service years, after demob he began to ply his skills in the pubs of north Manchester and, emboldened by his success, he wrote to BBC North's variety department at Broadcasting House on Manchester's Piccadilly in June 1953, asking for an audition. Comedy was not yet part of the repertoire, as he billed himself as a singer with a tenor/baritone range and jazz pianist. The verdict when he auditioned on 17 August 1954 was blunt. Producer John Ammonds's report read: 'Popular baritone. Badly out of tune. Quality of voice unpleasant,' while a colleague called Dawson 'a typical club singer. Very harsh,' and declared him 'no use for broad-casting'.[70] When Dawson asked for feedback, Ammonds mentioned the tuning issue and suggested that Dawson wait six months before re-auditioning, during which time he should work on the faults.

One audition he did pass was for a show called *Pick of the Town* at the Hippodrome in the Manchester district of Hulme, a bill put together by Liverpool-based variety agent Jack Billings, in October 1955.[71] Comedy was starting to creep into Dawson's act, for which he 'wore a ginger wig and imitated Quasimodo'.[72] In Dawson's version of events, Billings was caught trying to abscond with the show's meagre takings, which were re-appropriated by the cast and spent communally in the pub. At this time, Dawson was still living with his parents in the semi-detached council house at 21 Keston Avenue, Blackley, and he claimed that on the night of the Hulme show his mother pulled him indoors quickly, in case anyone saw him. Both Leslie senior and Julia had been in the audience, and their critical notice for their boy was simply 'You were bloody awful'.[73] With such successes, Dawson was unlikely to be earning a living from entertainment any time soon, so he kept up a succession of day jobs. Briefly a salesman for the Liverpool Victoria insurance company, he went on to a more enduring berth with Hoover, spending a total of nine years on and off selling vacuum cleaners and washing machines. He was lucky enough to have an understanding and accommodating manager called George Walker, who gave him time off for theatrical engagements when he could.

It was this post-demob period of daily drudgery and night-time novelty that shaped the Les Dawson a nation would come to love. Although a bright child, he had lacked focus. When he went out to work, he found his first job at the Co-operative Wholesale Society mind-numbing and back-breaking, but had scant concept of how to break out of a seemingly inevitable lifetime of menial work and penury. Like so many of his generation, his period of National Service was the turning point. The experience of submitting mindlessly and completely to authority sat badly with him, and the question became how to avoid authority figures or at least minimize their impact on his life. National Service showed him in no uncertain terms what he didn't want to do, and it also gave him a clue about what he did want to do, having been responsible for his real beginning as an entertainer. Once away from military strictures, the apparently free and easy life of the performer appealed.

Although he continued to harbour dreams of becoming a serious writer, slowly Dawson came to realize that his growing grasp of vocabulary could be put to excellent comic use. 'What I tried to do, before I started to get recognized, was to try and make a word picture,' he told Professor Anthony Clare in 1993. 'For instance, I used to use a thing in the opening of the act ... "The ashen-faced mourners hunched closer together as a cold grey fog embraced its clammy shroud, the wind howled like a lost soul in torment and from beyond the dark, brooding, rain-sodden hills, a demented dwarf strangled his pet raccoon" – one two three – "On a wonderful day like today" – which, looking back, it's a wonder I got out of these clubs alive.'[74] There were two reasons Dawson was allowed to survive. For one thing, he was distinctive, or, to put it as the punters might have done, a funny little bugger. One incident he related many years later illustrates his situation. Appearing on a radio show recorded at a Blackpool theatre with Liverpudlian comic Jimmy Gay, Irish comic Harry Bailey and singer Rosemary Squires, Dawson reported that he had received no more than 'polite applause', while Gay was rewarded with 'roars' and Bailey 'had them in the palm of his hand'. Coming off after his act, and sensing that the younger performer was upset, Gay told Dawson that he had no reason to be depressed, as he was very good and very different. Gay then led him to a spot near the pass doors by which the audience left the theatre, where they could hear the mutterings while remaining unseen. 'All talked about the jokes Jimmy and Harry had told, but never mentioned them by name, but all of them, despite not liking me very much, knew my name,' Dawson related in 1985.[75] The wise and kind Gay pointed out that they had all remembered Dawson rather than what he had said, and that personality not material was what made a performer a star. It seems likely that this is, like Paris, an example of Dawson misremembering or even embroidering a story. The only radio billing where Dawson is listed with Gay is for the 5 August 1962 edition of *Blackpool Night*. Rosemary Squires and Harry Bailey were not on that show.

The other thing that would endear Dawson to audiences was his lack of airs and graces. While many big names viewed fellow professionals as 'us' and the audience as 'them', to Dawson there was only ever one big 'us'. Even when he was in full flow with the mother-in-law and nagging wife jokes that would form the backbone of his future act, mothers-in-law and wives could laugh along, secure in the knowledge that they were nowhere near as bad as the proto-Fascist gorgons in the gags. Dawson always sought out good conversation, finding plenty in the clubs and pubs where he performed. 'People is [*sic*] what life's about,' he explained to Anthony Clare, outlining a theoretical situation where he and the psychiatrist 'were to go on to O'Connell Street [in Dublin] to a pub which we'd both enjoy enormously, just the two of us, and we'd talk about the world, we'd talk about psychiatry, we'd talk about philosophy, reincarnation, whatever you like. I wouldn't want that night to end, so I will keep you there as long as possible, till the whole of the Liffey and O'Connell Street is empty and dawn's rising.'[76] Dawson was intelligent and inquisitive, and only ever resorted to pretentiousness as a comic device, debunking it almost instantly. He was always listening, always picking up on what people were saying. Partly because he knew that some of it would make good material, but mostly because he was genuinely interested in his fellow men, and what they had to say.

He was also very interested in his fellow women. Despite being brutal about his physical shortcomings, never being 'the stuff of a young girl's dreams', but rather 'short and wide across the shoulders and with a tendency to run to fat', he doesn't seem to have wanted for female company in his twenties. There were the girls from the shows he worked in, including a stripper from a nude revue, to say nothing of the women from the audience who hung around afterwards to get to know the comic a little better. At one point, he claims he was ready to elope with the daughter of an Italian ice cream manufacturer, but when she failed to turn up at the rendezvous, he went to a pub, got drunk, 'picked up a red-haired girl and made love to her in a cemetery'.[77]

Elements of Dawson's early life resemble the plot of *Billy Liar*. Apart from the al fresco fumbling and the desire to break into comedy, Dawson's professional ineptitude seems to have rivalled Billy Fisher's antics at the undertaker's office. Hoover had posted Dawson to 'an area of tight slumland' called Moss Side. He was sent there, he claimed, because the area needed to be covered, though the company never expected to receive any orders – an ideal sinecure for a salesman of his self-confessed incompetence. However, while the work was merely something he did to meet his financial commitments, it furthered his insight into people and the way life was lived. 'It may seem incongruous that my mundane job . . . should be a veritable fount of experience,' he said years later, 'but going into divers homes was just that.'[78] Although Moss Side was to become notorious as the city's drugs, guns and gangland centre in the eighties, it was merely poor and rough in the fifties, when it 'teemed with a rich polyglot stream of humanity, from Irish to Dyak head-hunters'.[79] Whatever he thought of the rest of the work, Dawson enjoyed meeting and talking to people, and doubtless several of the sales he managed to close were achieved with the help of his sense of humour. There was repair work to be undertaken too, the simpler the better given Dawson's technical ineptitude. The repair job he remembered best was just before Christmas at a household where the husband had managed to mislay his whole week's wages. The festive season was looking grim until Dawson found that the small brown envelope had become sucked into the vacuum. Apart from life-enhancing moments like that, he viewed the day job as a necessary evil, with a professional performing career as his ideal, but the two jobs were similar in many ways, the main difference being one of scale and product. When Dawson traversed the north of England in his company van to make his appearances as a comedian and singer, he was still acting as a travelling salesman, only this time he was selling his personality and his material.

Dawson was to remain in Hoover's employ for most of the fifties, but not continuously. One substantial break in his Hoover service on Moss Side came when he moved from his home city to London. As 1955 turned into 1956, Dawson saw that variety star Max Wall was auditioning talent at the Hippodrome in Ardwick, Manchester, and decided to chance his arm. Wall saw something he liked in the rough and ready young Mancunian and suggested that he move to the capital for the sake of his career. Wall, at that time, was at the top of the tree; he had his own regular BBC Television show and was also appearing as time-and-motion man Vernon Hines in the musical *The Pajama Game* at the London Coliseum on St Martin's Lane. Dawson needed little persuasion to follow Wall's advice. Although Wall could not offer him any regular work, he could offer guidance and opportunities, in addition to paying for Dawson to have singing lessons with a teacher in Leeds named Madam Styles Allen. Dawson handed in his notice at Hoover and, after a wild night out with the lads on Friday, 3 February 1956, headed south.

Very soon after he arrived, it seemed that Dawson was in the right place at the right time. Musicians' Union members were on strike, refusing to take part in BBC Television shows, and Equity members were encouraged to come out in sympathy. As a result, the edition of *The Max Wall Show* scheduled to go out on BBC TV on Sunday, 19 February, was suddenly without an orchestra or a guest star, as Wall's *Pajama Game* colleague, the Canadian singer Edmund Hockridge, had been instructed not to appear by Equity. The orchestra was to be replaced by a pianist called Roma Clarke and an organist by the name of Lloyd Thomas, while Hockridge's place would be taken by

Wall's young northern protégé. Any nerves at the prospect of the live transmission were swept aside by the excitement. 'I was walking on air,' Dawson recalled later. 'People pumped my hand and London, dear old London was Disneyland after all.' He also claimed that 'all the newspapers carried the story about my "big break" into show business ... I recall one such banner line: "Non-Union Unknown Les Dawson Gets Big Show Biz Chance".'[80] If such a headline appeared, it wasn't in the *Daily Express*, the front page of which reported dutifully on the strike and Hockridge's absence, adding at the end, almost as an afterthought: 'Hockridge will be replaced by 24-year-old Les Dawson, who is "unknown" – and non-union.'[81] Nor was it in the *Daily Mirror*, which included a line about 'non-unionist' Dawson's involvement midway down its page seven report of the Hockridge withdrawal. Dawson wasn't mentioned at all in the *Daily Sketch*'s story on the strike, while the *Daily Mail* didn't touch the story either.

In the end, Dawson didn't get his moment of glory. He attended rehearsals at the BBC Television Theatre on Shepherd's Bush Green on Friday, 17 February, but Hockridge then returned, announcing that he would defy union orders. Dawson went back to his digs in Battersea, watching the show in a pub, where he also drowned his sorrows in booze. The 10 guineas the BBC paid him for his non-appearance, which would have been welcome under any other circumstances, came as cold comfort to the dejected Dawson.

He also had the misfortune to be associated with a falling star. It was at this time that Wall faced the moral outrage of the press after leaving his first wife for a beauty queen called Jennifer Chimes. The matter became a public issue on Tuesday, 15 May, with press reports of Wall's wife Maria being granted a decree nisi. Two days later, on 17 May, the newspapers reported Chimes's intention to wed Wall when her own divorce had come through. Divorce was a big issue in the fifties, especially when it involved an entertainer leaving his wife for a younger woman, and Wall soon found it hard to get the prestige bookings to which he had become accustomed. In many ways, he was being castigated for his openness and honesty. Affairs were common in show business, and journalists knew of many situations that they couldn't or wouldn't report. By doing the right thing rather than carrying on with Chimes in secret, Wall became a pariah.

In April, clearly aware of the moral outrage that was about to be directed at him, Wall had been telling Dawson to go back home to Manchester, there being little more he could do for the young man's career. Wall had enough problems of his own without trying to bat for an unknown comic, but there was also the risk that Dawson could be tainted by association. Wall was being cruel to be kind, but that was, naturally enough, not how Dawson saw it. On 13 April, Dawson noted in his diary that it was 'the date which marks the finish of any ambition I may have conceived would happen. Max Wall, after all his promises, and hopes for me, turned to me in his dressing room and said he thought it would be better if I gave the whole idea up of trying to sing'.[82] Wall had a point. As a straight singer, Dawson was distinctly average. His comic skills, as he later acknowledged, were not yet all they could be, either. 'I used to play the piano and sing, tell a few gags,' he told Roy Plomley in a 1985 TV documentary. 'The act in those days was dreadful. It really was bad.'[83] The act he demonstrated for Plomley involved a mid-Atlantic accent, a 'terrible grimace – all the fillings showing', and a great deal of pointing. 'And I'd go, "Hi there, I just love being here, ladies and gentlemen, I'm going to play you a little song, and I hope you like it"', upon which he would launch into some barely decipherable rock and roll. The net result was that he was paid off regularly.

Nonetheless, the experience with Wall was valuable, even if the direct influence seems hard to trace. So much of Wall's comic appeal was physical, with the oversized boots, the bald head, the tailcoat, the 'independent legs' and a routine in which he appeared to lengthen or shorten his arms by pulling or pushing them, that he seems an odd mentor for a comic as verbal as Dawson was to become. In fact, while Wall said few words, they were always impeccably chosen and enunciated. In a surviving recording of his 'Professor Wallofski' stage act, he describes his tuning fork and, in doing so, imbues the word 'chromium' with heaps of lecherous meaning, in a manner that Cosmo Smallpiece would have admired. Another similarity between Wall and Dawson is that they both used a piano as a regular prop.

In the long term, he never forgot Wall's kindness and early faith in him. In the short term, however, Dawson was understandably angry and bitter about his bad luck. 'What shall I do? Where can I go?' he asked his diary. 'My philosophy of life is now clearly etched, namely I don't give a damn whatever happens – I'll never bother about anything again ... What does a man do when his dreams crash around him? I who have just experienced it – go on the beer – lost – degraded and absolutely fed up ... Am I indeed destined for failiure [*sic*]? – no chance – Wall has no confidence in me at all. All is indeed lost now ... wasted and I could willingly die.'[84]

Nevertheless, before cutting Dawson adrift and tending to his own parlous situation, Wall had introduced his protégé to Betty Lawrence, a pianist who worked regularly at the Players' Theatre, a music-hall revival venue beneath Charing Cross station. She and her husband Jack befriended Dawson at a time when he needed friends desperately, and provided him with food, kindness and professional guidance, as well as employing him occasionally as a babysitter. Lawrence also helped Dawson make an amateur recording of a song called 'I Lie and Dream', which became his sign-off in his letters to the Lawrences.

Rather than admit defeat and return to his home city, Dawson stayed on in London for several months, working as a dish washer in restaurant kitchens while hoping for another chance at show business. It didn't come. By August, he was still ' trudg[ing] around the streets of this hostile city banging on agents' doors' to no avail, leading him to conclude, in a drunken diary entry, 'at 25 my life is over: it's been a good one and I'm thankful for those precious years.'[85] The one glimmer of hope that came from the wearying, grinding months spent in London was a booking from an agent called Al Heath, following an audition at the Max Rivers Rehearsal Rooms on Great Newport Street. Admittedly, it was only for a week's engagement in Hull much later in the year, working the fishermen's clubs, but it was an actual booking. Accepting this consolation prize, Dawson 'bade London a temporary farewell' and 'promised myself that one day I'd retrace my steps back to this indifferent city, and I'd win through'.[86]

On his return to Manchester, Dawson resumed his normal social round: pub-crawling with mates and consorting with unsuitable women, funded by occasional paid work as an entertainer in the same drinking haunts. The relative infrequency of his semi professional engagements can be gauged from the glee with which he recorded, on Sunday 28 October, that he was a 'paid artiste' at the White House. The publicans of North Manchester certainly got their money's worth, notwithstanding the certainty that he'd put most of his earnings behind the bar before the night was out. On that night, the punters saw a man 'sing; play the piano; yell rock an' roll and pound the ivorys [*sic*] with jazz; I drink heavy, sweat a lot and have a time with the crowd'.[87]

That Sunday gig was the opener of what was to prove a pivotal week in Dawson's life and career. However, on the Monday morning, there was one bit of business to be despatched before the journey to Hull, in the form of an audition at the ABC Television studios in the former Capitol cinema in the Manchester suburb of Didsbury. Independent television had reached the north-west in May that year, while Dawson had been struggling in London, with Granada providing the weekday programmes and ABC overseeing the weekend output. At the time, the audition would probably have seemed far more important to a fledgling performer than a week playing fishermen's clubs in East Yorkshire, particularly for someone who had come so near to getting national TV exposure not long before. Nothing, however, came of it at that stage, although it was Dawson's first visit to a studio that he would later return to in triumph.

Dawson drove from Didsbury to Hull on the afternoon of 29 October, thrilled to be on his way to do the work that he loved most. He nearly didn't get there: a sudden puncture caused his van to spin around in the road. He recorded in his diary that the incident was a 'narrow escape from death', and he seems not to have been exaggerating.[88] On arrival, the slightly shaken young performer was greeted by the fellow professionals who were sharing the digs that week. One of them, a female singer called Jessie Jewel, was booked for the same round of venues as Dawson, while another, the music-hall star Randolph Sutton, was working at the Palace Theatre in a nostalgia show called *Thanks for the Memory* with the comedian Billy Danvers, male impersonator Hetty King[89] and G.H. Elliott, always billed as 'The Chocolate Coloured Coon'. Both Jewel and Sutton were experienced entertainers compared with the Mancunian. The Brixton-based Jewel, often billed as 'the perfect "cheer-up" girl' had been active since the thirties, mostly in pantomimes and summer seasons, while Sutton was a big name from the past, best known for popularizing the sentimental song 'On Mother Kelly's Doorstep'. Jewel lived up to her cheery billing, befriending Dawson instantly, and joining him for drinks throughout the run, but Sutton was less welcoming. 'Frankly, throughout that week, he was to treat me like a lump of canine excrement,' Dawson recalled nearly thirty years later.[90]

To begin with, the hard-bitten Hull audiences shared Sutton's view of Dawson. In 1974, he recounted the experience on Michael Parkinson's BBC chat show:

> They virtually came straight from the trawler, with barbs, and salt caked on their faces, with a sockful of money, and they sat down and they drank to oblivion. An act was just superfluous. They didn't need an act. I died the death of deaths night after night. In those days, I used to sing, play the piano and get a few laughs. Particularly when I played and sang. One terrible night, they were letting bottles go, and pennies were being thrown. [Parkinson asks, 'What do you mean letting bottles go?'] Well, they used to shake them and take the cork off.[91]

Dawson described the overall effect as 'a sort of alcoholic El Alamein'. Alan Plater, who later wrote the scripts for Dawson's first foray into television drama, knew those Hull audiences well, having grown up in the city, and remembered a far more deadly way of giving duff acts the bird:

> It's a tough, warm city. They were lovely people, but tough people. We started our theatre in Hull in Spring Street in 1970, what's now become the Hull Truck Theatre. We shopped around for fund-raising and Ronnie Hilton was doing pantomime at the New Theatre. He said, 'Look, I'll do a late-night show at one of the clubs for you.' Bless him, we did a late-night show at the Stevedores and Dockers Club. A dockers' club, ergo a tough gig. The club were terrific. They said we'll give you the gate money, we'll take the bar. They raised a lot of money for us. They'd booked a comedian for the early part of the evening. He was from Doncaster and he wasn't very good. They didn't barrack him, the audience just started talking amongst themselves, and getting louder and louder and louder. This guy just gave up and walked off. That's tough. Full-frontal heckling is one thing, but to be totally ignored is something else.[92]

To perform to such indifference is disastrous for an entertainer, but Dawson's week wasn't an unbroken run of failure. Tuesday night's show was at the St Andrew's Club, with 'a real tough audience'. Dawson's coping strategy was to 'sup stacks of ale', but he and Jewel flopped miserably in front of the skippers and their families. However, on Wednesday, there were two gigs. The first, in the afternoon, was a show for pensioners, who proved appreciative. Meanwhile, in the evening, Dawson reported to his diary: 'I bring the house down – dancing and drinking!' Thursday at the Albert Club was a return to Tuesday's form: 'bad audience ... Jessie dies a death and I fare little better'.[93] So Wednesday went well, but was the exception.

The breakthrough, which entered Dawson's mythology through repetition on chat shows and in his autobiography, came on the Saturday night at the Empress Club on Hessle High Road. Once again, Dawson prepared with his customary skinful, finding a pub in a street called the Land of Green Ginger. This time, however, rather than steeling him to carry on with business as usual, the drink emboldened him to try something out of the ordinary. 'When my money had evaporated, I lurched to the club in truculent mood,' he explained, 'prepared to be humiliated once more but ready to curse back, and to hell with the consequences.'[94] Taking the stage, Dawson found that the drink had impaired his ability to stand or focus on the piano keyboard. The exact wording of what followed is lost in the mists of time, but the spirit of the material is consistent in all of Dawson's retellings of that night's events. Describing the venue as either a 'superbly decorated kipper factory' or a 'renovated fish crate' and giving them his low opinion of Hull, Dawson looked that audience in the eye and told them tales of woe firmly based in the reality of his everyday life. 'I don't do this for a living, oh no,' he explained to the Humbersiders, 'just for the luxuries in life ... like bread and shoes.'

To his utter amazement, they lapped it up. The knocking of their home town; the disparaging description of the club, which had recently been refurbished at considerable expense; the too-close-for-comfort jokes about poverty and failure. Suddenly, Dawson was getting big laughs, largely because a performer was meeting them on their own level. Instead of peddling show business schmaltz about how wonderful they were and everything was, a comedian was being honest with them and saying that everything was bloody awful. Unwittingly, Dawson had discovered that his own droll, sardonic personality, or a slightly exaggerated version of it, appealed to audiences. Worried it was a fluke, he tried the style at subsequent bookings and found that it had an amazing effect every time. He had found his voice. Bob Monkhouse later mused on the difference between 'sparse weeknight audiences'[95] and the weekend crowd, but the act that Dawson gave the punters that night was crucial. The weeknighters got what Dawson thought they wanted to hear, with a modicum of success, whereas the Empress audience got what Dawson wanted them to hear.

'It's about telling the truth,' said Alan Plater. 'This thing of any kind of creative artist, finding out who you are, sharing the essence of you with the audience. It doesn't work if what you're offering is a kind of made-up essence, a made-up persona. What you got from Les was Les.

You got the real thing. It takes all of us time to figure out who that is. Certainly when you're younger, insecure, desperate to make a name. Such early scripts of mine that have survived are just full of page upon page of me showing off.'[96]

While many comedians kept notebooks mainly to jot down existing jokes that they'd heard other comedians use, Dawson's jottings tended to be original creations. Lines that he noted down as they came to him in the mid-fifties would continue to serve him well until his death, and were rarely stolen by other comedians because only Dawson himself had the required delivery. A favourite joke formula of Dawson's throughout his career was the 'x is so y that z happens/happened'. Using the word 'formula' seems unfair, because it's what the writer/comedian puts in the places x, y and z that make the jokes. Most of them revolve around poverty, discomfort and disappointment, such as 'The house is so cold we put the milk in the fridge to stop it freezing'.[97] As a quick-fire gag, it's funny enough, but it becomes funnier and more absurd if you have more time to devote to it. If the house is so cold, why does it need a fridge? If the house is freezing, and the fridge is warmer, the pity seems to be that the fridge isn't big enough to sit in.

In Hull, Dawson learned the value of self-deprecation, with lines like 'What you are about to see is an act that has given a whole new meaning to the word "crap"',[98] and 'I'm the only one on this bill I've never heard of'.[99] However, the crucial thing is to use such material to get the audience on side, without them actually agreeing with your own low self-opinion. With many comedians relying on schmaltz or painting someone else as the victim, a comic who put himself down was a novelty, particularly one who did it eloquently. The self-deprecation would prove vital to the success of Dawson's act over the years. It gave him a licence to knock the audience, the venue and the town in which it stood, for example: 'Not the first time I've been in Hull, but last time I was here, it was shut', and 'I didn't believe you were a Yorkshire crowd, after all, you walk upright'.[100] Lines like that, without any leavening humility, would be likely to turn an audience against a performer. By laying into himself with equal fervour, Dawson would disarm the punters and get them laughing at the shortcomings of both their home town and their own lives. It was comedy that reached out to an audience and conspired with them, telling them that the man on the stage was 'one of us'.

Dawson also claimed, in his autobiography, that his flush of success in the closing days of the Hull engagement suddenly made him attractive to women who had dismissed him before. In particular, he claimed that he was set upon by his 'conical-shaped landlady', a woman with 'a face like a tin of condemned veal' whose 'legs were merely a trellis work for varicose veins' and 'whose bottom was so big, when she sat down she was taller than when she stood up'.[101] Curiously, however, his diary for the week contains no note of the conquests. He mentions flirting with the conical landlady's daughter, but that's as far as it goes. Perhaps it made a better story for the new-look Dawson's first groupie to be an ugly old dear rather than her relatively nubile offspring.

Dawson's new-found comic persona and his boosted confidence meant a steady improvement in the quality of his bookings when he returned to Manchester, moving up from pubs to the burgeoning club scene, and the round of dinner-dances thrown by employers, trades unions and social clubs. He also got his feet on the lower rungs of the variety theatre ladder. The less salubrious halls couldn't afford big-name acts, but they could afford naked women, so most of those that survived closure had given themselves over to striptease shows. In between the nude tableaux, while the scenes were being reset, comedians and singers struggled to entertain an audience to whom they were merely an unwelcome distraction. Among the halls taking this kind of programme was the Hippodrome in the tough Manchester district of Hulme, part of a small north-western circuit run by an impresario called James Brennan. Brennan and a Hippodrome sink had been the recipients of Frank Randle's ire over the infamous bar bill incident, and Dawson had already performed there once in 1955 as part of *Pick of the Town*. One of the promoters filling Brennan's halls with nudity was Arthur Fox of International Attractions Ltd, 168 Corporation Street,

Manchester. Fox advertised regularly for 'male production vocalists' to appear in his shows, and Dawson auditioned successfully for the *Penny Peep Show*, a nude revue starring one of the most popular strip-tease performers of the day, Pauline Penny. Dawson's name appears in no contemporary billings, but it seems likely that he worked with Penny and her company when the show hit Hulme for the week beginning Monday, 12 May 1958. As Dawson's Hoover boss George Walker recalled in 1971:

> He asked me if he could go on the Hulme Hippodrome to appear in the Pauline Penny show, which was a nude revue, as a lead singer. I agreed, providing he got all his work done for me. There was no question about that. The morning after the first night, I was called into the office by my boss, who said, 'I went to see a show in Manchester last night, and I'm sure there was one of your representatives on that stage.' I said, 'That can't be so.' He said, 'Well, you'd better go along tonight and find out for yourself.' I had to go along, and, sure enough, there was Leslie, surrounded by naked girls, singing 'Autumn Leaves'.[102]

At his manager's behest, Walker had attended the performance, knowing full well what he would see and hear, but any fallout seems to have been contained.

Competition among comics on the Mancunian scene was pretty stiff, and certain aspects of one gag-peddler's career had mirrored those of Dawson's progress thus far, albeit with greater success. Following his National Service, part of which was spent guarding Rudolf Hess and the other inmates of Spandau Prison, Bernard Manning had returned to Civvy Street as a singer, working with Oscar Rabin, a popular post-war bandleader. He had then settled back in his home city, and established a club in a derelict former Temperance billiard hall in Harpurhey, just off Dawson's favoured pub-crawl route, dubbing it the Embassy Club. So, while Dawson was still scuffling around, taking what gigs he could get, Manning – his senior by just six months – was in a position to offer bookings to other comedians. It helped that Manning came from a relatively prosperous family, his father being a greengrocer, while Dawson's father was still very much a council wage slave. Nevertheless, Manning would not come to national prominence until the early seventies, a few years after Dawson's big break. In Dawson's case, the delay was due to bad luck; in Manning's case, it was down to having found a lucrative niche as a blue comedian, with material utterly unsuited to radio or television. Dawson sometimes tried more ribald material when he felt that the audience would lynch him if he kept his patter too clean. He recalled one night at a social club in south Manchester where the high point of his act was a smutty limerick:

> There was a young woman of Hitchin
> Who was scratching her arse in the kitchen
> Her mother said 'Rose,
> It's the crabs, I suppose.'
> She said, 'Bollocks, get on with your knitting.'[103]

However, while such vulgar material might have amused Dawson privately, he regarded it as a last resort in professional terms, and a mere survival tactic when faced with a rough, unruly crowd.

For Dawson, even with material as clean as a whistle, a break into broadcasting still proved elusive throughout the late fifties. He kept auditioning for the BBC in Manchester, apparently to no avail. After the frank feedback from producer John Ammonds following his unsuccessful 1954 audition, Dawson tried again on 13 September 1956. Ammonds's fellow auditioner Lelliott was in attendance once again, this time joined by Ammonds's fellow producer Eric Miller, both of them failing Dawson yet again on tuning and harsh tone.

When Dawson next wrote for an audition in July 1958, he changed his emphasis, billing himself as a comedian rather than a singer. At the ensuing audition, on 21 August 1958, no comment was made by producer Billy Scott-Coomber about Dawson's tuning, the criticisms centring instead on his projection, piano-playing and patter. Once again, the verdict was no, but Dawson was gaining valuable experience of the auditioning process, and getting to know the staff of the

BBC North region's variety department, not least Scott-Coomber, an Irishman who had been a singer with Jack Payne's dance band in the thirties.

True love also seemed as far from Dawson's grasp as a radio spot, as he grappled with a succession of women who were less than ideal for one reason or another. One had a voyeuristic mother who liked to watch her daughter's sexual antics, unknown to the male partner in the exchange. As most of the liaisons took place in the back of Dawson's works van, this involved the old dear standing in the street peering through the steamed-up windows. Another of Dawson's lovers had 'more teeth in her mouth than a basking shark'.[104]

Julia would not have approved of the company her son was keeping. For all of the anguish and concern he put her through, Dawson was devoted to his mother. When she died in 1957, it had hit him and Leslie senior very hard. Leslie junior 'wept for that little woman who'd gone through so much'. In particular, he rued 'the nights I'd caused her heartache with my drinking; my neglect of her through the lonely war years when my father had been away; the way I had taken her for granted'.[105] The loss didn't bring an end to Dawson's waywardness. While many of his contemporaries had married young and were already raising families, Dawson seemed determined to prolong his adolescence for as long as possible. It took a chance encounter at a gig in 1959 to make him modify his ways and his outlook.

CHAPTER 2

A Plant in the audience

When the fifties became the sixties, Les Dawson had been an artiste for the best and worst part of a decade. Briefly professional, he had spent most of the period as a semi-pro, combining a day job with whatever gigs he could secure. At the start of his career, it would have been stretching a point to call what he did an act, but by the end of the fifties, he had developed the comic persona that would later serve him so well. All the same, he was making precious little progress.

His personal life, however, had turned the corner. One night in 1959, he had turned up to a booking at Crumpsall Labour Club, and been greeted by a slim young woman who reminded him of the actress Jean Simmons. The club, a cut above his usual run, had not only a decent piano but also a keyboard instrument called a clavioline, best known for providing the lead sound on the Tornados' 1962 hit 'Telstar'. The young woman asked if Dawson wanted to use the clavioline. 'No thanks,' the perpetual joker replied, 'I've already been.' The joke did not go down well with Margaret Plant, who turned away with distaste and left Dawson to his own devices.

A week or so later, Dawson bumped into Miss Plant again. He was at the Northern Sporting Club – a venue where he sometimes performed – with some friends, and Miss Plant was there with her sister Elsie, watching a wrestling match. She approached Dawson and asked if he was the comedian she'd met the previous week. On replying that he was, Dawson remembered that he had a spare ticket to the Hoover staff dinner and dance in Sale the following week, at which he was booked to do a spot, and asked her to be his guest. She refused, but was talked into it by her sister, who rationalized that it was for one night only. The following week, wearing a striped bow tie with his suit, he turned up at the Plants' house in his green Ford van, and met Margaret's father, Arthur, and her mother, Ada, greeting the latter with a cheery 'Hello, love'. Arthur Plant commented with amusement that Dawson had landed himself 'right in the shit' with Ada for being so familiar.[1] On the way to the function, Dawson and his date began bickering, with the argument reaching its height at a pelican crossing. Meg was on the verge of getting out of the van and walking home when the lights changed, and Dawson sped off.

At the dance, Plant proved to be a funny, sarcastic companion, holding her own in the banter. As the night progressed, Dawson realized that he was falling for his date. Meg was falling for Dawson too, the clincher coming during his act when he pointed and winked at her while singing 'Bye Bye Blackbird'. The conviction that she was something special was underlined when it transpired that Meg had worked with Julia Dawson at a rope manufacturer's in Crumpsall, and that Leslie senior had worked at the ICI factory in Blackley with Arthur Plant. Being over-familiar with Ada suddenly seemed not to matter. 'She was very strict,' Dawson told Paul Callan of the *Daily Mirror* in 1977. 'There's nothing stricter than REAL, down-to-earth working-class morality. There were four daughters and any young men "callers" had first to meet the Gorgon in the Hall.'[2] On that first night, Dawson shortened Margaret to Meg, a diminutive she liked, but which nobody had used with her before. After that first night, he also shortened the amount of time he spent with his mates, preferring to spend time with Meg and the Plant family.

Dawson and Meg were married on 25 June 1960, a year to the day after they had first met, at St Thomas's church in Crumpsall. While not having a real-life mother-in-law or wife was no obstacle to telling jokes about either breed, Dawson had now acquired two muses for the price of one. Les and Meg Dawson spent their honeymoon in Austria, a present from Leslie senior, into whose house on Keston Avenue they moved as a married couple. They couldn't yet afford their own place, and Les felt that a woman's touch would make it a family home again,

Leslie senior having neglected to look after himself properly since Julia's death.

Just as married life was beginning, another association – Dawson's on-off employment with Hoover – was coming finally to an end. He resigned and took a position as a salesman with a plasticware firm called Plysu, a match made in hell because Dawson, by his own admission, hated the dish racks and tea strainers he had to sell. His lack of enthusiasm for the product was reflected in his sales figures and he was soon out of a job. He then became a salesman for a company that made electrical fittings, posing far less of a menace than he had installing them in his Co-op apprentice days. However, while these jobs paid the bills, his heart was set on a show business career and, in Meg, he at last had the love and support he really needed. The semi-professional bookings continued, with November and December 1960 finding Dawson playing a GPO officials' dinner at the Lightbowne Hotel, a Royal and Ancient Order of Buffaloes dinner at the Farmyard Hotel and a dinner for the Manchester and Salford Co-op, but what he really craved was a radio or television break.

By the time Dawson was rewarded with his first booking for a broadcast, he had a decade of performing experience to draw upon, to say nothing of his near miss in London with Max Wall or his eight years of attrition on the auditioners at Broadcasting House on Manchester's Piccadilly. The breakthrough came on 8 February 1961, when he auditioned again in Studio 1 at BH. Although the audition had been set up by Bill Scott-Coomber, the session was run by a pair of young producers called Peter Pilbeam and Geoff Lawrence, both recently promoted from studio managers. Dawson gave them a flavour of his act, including a song and some gags, most of them about his musical abilities. In their notes, Pilbeam and Lawrence commented on his performance of the song 'Young and Foolish' that he had 'a bull voice' with 'no tone colour, just fff',[3] as well as remarking on his boxer's features – less of an issue for radio than for television. Had he been a straight singer, he would have failed the audition, but Pilbeam remembers his 'good, different line of chat', and that his 'very powerful, strong voice helped him comedically'.[4] The combination resulted in the word 'Yes' appearing on the audition form in red ink, passing Dawson as fit for broadcasting at last.

He made his first appearance on the North of England Home Service on 16 March 1961 as the second-spot comic in a Scott-Coomber production: the talent show *Aim at the Top* was recorded on 26 February in Studio 1 at Piccadilly and earned him a fee of 10 guineas. Scott-Coomber booked Dawson swiftly for his second outing, this time networked nationally on the Light Programme, appearing on *Midday Music Hall* on 17 April, recorded at the Playhouse in Hulme on 26 March, and bringing him another welcome 10 guineas. However, after this initial flurry of interest, it was to be over a year before Dawson got another BBC booking for the Light Programme's *Blackpool Night* series on 5 August 1962. James Casey, at that time best known for writing and producing the radio sitcom *The Clitheroe Kid,* as well as being the son of the great comedian Jimmy James, was the producer responsible. Already well aware of Dawson from the clubs and his earlier broadcasts, Casey remembers how the struggling comic secured his full attention:

He used to send me postcards, not saying 'Give me a broadcast', but that was the idea. I can still remember the odd one, like: 'A list of my forthcoming dates: a W.C. Fields benefit concert, and a tour of the African rainforests with Martha Hagerty's Trombone Romany Dwarfs.' I turned to my secretary and said, 'Book Les Dawson, that's the first bloody laugh I've had for weeks.'[5]

Dawson found himself summoned to the Jubilee Theatre in Blackpool on 31 July for an afternoon recording. The venue was on the top floor of the Co-operative Emporium store on Sheppard Street, a place he would refer to disdainfully in his act as 'this Co-op loft'.[6] With that, Dawson began a lifelong friendship and professional association with Casey.

At a time when the BBC was regarded as stuffy, Broadcasting House in Manchester was anything but. In London, the variety department tended to be headed by administrators, but its northern counterpart was run by people with a background in writing and performing. Before becoming a radio scriptwriter, one-time head of variety Ronnie Taylor had been a singer and pianist, while Jim Casey came from comic royalty. These funny, creative men made the northern variety department into an eccentric, slightly rebellious, largely autonomous enclave within the BBC, producing distinctive programmes, and fostering a special atmosphere in the offices, as former BBC Northern Dance Orchestra lead saxophonist Johnny Roadhouse recalled:

> Jim Casey was our boss, a very experienced man. Steeped in show business, he knew it from A to Z. He was a good man, a genuine person, and always a man you could go to with a problem. A father figure. You could always guarantee a genuine reply from him. No edge to him. He was great. Everybody knew everybody. If you wanted to go and talk to them, [you could] have a cup of tea with them in the variety department. You were part of the same family.[7]

Dawson had the good fortune to become part of Casey's extended radio family, with Casey and colleagues like Peter Pilbeam and Geoff Lawrence booking him whenever they could, at a time when nobody else seemed to know or care who he was.

Just over a year after Dawson's regional and national radio debuts, he finally made it onto television, giving what *The Stage* described as 'an excellent performance' on the 16 June 1962 edition of ABC's *Saturday Bandbox*, seen only in the Midlands and North ITV regions.[8] Also on that show was Jimmy Clitheroe, star of Casey's most successful radio series, *The Clitheroe Kid*, making it likely that Casey was watching. More significant, though, is the presence on the bill of the music-hall veteran Norman Evans, making one of his last public appearances before his death in November 1962. Dawson's later creations, Cissie and Ada, were clearly inspired by Evans's 'Over the Garden Wall' monologues, while another set of Dawson's later characters, a thoroughly miserable husband and wife called Mr and Mrs Despond, were obviously on moaning terms with Evans's Auntie Doleful. Having grown up with Evans, and thoroughly absorbed his work, it must have been a thrill for the young comic to appear with him. By the end, Evans was a very ill man. Following an early ileostomy, for Evans the garden wall had gone from being a prop to being a necessity, as ABC producer Royston Mayoh explains:

> It was brutal. The bowels didn't work. He was cathetered, and his under-carriage was locked into this tank. It was why he worked behind the garden wall. His wife used to sit on the steps, reading a book, while he was doing his act, so she could help him down. The courage of this man. The viewer, the punter, the consumer, saw this wall, and the man over it. We as professional programme makers, we saw the back of it.[9]

Dawson, whether wittingly or unwittingly, gave Evans his memorial. Without his influence on Dawson, Evans would today be an interesting, funny, comedy cul-de-sac. However, Dawson paid homage to and expanded Evans's comic vision: whereas Evans did both his Garden Wall and Auntie Doleful characters as solo acts, Dawson would develop and expand them into double acts. In a variety theatre, the performer interacted with the audience, who effectively, if silently, played the other part. On television, it was preferable to have another character to do the job.

It was around this time that Dawson began to be represented by Dave Forrester of the Forrester-George agency, which also represented Ken Dodd. Dawson had also acquired his first manager, Kevin McEntee, himself a singer, known professionally as Kevin Kent. By the early sixties, McEntee was working regularly as the compère at the Palace Theatre Club in Stockport, but had been part of a vocal group called the Kordites, who were regulars on the variety shows made by the BBC's North region. After the Kordites disbanded, he had formed another broadcasting group, called the Kevin Kent Four, which featured an 18-year-old Elkie Brooks on lead, as well as Northern Dance Orchestra flautist Peter Husband. As a result, he had excellent contacts in the Manchester show business scene, but he didn't have an office. Like many Mancunian musicians, he spent a lot of his time hanging around at the music shop run by the NDO's lead saxophonist Johnny Roadhouse at 123 Oxford Road. Not all shrewd businessmen are kind and generous, but Roadhouse was known for both qualities, and he came to McEntee and Dawson's aid:

> Kevin was a good lad, and Les was a very friendly bloke. On the first floor of this shop, there was a nice carpeted office with a nice desk. He said, 'Anywhere we can go hire to do business, to meet clients?' I said, 'We all know Les and like Les, come and do it for nowt.' So it became as his address: 'Les Dawson, 123 Oxford Road', and all his letters came to me. I used to pass them on. When I knew he was coming, I used to take away all of my paraphernalia, music shop stuff, so it looked like his own office. He used to come in there whenever he felt like it. Eventually, he found his own office, of course, and stopped coming. Letters used to arrive for months and months afterwards. I passed on the messages. Les was very appreciative. When he wrote one of his books, he mentioned me in his books, typical of him, he said 'an untidy shop'. He never forgot.[10]

Fairly regular work from BBC Manchester was soon guaranteed, on North of England Home Service series like *Air Break*, as well as nationally networked radio shows like *Startime*, *Workers' Playtime*, *Blackpool Night* and *A Night at the Varieties* on the Light Programme. Consequently, McEntee's goal was to establish Dawson's live reputation further afield, but the day job limited his opportunities. Apart from one-nighters in the northern clubs, from which he could drive back home over-tired and over-refreshed, only bookings that could be undertaken in holidays were possible. At various points in 1964, Dawson could be found at the Cavendish Club in Sheffield, Wetherell's in Sunderland and the Lyceum Cabaret Club in Bradford, as well as at the City Varieties Theatre in Leeds, a fine early Victorian music hall, best known as the venue for BBC TV's *The Good Old Days*. But there was one aspect of his public appearances that struck other acts as deeply unconventional. Dec Cluskey of the Bachelors remembers the first time he saw Dawson, at a club in Blackpool:

He amazed us because it was the first time we'd seen a comic sit in the audience drinking, and when he was announced, he literally stood up at his table. We were quite shocked at that. He got up and he thought nothing of it, but that's what he did. Maybe that's what he did in all the working men's clubs. It was not the done thing and, certainly, it's still not the done thing. There is a separation between the audience and the artist. We always say it's like showing kids Father Christmas three days before Christmas. You shouldn't show the audience the artist as a normal person. You have to retain that mystique, that glamour.[11]

Other than Dawson's round of the clubs and radio studios, though, he was making disappointingly little headway. In March 1964, Jim Casey and Geoff Lawrence used their influence to make a television pilot called *Two's a Crowd,* starring Dawson and the Liverpool comic Johnny Hackett. Speaking to *The Stage* at the time, Lawrence described Dawson's stage persona as 'diffident, self-effacing, apologetic, the sort of man who strips himself down in public "verbally". He is always ready to excuse himself for taking up so much of everybody's time.'[12] Unfortunately, the contrast with the brasher Hackett didn't find favour and the show remained a one-off, seen only by Northern viewers in a network opt-out slot. Similarly abortive was a week in the early summer of 1965 on the same bill as Billy Cotton and his band at the Opera House in Manchester.[13] On the opening night, the audience consisted of 'a few white blobs scattered around',[14] and these blobs greeted Dawson's patter with 'a silence like a forgotten grave in a disused cemetery'.[15]

Johnny Ball, then a young comedian working many of the same venues, recalls that Les was rated highly by his peers, but less so by the audiences. 'Les was a comedian's comedian – we all loved him, but he died on the club circuit in Manchester and didn't venture far afield,' Ball remembers. 'I recall twice, I think, telling him not to give the business up. The problem was, club audiences were energetic and wanted energetic entertainment, so a droll or melancholic just didn't get them off the ground. Also, it was an advantage to talk the same language and Les's flowery prose put them off.'[16]

There was a brief run in 1965 when it looked like Dawson was heading up to the next rung on the ladder, with four bookings from former *Goon Show* producer John Browell for *Light Up the Night* on the Light Programme in April and May, and a pair of shows called *Home and Away*, also featuring Elkie Brooks and Humphrey Lyttelton. The *Home and Away* shows, which were to be transmitted in the UK on the BBC Light Programme and overseas on the British Forces Broadcasting Service, were recorded in front of forces audiences in the German towns of Gütersloh on 29 September 1965 and Münster on 30 September 1965. Dawson provided a self-written spot in each of the German shows, submitting his scripts to producer Bobby Jaye well in advance. After the sessions, Jaye wrote to Dawson to say 'how much I appreciate the professional way in which you delivered your material, both on and off the stage!',[17] suggesting that the comedian had kept the cast and crew entertained as much as the audience, a recurring theme through Dawson's career. Less impressed was Denis Morris, head of the Light Programme, who, after the transmission of the second show on 13 October 1965, wrote to head of radio light entertainment Roy Rich to note that while he had initially shared Rich and Jaye's 'great hopes of Les Dawson's potential ... I thought he was well below the broadcasting standards we should expect' on the German recordings, observing also that a *Blackpool Night* performance had achieved an 'abysmally low' appreciation index, this being the qualitative panel-based research that the BBC conducted for many shows to complement the quantitative measurement of ratings. Morris was led to conclude that 'he no longer ranks among the potentially great, but maybe he is having a bad patch'.[18] Rich replied that he wasn't prepared to write Dawson off on the basis of a single show and a poor AI rating, and that he'd continue looking at ways to use him effectively. In fact, the German experience would be Dawson's last broadcast for nearly two years, so Morris's view seems to have held sway.

Even a summer season in Douglas on the Isle of Man in 1965, at the

Palace Coliseum theatre with Val Doonican and Jackie Trent, seemed to lead nowhere, despite the show being 'unquestionably the best summer revue to be staged on the Isle of Man for years'.[19] The main consolation was that Dawson fared better in the long term than the theatre, which was demolished at the end of the season to make way for a casino. Nevertheless, if all was gloom professionally, there had been some very good news on the personal front. The Dawsons had been trying, unsuccessfully, for a child throughout their five years of otherwise happy marriage. Meg had endured a series of miscarriages, and the couple were told eventually by a specialist that they would never be able to have children. Another doctor disagreed, and told them to keep trying, advising the checking of temperature to indicate when ovulation was occurring. It worked, and on 9 May 1965, at St Mary's Hospital in Manchester, Julie Helen Dawson was born.

By the end of 1965, the enlarged family was on the move, away from Leslie senior's house in Keston Avenue, Blackley, to a two-bedroomed bungalow at 2 Bradley Drive, Unsworth, Bury, where the family was soon expanded further with the arrival of a son, Stuart Jason Dawson, on 3 March 1967. From Unsworth, it was back to the day job as a salesman for Sun Electric, and one-nighters at venues like the Rhyl Sporting Club, as well as occasional longer bookings such as a Christmas show at the Gaumont in Doncaster. Dawson was now in his mid-thirties and watching with mounting disdain as younger, more conventional performers achieved instant success on television. His appearances on ABC's *Saturday Bandbox* and *Comedy Bandbox* in 1962 and 1963 had led nowhere, in contrast to the fortunes of the young Jimmy Tarbuck, who made his television debut on *Comedy Bandbox*, in October 1963. An edition of that show was watched by *Sunday Night at the London Palladium* executive producer Val Parnell, who promptly booked Tarbuck for the following week's Palladium show, an unheard-of accolade for a virtual unknown. Parnell's faith was rewarded fully. After the broadcast, the *Daily Mirror* reported that the newcomer 'was given one of the greatest receptions the show has ever known', with the paper's TV critic declaring the comic to be 'easily the best comedy find the Palladium has had for years'.[20] Within two years, Jimmy Tarbuck was hosting the Palladium show.

Tarbuck's meteoric rise must have stuck in Dawson's throat. He realized that it was make-or-break time. He needed to either go professional, or give up and stick with being a salesman. Having a young family and a bungalow with a mortgage made recklessness impossible. It was Meg who suggested the answer. Spying that ABC Television's top-rated talent show *Opportunity Knocks* was auditioning at Milton Hall on Manchester's Deansgate, she told Les to go along and try his luck. If he didn't get anywhere, he should give up. Dawson was against the idea, regarding the show as for amateurs, whereas he was an experienced semi-professional. Nonetheless, Meg's counsel prevailed, and on a wet Manchester morning, Dawson went to perform for the show's host and guiding light Hughie Green, and his production team: programme associates Doris Barry and Vic Hallums, producer Milo Lewis, and, crucially, a young director called Royston Mayoh. Mayoh was already well aware of the comedian's work, from the Manchester pub scene and his sporadic appearances on ABC shows. So Dawson had the good luck to have an ally from the off, but the audition process was not without its problems:

> We're up at the top table, looking down, and we had all the auditionees around. We didn't want singer, singer, singer. We'd have singer, comic, someone who didn't need the piano. If there was a band to set up, we'd give them time. It wasn't a variety show for our amusement, it was more to keep the atmosphere of the room up. At the back of us, visiting pros used to come. Tom Paxton turned up with Mary Hopkin and sat at the back. You'd see a pro coming in, and you'd say, 'Come and sit round the back.' I see what I think is Les Dawson standing at the door, just come in. He's standing there with Derek, my runner, putting the name down so he can come up to the desk and we can get the file out. I'm thinking, 'I know that face ... Les Dawson.' I said to Hughie, 'You see that guy? Bloody marvellous comic.' I went down and said, 'Excuse me, are you Les Dawson?' He said, 'Yes, who are you?' I said, 'Royston Mayoh', and

he knew my name because of the telly. I said, 'I used to watch you in the Yew Tree, the Cabaret Club and Wilton's. Come round the back and meet Hughie.' 'I can't do that, I'm auditioning.' 'What? For the show?' 'Yeah.' 'Right, OK. Fine. Are you sure about that?' I said, 'Cindy, get me Les Dawson out, quickly. Pull him up to the front. As far as I'm concerned, unless my memory's going, he's bloody marvellous. You'll love him. I can't even join in on this. He's my hero.' She said, 'He's not here. I can't find his form. He's not in comics. Hang on, I've got it, I think so.' One of the office girls had written in big letters 'Lesley' and put it under girl pianists.[21]

Having overcome the mistaken identity hurdle, Dawson then had to overcome the audition-weary Green's initial reaction at seeing his stage set-up, as Mayoh recalls:

I said, 'You are going to love this, Hughie. I'll give you my notes now. There's my notes,' before he came on. 'I just want to sit back and enjoy it.' Jack Dove [the accompanist] pulled the piano over. Green said, 'Oh, not a pianist, not another fucking pianist.' Of course, he sits down, he does it and Green was sick with laughter. When Green laughed, he went. He was wonderful when he laughed. He had such a laugh on him. And Doris, 'Dame Alicia Markova's sister, dear boy', was falling apart. First of all, it was 'I'm going to play you a famous piece by a man who isn't with us any longer.' It finished in half a bar, 'and then he died'. Then he'd sit down and talk about being a failure in the boom, and 'I was sent behind enemy lines with nothing but a yard of rubber tubing and a bag of radishes to put the wind up the Germans'. All that. Woof woof woof [*audience response*]. And then he finished with the out of tune. We put him on as soon as we could.[22]

Dawson's *Opportunity Knocks* appearance went out to the nation on Saturday, 20 May 1967, with that week's *Bury Times* reporting the booking in best 'Local Lad Makes Good' style, but putting his age as 24, rather than the 36 he really was. On the night, he found himself competing against Kay and Kim, the Glendoi Singers, Yvonne Marsh and the Rose Fletcher Pipe Band. Seated at the piano, Dawson regaled the Didsbury studio audience with his unique vision. Outlined in *A Clown Too Many*, he opened with a gag about a piece of music he would later choose as one of his Desert Island Discs. 'I toyed with the idea of playing Ravel's *Pavane Pour Un Infante Defunct* [*sic*],[23] but I can't remember if it is a tune or a Latin prescription for piles,' he joked, going on to observe that 'the neighbours love it when I play the piano, they often break my windows to hear me better'.[24] Another of his jokes that night introduced the national TV audience to the bathos for which Dawson would become famous, deflating a sentimental set-up with an unsentimental punchline:

> Mother used to sit me on her knee and I'd whisper, "Mummy, Mummy, sing me a lullaby do." She'd say, "Certainly, my angel, my wee bundle of happiness, hold my beer while I fetch me banjo."[25]

Opnox, as the show was known in the industry, worked on a system of postal voting, and when the votes were totted up the following week, Dawson had not won. However, on the night, the famous clap-o-meter, which gauged the volume of audience reaction, had judged Dawson to be the clear victor. 'He was as nervous as hell when he went on,' Mayoh remembers. 'He was sweating like a pig. He didn't want to let Meg down, you see. Meg was there and she was so proud of him. We all went to the bar after, and just got absolutely totalled in the ABC bar. The winning was academic. Before you appeared on it, you were 20 quid. After you'd been on television, you were now 50 quid. If you'd been on TV, you were a star in the clubs, whether you'd won or not.'[26]

In terms of booking his gigs, Dawson's association with the Forrester-George agency had come to an end some time before, at least partially because Dawson realized he would probably be getting the same amount of work without their help, and without having to pay any commission. He had also lost the services of Kevin McEntee, after McEntee decided to return full-time to performing, and so different agencies arranged different bits of work for him here and there. There is a letter in the BBC's files, dated 28 June 1967, from Joe Cash of the

Metropolitan Vaudeville Agency to producer Albert Stevenson, trying to interest him in seeing Dawson perform. By August 1967, however, Dawson had settled with the agent who would represent him for the rest of his career – Norman Murray, then of Fosters' Agency, one of the big old-time variety agencies, and later proprietor of his own firm. Murray, with his camel-hair coat and his tendency to call everyone 'Dolly' regardless of sex, was almost a caricature of the old-school show business agent. He was not universally popular. Royston Mayoh suggests that Iris Frederick, the casting director for ABC Television, avoided contact with Murray wherever possible, telling producers to deal with him directly. 'Anything we got went through Iris. Iris knew what the level was,' says Mayoh. 'Until Iris came, there was a lot of playing off one against the other. Iris wouldn't talk to him at one point. We, as producers, said "Well, you're going to have to, because we need things." "Well, do it direct." She hated him. Everybody did.'[27]

After his TV breakthrough, Dawson continued as a semi-pro, fearing that his new-found fame and improved remuneration would be fleeting. Dave Lanning, interviewing Dawson for the *TV Times*, captured a flavour of the comedian's life in that initial rush: 'Tonight, it's a club date in Lewisham. He travels second-class and will be on the one o'clock night train, dozing fitfully, back to Manchester and work in the morning.'[28] He admitted to Lanning that his sudden success was 'completely beyond analysis ... I'm no different. Neither is the act ... [but] for some reason people have been sitting up and taking notice'. One of those people was Mark Stuart, a dancer and choreographer who had moved behind the camera and become a senior producer at ABC, and who had helped train Mayoh as a director:

> Mark came into my office one day. In Teddington, the second floor was all light entertainment. We were all there: Keith Beckett, Mark Stuart, me, Peter Frazer-Jones, Peter Dulay. We were doing music programmes and there's a wonderful story about having the music up [in the office] and [ABC head of light entertainment] Philip Jones came out and shouted, 'Will you shut that music off, this is not a place of entertainment.' Mark

came into my office and said, 'That comic you've been banging on about, fellow from the north. Les Dawson? Do you rate him?' 'Yes, I do, I think he's marvellous.' 'Philip thinks he's crap.' 'Yes, well, Philip thinks anybody not born in London's crap, so I wouldn't worry about that.'

So he said, 'Anyway, I'm lumbered with doing the tech run for *Blackpool Night Out*.[29] Is he available? I need a front cloth act for the tech run because I've got a four-minute set behind.' You couldn't tape stuff and build, like you do now. 'He can do that, can't he? He doesn't need his piano?' I said, 'No, he can do it without the piano. He doesn't need any props. He's all right'.[30]

Since 1964, the company had been providing the ITV network's summer replacement for ATV's *Sunday Night at the London Palladium*, broadcast from the ABC theatre in Blackpool. At the start of each series, a non-broadcast pilot was recorded to check that all was as it should be, technically. Although the viewing public wouldn't see the results, a lot of people in a position to book acts would. On Sunday, 18 June 1967, as nervous as he had been at Didsbury for *Opportunity Knocks*, Dawson waited for his introduction from host Dickie Henderson. In so many ways, Henderson was everything that Dawson wasn't: a handsome, smooth, showbizzy performer, combining light comedy with polished song and dance. However, behind the perma-tan and grin was a kind, generous and well-liked man, and one who never begrudged another performer their share of the limelight. When Henderson gave Dawson a big build up, he meant it. Once on stage, Dawson's confidence soared. He ventured an early mother-in-law joke on the audience of holidaymakers. 'We often come to see the wife's mother here,' he explained. 'She lives in Birmingham but looks better from Blackpool ... I'm really enjoying this show, it's the first time I've played to a hung jury.'[31] Just like the fishermen and their wives in Hull over a decade earlier, the audience loved him. He was one of them, only funnier, conspiring with them, sharing their minor discomforts and major annoyances, and turning them into comedy. 'In show business parlance, that night, I "murdered" them,' he admitted, nearly twenty years later. Indeed, his success was so marked that Stuart offered him a spot in one of the forthcoming nationally networked Blackpool shows. Dawson accepted, but began to worry. Would he be able to recreate the magic of the pilot show? Had slaying the audience on the technical run been a fluke? When the same concerns had crossed his mind after the Hull epiphany, he had had far less to lose, and was able to test the new material over the course of the next few gigs. A national TV show was different. It had to be right, or else his career would be buried, this time possibly for good.

Sunday, 30 July 1967 was the big night, with Dawson at the bottom of a bill topped by the Shadows, with singer Julie Rogers, the Peiro Brothers and Chris Kirby. Dawson's fears were unfounded. For the second time in just over a month, he committed mass murder in Blackpool and left his victims grateful for the experience. One joke he used that night encapsulates the appeal of Dawson perfectly, acknowledging his own lowly status and using it to paint a wonderful mental picture:

> If you're popular in show business they give you a dressing room on the ground floor, if you're not so good, they put you on the first floor and so on. To give you some idea what they think of me, my room's full of falcon droppings, and the mice have blackouts.[32]

There was only one small problem with his bravura performance that night. He over-ran his four-minute slot by three minutes. The show was being recorded for transmission later that night, so an edit was possible, but there was a disagreement over which bit of the show should go. Royston Mayoh, who had gone along to cheer on his friend, remembers the discussion:

> The audience were over the moon with this thing. Dickie Henderson came on and said, 'Tonight, you've seen a star being born.' He wouldn't come out. Somebody pushed him out. I was in the audience and the tears were running down my face. I was just so overawed with our *Opportunity Knocks* finalist. He came off, and I went backstage. There

was a conflab with Mark Stuart, Philip Jones and Dickie Henderson. I'm walking over to say to Mark, 'Fucking great show', but they were in the middle of an argument. Mark says to Philip, 'You're mad, you're mad. You've got to leave it like it is.' Dickie's there saying, 'I'll tell you something. You touch one inch of that man's performance and you will not see me again. You want three minutes, take 'Umbrella Man' out. It was three minutes tonight. It was three minutes twenty years ago. It'll be three minutes in twenty years' time. I do that performance now, I'd do it exactly the same next week. There's nothing special about the perform-ance I did. But the performance that young man did was so special, you mustn't touch it. If you do, I won't be back.' Mark said, 'I'm with Dickie, neither will I.' Dickie was very important to Les. He had the clout. And Mark was important for putting him up.[33]

One appreciative viewer was George Melly, then TV critic of the *Observer*, who described Dawson as having both 'the face of a failed boxer who expects to be struck at irregular but frequent intervals by a stocking full of custard, and a genuinely comic persona; a rare gift in this age of synthetic mid-Atlantic matiness ... I think he may turn out to be a great comic if they don't get at him.'[34] That night in Blackpool turned Dawson into a TV comedian, making producers of variety shows keen to add him to their bills. His friend from the clubs, Johnny Ball, later to become a major TV personality and educator in his own right, thinks he knows why it happened, having seen him 'die' in the hostile atmosphere of the clubs many times. 'Once he did TV, he was perfect,' Ball observes. 'The camera just locked off on him and he did the rest. It was easy viewing, which allowed the audience to use their brains and ears in following his crazy train of thought. I recall even when he was a star and now packing them in in the major clubs – at the end he got a great ovation – but compared with many comedians, he didn't pull the roof in. They loved him for his TV image – but that was plenty.'[35]

Opportunity Knocks and *The Blackpool Show* had both been recorded programmes, but his first appearance after the Blackpool triumph was a live TV broadcast, from the stage of the BBC Television Theatre, on the 7 October 1967 edition of the *Val Doonican Show,* underpinning a bill topped by Cliff Richard and Rolf Harris. John Law, one of the writers on the show as well as being BBC TV light entertainment group's in-house script editor at the time, had promised Dawson an audio recording of his routine. Sending him the 3¾ IPS spool, Law said that he thought Dawson had got a good reaction from the audience and noted that the whole show had gone well 'give or take the odd Australian', [36] suggesting a degree of dissatisfaction with Harris's performance.

As well as renewing his acquaintance with Doonican, two years after they'd worked together in the Isle of Man, Dawson must have felt he was evening an old score that day, as the BBC Television Theatre had been the venue of his disappointment at the hands of Edmund Hockridge eleven years earlier. Even sweeter, the show's producer was John Ammonds, who had rejected him at his first BBC audition in 1954. Not that Dawson had any grudge against Ammonds, as they had kept in touch during the intervening years, with Dawson sending Ammonds friendly, amusing notes reminding him to listen to this broadcast or that. Over time, the producer had come to admire the comedian's work and distinctive outlook, noting that:

> He was very eloquent. His use of language was inspired. I used to love some of his routines. The one about the council house they'd got: 'Very damp, in fact it's the only place with gutters on the inside. The chap from the council came, we piped him aboard.' The mother-in-law one I liked best: 'The mother-in-law came round last week, it was absolutely pouring down, so I went outside, opened the door and I saw her there and said, "Mother, don't just stand there in the rain. Go home."' Very quick. [37]

The Val Doonican Show was not the only TV programme keen to enlist the newcomer's services in the winter of 1967 and spring of 1968. On Saturday, 4 November 1967, Dawson made his first appearance on a chat show, being interviewed and performing a little of his act on Simon Dee's top-rated BBC1 chat show *Dee Time*, along with guests that included Lotus Cars founder Colin Chapman and singer Vince Hill. The appearance was something of a coup, *Dee Time* being the hippest show of the day, but Dawson received what producer Terry Henebery described in programme documentation as a 'special low' 60-guinea fee, because it was assumed that Dawson could come down from Manchester on the morning of the show, not requiring an overnight allowance. At the time, an international star appearing on *Dee Time* could expect 100 guineas for an interview alone, while national stars received 50 guineas and all others 30 guineas. The 60 guineas for an interview and a spot suggests that, at this early stage, Dawson was somewhere between 'all others' and stardom.

The *Dee Time* appearance was followed on 30 December by a booking for *Mike and Bernie's Show* at ABC, with Mike and Bernie Winters, and a return visit two weeks later. Then, on 13 February, Dawson was back at the BBC for an edition of *Cilla* with Cilla Black, alongside Frankie Vaughan, Roy Hudd and Donovan. Later, in May, came a *Show of the Week* with Rolf Harris for BBC2, on which production Les met larger-than-life producer Stewart Morris for the first time, beginning a professional association and friendship that was to last until Dawson's death. Morris was a maverick and a risk-taker, pushing crews and production teams to the limit and beyond, asking for apparently impossible shots and almost always getting them. 'Stewart wasn't a great one for camera scripting,' explains Lydia Vine, Morris's trusted and respected production assistant for most of his BBC career. 'He would camera script any production routines or dance routines, but he liked to feel it on the night. You needed to lead him through a song or whatever, to tell him what was coming up and what he'd done before, but he had such a rapport with the cameramen that it was exciting, seat-of-the-pants time.'[38]

The presence of Dawson on a Morris-produced show was always welcomed by the production team, as it offered a brief respite from the tension. 'As a PA, it was always a great relief on Stewart's shows when Les came on because I knew it was eight minutes on one camera, and I didn't have to do anything,' says Vine. 'I think it was that show where I was desperate to spend a penny, and there was no hope until Les came on. There was a ladies' loo just outside TC8, so I raced out, came back and Les was still on.'[39]

Later, in June, John Ammonds also booked Dawson as guest on the fourth show of *Lulu's Back In Town*, a music and comedy vehicle for the Scottish singer who had come to prominence three years earlier with the hit 'Shout'. Luckily, both the *Cilla* and *Lulu's Back In Town* programmes survive in the BBC archives and show the newly famous Dawson at work. There are subtle, but noticeable differences in Dawson's technique and appearance compared with his later years on TV. He addresses the studio audience rather than the audience at home, his eyeline being a little over the camera lens and to the side, and is a little thinner, with a trendy sixties dinner suit on and a haircut to match, but that's all. When he had told the *TV Times* the previous year 'I'm no different. Neither is the act,' he was clearly telling the truth. The Dawson persona had been formed for some time, and was just waiting for the rest of the world to catch up.

Following an introduction in which Lulu described Dawson as 'a comedian who is bright and gay, full of energy and bubbling over with enthusiasm', he matched her irony with his opening line: 'Good evening, fun hunters', followed by the admission that 'I never expected to hear prolonged bursts of enthusiastic applause when my name was announced'. Anyone wanting to know what the phrase comic timing means would do well to observe the pause Dawson left here before the pay-off: 'I wasn't far wrong either.' This got an unsurprising woof from the audience and, from then on, Les could do no wrong:

You see, the trouble is that to get on in show business, you have to be born under a lucky star. Judging by the shape of my career, I must have been born under Fred Emney[40] ... It's funny, when I first got married, I promised the wife the world, which was understandable, because she looks like Atlas ... She started on about clothes and in particular that she's only ever had one dress since we got married. I said, 'What's wrong with that?' She said, 'Nothing, but we're doing the housework, and the train and veil are filthy....'. When we first got married, everybody thought I was a ventriloquist because every time I opened my mouth, she talked. She's never been the same since our honeymoon when she fell down a wishing well. I was amazed. I didn't know they worked ... She's a hell of a size. Every time she walks past a chemist's shop, the weighing machine jumps inside.[41]

After the stand-up routine, Lulu returns and chides Dawson for being so miserable, a cue for a song. The pair duet on 'And You'll Feel Much Worse', composed by one of the show's writers, a pre-*Goodies* Bill Oddie, and originally performed by him in the fourth show of the sixth series of the Radio 2 comedy series *I'm Sorry I'll Read That Again*. The Lulu/Dawson version is done as a much straighter vaudeville duet, while Oddie's original is clearly pastiche George Formby.

Dawson's jokes about his wife's physique wouldn't have been funny if they'd been true, but Meg was a well-proportioned woman. Also, the abuse was evenly balanced. Dawson paints himself as a terrible skinflint, forcing his mythical wife to wear her wedding dress for all eventualities. The extremity of the images is too cartoonish to be truly offensive. There is also no hint of domestic violence, the clear implication being that if any were to occur it would be Dawson himself on the losing end. In reality, Meg was no pushover, but Dawson loved her deeply and acknowledged the importance of the steel in her make-up in keeping family life running smoothly. If she nagged, she did it for a reason, as underlined by his radio producer and friend Jim Casey:

Meg was great. We got on very well, Meg and I. Of course, she had him absolutely under her thumb. I've been there when she's said, 'What are you doing?' He's said, 'We're just working.' She said, 'You've got to pick the kids up, they'll be out in ten minutes.' 'All right.' Here's this star and she's telling him. Another time, we were going to play golf and the kitchen was a bit flooded. He said, 'I've rung the fella and he's coming to sort it out.' She went on and on, then he said, 'We've got to go.' I whispered to him, 'You could get rid of all that water if she opened her mouth and swallowed it.' And he laughed his bloody head off.[42]

The peak of Dawson's first flush of fame, however, came on Sunday, 9 March 1968, when he finally reached the bill of ATV's *London Palladium Show*, alongside singers Tony Bennett and Dusty Springfield, and the Buddy Rich Orchestra. The Palladium show was regarded by performers as the number one TV variety booking, and so, at the age of 37, after years of struggle, the failure had become a success. Les Dawson had made it, this being underlined when Ammonds cast the comedian in his first starring vehicle, a situation-comedy pilot that was to open the new series of BBC TV's *Comedy Playhouse*. Since the debut run of the strand in 1961, several hit series had been developed from *Comedy Playhouse* one-offs, including *Steptoe and Son*, *All Gas and Gaiters* and *Till Death Us Do Part*. Normally, the decisions on which would progress to a full series were taken by the head of comedy, but for the 1968 run, *Radio Times* readers were asked to vote by postcard for the show they wanted to see more of. The *Daily Express* did not approve of this concept, regarding it as 'either a surrender of responsibility or a blatant publicity gimmick'.[43]

Dawson's sitcom pilot, *State of the Union*, was written by Ronnie Taylor, Ammonds's former employer as head of radio variety at the BBC in Manchester, and, in the producer's estimation, 'the nicest and cleverest boss I ever worked for at the BBC'.[44] Taylor had also been the creator of ABC's *Saturday Bandbox* series, in which Dawson had made his TV debut. The sitcom pilot featured Dawson as the secretary of a very small-time trade union called in to resolve a dispute concerning one of his eight members who took his dog, a St Bernard, to work with him. 'Les was supposed to be the union representative,' Ammonds explains, 'but he was siding with the management most of the time, running with both.'[45] Following a day of location filming on Monday, 18 March 1968, the piece was rehearsed between Monday, 25 and Friday, 30 March, at the North Kensington Community Centre in Dalgarno Way, with the recording following on Sunday, 31 March in studio TC4 at the BBC Television Centre, ready for transmission on Friday, 26 April, between 8.20 p.m. and 8.50 p.m. Unfortunately, *State of the Union* failed to impress the postcard-writing public, and so it did not progress to a series.[46] *The Stage*'s reviewer declared that, at times, she felt she 'was watching a particularly slow music-hall sketch', describing the plot and script as 'a trivial framework' and noting that Dawson 'looked at the camera so long and so steadfastly after some of his jokes that I felt he was either willing or defying the home audience to laugh'.[47] Ammonds recalls that Taylor's script 'wasn't one of his best. Even he was fallible. It was quite a funny idea, but it didn't seem to work out. Les, I think, got a bit annoyed with me, but I was as disappointed as he was that it didn't work. I don't know whether he was the right type of performer for sitcom.'[48]

Dawson's skills as a compère, honed over the years in the clubs, were never in doubt, however. In November 1968, he took over from Kenneth Williams as the host of BBC2's *International Cabaret*, a series transmitted from London's Talk of the Town, combining the cream of continental talent, including many death-defying, highly skilled speciality acts, with big international singing stars like Nana Mouskouri and Eartha Kitt, and other entertainers such as Dickie Henderson. Williams's links had been built on meandering monologues and feigned indifference or outright hostility towards the turns on the bill, so Dawson's approach continued the tradition in a subtly different manner. The show brought him into contact with one of the great names of British variety, Barry Lupino,[49] nephew of Stanley and cousin of Ida Lupino, and producer of the show. Unfortunately, despite his impeccable pedigree, Dawson was far from impressed with Lupino, whom he described as 'a perambulating distillery' with 'the smell of alcohol [hanging] about the room at the Talk like a dandy's aftershave'.[50] Dawson was no stranger to strong drink himself, but he held it well, and it rarely, if ever, affected his performance. In contrast, the producer did let it affect his work. 'There were stories of him being really sauced before programmes,' says John Ammonds. 'You can't really win like that. He was very fond of the bottle and it got in the way.'[51]

The *International Cabaret* series came between two long stage engagements: a summer season in Blackpool and a Christmas season in Leeds. The Blackpool run was at the Central Pier in Bernard Delfont's production *Star Show '68*. With fellow comedians Ray Martine and Jimmy Couton also on the bill, as well as singers Don Partridge, Solomon King and Steve Montgomery, a competitive edge could perhaps have been expected. However, each was such a distinctive performer that jealousy would have been futile. Martine, who made his name in the early sixties on *Stars and Garters*, Associated-Rediffusion's attempt to transfer London's pub entertainment scene to television, was very camp, very London, very Jewish and, on his day, very funny with lightly satirical material that sometimes tipped over into blue comedy. In contrast, Couton was joined for the finale of his act by a singing dog called Rex. Dawson found Martine's comedy 'acid and vulgar', but he enjoyed the southerner's company offstage and the pair became good friends. The show proved a hit with holidaymakers, and *The Stage* singled out Dawson's 'doomsday patter' for particular praise, declaring that he was 'certainly an originalist destined for the top'.[52]

The Leeds season, at the Grand over Christmas 1968 as part of a show headlined by Irish singing group the Bachelors, would help to propel him even higher. The stars of the show knew him from clubland, as did fellow supporting artists, the ventriloquist Arthur Worsley and the Hull-born comedian Norman Collier. The idea had been to present a variety show instead of the usual pantomime, and ensuring that the show was heavy on comedy made for a healthy atmosphere. 'We always had three comics,' Bachelor Dec Cluskey explains, 'and the theory behind that was that if the people were helpless with laughter, all we had to do was sing. We were very fond of that formula. It worked for us. The comics absolutely adored being on with us because there was no competition from the top of the bill. You couldn't win against a top of the bill.'[53]

Reviewing the Christmas season, *The Stage* praised 'this lively and swiftly moving show … [with] a rich assortment of music-hall and variety at its best', noting the 'lugubrious humour of Les Dawson'.[54] And at the end of its scheduled eight weeks in Leeds, the hit show moved to fill the Manchester Opera House from 19 January 1969, taking Dawson back to the scene of his disastrous week with Billy Cotton, only this time in triumph.

As well as being a success in its own right, the Leeds season had created two important associations. Along with Worsley, Collier and the three Bachelors – Con Cluskey, Dec Cluskey and John Stokes – Dawson became a member of the Grand Order of Water Rats, a group of entertainers devoted to charitable works that could trace its heritage back to the turn of the century and Dan Leno. Dawson would come to treasure this association, both for the good works the Water Rats performed and for the good company of his fellow Rats. Dec Cluskey recalls:

> One of the great nights at the Water Rats ball was when we all went up from the Great Room [at the Grosvenor House Hotel], and we were sat by the huge bar in the foyer, and there was a grand piano there. Les of course sat at the piano, and then Arthur Worsley decided to get Norman as a dummy and stick him up in the opening of the grand piano. You can just picture it. Les playing and Arthur Worsley and Norman. He was doing the 'back in the box ... I'm not going back in the box'. They were doing that whole routine, and slamming the lid of the piano. This Indian waiter came up and said, 'Oh no no no no, you cannot do that. This is the Grosvenor House. Now get off the piano.' He didn't know who Les was and he said, 'Excuse me, this piano is for professional players only.'[55]

The other vital connection made by Dawson during that Leeds season was with a producer from the newly established Yorkshire Television, which had based itself in the city. John Duncan had, with his Oxford contemporary Richard Ingrams, been part of an experimental theatre group called Tomorrow's Audience, until a royalty deal arranged by their business manager left them out of pocket. Ingrams had devoted himself, full-time, to the magazine he'd started with school friends Willie Rushton and Christopher Booker, *Private Eye*. Duncan, meanwhile, joined the BBC, initially as an associate producer on *That Was The Week That Was* and then on its successors in the satirical vein, *Not So Much a Programme ... More a Way of Life* and *BBC3*. By 1968, a desire to get out of London coincided with a call from his old BBC boss Donald Baverstock, who was heading to Leeds to start up YTV. Duncan regarded his comedy-producing as a digression, and wanted to move into serious documentaries and drama, but thought he stood a better chance of moving across with the new company, and so accepted the offer, working under head of light entertainment Sid Colin. Once appointed, he began looking for distinctive talent:

> I was using the telly to babysit my children one evening in London, knowing I was going to Yorkshire – it was *The Val Doonican Show* or something.[56] Anyway, there was this northern comic who came on and I just was absolutely bowled over, thinking, 'Why have I not heard of this man? He's a genius. Just what I need to start up in Yorkshire.' I didn't even know his name. I had to wait until the end of the bloody show to see what his name was.[57]

Thus armed, Duncan found that his man was appearing just two miles from the newly built YTV studios on Kirkstall Road, and so paid Dawson a visit at the theatre. Sitting in his dressing room, the pair had a drink and discussed the possibility of making a pilot show. Dawson sensed a kindred spirit in Duncan, a ferociously clever but self-deprecating figure in a business that thrived on confidence and bluster. Dawson latched onto Duncan's fundamental seriousness of purpose – just as the producer had always wanted to make highbrow television, the comedian harboured desires to be a serious novelist. The pair would develop a firm professional understanding and a good off-duty friendship. Just as an agreement was being reached, one of the show's dancers interrupted the meeting to invite Dawson to a party. Joking that he would attend if she promised to surrender to his advances, she replied with a pert 'No chance, Dawson' and turned to Duncan. 'We don't take any notice of what Les says.' The dancer's retort chimed with Duncan. 'After she'd left,' Dawson later recalled, 'Duncan turned to me and chortled, "That's it ... we'll call the show *Sez Les*."'[58]

CHAPTER 3

We don't take any notice of what Les sez

In Les Dawson, Yorkshire Television producer John Duncan had found a distinctive comedian, and knew the challenge was to build an equally distinctive show around him. To do this, he brought in young director David Mallet, who had come to Leeds after learning his trade in the US, working on Jack Good's pop music show *Shindig*. Like Duncan, Mallet was ex-public school, but this made no difference to the egalitarian Dawson. 'David was very posh and very west London,' recalls David Nobbs, who script-edited the later *Sez Les* shows, 'but that didn't interfere with Les getting on with him.'[1] The comedian was initially wary of the upstart, a reflex that Mallet understands completely: 'Would you trust a 21-year-old posh git from London if you'd been on the boards for twenty years?'[2] However, soon they found common ground: 'We got on really well and we used to have intellectual discussions.' Mallet loved Dawson for his speed in mastering the material. 'He was one of the few human beings I've ever met that could be given a script as he walked through the door, do that [mimes glancing at it] like that and go on to do a rehearsal,' Mallet recalls. 'He would do it right first time, and that was it. Didn't want to do it again. He was always late, but it didn't matter because he had total recall.' In return, Mallet's pragmatism endeared him to Dawson. Older directors, who had learned their trade when all television was live, regarded videotape editing as a last resort, and this became management orthodoxy. Barely out of his teens, Mallet had no such qualms. The technology was available and should be used:

> I used to let him wing it and I used to get into frightful trouble with the
> powers that be at Yorkshire, because, in those days, if your comic did

68

a stand-up, you wrote it out and it was timed. I used to say, 'No no no, you can't do that with Les Dawson, you've just got to let him rip.' He'd do six or eight minutes for a three-minute stand-up and then I used to cut it down. It was the early days of VT editing. It had just gone from cut to electronic, but when the electronic went wrong, they'd go back to the razor blade again. The early *Sez Les* were done as live, except they lasted fifty minutes, and then they were cut down by me to twenty-five minutes or whatever. There was no problem cutting down a six- or seven-minute stand-up to four minutes. With Les, he just used to throw it all into the pot. Quite often, some of them didn't work. It struck me that there was no reason to use the things that didn't work, just because they'd been scripted. Other people, I don't think, were prepared to spend the hours editing. I was.[3]

The idea settled on by Dawson, Duncan and Mallet was to place Dawson's earthy comedy in an oasis of glamour. A dance troupe called Les Girls was to be assembled, all ostrich feathers and long legs, moving elegantly around the most lavish sets that YTV's designers could supply. A strong supporting cast would be assembled for the sketches, including Brian Murphy from Joan Littlewood's Theatre Workshop in east London, and YTV announcer Redvers Kyle. Rather than using the theatrical layout still favoured by most comedy TV shows, much of *Sez Les* would be performed in the round, with audience rostrums in front of the performing area and on either side. This innovation was down to Mallet borrowing from what he had seen in the US: 'I lifted that from *Rowan and Martin's Laugh-In* and *The Andy Williams Show*. My influences were *The Andy Williams Show*, *Laugh-In* and *The Perry Como Show*. My influences were not Morecambe and Wise or whoever was variety in Britain. I'd been in America for two years, and I was only 19 when I went out there. I'd never seen British TV and it never occurred to me to do a theatrical thing with Les Dawson.'[4]

There was also the matter of music, about which Dawson had an idea. In April 1968, he had spent a week performing at the Mersey

Hotel, a large mock-Tudor pub in the south Manchester suburb of Didsbury, where ABC Television had its studios. Above the cabaret room was a ballroom, at the time being used by Syd Lawrence, who was an old acquaintance of Dawson's from the BBC Northern Dance Orchestra, for the band that he ran in his spare time. Tired of playing pop fodder on broadcasts in his day job, Lawrence had assembled a good amateur outfit to recreate the big band sound, with a particular focus on the Glenn Miller repertoire. Dawson went up to hear the band on the Tuesday night of his week at the Mersey and was knocked out by the standard of the musicianship. With the TV show in the offing, the following week Dawson took Duncan – a major jazz fan – to hear them play, and he agreed immediately that they were the perfect band for *Sez Les*. Moreover, the band were to be more than just 'noises off'. 'Normally, the orchestra wouldn't be seen on the screen but they decided to put our band on the screen and that was it,' Lawrence recalled in 1997.[5] There was only one problem: Lawrence was still on the BBC staff, and was unwilling to chance his regular gig for the sake of an ITV show that might not last. Duncan called in his old *That Was The Week That Was* colleague Dave Lee as musical director for the first series, but when the second run got the green light, Lawrence felt secure enough to jack in his £17 10s-a-week post with the Northern Dance Orchestra and become a full-time bandleader. In reality, Les loved the Lawrence orchestra to bits, but on screen, the insults came thick and fast. 'Despite his advanced age just wait until you hear Syd play that trumpet. I'm not saying it's a loud noise but they're repointing the walls at Jericho,' reads one jibe in Dawson's script notes.[6]

The first series of *Sez Les* swung into action at 10.40 p.m. on Wednesday, 30 April 1969, shown by most ITV network companies, except Tyne Tees and Scottish Television. It was regarded, at first, as a late-night show. The *Daily Express*'s reviewer Ron Boyle said he was 'furious' initially at the late scheduling, and thought it 'a dirty trick on both Yorkshire and Dawson', but admitted that 'it fits this mood of the evening to perfection'.[7] The choice of slot was perhaps partly because

of its cabaret flavour, but the attitude of YTV managing director
Donald Baverstock had an effect as well, as David Mallet remembers:

> Donald Baverstock, at his best, was some sort of genius and, at his
> worst, was a nightmare. I always remember seeing him in the Yorkshire
> Television canteen, and it would have been about half-past six, and there
> was a new light entertainment show – thank God it was nothing to do
> with me – and the pilot or the first show was going to be recorded at 7.30.
> He'd been in the bar, came in and cancelled the show and walked out.
> He just didn't like the idea. Donald Baverstock hated Les Dawson. Hated
> the show, hated Les Dawson, hated northern comics. He fucking hated
> anything to do with common northerners. How did he end up there?
> I don't know. He regularly ranted about 'that crappy show'.
>
> One night, in the bar, Donald and Les were at the same bar, I thought,
> 'Fuck this, I'm 21.' I said, 'Donald, I'd like you to meet Les Dawson,' and
> you could see him pulling back. Les stuck his hand out. They got into
> a discussion about Freud and Nietzsche, and suddenly Baverstock did
> a complete 180 in twenty-four hours. That show suddenly got a better
> place on the network. The two of them, they closed the bar that night.
> I remember, it was 11.15 and the double whiskies had gone down, I don't
> know how many, and they virtually strolled off arm in arm. It was the
> most extraordinary sight I'd ever seen. Before that, Donald Baverstock
> wouldn't even entertain the notion of a light entertainment show from
> oop north.[8]

Sadly, none of those early *Sez Les* shows survive, but the *TV Times*
billings do, and each resembles a miniature Dawson performance. For
show one, Dawson announced that it was:

> the show that takes you out of yourself, and forgets to put you back in
> … What to put in the show? I've always been a big band fan (everywhere
> I go, I'm banned) so I thought of the great Syd Lawrence Orchestra play-
> ing the Glenn Miller sound. Someone would have to write this show, so
> I put an ad in the papers – 'free ink supplied'. A horde of literary vagrants
> came flocking to Leeds. They attempted to curry favour by plying me

with strong drink. Well done, Mike, Dave, John. You got the job. To allay the doubts of those born South of Potters Bar, I hired a southerner, Brian Murphy, to assist me in the sketches. Also on hand are Redvers Kyle and the Skylarks.[9]

In following weeks, the listings have the distinct flavour of having been either written by Dawson himself or ghosted by someone who appreciated his humour. Show three promised that 'Les Dawson occasionally hits a high note of humour which is only perceptible to dogs, and certain other quadrupeds, so don't be alarmed by the whining in the hall, and the mooing in the garden as the show gathers pace,'[10] while in the show two listing, reference was made to the star guest, top American singer Roy Orbison, spending 'three days at Keighley roundabout waiting for a lift'.[11]

That initial run ended on 18 June 1969, and was followed swiftly by a second series, beginning on 10 September. At the start of the series, ITV was still transmitting in black and white only, but the last show of the series, on 19 November, went out in colour, the 625-line PAL network for BBC1 and ITV having been switched on just a few days before. With Dawson busy in clubs and theatres, there was a hiatus of nearly two years before series three of *Sez Les* began in 1971, but Yorkshire had ways of keeping its top comedian on screen. Canadian-born scriptwriter Ray Cameron and Mike King of the singing group the King Brothers had created a quick-fire panel game called *Jokers Wild*, in which comedians like Ted Ray and Arthur Askey competed with personalities like Michael Aspel and singer Lonnie Donegan to tell a joke on a given subject uninterrupted, under the chairmanship of Barry Cryer. From the start in July 1969, Dawson was a regular panellist and sometime team captain, and the apparently unrehearsed, impromptu nature of the show suited Dawson down to the ground. In addition, Dawson's tendency to dress up his jokes in florid language meant that, more often than anyone else on the show, he got to the punchline unmolested, the other competitors having either failed to recognize the old groaner he was telling until it was far too late or decided to just let him get on with it. 'It was solidly based on jokes, so one of the comics would say, "These two men go into a pub" and *bzzt*, and another would chime in with a pub joke,' Barry Cryer explains. 'And they'd all join in, buzz, buzz, pub, pub. Les would embark on some rambling monologue and the other comics would just sit back: "Les is on now." That's very rare. The other comics went, "No, it's Dawson talking. We're listening."'[12]

For a fairly typical Dawson contribution, take how he responded to a request for a joke on clergymen:

A few years ago, I struck a very bad financial patch. The wife had fell off her bike on the Wall of Death, and it cost a fortune to get rid of the clinkers. She got another job, but she had to give it up because she kept getting a rash off the diver's helmet. Just after that, I was drummed out of the Lighthouse Plasterers' Union because I cheated at Monopoly. And then to crown it all, on the Great North Road, my son, my eldest lad, was fined £10 for smacking a duck with a telescope. To escape from the scandal we went to a village that was so small the speed limit signs were back to back. It was a very poor village, the wishing well was full of IOUs. We loved it there, in that cottage. It was an old cottage, the mice wore powdered wigs. The only thing we didn't like was the local vicar. He was a long-winded bore. One day we went to church, and his sermon was long, it was a drowsy day, bees were humming outside, everybody was nodding off and he said, 'Look at you, sinners, you come here in a place of worship and you cannot keep awake to listen to what I am saying. The only person who is listening to me is that poor benighted soul you have the audacity to call the village idiot.' The idiot replied, 'Aye, and if I weren't so bloody daft, I'd be asleep with them.'[13]

On the recording, the laughter that greets each line shows how, with Dawson, the journey was often more important than the destination. In the same edition of the show, Cryer had said of him that 'when he tells a joke, I always bring sandwiches', causing Dawson to laugh and narrowly avoid spraying a mouthful of water over the desk. The camera cuts back just as he's turning away, choking on his chuckle.

On breaks from his *Monty Python's Flying Circus* duties, Cryer's friend and *Frost Report* colleague John Cleese made semi-regular appearances on *Jokers Wild*, encountering Dawson for the first time. His patrician manner masked a certain nervousness, as Cryer realized on the way to the recording of Cleese's first appearance:

> We used to get the breakfast train from King's Cross, and Ted Ray, everybody, oh God, over breakfast, never stopped. Not rudely, John was sitting over the aisle with his hands over his ears, reading a Penguin book, and I said, 'Are you all right?' and he said, 'Oh they're wonderful, but I'm unnerved. I shouldn't be doing this show. I'm not a comic.' I remembered this, we got to Leeds, John and I were chatting and I said, 'Do it on the show.' He said, 'What?' I said, 'Have the book on the show.' So we fixed the whole thing up. It came to his turn, I pressed the button and a card came up and I said, 'Mr Cleese.' 'Yes? What?' I said, 'Mothers-in-law, Mr Cleese.' He had a joke ready, of course, but it worked a treat because he was completely isolated in the middle of *Jokers Wild*, reading.[14]

Cleese's mock disdain was amplified by the fact that, instead of peering at a book, as he had on the train, he was concentrating on *The Times* crossword. To many, Cleese and Dawson occupied different comic worlds, but they would later coincide to great effect. Part of what made that possible was that Dawson was never a conventional quick-fire comedian. He had his own surreal, mocking orbit, into which the likes of Cleese could fit without too much trouble. In some ways, Dawson was an arch-subversive, taking cerebral, wordy material into the mainstream as often as he possibly could. Also, all of the Python team were still jobbing writers, with Terry Jones, Michael Palin and Eric Idle turning up regularly in the credits of the early *Two Ronnies* shows, and Idle collaborating with Graham Chapman and Barry Cryer on co-writing the Ronnie Corbett situation comedy *No, That's Me Over Here*. Cleese and Chapman also contributed a great many scripts to LWT's *Doctor* ... sitcom series, as did Bill Oddie and Graeme Garden, who, by 1971, were already established as two-thirds of *The Goodies*. Of course, Oddie had been writing links for Lulu back in 1968, while

Chapman sometimes performed the same service for Petula Clark, later observing that 'sketches … came easily enough … but trying to think up seven different introductions to "The Other Man's Grass is Always Greener" and ten for "Downtown" and the odd humorous remark for such people as Anthony Newley, Sacha Distel and Johnny Mathis was really quite a feat'.[15] So, the dividing lines between old and new comedy were nowhere near as clear as is sometimes made out.

The interim period also saw Dawson making guest appearances on other shows, including a triumphal return to *Opportunity Knocks* in a special edition transmitted from the aircraft carrier HMS *Hermes* on 10 November 1969. He also popped up twice for Thames Television on *David Nixon's Magic Box* in the spring of 1970, and renewed his acquaintance with Lulu on her BBC1 show on 25 July 1970, guesting alongside Dudley Moore. On that *It's Lulu* appearance, the Scottish singer introduced Dawson by admitting, 'I'm a wee bit worried about our next guest, because the idea is for him to come on and make us all laugh, but I've got a feeling we're going to have to make him laugh.' To a flourish of 'Put On a Happy Face' from the Alyn Ainsworth orchestra, on walks Dawson, to be asked by Lulu why he's always so miserable. 'Well, you see, Lulu, some people have a split personality,' he explains. 'Mine's shredded. Let's get one thing straight, this misery's only a stage image. In my private life, I'm a normal, average, happy-go-lucky manic depressive.'[16] Or at least that's what he's meant to say. He fluffs the line just after 'happy-go-lucky', laughs and garbles the punchline. Making himself laugh at the mistake was a rare slip, as he usually ploughed on, but he was far from immune to jumbling up his words, unless watched carefully by a producer and told to slow down. 'He always had terribly difficult diction,' David Mallet argues. 'He had a tendency to trip over the punchline.'[17] The spot is remarkable for the early presence of what would become a signature Dawson gag: 'Last week, the wife's mother came to stay with us. As soon as I heard the knock on the front door, I knew damned well it was her, because all of the mice were throwing themselves on the traps.'[18] This line would remain in his repertoire until the end of his career. At this stage,

Dawson still had a very noticeable tendency to acknowledge laughs with a Groucho-esque flutter of the eyebrows. It was a habit he would later grow out of as his confidence increased, and he felt more able to let the material stand on its own.

In August that year, Dawson made his debut as a guest, along with singer Ronnie Hilton, Hollywood star Stephanie Powers and host Bob Monkhouse, on ATV's Sunday evening game show *The Golden Shot*, the first of several appearances on the show over the next two years. With the show transmitted live or recorded as live, Dawson was the ideal *Shot* guest, being able to provide a monologue to the required length, and also to act as foil to the quick-witted Monkhouse in bits of comic business. On that first visit, the script required him to dress up in drag as the show's unlikeliest-looking 'Golden Girl', alongside the real article, Anne Aston. There were also references to Dawson giving Hilton a lift down to the Birmingham studios from Scarborough, where the pair of them were appearing in summer season with Monkhouse at the Floral Hall, in a production called, with unsurprising opportunism, *The Golden Show*. Monkhouse later commented that 'I took top billing ... but it was Les who was the hit of the show'.[19]

In the Scarborough show, Dawson took part in the opening number, then returned for some cross-talk with Monkhouse early in the first half, with the pair sticking to the summer season rule of making as much fun of local place names and people as possible. One of Dawson's staple jokes, scribbled into a notebook in the pre-fame years and honed during his club and pub years, concerned a chap at the bottom of a swimming pool apparently holding his breath while onlookers gather round to admire the man's stamina. After watching for fifteen minutes, Dawson comments to the pool attendant that it's a remarkable feat, to which comes the surprising reply: 'He's nothing but a bloody show-off. He's been down there a month.' For the Scarborough season, this well-polished gag, which would see further service in Dawson's stage shows and radio performances, was claimed to have occurred at the open-air pool in Peasholme Park. Monkhouse responded in local mode by mentioning a seller of novelty items who strode up and down the prom shouting 'RUBBER BALLOONS!', seemingly for the simple laugh of recognition. The pair then went on to tell a tale, apparently concerning an ample female member of the audience who had leapt onto the stage to throw herself at Dawson. 'She was a hell of a size,' Dawson observed to Monkhouse and the punters. 'She must have been built when meat was cheap ... I've never seen a woman with so many double chins. She looked for all the world as if she were resting her head on a pile of crumpets.' Having achieved her goal, she promptly fainted, at which 'Her dress burst open. She hadn't got a thing on underneath. I felt like a pigeon going across the Pennines.' Dawson then mused on the various options open to him in treating her condition: 'Well, I didn't know whether to rub her forehead, rub her wrist or ...' This was as far as he got, as the punchline was left to Monkhouse, shouting 'RUBBER BALLOONS!'[20]

Dawson returned at the end of the first half to do his solo spot. It was the last time he'd appear as the second comic on any bill. He opened by complimenting the previous act, singer Jane Fyffe, on her performance. 'I should know what I'm talking about,' he asserted, 'because all of my family were good singers. We had to be, we had no lock on the toilet door.'[21] Next, he seems to play against his image by announcing that 'things are looking up' career-wise, but, unsurprisingly, it was a set-up for a let-down. 'Later this year, I've been engaged as the entertainments officer aboard a Norwegian whaler,' Dawson announced. 'It'll be a very challenging post, because apart from organizing ship's concerts and whist drives, I shall also act as bait.' He reported that there was also the prospect of a winter return to the US, because the last time he had performed there he had overheard the ambassador saying 'It'll be a bloody cold day before we have him back again.' His mother-in-law got off lightly, his ire being reserved for his wife's father, a man of vile habits, including dropping his cigarette ends on the living room carpet, with the result that it's 'so full of holes the mice use it as a crib board'. Normally, said Les, the old man was inclined to pick up cigar butts in the street and smoke them, but 'he had to give it up last winter as he made some terrible mistakes in the snow'.

Over Christmas 1970, during his season at the Grand in Leeds, playing the Robber-in-Chief in *Babes in the Wood*, Dawson had three television bookings, all for ITV. The first was *A Gift for Gracie* on Christmas Day itself, a big show from YTV starring Gracie Fields. Although colour television had been introduced on the network, a union dispute over extra pay for colour work resulted in a work-to-rule on commercial television in late 1970 and early 1971, where programmes were once again made and transmitted in monochrome. This ruling affected Dawson's second guest spot, on London Weekend's *Holiday Startime*, transmitted on Boxing Day 1970 and hosted by Australian actress and singer Maggie Fitzgibbon. The comic competition on this festive show was pretty stiff, with Peter Cook offering an E.L. Wisty monologue, horror actor Vincent Price sending himself up with a drunken cookery lesson and Thora Hird in a sketch with Arthur Lowe. Even so, Dawson held his own admirably, despite some unnecessary business at the start of the show with a 'joke computer'. Being 1970, the 'computer' is the size of a large coffee machine, although, oddly, it is missing the spooling reels of tape that props departments usually threw in when called upon to build a fake computer.

The third appearance, in a one-off called *The Syd Lawrence Band Show*, was only part-networked. Introduced by band singer Kevin Kent, Dawson opened by saying, 'Of course, Kevin and I are old friends. I knew him when he was Rommel ... It's a great pleasure to be working again with the wonderful sound of the Syd Lawrence orchestra. That's one thing about me. I've always been polite as well as tone-deaf.' After his routine, Dawson hot-footed it off to sit among the band for 'In the Mood', grabbing Lawrence for an impromptu jive as he passed, amply supporting his claim that he was once the North Manchester jitterbug champion.

Sez Les returned on 16 August 1971, cross-promoted the following Sunday by Dawson making another appearance on *The Golden Shot*. The game show took 'Boy Meets Girl' as its theme, with Dawson appearing first on as Adam in the Garden of Eden, dressed in long johns with a strategically placed fig leaf and smoking a cigarette:

Les: Good afternoon, I'm Adam, the one-man population explosion. [*Looks at cig in hand*] Hey what am I doing with that? They haven't been invented yet. [*He throws it down and stamps on it … and then recoils, and nurses bare foot*] And shoes haven't been invented either! I'm fed up too. Do you know what that Eve went and did? Put my best suit in the salad … Do you know she even takes that snake to bed? I mean if I have to go to bed with a snake, give me a bad adder, like Anne Aston. [*Rubs hands together eagerly*] Well now to forget the Good Book and start the loose leaf system![22]

For the most part, Dawson was left to come up with his own lines for game show appearances, but this gives an insight into the standard rather corny material (in this case written by Wally Malston) that the guests could be expected to peddle in order to keep the show moving. His later spot in the same show, presenting a prize to a contestant, is either written by Dawson himself, or by Malston in consultation with the comedian, as it is far more obviously in his distinct voice, using a couple of his standard lines. Aptly enough, the prize is a piano:

Do you remember when just about every home had a piano in the parlour or front room? And when Mum and Dad were so proud to let their little boy have piano lessons. I used to play the piano. Everybody loved my playing. Mum, Dad, relatives, all the neighbours. In fact they even broke all our windows so they could hear me better. [*Plays a bit more*] I wished now I'd stuck at it. I might have been able to play like this [*then plays a few bars very impressively of any tune*] 'course we didn't have a piano as good as this. This is a fabulous instrument. Marvellous tonal quality. It has all over iron frame. There's all the qualities of a larger model in this six-octave unit. It's 3' 3" high, 3' 8¾" long and only 1' 7" in depth, so will fit anywhere. It's another proud example of the British piano industry who make 18,000 a year, of which over half are exported. We'll gladly export this one to your home next week.[23]

The way the monologue gives way to a sales spiel says a lot about the time in which it was delivered. Against a backcloth of industrial unrest, a great deal was being done to promote British products and services, particularly as items for export. ATV, the company that made *The Golden Shot*, did much for British exports with its ITC division producing filmed adventure series like *The Saint* and *Danger Man*, which were snapped up by overseas networks. This success was acknowledged when ATV won the Queen's Award for Export in 1967 and 1969. The detailed description of the prize piano also gives a little inkling of what Dawson might have been like back in his Hooverselling days.

Back on *Sez Les*, while Dawson always crafted his monologue at the start of the show and wrote the odd sketch, it was other writers who supplied the majority of the material. 'Les couldn't write classic sketches,' David Nobbs avers. 'It wasn't his kind of thing.'[24] His attitude to the whole set-up was curious, taking the monologues very seriously, but rarely complaining about anything offered up by the other writers. 'He never even thought about a script, he never thought about anything,' David Mallet explains.[25] From series three onwards, the bulk of the script came from Peter Dulay, son of an old-time comedy magician called Benson Dulay, and an experienced variety performer himself. The name Dulay had been adapted by Benson Dulay from his real family name, Dooley, and his son was very particular about its pronunciation. 'He pronounced it "Du Lay" always, like Madame "Du Barry",' notes David Mallet. When Max Wall bowed out of the London production of *The Pajama Game* in 1956, Dulay had taken over the role of Vernon Hines, the factory time-keeper. Dulay then moved from performing into television production, working at ABC with Ronnie Taylor, Mark Stuart and Royston Mayoh.

So, when he came to work on *Sez Les*, he had been aware of Dawson and his work for longer than most. For better or worse, Dulay's idea of what constituted comedy did tend towards the more traditional. 'His strength was rock-solid visual slapstick gags,' Mallet explains. 'Les was terribly good at [it], but he didn't know he was good at it until he got with Dulay. When Peter Dulay got comedy right, he was right bang on, because he understood how to deliver it.'[26] One such example is a sketch set in a hospital ward with Dawson as a troublesome visitor bothering a friend in traction: 'We did laugh when you stood on that window ledge and said "I can fly! I can fly!" We'd have stopped you, but we thought you could.'[27] He torments the near-mummified figure with gossip about his wife, then adjusts the bed and the pulleys and uses the patient's plaster cast to crack a Brazil nut. It ends with the patient – swathed from head to toe in bandages – disappearing out of the window, having been raised up by Dawson so he can get a better view of the world outside. With the other performer mute save for the odd groan, it's effectively a solo sketch for Dawson, and one that he pitches perfectly. Mallet had seen the basic idea done before on an American show, and described it to Dulay, who wrote it up for Dawson.

In the opening show of the fourth series is another noteworthy slapstick-heavy sketch, set in a china shop run by a pair of old queens. One of them is played by Roy Barraclough, later to become Dawson's closest comic collaborator and, in his own right, a star of *Coronation Street*, wearing a shirt open to the navel and a medallion; this was the first time he had appeared on television alongside Dawson. As the sketch opens, Barraclough is seen mincing around and putting plates on a precarious-looking display. In walk Dawson and a colleague, in overalls and caps, answering an advertisement for odd-job men. The comedy value of the two labourers carrying each plate as slowly and gingerly as if it were a ten-foot-tall glass statue is undermined fatally by the depiction of homosexuality, which is, even allowing for the attitudes of the time, unpleasantly crude. Lines like 'Listen, Whittaker, whatever you do, don't get separated', as Dawson warns his colleague not to find himself alone with the shop's proprietor, get undeservedly massive laughs.[28] The effeminacy of Barraclough's character is as nothing compared to that of his partner, resplendent in a gaily coloured bow tie-cum-neckerchief, who takes exception to the plates being put out by Dawson due to jealousy, the designer being a 'close personal friend' of Barraclough's character. This tension inspires a lovely bit of business that almost redeems the sketch. When

Barraclough's character seems to be prevailing in his insistence that the plates should stay, Dawson and mate load the display, but when the other seems to be winning, they begin removing the plates. This continues back and forth, with Dawson's face cataloguing the changing tide, until a cry of frustration from one of the proprietors causes one of the plates to be dropped. Fainting with shock, he then collapses onto Barraclough, and the pair fall backwards onto a display case, which topples into another, with every fitting in the shop following like a cascade of dominoes until every piece of stock has been shattered but one. Dawson triumphantly places the lone plate on the display, with a flourish reminiscent of W.C. Fields, then leaves the shop, the closing of the door causing the plate to fall to the ground and break, the tag marred only slightly by the obvious intervention of a scene-shifter's hand nudging the plate off the display.

While such material did nothing for gay liberation, Mallet felt that Dulay's influence set the show back in more fundamental ways. 'The Dulay material ... assumed that Les was an old northern on-the-boards comedian,' says Mallet. 'There was a lack of variety of types of material'. Mallet was particularly unhappy with a recurring character called Superflop, a lavatory attendant who responded to crises by turning into a super anti-hero and promptly making them into disasters. 'It wasn't very funny,' the director admits. 'The opening routine of Superflop was a minute and it was the same every week. You just want to kill yourself now when you watch it. It went down very well in budget terms, but I did it and I'm ashamed of myself for making it so long. Some of the gags were weak, I thought.'[29] However, the segment became mildly notorious not for its quality, but for the name of the character in Clark Kent mode, Leslie Bottieball. This moniker was noticed with disapproval by the general manager of the 21 Club and Churchill's Club in London's Mayfair, one Leslie Botibol. 'I was very annoyed at the time,' Mr Botibol told the *Daily Mirror*. 'I was always receiving letters, comments and phone calls in the club from friends who said I should be living in the gents.'[30] Following a complaint from Mr Botibol's solicitor, Yorkshire Television agreed to edit the character's surname out of future repeats,[31] and paid the aggrieved party £200 to cover his legal expenses. In return, Mr Botibol invited Dawson to dinner at his club. 'Generally I think Les Dawson is an excellent comedian,' said Mr Botibol. 'He makes me laugh – especially now he is not mentioning my name.'[32]

Sez Les also made the news when former dance band leader Bert Ambrose was rushed to Leeds General Infirmary during rehearsals on 11 June 1971 after suffering a heart attack. He was at the studio as the manager and lover of the singer Kathy Kirby, who was guesting on the show. Ambrose died at the hospital. 'I was the one who told Kathy Kirby,' recalls David Mallet. 'I had to come down because the floor manager, Rusty Buckley, didn't dare tell her.'[33] The recording went ahead as planned, but a distressed Kirby loses the time on *Come Rain or Come Shine* and manages to get half a bar ahead of the band. The result is an unholy mess.

For the fifth series, beginning on 29 July 1972, each edition was extended to forty-five minutes, and the show was promoted to Saturday teatime, before the quiz *Sale of the Century*. 'Despite the fact that we've been given an earlier programme and a forty-five-minute duration,' Dawson announced, 'I can assure our fans that it's still the same cheaply produced bilge.'[34] Actually, the quality of the material had improved considerably, perhaps due to the arrival of future situation comedy writer Richard Ommanney on the team. The first show opens with a visual gag involving a top-hatted Dawson descending a Hollywood-style staircase with increasing difficulty as the steps become larger. By the bottom, the treads are nearly half Dawson's height. Having reached the bottom, a female hand is seen in shot. Dawson croons lovingly to its owner, who, it soon emerges, is approximately twenty feet away, at the end of an extremely long arm. Having reached her face with some difficulty, he is rewarded not with a kiss, but with a faceful of smoke blown from the cigarette she is smoking in a long holder. Later in the same show, a simple prop joke, involving Dawson as a wine waiter removing a cork as long as the bottle it encloses, is rendered joyous by the sommelier

Dawson chuntering on pretentiously about the virtues of the contents of the bottle as the freakishly long stopper is removed. While 'lugubrious' was a word much applied to Dawson, here he has serious competition from John Vyvyan, a toad-faced character actor and unsmiling veteran of so many British comedy shows, including *Hancock's Half Hour*, as one of the diners, while Damaris Hayman, who also worked with Hancock later in his career, plays Vyvyan's companion.

The fifth series of *Sez Les* also featured a guest appearance from a young and relatively serious Richard Whiteley, then working as the presenter on Yorkshire's regional news magazine *Calendar*, interviewing Dawson as a man who claims he can catch raspberries, of the blown rather than the edible kind. Having made his debut in the previous series, Roy Barraclough also began to appear more regularly in this run. In one glorious quickie, Dawson and Barraclough are a pair of ventriloquists meeting in a pub, greeting each other through closed mouths and counting doggedly as they drink their pints of bitter in one gulp. Barraclough turns up again as the film director in a long but enjoyable sketch about a scene hand, played by Dawson, being pressed into service as a stuntman:

DIRECTOR: Now come on, Hugo, baby, for the last time, it needs more pace. Now can I go for a take this time? I'm two weeks behind schedule as it is.

LEADING MAN: If the casting department paid as much attention to getting me a decent stand-in as they do to picking these bosomy blondes for the orgy scenes, we'd be on time.

DIRECTOR: OK, so we've had a few accidents. What's a stuntman here and there? ... OK, stand by, roll 'em. Action ...

LEADING LADY: Humphrey, I beg you, please stay the night, we're completely cut off by the floods and the only bridge is all but washed away. There's no danger of my husband returning now.

LEADING MAN: But if he were to come through that door at this moment, what would he say?

[*Dawson enters in flat cap and brown coat*]

SCENE HAND: I've got a cactus here, where do you want it?

DIRECTOR: CUT! Didn't you see the little red light? You do not come barging onto a set when the little red light is up ... OK, get the stand-in.

ASSISTANT: I'm sorry, the stand-in hasn't turned up, we haven't got one ...

DIRECTOR: You, little man, put that plant down. Get him a costume.[35]

With the story requiring the storm to batter both the house and the leading man, when he opens the window to take a look, the stand-in's job is to take the battering. Naturally, the hapless scene hand gets drenched and, when the leading lady's husband returns, is beaten up. The scene ends with the husband having shot the lover, and the leading lady having shot her husband in retaliation. Bemoaning her sudden loneliness, she wishes she had a son to carry on the name. At which, the beaten and bruised scene hand pops up from behind the bed, declares this a job for the stand-in and leaps onto the bed with the leading lady. The scene is slapstick-heavy like a lot of Dulay-era *Sez Les*, but all of the physical activity serves the comedy.

However, despite the upturn in the quality of the sketch material, only the monologues with which he opened each show, and the withering introductions to the guest artists, stand out as distinctive Dawson, perhaps unsurprisingly as they were still his main writing contribution. In the opening show of the fifth series, he refers mockingly to 'Syd Lawrence and his Arthritic Rhythmaires, playing their usual band of musical earache' and the dancers, billed as 'Les Girls', are dismissed as 'a job lot from a chilblain clinic'.[36] Meanwhile, singer Labi Siffre, who became a *Sez Les* semi-regular, was described as having a name 'like a form of industrial bronchial catarrh',[37] and big US star Neil Sedaka was introduced as 'the American name for Jeyes Fluid ... direct from a one-night stand at Goole Floral Arcade'.[38] Sometimes, the digs were aimed at performers who weren't on the show. Discussing the insecurity of show business, Dawson once announced that 'I shouldn't be here now. I should have been on tour in a revival of *The King and*

I with Flora Robson. They had to cancel it. She wouldn't have her head shaved.'[39]

When writing monologues, a favourite technique of Dawson's was to build an edifice of several unrelated statements of nonsense purporting to be fact, all couched in the most purple prose he could manage, before reaching a punchline that knocked it all down. 'In the court of Louis XIV, ladies used to paint their faces with a tincture of lead oxide to keep away the signs of old age,' began one such preamble, continuing 'and there is, in Bolivia, a tribe of dwarf cannibals who keep their skins youthful and pliant by smearing their bodies with python fat and gazelle droppings. And in 1848, a Dutch harp tuner from Norwich claimed that you could keep away grey hair and crows feet by rubbing your face in a mackerel's liver. The reasons I mention these tips on how to stay young are because when you see the show it'll put bloody years on you.'[40] Indeed, many of Dawson's monologues consist of a very loosely themed collection of one-liners that work independent of context. It's the pacing of Dawson's delivery that elevates them into something more coherent.

Dulay's collaboration with Dawson continued outside the YTV studios. In December 1972, Dawson returned to the Grand Theatre in Leeds for another Christmas show, *Goody Two Shoes*, directed and co-written by Dulay. Not one of the traditional pantomimes, *Goody Two Shoes* was an entirely new production, based on an eighteenth-century children's story about an orphan girl who is given a pair of shoes as a reward for being virtuous. Dawson was called in to play Lazy Les, one of the baker's men, the others being up-and-coming comedian Brian Marshall as Simple Simon and Eli Woods as Wandering Willie. Woods, who had been Jimmy James's longest serving stooge, had become part of Dawson's repertory company both on TV and, through his cousin, Jim Casey, on radio. Meanwhile, Dawson's old colleague from the 1970 season in Scarborough, Ronnie Hilton, came in as Pete the Puppeteer, and Mary Oakley from *The Black and White Minstrel Show* took the title role. In its review of that year's Christmas shows, *The Stage* referred to *Goody Two Shoes* as 'one of the best pantomimes presented there in recent years', with 'clever, novel specialities' and 'a lively pace'. Dawson was singled out as 'a real hit'.[41]

Even without Dulay's support, Dawson had been keeping a very full diary of live engagements. In the summer of 1971, he joined singer Ronnie Hilton, with whom he had worked at Scarborough the year before, for a season at the Queen's Theatre in Blackpool. His fellow performers on this run included Dora Bryan, sharing Dawson and Hilton's top billing, and an up-and-coming young man called Lennie Bennett as second-spot comic. It was the first time Dawson had been back to the Lancashire resort for an extended run since his Central Pier season in 1968, despite Blackpool being the scene of so many early radio and TV triumphs and practically home turf for a Mancunian in need of sea air.

In *The Stage*'s write-up of the show, which did good business throughout the run, the reviewer claimed, erroneously, that Dawson was 'the embodiment of the cloth-capped Northerner'.[42] Northern he was and proud of it too, but Dawson's appearances in a cloth cap were few and far between. In his TV appearances of the era, he is often to be seen wearing a hat but it's almost always one of the pork pie variety. Nonetheless, during the Blackpool season, his 'almost funereal . . . quips' were 'always clean and palatable – and always laughter-evoking'.[43]

As soon as Julie's school holidays began, Dawson moved the whole family to join him in Blackpool for the rest of the season. Meg was heavily pregnant with their third child, but found the energy to join her husband on explorations of the surrounding area. On visiting the refined, genteel district of Lytham St Anne's, seven miles south of the bustling resort, the Dawsons agreed that it would be an ideal spot to put down roots – close enough to be handy for the entertainment Mecca of the north-west, and yet sufficiently distant to allow a different pace of life at home. It would be four more years before they finally moved there, but the seed had been sown. On the night of 17 July, Meg was rushed to Fairfield Hospital in Bury, where Stuart had been born, to prepare for the birth, which followed on 20 July.

As Dawson told the story in his memoirs, he was on stage when he heard the news of the new arrival, brought to him by Jimmy Tarbuck, who was clutching a bottle of champagne and offered to stand in for him while he made for the hospital. Once again, this appears to be a nice story but nothing more. According to a contemporary report in *The Stage*, 'the comedian ... was at the Manchester maternity hospital at 3.30 in the morning when Pamela Jayne, his 7lb daughter, was born'. The article added:

> The second-house audience was given the 'Mother and child both doing well' report the following night after the walk-down. Dora Bryan sharing the spotlight with Les made the surprise announcement. Whereupon Ronnie Hilton – the other principal – emerged from the wings pushing a battered old pram. From it he extracted a chocolate-coloured doll which Les accepted with an exaggerated show of affection and exclaimed: 'Well now, isn't that just like the wife – she burns everything!'[44]

Summer 1971 in Blackpool was followed by Christmas and New Year in Birmingham, starring in *Robinson Crusoe* at the Alexandra Theatre, and working alongside Jack Tripp, a relative unknown outside the world of theatre, but one of the most respected pantomime dames in the business. Dawson's main recollection of that Christmas season in Birmingham was less of the show or the city than of Derek Salberg, the theatre's proprietor and the show's booker. On first impressions, Dawson was underwhelmed and depressed by this 'small agitated man with worry lining every crease in his face', who dismissed all of Dawson's ideas and left the comic feeling 'like stowing away on a freighter, only there aren't many in Birmingham'.[45] Despite very favourable reviews and good business at the box office, all Salberg would say was 'Could be better'. Sensing the tension, Tripp advised Dawson not to worry about it. The simple fact was that Salberg was a contrarian, and whatever anyone said, he'd say the opposite. When Salberg called in at Dawson's dressing room before the next show, the star apologized profusely for his performance and for the lacklustre business, which he felt sure was all his fault. Salberg replied that the season was doing the best business the theatre had had for years and that Dawson was largely responsible. Dawson burst out laughing and cried 'Got you, you old bugger'. Salberg fixed Dawson with a glare and then burst out laughing himself. From that moment on, the pair became good friends, and Dawson came to admire an 'old school … gentleman' of the theatre.

In the summer of 1972, Dawson took a break from the conventional summer season variety show and branched out into farce, appearing in *Don't Tell the Wife* at the Pier Theatre in Skegness. Dawson's character was a plumber called Alf Willis, whose wife has become convinced that her husband is pursuing other women. In fact, he is devoting most of his time and effort to resisting the advances of their French lodger, Georgette, who was played in the Skegness run by the very glamorous Valerie Leon, best known for her appearances in the seventies Hai Karate aftershave commercials. *The Stage* reported that Dawson had made 'a tremendous success' and 'quickly … adapted himself to the legitimate stage'. At the end of the month, another Cree farce – *The Mating Season* – moved in, with Sid James in the leading role.

The longer theatre runs were punctuated by shorter engagements at clubs all over the north. In November 1971, Dawson headed a variety bill at the Talk of the Midlands in Derby, while April 1972 found Dawson at the Club Fiesta in Stockton, and, in August, he could be seen at the Golden Garter in Wythenshawe. The slightly overblown and grandiose names of these establishments were meat and drink to the comedian, who invented a fictitious seaside nightspot called Talk of the Groyne.

Back in the television studios, along with the zealous and converted Donald Baverstock, Dawson had another intellectual ally in the form of John Cleese, who had already encountered Dawson on *Jokers Wild*. Mallet immediately saw the comedy potential of such an unlikely pairing.

> I'd always been a fan of him in *Python* and I remember thinking, 'Public-school educated, six foot six, and Dawson – probably five foot four.

Wouldn't it be great to have Cleese, rather than any of these northern comics for him to play off', and for some reason Cleese accepted. We did loads and loads of quickies. I'm sure they're all wiped now. The Foreign Legion was the first one, in a foxhole, the two of them with the height difference. Cleese says, 'Dawson, what's that chap doing over there?' 'I think he's flashing, sir.' Cleese doesn't do anything, he just looks Marvellous.[46]

Not everyone realized what a coup it was for *Sez Les* to have Cleese around. Scriptwriter David Nobbs's 'main memory of [Dawson's manager] Norman Murray was when we did sketches with John Cleese, and Norman Murray said, "That lad's good, who is he?" I just thought it was absolutely astonishing. *Monty Python* was up and running and may have been almost over. It was astonishing. So I dare say that Norman wasn't fully in touch.'[47]

As well as Dawson and Cleese worked together professionally, it was nothing compared with their off-screen respect for each other. 'They both got on,' Mallet relates. 'From the day they met, they were like *that* [crosses fingers]. Everyone said they'd hate each other, and everything else like that, but they were like *that*. Cleese was in awe of Les. The language, the verboseness and all that, while Les looked up to him, like an officer.' Even the potential tension of their differing approaches to rehearsal didn't get in the way of their friendship. 'They were very different,' Mallet observes. 'Cleese liked it buttoned down, and Les wouldn't button anything down until the moment. People say he was lazy, but I don't think it was laziness. This is I think an important point. Anybody that can come in at eleven, an hour and a half late, read a seven-page sketch and just do it, and you're out by twelve o'clock. I'm not exaggerating. I never saw Les glance at a piece of paper in my whole life. Les wasn't lazy, he was brilliant.'[48]

Radio remains the ideal medium for a comedian who gives their best on the first read-through. Indeed, publicity shots showing performers at the microphone with a script are not posed: it remains the way that much radio comedy is done, even today. At his peak, Tony

Hancock was another who could grasp the nuances and tone of a script on first read-through. Even with his television fame growing, Dawson remembered the medium that gave him his first national exposure, continuing to broadcast on the radio despite his other successes. Moreover, he stayed with the BBC Manchester team who had given him that chance, headed by Jim Casey, out of a combination of professional respect for their skills and gratitude for taking a chance on him when nobody else would. There's an old show business maxim that instructs turns to be nice to people on the way up, because you'll meet them again on the way down. Dawson grasped that basic truth, less out of self-preservation and expediency and more because his roots and fundamental sentimentalism never allowed him to overlook or forget kindness. Casey has a telling story about the newly famous Dawson: 'When he got his first big car, he took me out after a rehearsal and said, "Jim, come outside. Look at that. Isn't that beautiful?" I said, "I wish you well to drive it, son." He said, "That's thanks to you, that." I said "Sod off." He was so thrilled that he could get an expensive car. It was all a genuine thrill that life was great and successful.'[49] Cars would be an enduring passion of Dawson's, his proudest automotive possession being the Jaguar E-type that he kept alongside more sober, but still powerful, family saloons.

Reviewing one of his early radio appearances after his *Opportunity Knocks* success, Gillian Reynolds in the *Guardian* observed that while Dawson 'fit[s] into radio comedy perfectly', the experience of listening to him is helped by 'remember[ing] his plump-poker face'.[50] By the time Dawson had his own radio series, his face was well known enough for the audience at home to have a good idea of his visual reactions to the sound gags. His first starring vehicle for the wireless had been a run of six shows in early 1970, titled *Les Dawson – Man of Fiction*, broadcast only on the northern transmitters of Radio 4, as the Home Service had been renamed in 1967. This was followed, in December 1971, by a networked series, written and produced by Casey, called *Our Les*, a sitcom about a pair of brothers who cleaned windows by day and did a club act by night. 'I rang him up, and he was at the

Grand, Leeds, in pantomime,' Casey recalls. 'I went over and I said, "I've written this script, it's a situation comedy, we'll read it, tear it to pieces and put it back together again." He read it and said, "I wouldn't change a word. That's more like me than I am." I said, "Well, I'm going to put it up, do a pilot, and see what they say." He said, "Well, if they don't like it, they can get stuffed."'[51]

Dawson's pessimism was not unfounded. Casey always had to negotiate a path through the internal politics of the BBC to get Manchester shows placed. London producers wanted all of the best slots for themselves, and without forceful lobbying from elsewhere in the Corporation, they tended to get them. As Casey admits:

> I was a bit of a rebel. My boss, who always kowtowed to anybody with initials, head of whatnot, he went through for the meeting with light entertainment [in London] and the controller of Radio 1 and 2, and came back and said, 'Well, you've only got the one series on, *The Clitheroe Kid.*' I said, 'What? Can you arrange another meeting? I'm coming to another meeting.' So he arranged another meeting with the head of light entertainment [Con Mahoney], and the controller of Radio 1 and 2, Douglas Muggeridge. Douglas was a fan of mine and we went to this meeting and I came away with three series. One was Les, which they didn't want at first.

Casey was able to call Dawson in triumph and tell him that the show had found a home on Radio 2, the former Light Programme. The cast consisted of actors rather than comic performers, with Colin Edwynn playing Les's brother. The script was written to play to Dawson's bathetic strengths, particularly when it came to the depictions of the brothers' act, with Dawson's character thinking 'he was very clever to change Chicago so that if they were in Scunthorpe he'd sing "This is our kind of town, old Scunthorpe is"'.[52] Amusingly, the same song had been employed in one of the big production numbers at *The Golden Show* in Scarborough, and the same switch had been employed, with the North Yorkshire resort standing in for the Windy City. The joke appears to be that big stars in a big show can get away with it, whereas a down-at-heel act pulling the same stunt can only appear shabby.

Getting the show on air did not mean that the production was home and dry. One of Mahoney's underlings took exception to one mild reference to effeminacy and brought it up at the next meeting. Casey expressed surprise that it was an issue, given the rampant campery that had recently been on display in Kenneth Williams's series *Stop Messing About*. The comment may well have touched a raw nerve, as the series had been dropped, as Williams noted in his diaries, because 'there'd been complaints about how dirty the script was etc.'[53] *Our Les* went well enough, but Casey never felt it was the best vehicle for Dawson as a radio performer.

If Dawson's early years of fame sound like a mad rush of work with precious little time for reflection, that's because they were. After fifteen years of not quite making it, he was keen to make the most of the opportunities now open to him. He paid a heavy price for this decision, seeing very little of Meg or their young family. To some degree, Dawson's professional life led to an emulation of the estrangement that had occurred between him and his own father during the Second World War, although his own periods of leave were longer and more frequent. For summer seasons, it was possible to uproot the entire family, but for weeks here and nights there, it made no sense. 'So many things were happening for me, that my home life became non-existent,' he explained in *A Clown Too Many*. 'Julie and Stuart were growing up without me being there to see them develop. When I did get home, Meg was fully in control and I felt that I wasn't needed ... she had to be a father as well ... [and] the pain of seeing their closeness caused anger.'[54] Sadly, the anger wasn't enough to keep him in Bury. 'I fretted at the inactivity at home and longed for the travelling again,' he admitted. 'I had changed, for the worse, really: I was too ambitious for my own good.'[55]

Even television work in Leeds, from where Dawson could, theoretically, return home to Bury at night, became an overnight stay.

A man of Dawson's capacity for drink, conversation and carousal needed little persuasion to immerse himself in the bibulous culture that pervaded broadcasting and show business at the time, and so it became prudent to stay on the other side of the Pennines, for the sake of his driving licence. 'I'd wake up in unfamiliar places and see a stranger in the mirror,' he wrote in 1985, adding that 'it would be years before common sense took charge'.[56] One of the more constructive pursuits of those early years as a nomadic entertainer was the novel he had begun to write, on which he worked in idle moments. Sticking to the principle of writing about what you know best, the manuscript concerned a struggling club comedian who hits the big time on TV, but has to choose between his career and his family.

Perhaps unsurprisingly, Dawson began to fear for his marriage around this time, his paranoia being heightened by Meg's receiving mysterious telephone calls. Whenever Dawson himself answered the telephone, the line would go dead. He became convinced that Meg was having an affair. He also had a vague sense that his career had peaked and that the only way in terms of ratings and approval was down. The latter impression was underlined when he was booked to appear as a star guest on the All-Winners Final of *Opportunity Knocks* on 20 December 1971. Suspecting that he would find at least a few friends in the bar at Thames Television's Teddington studios, he was most upset when his old friend, Thames producer Royston Mayoh, steered him to an ante-room laden with bottles of Scotch whisky and explained that the bar was in use for an executive party, a story that Dawson didn't believe for one minute. Mayoh went to attend to another matter, leaving Dawson to drink alone.

Finally called to make his appearance at the close of the show, Dawson was going through the motions of banter with Hughie Green and Irish comedian Frank Carson, discussing Green's birthday and the present that Carson had brought for the host, when a tall figure emerged from behind the set. Green suggested that Dawson open Carson's present on his behalf. Calling Carson a 'creep', Dawson began removing the wrapping paper, to reveal a red book. Realizing that he was in the middle of a *This Is Your Life* sting, he laughed awkwardly, but the laugh turned to shock as Eamonn Andrews stepped forward, and put his hand on Dawson's shoulder. Green and Carson were now laughing and clapping uproariously. The telephone calls and his pariah status at the studios were all explained as Andrews said, 'Tonight, Les Dawson, *This Is Your Life*'.

'You're asking your loved ones to tell lies for the first time, and Meg wasn't very happy about that,' observes Royston Mayoh, himself a director of many editions of the show. In the case of the Dawson show, others produced and directed, but Mayoh was crucial to the preparations, knowing both Andrews and Green well, and being able to keep the secret. 'Many times we cancelled the show because we'd heard that the subject had heard about it. Eamonn was absolutely resolute that if there was any doubt at all that the subject knew, you didn't want to be there.'[57]

One element of the preparations for any *This Is Your Life* was the stagger-through the evening before the recording, at which the director would take the Andrews role and run a rough rehearsal with any guests that were overnighting. Usually these would be family members, which meant there was a chance to check on the details in the script. As Mayoh remembers:

> Oftentimes, within the first sentence, a voice would come from the back: 'Excuse me, it wasn't 1946 at all.' Everybody's got a different memory. [Scriptwriters] Roy [Bottomley] and Tom [Brennand] were there, and the producer was there and the three researchers were there, and I was reading it as Eamonn. We'd stop and talk about it. It was important for me as a director, because I could make notes on what I was looking for. I could make notes on the passion that was around there. Auntie Mildred – when she comes on, I've got to get a close-up of her because she's going to 'go'. It gave me clues on what I was looking for.[58]

In the case of Dawson's *This Is Your Life*, the line-up included Meg and their children, Dawson's childhood friend Ken Cowx, mentor Betty Lawrence and his old Hoover boss George Walker, as well as

Dickie Henderson, remembering the big night in Blackpool where Dawson had gone from being an *Opportunity Knocks* audience winner to a fully fledged TV comedian. At the end of the show, some scenery flats were removed to reveal the Syd Lawrence Orchestra, who played out their benefactor in swinging style, before rushing to play a gig in Exeter. Lawrence's professionalism meant that there was no chance of cancelling the concert, but equally he was unwilling to miss Dawson's big night, so he had chartered an aeroplane at considerable expense to ferry the band to the engagement. 'Syd and Les were in heated discussion about Glenn Miller, who perished in an air crash,' recalls drummer Fergie Maynard. 'Syd had always avoided flying and was extremely nervous. I suggested a few double brandies, as did several of the orchestra. I boasted that I had been in the band of 2nd Battalion, the Parachute Regiment and had taken off twenty-three times, and never landed once, but that didn't help. On landing at Exeter, I was the greenest looking member of the orchestra, but Syd forgave Les.'[59] While all this was going on, Les, having sown the seeds of fear in Lawrence's mind, was otherwise occupied. After the recording, relieved that their marriage was not on the rocks, Dawson and Meg returned to the hotel room that had been paid for by Thames and 'made love … in the manner of a teenage honeymoon'.[60]

One notable absence was Leslie senior, who had died on 10 April of the previous year, aged 65. He had never really recovered from the loss of his wife thirteen years earlier. In a note he left for his son, he said that 'when she died, something in me died also'.[61] For the last few years of his father's life, Dawson had been trying to persuade Leslie senior to join them in the bungalow in Bury, but he'd stayed at the family home in Blackley, and Dawson had been upset to notice how little his father cared about its upkeep. Had he moved in with Les and Meg, it would have been a tight squeeze, the bungalow having been purchased at a time when the Dawsons seemed unlikely to have children. By 1972, with two daughters, a son and luxuries like a baby grand piano, the place was bursting at the seams. A bigger house was needed, but while any new abode would score on size, it would miss a feature of the bungalow that hadn't figured in the estate agent's particulars, a supernatural presence known to the Dawsons as the Grey Lady. The figure first became apparent when Dawson spotted his eldest daughter Julie, then aged 4, seemingly talking to the hallway wall. Asking her why she was talking to the wall, he was surprised to hear her reply that she was talking not to a wall but to the Grey Lady, a kindly soul with a limp. Stuart also claimed to have seen a figure with 'a poorly leg' at night. Dawson was perturbed. 'Years later I was to become interested in the paranormal, but at that period it put the willies up me,' he admitted. Meg later attended a talk by a psychic who told Meg that while there was a presence in the Dawson family home, and it was lame, it was 'an element of Good'.[62]

Dawson's fears for the well-being of his career weren't merely the usual insecure musings of a turn. At one point in the seventies, he was a constant fixture on television, with *Sez Les*, *Jokers Wild* and numerous guest spots. The height of the glut occurred in 1972, with thirteen editions of *Sez Les*, a six-part sketch series without the Syd Lawrence Orchestra called *Les Sez*, and twenty-two editions of *Jokers Wild*, to say nothing of a pair of *Golden Shot*s and an appearance on *The Good Old Days*. The sheer number of shows that Dawson did at Yorkshire appears to have been the result of an oversight on the part of his agent, Norman Murray. Vernon Lawrence, who came over from the BBC when Paul Fox replaced Donald Baverstock as head of Yorkshire Television, and would become Dawson's producer, recalls the situation with regard to Dawson just before his arrival at Yorkshire:

> His agent and Yorkshire had done an incredibly stupid deal. They'd paid him a fortune, which he was very happy to accept, his agent was delighted with and so was Yorkshire Television, but when they sat down to work out how the deal would work, what they failed to do was to say how many specials, how many half-hour shows he would do within a year, of each year's money. So he was totally over-exposed by Yorkshire.

The agent didn't care, Les didn't mind. That was the only way they could make the contract work. Totally hypothetical figures, but if it was £100,000, they should have said a series of seven half-hours, four specials and that will do you. In actual fact, they landed up doing three [series of] seven half-hour[s] ... *Les Sez*, *Sez Les*, and what have you. So it was a question of trying to make it work.[63]

There was a very real risk that viewers would become sick of Dawson. There was also another concern. Dawson had a tendency to rely on the stocks of original material that he had built up in the years before he became famous. The joke about the mice throwing themselves on the traps when the mother-in-law visited was in the Dawson jokebook from at least 1970, when it turned up on *It's Lulu*, and would be reused regularly through the rest of his career. He would continue adding to the repertoire but some favourites would recur repeatedly. In the course of time, they would come to be regarded by the audience almost as greatest hits, and their absence would be more notable than their reappearance. However, at this early stage in Dawson's career, over-exposure could have been fatal. Variety comedians had used the same jokes and the same acts for years on the halls, but television was a voracious consumer of material. Television would show any cracks all too clearly.

With Dawson chained to his ludicrous contract, the wrong choice of writers could have been a calamity. Fortunately, disaster was averted with the arrival of new writers, who would help Dawson show that he was much more than just another northern variety comedian. Mallet and the show's producer, Bill Hitchcock, considered the options, along with their boss, John Duncan, now promoted to YTV's head of light entertainment. Thinking of writers who they felt would be more in tune with the comedian, Duncan suggested David Nobbs, while Mallet put forward the name of Barry Cryer. In turn, Nobbs had noted the talent of a young Lancashire-based writer called John Hudson, who came in and made a significant minority contribution to the weight of material. 'Their humour was what you might call up-to-date,' Mallet observes, while the previous scripts 'really came out of English variety, on-the-boards stuff'.[64] Both Nobbs and Cryer were part of the extended family already. Nobbs had been working at Yorkshire as an in-house script editor, while Cryer had worked with Dawson for several years on *Jokers Wild,* and with Nobbs on *The Frost Report.* Nobbs's first television writing credits had been on *That Was The Week That Was,* on which John Duncan had been associate producer, with responsibility for rehearsing the sketch material. Though he had made his name in satire, Nobbs loved working for old-school comedians like Ken Dodd and Frankie Howerd in equal measure.

The call to work on *Sez Les* came at exactly the right time for Nobbs, who had been working on a critically mauled situation comedy for Jimmy Edwards, called *Sir Yellow.* To be transferred immediately to a hit show minimized any potential damage to his reputation, and to work with a comedian he admired already was a bonus. 'I was absolutely thrilled because none of the other things I'd been doing at Yorkshire had really worked,' Nobbs explains. 'I was absolutely delighted to work with Les. I loved the fact that he was such a great wordsmith. He obviously loved words. I remember the first thing I saw him do, I remember in his monologue he was talking about visiting the all-night windmill and it just struck me as such a funny concept.'[65]

Dropping Dulay was a major change, and, with the show still doing well, Dawson could be forgiven for worrying, initially, whether it was the right move. However, any reservations about the new regime disappeared quickly. 'I should think he was very cautious,' observes Nobbs. '"Who is this chap, are they saddling me with somebody?" Although the fact that I was John Duncan's choice might have helped. I don't think it took very long. I think it's a very valid point. You do want to know that people are on your side, and don't have secret agendas. We had a lot of fun.' While many comedians are intensely aware of the politics of the industry, and try to exploit the politics for their own ends, Dawson tended to resist doing that and just ploughed on. 'I think by nature he was slightly naive, because his good nature led him into naivety. It wasn't stupidity, it was essential good nature.

He wanted to trust people. He wanted to have a team around him. That was his comfort zone. His comfort zone was in the team of friends, and then you could take the comedy anywhere you liked.'[66]

Both Nobbs and Cryer were university-educated: Nobbs had written sketches for the Footlights revue while a Cambridge student, and Cryer had begun an English degree at Leeds, his hometown university, before abandoning his studies to work in the theatre, later moving into cabaret and revue. Both had a level of education that Dawson had missed out on, but the comedian had the intelligence to match them. Equally, all three shared a love of the absurd and a delight in bathos, particularly the creation of improbable names. Dawson even acquired the middle name 'Makepeace' for some sketches. Nobbs and Cryer were skilled writers who could turn out conventional variety gags and sketches if they wanted to or were required to do so, but it ceased to be the default setting for the show.

The division of labour remained the same as before. 'All the monologues were Les, we never touched the monologues at all,' Nobbs explains. 'We wrote most of the rest and we devised a form, whereby there were an awful lot of quickies on the show.' Quite a number of the quickies involved a new character, created by Nobbs and Cryer, called Cosmo Smallpiece, a myopic pervert with a centre parting. Usually cast in the role of weatherman, newsreader or presenter, Smallpiece would begin soberly, reading whatever bulletin he had to impart. Soon, however, he would see filth and innuendo in everything, and begin letting his libido rise to the surface, usually ending with a cry of 'KNICKERS! KNACKERS! KNOCKERS!' as he was being pulled off with a shepherd's crook.

None of the characters Dawson had played in his television shows before had taken hold in the way that Smallpiece would, but he wasn't the most important introduction under the new regime, for it was at the start of the Nobbs and Cryer era of *Sez Les* that northern housewives Cissie Braithwaite and Ada Shufflebotham made their debut. The idea of depicting a pair of northern gossips came originally from Cryer, remembering an old variety act called Collinson and Breen. Bill

Collinson had originally been the straight man to Alfie Dean, who, by virtue of being over a foot shorter than Collinson, usually played a wisecracking miscreant child to Collinson's pillar of slightly seedy respectability. In his *Cavalcade of Variety Acts*, Roy Hudd remembered a sample Collinson and Dean joke: 'If I've got £2 in this pocket, £2 in this pocket and £2 in my back pocket – what have I got?' 'Somebody else's trousers.'[67] The act split when Dean went into the army during the Second World War, but Collinson paired up with another diminutive partner, Bobby Breen, and resumed the act as Collinson and Breen. 'I called them Mrs Collinson and Mrs Breen,' explains Cryer. 'Les got it. He got the joke. Him and Roy Barraclough. And then Les really steamed in. He was lovely. He said, "Oh Baz, I'm sorry, I've written a couple." I said, "Oh, go on." He said, "This Mrs stuff doesn't work, though. They're Cissie and Ada." And he was right.'[68]

What carried over from the old variety turn to the new characters was that one was outwardly respectable, while the other sought to drag both down to his level. In their own quiet way, Cissie and Ada were a perceptive satire on class, social pretensions and human nature. Cissie thought herself refined, while Ada knew she wasn't but still she had a strange, selective sense of decorum, mouthing what she believed to be unmentionable things, while giving full voice to statements that reeked with innuendo. What shines through is that, whatever Cissie thinks she and her never-seen, much-referenced husband Leonard are, and however much Ada knows that she and her equally unseen Bert aren't, the pair are firm friends, having almost certainly known each other all of their lives. And they are as one when it comes to gossip. Cissie certainly doesn't disapprove when Ada says of one neighbour's exploits during the war that 'she had more soldiers than Eisenhower'.

Writing the dialogue for Cissie and Ada came easily to Dawson, as the archetypes had populated the streets of Collyhurst in his youth. Their first on-screen encounter occurred in the second show of the seventh series of *Sez Les*, transmitted in July 1973, in the setting of a launderette:

CISSIE: Morning, Ada. Late this morning.

ADA: I thought you were. I'm on me second spin.

CISSIE: So you are. What a morning I've had. I've been stuck in that surgery for an hour and three-quarters. It's my old trouble back again.

ADA: Oh not again.

CISSIE: Last night I were up at screaming pitch with it, so this morning I decided I'd take my elastic stocking off, wash my feet and go to the doctor's. Anyway, he took one look at my feet and said he'd never seen anything like them. My toes were like globe artichokes.

ADA: I must say you've been a martyr to those feet. A martyr. Actually, I saw our Lillian at the shops.

CISSIE: How is your Lillian?

ADA: Well, she's not been the same since [*mouths indistinct phrase and gesticulates towards abdomen to indicate major surgical procedure – lip-reading what Dawson says, it looks like 'George left her. She's had it all taken away, you know?'*]. I saw her walking, she's always had trouble with her thighs. They've always chapped her legs. I said to her, 'You'll have to get that seen to, or else you'll be hobbling.' So she said, 'I was just going into Johnson's the Butcher's,' because she's partial to a bit of mince.

CISSIE: Oh yes, and there's not a bit of fat on it.

ADA: Ooooh yes, and his black tripe is always fresh, you know. I'd gone in there and I said, 'Get those legs seen to.' Any she took my advice. She went to Dr Markham's.

CISSIE: Down by the bridge?

ADA: Yes, CISSIE Markham's husband.

CISSIE: Yes, she used to play the organ for choir practice.

ADA: That's the one ... She walked into the surgery as I live and breathe, with those awful legs, and within two minutes he'd cured her.

CISSIE: Why, did he operate?

ADA: No, he took two inches off her wellington boots.[69]

From the beginning of Nobbs and Cryer's involvement, *Sez Les* became more of a pure comedy show than the variety show it had been before. Also, Mallet was changing the way the show was produced to the way he had always wanted. Although he had won the battle on videotape editing, he was still expected initially to record complete shows at one session. Having seen the way American television production worked, he wanted to record in chunks and then assemble the shows later. It didn't matter if the studio audience didn't get a complete bill as long as they laughed at what they saw. The management saw it differently. 'They just thought it didn't make sense if you didn't start a show at the beginning and finish at the end,' he outlines. 'I tried to do the Les Dawson shows non-sequentially in bits, and it wasn't terribly popular.'[70] However, when the Syd Lawrence band became more successful, it made sense to record their contributions in a block and edit them into the shows through the run. In the case of the fifth series, Lawrence band drummer Fergie Maynard remembers that with twenty-eight live dates booked in the month of recording, the remaining two days were given over to taping all of the band's numbers.[71]

From this base, Mallet increased the proportion of non-sequential recording with each series until the shows were produced that way entirely. This helped alleviate Dawson's tendency to get bored with the overcooking of material. 'We used to call it Black Thursday,' explains Barry Cryer. 'We'd rehearse in Leeds. Les could pick up a script like that. He got bored by the Thursday, and he was messing about with the sketches. We'd say, "Les, we're doing it tomorrow. Will you get *back*? Because you were funny on Monday."'[72] Mallet and Cryer would go on to work with Kenny Everett, and Cryer notes that despite the apparent differences, they were 'very similar animals. Do it first time, brilliant, and then "Can you do it again?" Not as good. First take with both of them was always the one.'[73] As well as suiting Dawson's rip-and-read approach to rehearsal and performance – allowing them to record an item moments after it had been written – this mode of production meant that the series could make the most of special guests like John Cleese, recording a lot of material on the days they were available and spreading it through the series.

One of Cleese's performances stands out for Mallet and Nobbs, effusive in their praise for Cryer, who wrote the joke. The scene is a bookshop, run by a sober-suited and imperious Cleese, into which a figure in a flat cap and raincoat skulks, looking furtively around him, sniffing and wiping his nose on his cuff. Reaching the counter, the customer, played by Dawson, opens his mouth, and in a catarrhal Scouse accent asks, 'Hello dere, la'. Have you got any dirty bewks?' Making the most of the height difference between them, Cleese looks down his nose at the Liverpudlian pervert and says absolutely nothing. There then follows a full thirty seconds in which Cleese merely furrows his brow and allows his face to register clear contempt and disgust for the customer and his sordid request. At the end of the pause, it looks as though Cleese is about to tell Dawson to get out of his shop and never darken the doors again. Instead, out of the side of his mouth comes a killer punchline: 'Yer. What do you want?'[74] 'On paper,' says Nobbs, the sketch 'is absolutely nothing'.[75] The joke is the audaciously long pause and the build-up of expectations, to say nothing of the physical disparity between the two performers and Dawson's decision to play the character as one of Ken Dodd's Diddy Men in human form.

Soon the new team settled into a happy, almost family, relationship. 'We very much encouraged people. Don Clayton, who was the floor manager, wrote several quickies for the show, and he had a tremendous thrill from that,' says David Nobbs. The process of getting to know each other was aided greatly by the lunchtime sessions in the YTV bar or one of the pubs near the studios, during which a fearsome amount of alcohol was downed, in the manner of the time, as Nobbs remembers:

> He [Dawson] did drink a great deal, but it was never a problem. Never ever a problem. A lot of double whiskies before the show. Phenomenal amounts sometimes. But we drank a lot as well. My drink in those days, in the bar at Yorkshire Television, was a gin and double Cinzano Bianco. I used to buy the first round because I didn't expect anybody to buy that. And I'd sip it. When anybody offered me a drink, I'd ask for Cinzano or a gin, and by the time I'd finished my first gin and double Cinzano,

three rounds would have elapsed and I would have had another gin and double Cinzano, and by the end of the lunch break I would have had a third. This meant that at least seven rounds had to have been bought for this to happen, and then we all went and did good work again in the afternoon. Astonishing. You build up resistance and your body gets used to it.[76]

It was in the bar, however, that one of Dawson's most notable idiosyncrasies was most apparent. His friends and colleagues found him endlessly generous with praise, laughter and his time. If anybody wanted a fête opened, Dawson would drive to wherever he was required and do the necessary without a murmur. Despite this, he showed a remarkable reluctance to buy drinks. On one occasion recalled by David Nobbs, Barry Cryer and latter-day *Sez Les* producer Vernon Lawrence, Dawson had returned from the bar after an age with a tray of drinks, apologizing for the length of time it had taken him to get served. Floor manager Don Clayton piped up and replied, 'I have no problem. They *know* me.'[77] To his credit, Dawson loved Clayton's aside and laughed heartily.

The reputation sometimes made it onto the screen, as in an edition of *Jokers Wild* where Jack Douglas was on the spot, having to find jokes based on the subject of eternity. 'Jack told a joke [that] hinged on the fact "Eternity is waiting for Les Dawson to buy a round", and Les walked off the set,' says Barry Cryer. 'He walked off. We were recording. "Ah ha ha. Oh er um." We filled in and prattled about. Les had run or whatever – you could get to the bar very quickly – and came back, staggering with a tray with about five or six pints on, to enormous applause from the audience. I said, "Oh, you're back." And he gave everybody a drink except Jack Douglas.'[78]

The worst instance of Dawson's short arms and long pockets came at an end-of-series dinner, remembered with great dismay by David Nobbs:

Les invited us all out to dinner at a restaurant in Horsforth. He said, 'I want the people who've really contributed to this show. These are the ones I want.' Brenda Fox, who was wardrobe, was one of them. Les accurately identified all the people who had really made it on the show. When we got to the restaurant, the bottles of wine were on the table. The red was Spanna, an Italian wine that Les liked. I think there was white and so on, and we all sat down and had a meal. Duncan Wood was accompanied by Jackie [O'Gorman], who was a vision mixer, who had been ill that day and had been replaced on the show but was well enough to come to the dinner in the evening, so there was already a bit of tension. We had a very pleasant dinner and, at the end, Les said, 'I think the gentlemen should pay for the ladies, so it's divided by eight.'

Barry Cryer and I had suspected this might happen, just wished it hadn't happened. Others had no money on them, so we had to lend them money. Bob MacGowan [the show's designer] was so embarrassed he went off round the edge of the room, he couldn't stand it. Les called out, 'That's right, Bob, build a set around your wallet', which was the most inappropriate remark you could imagine, and [producer] Vernon Lawrence got so embarrassed that he rattled ice around and made a joke about an Eskimo peeing. It was an evening of enormous embarrassment, and you wondered afterwards, 'Did Les intend to pay, and just get an attack of meanness, or did he always assume that everybody would think it was?' That's how it goes with Les. Monumentally insensitive to say that to Bob MacGowan though. I suppose there was a bit of tunnel vision. A nice man, but flawed. I'm trying to tell the truth, which I think is quite important. It saddened me. It doesn't show Les in a very good light, but it's part of him, and I feel I should tell it, because I'm telling you how I admired him in many ways.[79]

Nobbs adds that, despite the awkwardness of the situation, 'nobody bore a grudge' towards Dawson. But why should such thoughtless behaviour have been tolerated? The key was in how Dawson treated people when money wasn't the issue. Vernon Lawrence is clear on the strange dichotomy of Dawson's personality:

Les was an anomaly, in as much as he was one of the meanest men I've ever met, and at the same time one of the most generous men I've ever met. He was very mean with his money, but very generous with other performers. On a show, he didn't want all the laughs, which the majority of them do. In other words, he had that Jack Benny philosophy, which is wonderful, that it's called the *Jack Benny Show*, or it's called the *Les Dawson Show*, and you can only do better by creating a wonderful show.[80]

Dawson's lack of side and willingness to take a joke bought him a lot of goodwill. Nobbs recalls one location shoot near the YTV studios:

Les asked, would I mind going to the corner shop to get some fags for him, because he was in costume and he didn't want to go. I went into the shop and a little old lady came in and said, 'What's going on in the street?' I said, 'They're filming.' She said, 'Filming? Who's filming?' I said, 'Yorkshire Television.' She said, 'Yorkshire Television are filming in our street?' I said, 'Yorkshire Television are filming in your street.' She said, 'What are they filming?' I said, 'They're filming *The Les Dawson Show*.' She said, 'Yorkshire Television are filming *The Les Dawson Show* in our street?' I said, 'Yorkshire Television are filming *The Les Dawson Show* in your street.' She said, 'If I went down the street now, would I see him himself, Les Dawson, in our street?' I said, 'If you went down your street now, you'd see him himself, Les Dawson, in your street.' She said, 'I don't like him.' The great thing about Les was that he loved that story. I couldn't wait to tell him, knowing that he would slap his sides in joy.[81]

Many stars would have thrown a hissy fit had such a story got back to them. Dawson's glee at the old lady's dismissive response gives an indication as to why he was liked, even loved, by his fellow members of the Yorkshire Television family, from the tea ladies to the top executives. In David Mallet's assessment, 'he was totally unstarry'.[82] This down-to-earth manner explains both his generosity of spirit and his financial meanness. He had grown up without material possessions or comforts, but what he, his family and his neighbours had to offer each other had been time and kindness, and this attitude had persisted into his adult life and his professional life. Nothing was too much trouble as long as it didn't involve cash, which was to be preserved for fear of ending up poor again. Dawson's penny-pinching wasn't the result of a miser's love of money above all else. If it had been, he would have realized the considerable monetary value of his time. In many cases, turning up to open a fête cost him far more in real terms than writing a sizeable cheque in support of the cause. Nevertheless, for all of his keenness to preserve his income, when it came to family matters, Dawson's spending was subject to different rules. Nothing but the best would do. Throughout his career, he spent as much as he made, and, as a result, found it hard to take time off, always having to accept whatever work he could get to maintain cash flow. In time, this punishing schedule would catch up with him.

Through the first half of the seventies, Dawson had one of the best comedy shows on television, with writers who could take his flashes of inspiration and turn them into tailor-made material; he also had a diary full of live engagements, to say nothing of his radio work. The slum boy was now very unlikely to head back to obscurity. Some stars kill their own careers through arrogance, Simon Dee being the best-known example, but Dawson had no such delusions of grandeur, and producers and writers loved working with such an easy-going turn. The call to appear at the 1973 Royal Variety Performance confirmed his increasingly high-profile status.

CHAPTER 4

Les is more

The bill for the 1973 *Royal Variety Performance* was, even by the usual standard, a high-quality offering. Comedian Dick Emery hosted, Rudolf Nureyev and Lynn Seymour gave the audience a little ballet, and there was music from Cliff Richard and Nana Mouskouri as well as bill-toppers Duke Ellington and his Orchestra. Ronnie Corbett joined Dawson in representing comedy, while singing duo Peters and Lee provided the *Opportunity Knocks* connection. Dawson found the occasion daunting, and not even the sight of Ronnie Corbett, with whom he shared a dressing room, mistakenly putting on Dawson's dress shirt and almost disappearing in the mass of fabric could lighten the mood. 'The knots inside my gut tightened unbearably,' Dawson recalled over a decade later. 'I heard the laughter that Ronnie Corbett received and my heart sank; how could I, a red-nosed club and pub comic ever hope to entertain the Queen? Had I bitten off more than I could chew?'[1]

Once again, a story has been rejigged by Dawson for dramatic effect. Dawson was the penultimate act in the first half, between Cliff Richard's performance and Nureyev and Seymour. Corbett appeared in the second half, just before Duke Ellington. Dawson knew that changing the order for the retelling so that he could hear Corbett storming the Palladium would ratchet up the tension. Whatever the running order, Dawson took to the stage without announcement or fanfare, and declared: 'In 1645, Prince Rupert's mercenaries smashed Cromwell's left flank at Naseby; and in 1871 the Franco-Prussian War ground to a halt at the siege of Metz; and in 1903, from the Kyles of Bute, came the first report of an outbreak of sporran rash.' None of this, he admitted, had 'got anything at all to do with the act, but it shows how your mind wanders when you're worried'.[2] They laughed. The first hurdle had been surmounted. Often, when delivering this sort of joke, Dawson would allow himself a mock-nervous little smile and a chuckle on the punchline, building complicity with the punters, but he was too tense for such luxuries of confidence tonight. Mock nerves had given way to real nerves. With time of the essence, another gag was called for. 'The last time I appeared at the Palladium, I had the audience with me all the way,' he told the distinguished audience. 'Luckily, I shook them off at Watford.' More laughter, this time longer and louder. Time to hit them with a reflection on the changing nature of stand-up comedy:

> It's always difficult to know what to do on these occasions. In the days of the old music hall, comedians would walk on the stage wearing a red nose and blowing raspberries. They were, of course, on reflection, third-rate inferior performers destined for theatrical obscurity. Tonight, to enhance my claim as a cultural performer, I should like to play for you on the pianoforte not one but two numbers. The first one is a classical rendition, 'In An Eighteenth-Century Drawing Room', swiftly followed by the theme from *Love Story*. Thank you for your indulgence.[3]

Dawson then sat at a white grand piano, and began to play Mozart's Piano Sonata number 16 in C major,[4] a piece that the composer regarded as an exercise for beginners. After a bar or so, notes were creeping in that had not been in Mozart's score. Some were sharp, some were flat. Enough were right to allow the listener to keep track of the piece and recognize what Dawson was playing, but enough were wrong, and there appeared to be no neat pattern as to when they would occur and how wrong they would be. On top of this, Dawson maintained a visage of fierce concentration, as if every last note was being wrung out of his soul. Without a pause, Dawson continued into a woefully discordant version of the well-known romantic theme to the 1970 film *Love Story*, turned to the audience with a hint of a Las Vegas smile, then abandoned the keyboard, walked to the microphone, said 'Oh well', put on a red nose and blew a raspberry.

Dawson had been delighting friends, colleagues and live audiences with his deliberately bad piano playing for years, and he had occasionally made use of it on television, including in the third show of the fourth series of *Sez Les* in January 1972. Gary Husband, now a world-renowned pianist and drummer, had many chances to observe Dawson at the piano, being the son of Peter Husband, who worked as Dawson's musical director at YTV for many years. He says that Dawson was a good straight pianist, and needed 'that knowledge to be able to select so skilfully and consistently those funniest and ugliest bum notes – a very clever art… and mystery to a lot of pianists, including me'.[5]

Featuring the routine in the *Royal Variety* show had the advantage of minimizing the chance of any verbal slip-ups, as well as allowing any genuine mistakes to be disguised and passed off as part of the shtick. The routine was still in the early stages of development. In the 1972 version, Dawson grimaced every time he hit a bum note. In the 1973 *Royal Variety Performance*, the grimacing has been toned down, with the red nose and raspberry punchline an admission that the music was of a poor standard. Dawson would soon come to realize that it became even funnier if he maintained that there was absolutely nothing wrong with his playing. Nonetheless, it was funny enough on the night. Dawson had survived. Billy Marsh, agent to Morecambe and Wise, greeted Les backstage with 'Great, Les, you've never worked better', while Dawson's own agent, Norman Murray, was 'wreathed in a cloud of grins'.[6] In the final line-up, Dawson admitted to the Queen that he had been nervous, to which she replied appreciatively that he had no need to be, and that she had enjoyed his act. Her appreciation was as nothing compared to that of her husband, Prince Philip, with whom Dawson became a firm favourite. The only sadness that November night was that neither Leslie senior nor Julia had survived to see it.

Although it seemed to be business as usual at Yorkshire Television, with a special on Boxing Day 1973 called *That's Christmas Sez Les*, and a contribution to the previous day's *All-Star Comedy Carnival*, change was in the air. John Duncan had tired of office politics and the people above him in the hierarchy who didn't seem to understand what he did, still less appreciate it. When he had taken over as head of light entertainment, he had given Donald Baverstock an eighteen-month plan to restore the company's fortunes:

> At the end of the eighteen months, I said, 'Right, I've done it.' And what did I get? I got a bollocking for not being in my office at nine o'clock. At the end of that real struggle. Ward Thomas [deputy chairman and joint managing director] was the man who did it. Dropped me a memo saying where was I? I absolutely got him by the balls and twisted them because I said, 'If your snooping had been more thorough, you'd have found me in the dubbing theatre at 8.30. Fuck off.' That didn't make me any friends in high places, but I thought, what a bloody reward for that. Baverstock was still around, and according to him, and I believe him, he did back me up a lot, but they didn't want him either by that point.[7]

In June 1973, Baverstock had resigned, to be replaced by Paul Fox, who had been controller of BBC1 for the previous six years. David Nobbs is of the opinion that the new order was not as in tune with Dawson as the previous management had been. 'Very few people are big enough to take enthusiastically the creations of the previous regime,' his assessment begins. 'I think there was a bit more to it than that in Paul Fox's case. I think Paul Fox wanted to de-clothcap Yorkshire [Television]. I think it was right that while it had some regional roots, it didn't see itself as a regional company. It saw itself as a player in the national game and did it very well. Nonetheless, in nodding to northern humour, it had a northern master, and did they realize that he was absolutely one of the greats of all time? Did they realize that? The answer I think is no.'[8]

As Paul Fox came in from the BBC, John Duncan went in the opposite direction, to become an executive producer at BBC Manchester, but once again found himself tiring of office politics, and eventually left television to open an antiquarian bookshop in York. Duncan had always regarded himself as a square peg in a round hole when it came to entertainment. 'I didn't want to be stuck in LE because I wasn't any good at it,' he claims. 'My background was Oxford and all the serious plays. *Tamburlaine the Great. Faustus.* All that stuff. I was never known for being a funny man at all. I saw the problem, addressed it and did my best, but I knew I didn't have the gift that Dick Clement and people like that had. I didn't have that flair for LE. You can't do it just by calculating, thinking and even by knowing the right names. You've got to have the flair somewhere beneath.'[9] In his autobiography, *A Clown Too Many*, Dawson disagreed heartily: 'If I had my way, he'd be back in the studios. He had ideas and he was never afraid to stand by them.'[10] David Mallet concurs with Dawson: 'People constantly underestimate John Duncan. John Duncan gave the nation Les Dawson, the Syd Lawrence Orchestra, *Jokers Wild* and a thing called *Rising Damp*.[11] He was absolute fodder for management types, because his satchel clinked with beer bottles. All those stories were true. A very reluctant executive, and quite a reluctant producer, [but] people don't realize what a terrific, classic producer he was.'[12]

He was replaced by Duncan Wood, who had been head of comedy at BBC Television under head of light entertainment Bill Cotton Jr. Although there was no personal animosity between Wood and Mallet over *Sez Les*, the producer observes that his new boss 'hated the way I did it, or was doing it. He was much more comfortable with people from his side of the tracks. Pretty much everything changed. They didn't want the dancers, they didn't want the music acts. It became a sketch show and my point was and is that Les Dawson couldn't necessarily hold too long a sketch show.'[13]

The first changes became apparent in the 1973 Christmas special preceding the eighth series. 'Caribbean Clipper' was no longer the theme tune and Syd Lawrence's orchestra was no longer a fixture. Instead, the session orchestra that had provided backing for guests was brought out front, under the direction of Johnny Pearson. When the series proper got underway on 25 January 1974, it was back to a half-hour after the previous run of forty-five-minute shows, and the musical director was Peter Husband, who had known Les since his days as a flautist with the BBC Northern Dance Orchestra.

For the time being, the dancers remained, taking part in a running joke at the beginning and end of each show, holding large polystyrene letters spelling the name 'LES DAWSON', which would then become rearranged as the dancers moved around. Dawson would make his big entrance, find himself faced with an anagram like 'SODNWALES, SLOW DANES' and try to rearrange the letters into the correct order before flinging them to the ground in frustration. A similar idea would appear a year later in the opening titles of guest star John Cleese's own sitcom, *Fawlty Towers*.

Another recurring theme in the eighth series was based on the fact that, alongside his TV work, Dawson had been trying to break into the pop charts as a singer. The 'bull voice' noted by Peter Pilbeam at the 1961 BBC audition had not improved noticeably, but the comic could carry a tune, and with his heightened profile, some producers thought it worth a try. His first vinyl outing had been a non-comedy single for Chapter One in 1969 called 'Send Her Roses'. The follow-up was 'Promise Me' for Decca in 1971, also performed completely straight.

Three years later, with the aid of an orchestra conducted by Brian Bennett, who as drummer with the Shadows had been present at Dawson's initial TV triumph in Blackpool, he tried again with an up-tempo number called 'Spread It Around'. The song's optimistic lyrics by Jokers Wild creator Ray Cameron played against Dawson's public persona, but were very much in keeping with the man's real life bonhomie. They refer to feeling good, getting out of bed on the right side, experiencing uncontrollable laughter, and the value of spreading your jollity as far and wide as humanly possible. The effect is not unlike a funky version of the children's song 'Magic Penny', which tells us that if you give love away, you get far more in return. To add to the joy, Dawson ad libs various instructions to the band.

Resplendent in bow tie, waistcoat and straw boater, Dawson performed the song in the third show of the eighth series, supported by the show's dancers, then walked over to a map of the world into which lights had been installed, each representing the sale of a record. Checking up on sales after a week in the shops, a solitary bulb was illuminated, indicating one sale, in Ceylon, using the name that Sri Lanka had abandoned two years earlier for comic effect. Enter John Cleese in tropical gear and pith helmet, announcing, 'Now look here, I plant things in Assam, and I bought one of Des's records and I must say it has a certain snap', breaking the record in half. The following week, the map reappeared, with a lone light in Africa indicating a single sale to a tribal chief played by Roy Barraclough, who had bought it for his wife to use as a traditional African lip plate. A week later, Japan lit up, and it was reported that twenty-five copies had been sold, but only to be piled up and chopped in half as part of karate practice. Unfortunately, the jokes weren't too far off the mark, as the single failed to make an impression even on the lower rungs of the hit parade. In the final show of the run, singer Ronnie Carroll appeared, singing the song, interrupted by Dawson as W.C. Fields announcing that Carroll sings it 'better than that little bum'.[14]

At the end of the ninth series, David Mallet bowed out as producer. 'Paul Fox came in and didn't like me particularly,' Mallet recalls, 'and then, about a year afterwards, he brought in Vernon Lawrence, a very nice bloke. Paul Fox wanted it done the Vernon Lawrence way, so they just let me go. They didn't fire me. I didn't work for Yorkshire, I was freelance. That [*Sez Les*] was my mainstay, and I used to do *Jokers Wild* as well, and the Christmas pantomime, which was a big deal back then. Just one day, they didn't renew it.'[15] Lawrence's first production was a musical special, *Sounds Like Les Dawson*, transmitted on 4 December 1974, and David Nobbs's main memory is of the instant critique provided by those present in the studio gallery at the start of the recording:

> There was Barry Cryer, me, Meg, and Bob MacGowan, and David Mallet, the old director of the previous shows, was in there too. There was a precredits quickie, and David Mallet said, 'I wouldn't have shot it that way.'

Barry said, 'That wasn't really what I meant.' Meg said, 'He promised me he'd never wear that shirt again,' and Bob MacGowan, in about five or six seconds, drew a magnificent little picture of a parachutist about to hit the ground, his parachute not having opened.[16]

The quickie in question spoofed the Coca-Cola commercial of the time, where a choir of various races sings 'I'd Like To Teach the World To Sing'. Instead of perfect harmony, this assembly ended in a fight after Dawson is accused of singing flat.

After the titles came a musical number from the Second Generation dance troupe, in which each lithe and lovely member introduced themselves by name, and then introduced the star of the show. From behind the mass of glamorous hoofers shuffled Dawson in his evening suit, making his way through the throng with Irish jigs, before being presented with a small harp. As the orchestra quiets down, he announces, 'I don't know how those kids do it. I do get winded these days. I went to the doctor the other day, and asked what's good for wind? He gave me a kite.'[17]

This special also contains a sketch in which Dawson plays Ludwig van Beethoven, failing to hear anything said by his Germanic doctor, played by Roy Barraclough, shouting his garbled replies in a northern accent ('What seems to be the trouble?' 'Ten past nine.') and displaying a laugh that resembled the opening figure of his Fifth Symphony. This resulted in some very unfriendly mail for the writers. 'We got letters saying "You miserable people of no talent. Here you are, mocking one of the greatest composers of all time",' recalls David Nobbs. 'Les was very funny as Beethoven, I can assure you, the sheer impossibility of it.'[18]

Unsurprisingly for a musically based Dawson show, his out-of-tune piano playing is featured, but the discordant accompaniment and thus the joke is rather obscured by the lusty, tuneful singing of the Second Generation, dressed in flat caps and clogs. Officially, Cissie and Ada are absent from this show, but Vera the violinist and Dorothy the cellist of the Madge Longbottom Trio sound and look awfully familiar as they

mourn the sad passing of Miss Longbottom during a recent performance. 'I can never forget that afternoon, it's etched upon my memory,'
notes Dorothy/Ada through her tears. 'How can I ever forget it? We'd
just brought *The Student Prince* to a climax and we were poised, ready
to launch ourselves on *The Vagabond King*.'[19]

After the baptism of fire in the gallery, Lawrence soon became very
much part of Dawson's television family. Perhaps most importantly,
he shared everyone's enthusiasm for a relaxing drink after a hard
day's work. 'When I'd finished a show, I'd go into the bar, and do you
remember those Swedish long, tall glasses? I used to have a quadruple
whisky in that, with ice, topped up with lemonade, in that hand, and
another one in this hand,' he recalls. 'Then when we went out to eat, I'd
drink red wine, and about midnight, I'd be like that [asleep] at the end
of the table, and I could hear them saying, "Oh, poor man, he's given
his all for us. Isn't he wonderful? He's utterly drained." I was utterly
pissed. I'd quietly passed out.'[20]

Despite drinking enough to stun a shire horse, Dawson retained
amazing stamina. His writers marvelled at his fearlessness and willingness to do anything they wrote, no matter how arduous. 'The thing
I think that was his greatest strength for us was that he'd turn nothing
down because it was difficult,' says Nobbs, admiringly. 'We had the
man up on a Kirby wire, playing the piano. Les up one Kirby wire, the
piano on another Kirby wire. The very first note he plays, the piano
crashes to the ground in a thousand pieces. Nobody else would have
bothered.'[21]

Vernon Lawrence remembers with delight the flying piano but cites
another Nobbs and Cryer creation as the high-water mark of Dawson's
physical fearlessness: 'The bravest thing I ever saw Les do was called
Jock Cousteau, the underwater bagpipe player. That was just amazing.
We got a bagpipe player in the studio and [Les] mimed it, and thank
God he put on white trunks underneath his kilt. Down he went into
this water, and just rolled over. It brought the house down. It was amazingly courageous.'[22] In the sketch, from the 1974 special, *Les Dawson's
Christmas Box*, Dawson is dressed in an outsized tam-o'-shanter.

He announces, in an accent that veers between the Gorbals and the Isle of Arran, that 'the water in this tank has been passed by the public health inspector [pause] with the help of an elderly horse'. At this point, Dawson corpses. Announcing that he will play 'Scotland the Brave' while submerged, he walks down the steps into a tank full of murky-looking liquid, never letting the manic grin clamped around the mouthpiece of his bagpipes slip, even as his kilt rises.[23] It's an incredibly elaborate set-up for what is effectively a throwaway gag, but it proves worth all of the effort.

Dawson's willingness to listen and laugh made what can be an annoying trait in other comedians endearing in him: a tendency to crack jokes or do bits of business all of the time. For example, the late Norman Wisdom was always falling over, and the joke invariably wore thin. Les got away with it. Barry Cryer uses the proper theatrical term for the condition: 'He was never "off".' The crucial difference was that Dawson was 'warm and lovely. He loved making people laugh, and he'd always be "on". That's why I loved him, the compulsive.'[24] Lyn Took remembers an occasion at the Montreux television festival when she and her husband, writer Barry Took, went to dinner with Les, Norman Murray's colleague Anne Chudleigh, and, from YTV, Duncan Wood and Vernon Lawrence:

It was a long, thin room in the upstairs of a restaurant overlooking the lake, and when we walked in it was empty, except for [agent] Roger Hancock sitting at a table just by the door with three other people. So we joked with him and said we didn't want to sit near him, and we walked to the other end of the restaurant, and sat at the table at the other end of this long, thin room. Les started this running commentary, which was obviously like all his material was, and it was very funny, and Barry kept trying to stop him, and get him to go into normal conversation about something, which worked sometimes. Vernon started this thing by saying 'One point to Barry, one point to Les.' In the meantime, we were ordering and eating, and not really thinking that much about it, but then we got really caught up in it. I had bought a little bell in the afternoon, which I thought was just a cute little souvenir, just a tiny metal bell. Vernon took it out of the bag, which was hanging with my handbag, and put it on the table. Every time Barry scored a point he put a coin underneath it, and said, 'This is really good. It could make us rich.' He was just being really silly. Les went on and on, and we did talk about other things as well, because we weren't just sitting listening to Les, although it was quite difficult not to. We did converse about other things, about what we'd been doing and what we thought about what was going on in Montreux, but every so often, Vernon would lift this bell and put a few cents under it.[25]

In 1974, Dawson and his team were enticed to West Berlin to make a one-off special for the television channel operated by Sender Freies Berlin (now Rundfunk Berlin-Brandenburg), entitled *Dawson und Dixie, oder was ist komisch*. At the time, dubbed British comedy programmes were very popular on German television, and there was a brief vogue for specials made expressly for German viewing. In 1972, Westdeutscher Rundfunk had produced two *Monty Python's Fliegender Zirkus* shows, with the cast learning their translated lines phonetically, and the Goodies had featured as comic relief in a series co-produced by the BBC and ZDF to showcase Engelbert Humperdinck and the Young Generation song and dance troupe. For Dawson's Teutonic outing, the 'dixie' of the title was supplied by Kenny Ball and his Jazzmen, who were regulars in TV variety at the time. The show also featured Paul Kuhn, a jazz pianist-turned-bandleader who had become a fixture on German television over the previous twenty years. The sketches included some tried and tested *Sez Les* favourites, including the quickie where Dawson, as a street sweeper, is seen to lift a fake pavement and sweep all of the dust and dirt under it. Unfortunately, despite being a visual joke, something was lost in the translation, as he told Michael Parkinson in 1974:

When we got there, a fortnight before the show was actually due to go, two of us went to suss the scene out, see what they wanted. The German mentality is something I'd never previously come across, because it's all, you know, faces really like flint. Hard, unyielding. So, they had a girl with braided hair, who looked a bit like Danny La Rue, and she said, 'You tell me vot you are going to do vich is funny? All mein colleagues around the table.' So in this atmosphere, I said, 'Well, the first thing we'd like to do, there is a man sweeping the street. He looks one way', and this is what broke me, she said, 'Man who looks ein fahrt?', which is German for 'one way' … I say, 'He then lifts up the pavement, and brushes the dirt underneath it.' And there was a silence like a forgotten tomb. She said, 'I think I should tell you that in Germany, the pavements don't lift up.'[26]

Through the fifties and sixties, television had gradually taken over from radio as the pre-eminent broadcasting medium, but Dawson remained loyal to radio, and to Jim Casey, even though its poor-relation status persisted for some years. BBC Radio comedy in particular showed a worrying tendency to rely on audio adaptations of television hits like *Steptoe and Son*, *The Likely Lads* and *Dad's Army*, rather than originating its own formats and shows. Warhorses like *The Men from the Ministry* and *The Navy Lark* trotted on dutifully, along with panel games like *My Word* and *Just a Minute*, but TV was making all the running.

Up in Manchester, Jim Casey's fiefdom proved one of the exceptions to this rule. Although BBC North's radio LE department had its own warhorses, such as *The Clitheroe Kid*, written and produced by Casey, the Manchester team – which included producers like Peter Pilbeam, Geoff Lawrence and Mike Craig – was still creating new hit shows, mostly for Radio 2, as the Light Programme had become in 1967. *Castle's On the Air*, starring multi-instrumentalist and entertainer Roy Castle, ran happily for several years, while Morecambe and Wise's main writer, Eddie Braben, brought his Liverpudlian surrealism to the wireless in *The Show With Ten Legs* and *The Show With No Name*. Dawson had kept up his links with Casey through the situation comedy *Our Les*, but both Dawson and Casey felt that they could have more fun without the constraints of an established framework. Eventually, the bosses in London, including head of light

entertainment Con Mahoney ('a bit of a twit' in Casey's sage estimation), reached the same conclusion. 'They then said they wanted
a stand-up spot show,' Casey relates, 'and I said, "Well, that's much
better for me, much easier."'[27] Carrying Daphne Oxenford and Colin
Edwynn over from *Our Les*, and using 'Put On A Happy Face' from the
1960 musical *Bye Bye Birdie* as the heavily ironic theme tune, *Listen to
Les* launched on Radio 2 at 7.02 p.m. on 6 July 1974. In the early shows,
Colin Edwynn's introductory exhortation varied from week to week,
but for most of the show's twelve-year run, it was 'If you can't laugh at
your problems, then laugh at his, as you *Listen to Les*'.

As with the TV shows, Dawson wrote the monologues while another
writer, in this case, Casey himself, supplied the majority of the
sketches. In some ways, Casey's CV was closer to that of Peter Dulay
than those of Cryer or Nobbs, but he had inherited from his father
a whimsicality and a turn of phrase that elevated even the corniest
gags. In this regard, he and Dawson were well matched. Casey also
aided Dawson greatly by seizing on passing comments that had comic
potential. Offstage, Dawson was inclined to throw off funny lines and
lapse into amusing characters and voices, with no apparent idea that
they might work onstage too. 'He was great at creating characters,
but he never knew quite what to do with them,' notes Jim Casey. 'We
had one who'd just say, "Is that George, eh? George likes women, you
know." What happened was that I went to see him in Southport, and
when I went backstage, he was knocking on the other artists' doors
and saying, "Is George there? George is my friend." He saw me, said,
"Hello Jim." I said, "He's in on Sunday." He said, "Who?" I said, "George."
"Is he?" "Of course he is, that's a bloody marvellous character."'[28] The
name of the character was Albert Clutterbuck, and George was a mysterious associate that he referred to frequently, as in this visit to a
dating agency run by a Mrs Willis, played by Daphne Oxenford:

MRS WILLIS: Now sir, you are …

ALBERT CLUTTERBUCK: That's right, me sister is a miss, but I'm a mister.
We look the same but for her moustache.

WILLIS: Very droll. Could I please have your name?

CLUTTERBUCK: Why? What's wrong with yours?

WILLIS: Really, sir, would you please be serious? What is your name?

CLUTTERBUCK: Albert Clutterbuck. Clutterbuck was me dad's name.

WILLIS: Naturally.

CLUTTERBUCK: Albert was me mother's name. They got on well, they played the violin together. They were always on the fiddle.

WILLIS: You really are quite a wit. Now you are lonely and you are seeking a companion. Someone to love.

CLUTTERBUCK: That's right. I loved Winnie, but I lost her.

WILLIS: Oh, I'm so sorry. When did she die?

CLUTTERBUCK: She didn't die. I just lost her. Down a hole…

WILLIS: But you went to the police, I assume?

CLUTTERBUCK: No, but George did. George is my friend. George got me a woman once with big feet. She was lovely, she used to kick-start Boeings. George bought me some goldfish once.

WILLIS: Did he?

CLUTTERBUCK: Yeah, but I didn't like 'em. I'd sooner have cod and chips.[29]

Clutterbuck was basically Cosmo Smallpiece's Neanderthal cousin and, with Cosmo established on television, it was natural that he should join Dawson on radio. Casey recalls relishing the chance to write for such a free-spirited pervert. One run of sketches involved Cosmo as a telephone pest, 'ringing up, saying "Oooh, I hope it's a woman. If it's a fella again, I'll ring the wife. I want to come over there, I want to cuddle you. Will you stop telling me what the time is?" So, he rang the time clock, and he rang the police station by mistake. The one I loved was when he started talking: "Oooh, it's a woman. I want to … you what? You're disgusting" and he hung up.'[30]

One of the early *Listen to Les* shows, from 1975, features a version of a monologue that would become part of the core Dawson repertoire. Later adapted so that it could be presented by Dawson speaking as himself, claiming to be a celebrity using his fame to raise awareness about ecological issues, in this manifestation he delivers it as an effete scientist by the unlikely name of Professor F. Fluent. It concerns the welfare of the blue-nosed fruit duck, an animal endangered by its perilous breeding habits and oil slicks on the cliffs of Dover:

> The fruit duck is a delightful little creature that hangs from conduit and spits at fish … The female, when ready to mate, stands on the edge of the cliffs and goes [*blows raspberry*], then lifts up its feathers and blows sand down its beak. The male duck, perched on a rock, hears the saucy invitation, crosses his eyes, hops on one leg and rubs chalk on his chest, and as he does this, he replies with three staccato rasps like so [*blows three raspberries*]. If the female does not throw an egg at him, this means that she is ready to accept him as a mate. He then takes a few paces backwards, braces his legs and runs at the female duck in a series of skips and low swoops. Here is the tragedy of it all. Just as he is about to dive onto his mate in a fit of emotion, he skids on the oil slick and overshoots the target. He then falls over the edge of the cliff and knocks himself out. Some male ducks have fell as many as ten times, and they become impotent and prefer a drink with the lads.[31]

The radio shows were also home to a great many sketches featuring one of Dawson's favourite characters, an impoverished actor laddie with a fruity voice that invoked the cape and cane instantly, known variously as Rathbone Mole and Quentin Sadsack. In one sketch, he is arrested when his attempt to help a gent with a problematic cigarette machine is mistaken for an attempt at robbery:

> SADSACK: Do I evince that you are having difficulty with this metallic vendor of tobacco?
>
> FRUSTRATED SMOKER: No, the cigarette machine's stuck.
>
> SADSACK: Then allow me to assist you, my good fellow. In similar straits, I have found that a smart blow delivered on the coin slot produces the desired effect.
>
> [*FX: window breaking*]
>
> FRUSTRATED SMOKER: Hey, you've pushed it through the shop window.

SHOPKEEPER'S WIFE [*from window above*]: Charlie, call the police, we're being robbed.

SADSACK: Don't be alarmed, madame, it was merely an unfortunate misadventure.

SHOPKEEPER'S WIFE: Ooh, there's two of them, Charlie. Vandals! Thieves! Let the dog out ...

[*Frustrated smoker flees*]

SADSACK: Get back, hound. Desist you villainous quadruped. Release my nether garments. You carniv ... oooooh. [*FX: another window breaking*]

POLICEMAN: It's all right, call off the dog, Mrs Woman, I've got him.

SADSACK: Ah, a most propitious arrival. That whelp was on the verge of masticating my buttocks to shreds.

POLICEMAN: Just come quietly, Jimmy, and there'll be no more trouble, all right?

SADSACK: What do you mean come quietly? Are you inferring that I am being placed under arrest?

POLICEMAN: Well, I'm not inviting you to the policemen's ball.[32]

In *A Clown Too Many*, Dawson suggested the sketch was based on real life. The machine having taken numerous customers' coins without issuing any product, Dawson said he 'banged the side ... and money spilled out all over the pavement and the newsagent lifted up his living quarters' window, and blew a whistle for the police. They duly arrived with an insane dog who proceeded to take the sleeve off my sports jacket.'[33]

Dawson enjoyed the radio bookings because he admired Edwynn, Oxenford and Casey so much, and also because it was quick work, with time for socializing between rehearsal and recording. As Jim Casey recalled:

We did two shows on a Sunday, and ... I started rehearsing later every week until eventually we were meeting at four o'clock, rehearsing and recording two half-hour shows. We'd finish rehearsing at seven, including having some tea, then he'd be off to the pub. I remember. I very rarely went. I'd go afterwards, but on the odd occasion I went before the eight o'clock, and he'd have had about four or five whiskies before I got there. Colin Edwynn would go with him and have half-pints, while Les had double whiskies. Colin said, 'You know when you came last week? You didn't half put a damper on it.' I said, 'He'd had five double whiskies.' He said, 'Ah, but he was cutting down because you were there.' He could take it. He was a very heavy drinker. It didn't seem to affect him as much as other people.[34]

Until Duncan Wood arrived at Yorkshire Television, Dawson's shows had been pure variety. An extremely experienced television producer, Wood could put together variety shows when required to do so, and had worked extensively with Ken Dodd at BBC Television in the sixties, but his forte was situation comedy, having produced all of the *Hancock's Half Hour* television shows and most of *Steptoe and Son* before rising to become head of comedy. Some producers who move from the studio gallery to an executive job find the job constricting and return to production as soon as they can. Others take to executive life as if born to it. Wood was in the latter group. 'He was a very thrusting executive, if you know what I mean,' says David Mallet. 'He had his opinion and he wasn't really interested in discussing.'[35]

Given Wood's pedigree, putting Dawson into a sitcom was a logical step, and Wood's long-standing connections with *Hancock's Half Hour* and *Steptoe* writers Ray Galton and Alan Simpson made it natural that they should write what would be Dawson's first sitcom since the abortive *State of the Union* pilot. Alan Simpson recalls that it was 'commissioned by Yorkshire Television as their Montreux entry'. The writers went up to Leeds to meet their new leading man, and found him perfect company. 'That was the first time we'd ever met him,' Alan Simpson relates. 'Obviously, we knew his work. That was the first time, and we clicked straight away because he was one of us. He was one of the lads. I remember the first time we went up there he took us out to a nightclub, Cinderella Rockefeller's. That was the first social occasion and we hit it off straight away.'[36] The subject of the show was to be that emerging seventies phenomenon, the cheap package holiday.

Rehearsals took place in London, with the team going up to Leeds the night before the recording. Like everyone else, Galton and Simpson found Dawson very easy to work with. He had learned the script thoroughly, as was his tendency. 'We never had any problems with Les, really, in terms of temperament,' Simpson observes, adding that 'He was a writer himself. It helped in that respect. When they're writers themselves, they respect it, because they know how bloody hard it is to write it, so they respect the effort that's gone into it and the quality. The only problem we had with Les was stopping him putting his little wheezes in. Like a lot of comics, they don't have any faith in the script, so if they see a chance to put in "She had a face like a sackful of spanners" or one of Les's typical one-liners, they'd slip it in. And we'd say, "You don't really need it and it spoils what comes after. It's spoiling the build-up to the proper joke." I think he saw the point, and, anyway, [as] he got more confident with the material, he realized he didn't need it.'[37]

Holiday With Strings was transmitted on August Bank Holiday Monday, 1974. In the opening scene, Dawson, in raincoat and sou'wester, pushes his racing bicycle (with brown ale in the bottle on the handlebars) into a travel agency and shakes himself dry, much to the consternation of one of the staff. Dawson apologizes, revealing that 'my mother used to go to work, and I was brought up by next door's Alsatian'.[38] A confrontation follows as he is told to leave the bicycle outside, and Dawson threatens to take his business over the road to the Co-op, 'and let's face it, the divi on a round-the-world cruise must be worth a bob or two. I hold the Co-op in high esteem. They buried the mother-in-law.' At the prospect of losing business, the manager of the shop, played by Frank Thornton, intervenes, but it soon becomes clear that Dawson doesn't have the required funds. Blanching at the £1,750 cost of a cruise, he reveals that his holiday budget is £22, and is banished from the shop with a sheaf of cheap package-tour brochures.

The next scene has Dawson on location at Leeds airport. Inside the modern terminal, he shows his ticket to an air stewardess who directs him to a grotty tent on the apron of the runway, the base of operations for Kut-Price Holidays Ltd, reminiscent of the early post-war Heathrow. 'That's what it was like,' says Ray Galton. 'It was an army training ground, Hounslow Heath. It was a row of tents.' Inside this monument to a lost age of air travel, Mollie Sugden, who is in charge of check-in, tells Dawson to weigh his luggage. When he informs her that the scales don't seem to be working, she asks if he's put a penny in. This gets a massive laugh from the audience, as does the revelation that Dawson has to weigh himself too. Even with no luggage, he's still too heavy, and replies, indignantly, 'I'm not having a leg off', but is charged £3.50 excess just for himself, with no cases, only a couple of shirts stuffed in his pockets. Once on the flight, there isn't enough food for all of the passengers, so a raffle is held by the stewardess, played by Patricia Hayes, who still thinks she's a bus conductress. Such corner-cutting was deemed richly comic in 1974, but it's almost as if Galton and Simpson could see the future. 'The whole point of *Holiday With Strings* really is that it was fiction, that it was impossible,' says Alan Simpson, but now the truth is as strange as the fiction, as Ray Galton observes: 'Ryanair a couple of weeks ago were talking about making you pay to go to the lavatory. Well, we did that. We put it in that you had to pay to go to the lavatory on the aeroplane, and they were having a whip-round so that they could land and get some petrol to get over the Alps.'[39]

The aircraft in question is a Bristol freighter that looks distinctly un-airworthy. The fuselage is covered with graffiti, including 'PORKY' and 'LEEDS FOR THE CUP', and when Dawson inspects the tyres, their condition is not all that it could be. 'We did write in that it had to have a crossed plaster on the tyre, which you always used to get in *Comic Cuts*,' notes Alan Simpson, and sure enough, the props department obliged the writers in their comic-book fantasy. On board, Hayes as stewardess announces that 'We shall be flying at a height of around three or four thousand feet until we reach the Pyrenees. You will then be transferred to a coach and we will meet you on the other side.'[40]

Dawson is seated next to a camp coal miner called Peregrine, played by Roy Barraclough, who asks, 'Are you going to Tossa? Are you going all the way?', much to Dawson's consternation. Eventually, Dawson and Peregrine reach a truce and play cards until the pilot announces the aforementioned refuelling stop and whip-round.

The final scene is set back in the estate agent's, two months later. Dawson enters, pushing a butcher's bicycle, wearing a poncho over his raincoat and a sombrero in place of his sou'wester. Informing the manager he wishes to make a complaint, Dawson is informed that complaints must be addressed to the tour operators. 'Certainly,' Dawson replies. 'Which prison are they in?' The company, it transpires, went bankrupt 'just after the plane crash-landed and just before the hotel fell down'. Asked why it's taken him two months to complain, he explains that he cycled home to Leeds all the way from Tossa del Mar, having stolen the bicycle, and been 'pursued to Perpignan by three irate Basque slaughtermen astride elks brandishing cleavers'. Dawson asks if there are any more cheap package tours to Tossa del Mar. If so, the travel agents can return the bike and the delivery of 'this kilo of mince and these two pounds of Andalusian chipolatas'. He then storms out of the shop.

The lines about the elk-riding slaughtermen and the chipolatas are classic Galton and Simpson – redolent of the 'château-bottled Albanian burgundy' that the fictional Hancock was seen to drink. However, they are also clearly in the same register as many of the lines that Dawson wrote for himself. *Holiday With Strings* was a good match of writers and performer. As with their Hancock scripts, the writers took pains to leaven the leading character's pomposity and irateness with a certain amount of vulnerability and sympathy. They had also used the circular ending that marked out many of the best Hancock shows, not least 'The Blood Donor', in which Hancock cut himself slicing bread and ended up being given the blood he'd donated only hours earlier. There were other parallels. 'I think we approached it in the same way as we did *Hancock's Half Hour*,' says Alan Simpson, 'trying to exploit what we saw in front of us.' However, the writers always dismissed suggestions that they were writing as if for Hancock. 'That's the way we wrote anyway, whether it was Hancock or anybody else,' Ray Galton explains. 'We were asked by Leslie Bricusse to write a musical of Noah. When we finished it and sent it in to him, he said, "Wonderful, wonderful, but do you realize that every word of Noah is Hancock?" We said, "Don't be ridiculous, we haven't written Hancock for years. This is the way we write."'[41]

While this may be true for Galton and Simpson, others close to Dawson sensed that there was a deliberate attempt on the part of the producer to emulate the writers' earlier success. 'Duncan wanted another Hancock,' claims David Nobbs. 'Duncan was obsessed with Hancock. It's only in hindsight that you see that. They were really trying to put him in what I thought were the wrong clothes.'[42] Critical response to *Holiday With Strings* was broadly favourable, if not an actual rave. In *The Times*, Leonard Buckley noted Galton and Simpson's involvement and said, 'Les Dawson ... was entirely himself ... [and] gave us a package of good corned beef. But the acting of poor Tony Hancock, for whom they also wrote, would have turned it into glorious ham.'[43]

Dawson's next show for YTV was another special, this time written by Cryer and Nobbs, under the title *Dawson's Electric Cinema*. In it, he reminisced about the fleapit run by a fictional Dawson family, playing almost every member of the staff himself. Standing in the ruins, he brought to mind 'the smell of freshly peeled oranges ... the crackle of ha'penny bags of monkey nuts, the swish of red velvet curtains on brass rails and ... that special feeling of excitement when the lights dimmed and that shaft of light came from the projection box'.[44] The show is an interesting diversion, but is memorable mainly for a cameo appearance from 8-year-old Stuart Dawson, playing his father as a boy, and for the lovingly shot silent movie custard-pie fight sequence at the close. Neither Mallet nor Lawrence were involved, with production duties being undertaken by Ronnie Baxter. David Nobbs feels that the producer misjudged the star: 'I didn't think it was good. Ronnie Baxter kept saying "Smile, Les". We wanted to say "Les doesn't smile, that's not the point." I think he tried to make him more like other comedians. Maybe history will say it was right, but we were struggling with it.'[45]

While Wood was trying various new ideas for Dawson, YTV's head of drama, Peter Willes, who had nurtured Harold Pinter in the early days of commercial television, sounded out the star about doing some work for him. Having grown up in the thirties depression, Dawson had a tendency to view all work as good work, but an approach from the drama department intrigued him more than the usual offers of club dates. Willes knew exactly who he wanted to write for the comedian. Jarrow-born and Hull-raised, Alan Plater had made his name in the early sixties as a writer on *Z Cars*, before developing through the later part of the decade and into the seventies as a television playwright of stature, conscience and, most importantly, humour. It was a time when drama was strong on social issues, and the very left-wing Plater more than did his bit to highlight these, but never lost sight of life's absurdities and their comic potential. 'It caused a little bit of friction, I gather,' Plater related later. 'Peter Willes said, "They won't like it in light entertainment, Duncan Wood will think I'm poaching Les." I said, "Well, you are poaching Les." It was all very informal in those days, amazingly casual.' Although Plater had not been a slum child, the writer and the performer had a similar upbringing in one important area:

> When I got the call [asking,] 'Would I like to write something for Les?', I said 'Absolutely'. I was a fan, and when I got the call, and I can't remember what route it took, whether I got the call from Peter Willes or via Peggy Ramsay or whatever, would I like to write three plays for Les, I was 'Absolutely, deal me in.' I've always loved comedians. My formative years in theatre were actually going to the music hall with my dad. It was in Hull, so it was generally the Tivoli, occasionally the Palace. The Palace closed during the war, it was bombed, but the Tivoli ran through the war. My mum was a bit ambivalent. She liked some things about variety, but other things she didn't like. Dad used me as an excuse for going.

'Well, the lad would like to see . . .' whoever it was. So I got to see the great comedians like Jimmy James, Norman Evans. I saw Norman Evans do the 'over the garden wall' thing at the Tivoli in Hull. I can remember specific lines. 'I'll kill that cat. I could smell it in the custard on Sunday.' That's genius. I wish I could write lines that good.[46]

An introduction was furnished, and Dawson told Plater of a concept that had occurred to him. 'The idea of *The Loner* was him,' Plater explained. 'A man living on his own halfway up a hill somewhere in Yorkshire. He walks down the hill into an adventure each day. We talked, and it was a joint concept, if you like. I hate the word, but it was a joint concept. So, I just went back home and I wrote them, and we did them.'

On a drama series like *The Loner*, Dawson's attitude to rehearsal and the material was markedly different to *Sez Les* and his initial encounter with Galton and Simpson. There was no Black Thursday, no drifting off, no insertion of gags. 'He had huge respect for writers and writing, and he wouldn't alter a syllable,' Plater noted. 'He didn't alter one syllable of anything I'd written. Not one dot or comma. I said very light-heartedly to him, "Are you word-perfect?" and he said "Yes". I thought he was joking.'[47] Dawson's willingness to stay on the script shows how seriously he took the project, and his respect for Plater's craft was underpinned by his own ambitions: 'We were in the bar at Yorkshire Television, which was where so much business was done in those days. He [Dawson] said to me, "Of course, I don't want to do what I do. I want to do what you do. You're what I want to be." He wanted to be a writer, so he went to Paris, because that's what writers did. A lovely kind of romantic notion. He just loved the idea of writing.'

Like so many others, Plater relished the 'ornate and rococo' elements of Dawson's work, and the way that he would suddenly drop into mild vulgarity:

I remember seeing him in summer season at Scarborough, doing that thing about the beautiful garden. This rhapsodic description of this garden that he'd seen. 'Eventually, I said to the man tending his flowers,

'How do you do it?' He said, 'Horse muck.' But he then tagged it. He said to the gardener's wife, 'Couldn't you ask him to say something better than horse muck?' She said, 'It's taken me years to persuade him to say horse muck.' The double-tag thing. I can't think of another comedian in our time whose routine was so ornate and verbally rich.[48]

The three half-hour playlets were transmitted on Wednesday nights at 9.30 p.m. between 7 May 1975 and 21 May 1975. The first of the run, 'Dawson's Complaint', begins with a shot of a flat-capped Dawson striding with purpose and a little pomposity out of a solitary house on a Pennine hillside and announcing, 'At ten o'clock on a sunny May morning, I set out unwittingly to change the world. This is the story of my failure.'[49] Straight away, the pomposity is deflated and Dawson's underdog status is defined.

His first port of call is the local shop. Even though Dawson is a regular customer, the shopkeeper, played by George Malpas, fails to remember his name. Already a little riled, Dawson responds to the shopkeeper's offer of 'lovely deep-frozen runner beans' with the admission that he is not there to buy anything, eliciting the reply 'It's a shop. You buy things in a shop.' Dawson admits that he is there to register a complaint, but begins to explain the grievance in deliberately oblique terms. First he asks for some paper. The shopkeeper delineates the various types of paper on offer: 'There's your kitchen roll, your toilet roll, your tin foil or your writing paper smelling of lilies of the valley ...' Dawson explains that he requires some paper that can be written on, but that he isn't going to write anything on it. He settles for the margin of the sports page of the newspaper, and, producing a pen from his pocket, moves it across the paper, leaving no mark. All is explained: 'The bloody pen won't work', to which the shopkeeper replies haughtily that 'you can't expect miracles for a shilling'. He produces a box of pens from the deep freeze (pressed on this issue, the shopkeeper replies 'I have my reasons'), but none of them work either. The shopkeeper tells Dawson that he'll have to take it up with the supplier of the pens, Brighouse Office Supplies, a London-based company registered in Brighouse for tax reasons, a concept that baffles both the shopkeeper and his irate customer. The scene is a joy, with two people having two apparently separate conversations, yet reaching a satisfactory conclusion. Neither side wishes to give away more than it has to, but eventually an accommodation is arrived at.

Dawson is next seen in location footage, shot among the sixties blocks by London's St Paul's Cathedral that drew the ire of the Prince of Wales in the eighties and were later demolished. Dawson declares the capital to be 'the city of flashing lights, corridors of power, fixed smiles'. Next stop, the offices of Brighouse Office Supplies, with bells, buzzers, an illuminated map of the world on the wall (almost certainly not a conscious call back to the 'Spread It Around' map on *Sez Les*) and a receptionist who fields a call to a sales representative with 'I'm sorry, I'm afraid Mr Harrison died yesterday. Yes, I'll ask him to call you back.' Dawson finds himself in a conference with a senior executive, Mr Harding, played by *Porridge* and *Last of the Summer Wine* star Brian Wilde, where it soon becomes apparent that Mr Harrison's predicament is not unique. 'Well, of course you must understand that we all work under tremendous pressure here, Mr Nesbitt,' Harding informs Dawson, who gently corrects him on the mistaken identity, and receives the response, 'Sometimes it's very difficult just to focus one's attention. Most of us die at forty.' When Dawson gets to the point of explaining the reason for his presence, Harding dismisses the writing implement as inferior, announcing, 'Oh, what a rotten little pen ... Are you a rep? I don't see travellers.' Dawson replies, 'I'm a consumer, except that I've got nothing to consume, seeing as how the pen won't work. That's why I'm complaining to you, the source, the corridor of power.' Harding tries to abdicate responsibility, expressing surprise that Dawson should have expected him to do anything about the pen, and admitting that his main concern at the moment is deepfrozen runner beans. Dawson pleads 'on behalf of all the people who keep buying these rotten pens. The milkman on his rounds making up his cash returns. The lads in the betting shop working out what they've got to come back on a two-way Yankee. The shepherd in the hills.' Harding's only reaction is to consider diversifying into sheep. Checking the documents, Harding finds that the office supplies division has been sold on to a mysterious outfit called Global and Brotherhood Insurance of St Ives, based in the north of Scotland. As he's leaving the office, Dawson asks Harding how old he is. Receiving the reply '39', Dawson says solemnly 'I'll say goodbye, then.'

Dawson is next seen in a baronial hall, being offered a drink from a crystal decanter by the ancestral pile's owner, Lord Ross and Cromarty, played by Cyril Luckham. Ross and Cromarty is 'old money': 'Six or seven hundred years ago, one of my ancestors did a few unconventional favours for the monarch of the day, and he was given this place for services rendered and for keeping his mouth shut. You could say I've been lucky.' When his Lordship asks what Dawson thinks of the deer heads that are hung up, he replies, 'Must have been going at a fair lick when they hit the wall', which is just about the only overt joke in the whole half-hour. The conversation with Lord Ross and Cromarty continues in the same manner as the previous conversations. With the exception of the occasional hilarious interjection, most of the really funny lines are given to the other actor, and Dawson's main job is to react in confusion. Dawson's lack of insecurity enabled him to deal with this rather better than many comedians would have done.

Lord Ross and Cromarty is friendly and conciliatory, treating Dawson as an equal, but at the same time being utterly unable and unwilling to resolve the predicament by giving him a pen that works. 'I'll have some enquiries made. I'll see that somebody gets the sack,' His Lordship offers, to Dawson's horror. Ross and Cromarty replies, 'You can't stop an assembly line once it's running. You might as well try to stop a mad runaway stallion ... You can't expect us to stop making things. It's the way we all make our money. Consumer goods, I believe they're called. You see if that pen of yours lasted forever you'd never buy another one, and the whole organization would grind to a halt.' Dawson responds by proposing to 'raise an army of angry milkmen, gamblers and shepherds from the hills' to 'overthrow you, Whirlwind

Office Supplies, and Global and Brotherhood Insurance, by a force of arms'. His Lordship states quite clearly that the revolution wouldn't stand a chance. He has the ear of the chief constable and, in any case, Dawson almost certainly has a vested interest in not leading the charge. Flummoxed, Dawson claims to have no vested interests, but quickly realizes that he is himself a customer of Ross and Cromarty's insurance empire, with a shilling-a-week policy guaranteeing that 'if I die of bubonic plague after the age of 65, the person standing nearest to me gets £200'.

> Lord Ross and Cromarty: Well, there you are, you'd be jeopardizing your own investment and to put it another way, you own a tiny proportion of this pen, so if it doesn't work, it's your responsibility.
> Dawson: It's a mess, isn't it?
> Lord Ross and Cromarty: We can still be friends.

Dawson returns to his Pennine retreat, having realized that 'If I want to get a pen that works, I've got to dismantle the whole structure of society'. Deciding that he might as well have some runner beans, he returns to the shop and finds them sold out, and is offered a woolly vest as a substitute. The whole situation appears to be an allegory for the incompetence of British industry at the time, particularly the misguided over-expansion and lack of quality control. What film director Lindsay Anderson hadn't quite pulled off in three hours of *O Lucky Man!*, Dawson and Plater managed to achieve in twenty-five minutes. Plater later confirmed the political undertones:

> It was a fully frontal attack on global capitalism, but we didn't say so. That was one of my favourite devices, in those days, certainly. I did a television play for Yorkshire, and it was four days in the studio, a ninety-minute play. I think it was on the third day that the director turned around to me and said, 'I've just realized this play is political.' I replied, 'This is about the right time for you to realize it. If you'd realized it at the read-through, you'd have said, "This is political, do something about it."'[50]

The second in the series was 'Dawson's Connection', in which the anti-hero is thrust into the role of unwilling detective after being buttonholed in a pub by a mysterious man in a cloth cap. The man quotes the metaphysical poet Andrew Marvell at him, and when Dawson finishes the poem, unwittingly giving the code, the man leaves a parcel. Plater and Dawson were both fans of hard-boiled detective fiction, so the introduction was written with love and delivered with obvious relish in voiceover: 'It was around ten o'clock on a sunny May morning, when I set off down these mean streets, heading downtown. I was walking into trouble, all on account of being erudite. Not only that, I read a lot. I don't often drink at Harry's Bar, but it's next door to the reference library. Handy if you want to check somebody's credentials between rounds.'[51] Dawson asks the landlord if he recognizes the poetry-reciting stranger in the 'Monty Burton suit', getting a reply in the negative but a suggestion that he should try the district attorney's office. The next line punctures the amusing incongruity of a Yorkshire publican talking in such terms, with Dawson rationalizing that as there is no district attorney, there will be no office, so the next best thing would be 'Sergeant Hardaker of the 79th Precinct'. He then traces his way to the police station under some genuine Yorkshire lattice-work railway bridges that nonetheless have a faint whiff of Chicago about them, a triumph of the location finder's art.

Sergeant Hardaker, played by Roy Kinnear with a rich range of furrowed brows and worried sideways looks, enquires about the parcel, to which Dawson replies that it's all down to Andrew Marvell (who had, incidentally, been born at Winestead-in-Holderness, near Hull, Plater's adopted home town). Noting the name down, at first with only one 'l' – on which Dawson picks him up – Hardaker asks for Marvell's address, with Dawson replying that he can't supply it as he died in 1678. He then tries to explain the situation further, but doesn't get past 'This parcel is ... this parcel ...', at which Hardaker cuts in with the observation that the statement 'This parcel is this parcel' is 'a bit Gertrude Stein-ish for a Thursday'. Dawson's only concern is to offload the package, but Hardaker points out that lost property is already packed to the gunwales, with items like 'one set of bagpipes in hunting Stewart tartan, one gents' bicycle, one set build-it-yourself kitchen units in imitation plastic mahogany, one ladies' bicycle, one set complete works of Andrew Marvell [peers at book] spelt with one "l", thick as two short planks, some people'.

Dawson then walks around town, most of the locations being in and around Sowerby Bridge near Halifax, trying to lose the parcel. He posts it through a car window, but the motorist hurls it back at him. He leaves it on a bus, only to have it thrown at him by the conductor further down the street. He chucks it over a bridge, but it is thrown back by an angler below. In desperation, he visits the Citizens' Advice Bureau, staffed by Sharon Maughan – then starring in Yorkshire's drama series *The Main Chance* and later known for her part in the long-running Nescafé Gold Blend coffee commercials – who announces proudly that there's nothing Dawson can enquire after on which they won't have a file. Just as Sergeant Hardaker called back to the 'erudite/read a lot' joke from the opening voiceover, so does the citizens' adviser. She informs Dawson that he would be justified in opening the package to see whether there are any clues to ownership inside. The contents turn out to be a thick wad of £5 notes. She rationalizes that Dawson has blundered into a criminal conspiracy. The man who was meant to collect the parcel had been primed to complete the Marvell quotation, the criminals having not reckoned on one of the punters being a poetry lover and recognizing the line in innocence. Dawson is told to return to the pub. As he leaves, he tells the adviser, 'You're very beautiful, has anybody told you that?' Checking her card index, she is able to inform him that someone has indeed done just that at some point in the past.

Back in Harry's Bar, Dawson tries the Marvell line first on the landlord, who thinks the next line is 'Nor iron bars a cage'. He silences the pub by telling them to give their attention to the chap coming round with a riddle. All of them come up with wrong next lines, including one who supplies the punchline to a mildly risqué joke: 'It must be "The first time it made me sick, the second time, me hat blew off."' Dawson's attempt to hand the parcel back to its rightful owner results in an unpleasant scuffle by the dartboard, but the answer comes when he retreats into the Gents. In there, he is informed by a lurking assailant that the parcel is intended for Big Sam who 'runs the Bradford mafia' and that they could have both 'ended up in the canal with a loom round each ankle'. Dawson is given some forged fivers for his trouble, and, with pride restored, returns to the bar where, instead of his usual half of bitter, he asks for a Scotch on the rocks. 'No chance, you'll have it lukewarm, like everyone else,' the landlord replies. As he looks at his new-found wealth, Dawson realizes something with horror and asks the landlord's advice:

DAWSON: Tell me, you're a man of the world.
LANDLORD: I've been to two rugby league cup finals.
DAWSON: Have you ever known the Queen to wear a cloth cap?

The third playlet was 'Dawson's Encounter', based loosely on the film *Brief Encounter*, in which Dawson strikes up an unlikely romance with a woman he meets in a restaurant, played by Gillian Raine, real-life wife of Leonard Rossiter. The woman, who never gives her name, admits to liking people with a sense of adventure, such as men who almost won the Nobel Prize or a ballooning record. She admits that they might have been lying, but adds that she might be lying too. They repair to Harry's Bar, the same down-at-heel back-street boozer as in the second show, marred, in Dawson's estimation, by an over-loud jukebox, but with an acceptable line in bitter and Scotch eggs. He admits to turning the jukebox off with his boot if he doesn't like the record. The woman confesses to a liking for Gregorian chants after being given an LP of plainsong by mistake in the sleeve of *The Student Prince*. She leaves, but accepts his invitation to meet the next day, when he'll demonstrate his jukebox sabotage technique.

At their tryst the next day, Dawson asks the woman to tell him more about herself. She asks whether he wants truth or lies, to which he says he'll take either. She reveals a desire to 'trample barefoot on potato crisps', a liking for *Jane Eyre* and rainbows, and admits to being slightly married ('He went to Carlisle to sell a piano, and he hasn't been back since.').[52] Dawson heads to the jukebox and selects a record, 'the Drinking Song' from *The Student Prince*, not by Mario Lanza but by the Big Ben Banjo Band. The stylus lands on the disc and from the speaker comes a Gregorian chant. Dawson claims to have sneaked into the pub in the middle of the night and switched the records. By the next day, the landlord has grown tired of the chants, and tells the couple, 'Be happy. Gaze into each other's eyes. Think dirty thoughts if you must, but if I hear those flaming monks again, you'll be out on your neck.' It is noted that Dawson has told the woman nothing about himself, but she rationalizes that 'the more you know about a person, the less exciting they are'. What Dawson does tell her is of his quest for something unattainable in a mundane, humdrum world. Reginald Marsh, the actor playing the landlord, later told Piater the soliloquy contained his favourite line in anything he'd worked on, namely 'Yes, I once thought I saw a bright light shining on the road to Damascus but it turned out to be the sun reflected off some bloke's cucumber frame.' The playlet ends with the woman telling Dawson that they can't meet again. Their relationship is better in the mind, and she's running away before it becomes too real. It's an odd, affecting, warm, surreal piece of television.

Dawson's performances are sometimes breathless, with the odd fluffed line, but his appreciation of the quality of Plater's work is clear. He and the playwright remained friendly after the project had finished, and talked regularly of working together again. 'The unfulfilled dream [was that] we were going to put *The Loner* on stage,' Plater revealed. 'It was going to be a series of, I don't know, three one-act plays, with him linking the stories with a little stand-up routine. There was a deal of interest. I think – mind it was a long time ago – I had the Sheffield Crucible in mind as a launch pad, and I might even have talked to them about it. I think I wrote to Les and he was up for it, but it was availability, and he was always busy.'[53]

The fictitious Dawson created by Plater is a man struggling to understand the ways of the world, meeting them only with baffled resignation. He is at once a more innocent and more proactive version of Dawson's stage persona, the man who's seen it all, endured it all and who declares himself ready for more of the same with every line. Dawson fits well into the universe of Plater, where strange publicans, eccentric policemen, useless businessmen and cheerful subversives proliferate. Most of all, Dawson, as written by Plater, is an immensely likeable character.

Returning to the embrace of the comedy department, Dawson renewed his acquaintance with Galton and Simpson, this time for a seven-part situation comedy series called *Dawson's Weekly*. Once again, the comedian played an exaggerated version of himself, this time dressed in bikers' leathers studded with 'LEEDS DARBY & JOAN CLUB', and riding a moped. Like Plater, Galton and Simpson wrote the fictional Dawson as a loner, an outsider, and placed him in situations where he faccd, at best, indifference and, at worst, outright hostility.

In the first of the series, 'Les Miserables', Dawson visits the psychiatrist. He takes his place in the waiting room with a man peering at his fellow patients through a hole cut in his newspaper. One of the patients is a congenital liar who claims to own every property for sale in *Country Life* and is trying to sell some of his holdings to the kleptomaniac woman next to him. Dawson has been referred by his GP who says he has acute melancholia. 'Abject is more the word, with dirty great big dollops of manic depression thrown in,' Dawson tells the shrink, adding that he came 'grumbling out of my mother's womb'. Since then, his condition has been made worse by the catalogue of global disaster:

> Pestilence, famine and plague. You've got starvation, inflation, deflation, inflation. You've got assassination, taxation, nationalization, floods, earthquakes, typhoons, droughts, oil strikes. You've got balance of payments, you've got dollar crisis, oil crisis, pound crisis, germ war, nuclear war, civil war, Max Bygraves. That's not all. You've got gay lib, women's lib, pollution, disease, slums, disease, pollution, corruption. You've got

alcoholism, you've got overpopulation, underpopulation, prostitution, rape, shootings, lootings, and that's only down our street.[54]

Lists are a comedy staple, and a good one is comedy gold. The right-wing Jimmy's list of what's wrong with Britain ('namby-pamby probation officers, rapists, papists, papist rapists, foreign surgeons … Wedgwood Benn, keg bitter') and Reggie's list of the sort of nutters who would join Jimmy in fighting these baleful forces ('thugs, bully-boys, psychopaths, sacked policemen, security guards, sacked security guards, racialists, Paki-bashers, queer-bashers, chink-bashers, basher-bashers, anybody-bashers') in David Nobbs's *The Fall and Rise of Reginald Perrin* is perhaps the high-water mark of the genre.[55] Dawson's list of causes of depression is let down slightly by a couple of fluffs, but it has two good punchlines – 'Max Bygraves' and ' … that's only down our street'. Bygraves becomes a leitmotif throughout the series, occupying a similar position to Des O'Connor in the world of Morecambe and Wise.

The choice of Bygraves was largely down to his massive popularity and his bland, likeable profile. 'Everybody used to make fun of Max,' Alan Simpson notes. 'He was so popular, he was as popular a singer as he was a comedian. He wasn't a character comedian. He was one of the first ones to make films in his own right. *Charley Moon* and films like that. Expensive productions and successful.' Ray Galton adds: 'That sort of thing happened more in America than over here, where they didn't find it strange that a singer could act, and perhaps have a love affair.'[56]

Bygraves aside, the psychiatrist tells Dawson there's nothing wrong with him and, after the commercial break, Dawson has taken to his grotty bedsit, parts of which are recognizably recycled from the *Rising Damp* set. The rain is pouring down outside, the radio is full of depressing news, his piles are giving him merry hell and his lighter won't work. Just when he thinks matters couldn't get worse, the radio announcer introduces *Desert Island Discs*. The castaway is Max Bygraves. Then, as if that weren't bad enough, a neighbour, played by

Roy Barraclough, bursts in, having observed Dawson's hermitage and become concerned. 'I'm a bit worried about you,' he tells the recluse, as he sits on the bed. 'I'm a bit worried about you too,' Dawson replies, uncomfortable at the proximity of his visitor, who's brought him some coq au vin. Soon, however, the visitor is revealing to Dawson that he has depressive tendencies of his own. He blames his upbringing: 'Brought up in an orphanage, I was. My dad died three years before I was born.' The more he explains his situation, the more depressed he becomes himself. Dawson admits it's the saddest story he's ever heard, and soon he's feeding his unwanted guest the chicken dinner and singing 'I Want To Be Happy' with jazz hands and high kicks. When this has no effect, he leaves Barraclough moping in bed and goes to the pub. The episode serves well to set up the bellicose sitcom character version of Dawson, and the dynamic between him and the lonely, slightly pathetic soul played by Barraclough. The series is not episodic in structure, with no story arc across the seven episodes or any real sense of continuity. And while Barraclough recurs in all but two of the run, playing the same character throughout, there's never any sense that he's renewing his acquaintance with Dawson. Each meeting is a clean slate, leading to much the same conclusion.

Dawson's Weekly highlights one of the most curious contradictions of Dawson's career. Racist jokes were, throughout his career, notable only by their absence. In the final episode of *Dawson's Weekly*, set on a sleeper train, the steward is played by singer and comedian Kenny Lynch. This must be the only time that Lynch appeared on television in the seventies without reference being made to the colour of his skin. However, Dawson appeared to have no problems with jokes about homosexuals that now cause discomfort in the more liberal viewer. The china shop sketch in *Sez Les* was the low point, but the fifth *Dawson's Weekly*, which finds Dawson in a post office trying to buy a postal order for his pools coupon, comes close in places. It is, by far, the least satisfactory show of the series. Barraclough turns up, standing behind Dawson in the queue. They fall into talking about politics, but when Barraclough mentions that he voted for the

Gay Lib candidate, Dawson lets him move in front, for fear of sexual assault.[57] The episode relies just a little too much on misunderstanding and innuendo ('What's your favourite team?' 'Queen of the South.' 'I thought it might be.'), and the predictable closure of each window as it is Dawson's turn to get served. Moreover, without the gay jokes, it would be about half the length. Barraclough's male nurse in show four is also the recipient of a number of unpleasant effeminacy jibes. Declaring himself willing to donate any part of his body for transplant if Dawson needs it, he reflects ruefully, 'I'm sure you'll put it to better use than I have.' Dawson replies, witheringly, 'Well, different, anyway.' These jokes, along with various other references, do lead to the conclusion that Dawson was at least slightly uncomfortable with the concept of homosexuality.

In looking at the apparent homophobia, the recurring Barraclough character is interesting because, in most of *Dawson's Weekly*, he is quite clearly heterosexual, or versatile at the very least, despite being as camp as a row of tents. In 'Where There's A Will', he is seeking the companionship of a woman. In the final episode, he scuppers Dawson's amorous plans and gets the girl. Only in 'All Pools Day' is there an explicit suggestion of homosexuality. It's likely that his effete, well-meaning presence and Dawson's reaction to it says more about Dawson's personal attitude to homosexuality than about seventies comic attitudes per se, or Galton and Simpson's outlook. Dawson claimed to have been set upon by an older male colleague in his early days as a Co-op worker, saying that it 'left a mental scar for a considerable period'.[58] Unsympathetic gay characters also recur in Dawson's writing. Perhaps it shouldn't be surprising that a man of Dawson's generation and upbringing should be at least a little homophobic, but it sits curiously with his enlightened outlook in so many other areas. Dawson got on well with Jack Tripp, his pantomime colleague at the Alexandra Theatre in 1971, who lived openly with his male partner. He had many other friends and colleagues in the profession who were gay, not least his *Jokers Wild* colleague Ray Martine, who bordered frequently on camp caricature.

143

Plater's Dawson and the Dawson of *Holiday With Strings* are both capable of indignation and anger, but the Dawson of *Dawson's Weekly* rises very quickly. There is less light and shade. In addition, where the Dawson of *The Loner* is well meaning and vulnerable, the character in *Dawson's Weekly* is snide, devious, on the make and, frequently, an irritation. Perhaps the less subtle characterization can be attributed to the fact that, once commercials are taken into account, an ITV half-hour is closer to twenty-five minutes, so there's less time for character development. Being a one-off special, *Holiday With Strings* had the luxury of a thirty-five-minute slot, with the programme itself running just under the full half-hour. Plater had only twenty-five minutes for each episode of *The Loner*, but did not have to allow for 'spread', the lengthening that can occur on comedy shows when all is going well and the audience are laughing long and loud. Whatever the cause, *Dawson's Weekly* has some nice moments, but does not work anywhere near as well as *Holiday With Strings* did.

For comedic reasons, Dawson was always depicted living in grim surroundings. His 'Pennine retreat' in *The Loner* was a solitary house perched high on a Yorkshire crag. In *Dawson's Weekly*, his bedsit was grotty in the extreme. In real life, Dawson's domain was anything but grim. The three-up three-down Bury house with the benign 'presence' was warm and homely, but Dawson and family had swapped it for a larger house; *The Stage* reported the sale in August 1974, just before *Holiday With Strings* went out. After trawling most of the north-west, Dawson and Meg had found the ideal property, a large detached house called Garth in Islay Road, Lytham St Anne's, just south of Blackpool. The move took place on 19 February 1975. They were sad to be leaving Bradley Drive, Meg in particular. 'Our luck changed as soon as we put down a deposit on this house,' she told the *TV Times* in a two-page feature published the week *The Loner* began. 'I'd lost four babies and was told I could never have any, but I was pregnant within days. Les started getting better bookings, too. We were on our uppers when we moved in; we were nobodies. Now that Les is, well, a success, our neighbours don't treat us any differently. Knock on any door and they'll help. I just wonder what our new neighbours are going to be like.'[59]

The *TV Times* feature shows the happy family shifting its chattels into a van supplied by He-Man Removals of Rochdale, and also shows how necessary the move was. Dawson's main indulgence, his piano, had been crowbarred into a room that left little space for anything else. The process of getting the family and their trinkets moving takes 'only slightly longer than the retreat from Moscow', hindered by screwdrivers going missing and sibling horseplay. 'Stuart (7), rugby tackles 3-year old Pamela, and they land in a heap at Les's carpet-slippered feet. "You asinine little whelp," he booms in his best W.C. Fields voice. He's calming Pamela with a rambling story about Morecambe whelks and the Raspberry Duck of Sumatra when the removal men arrive.' Dawson jokes with the Rochdale He-Men, pretending to mistake them for bailiffs, wailing 'Please don't take my home. I would have paid you in time. Leave me the telly please – it's the only comfort I have.'[60] Amusing when you're a top entertainer, but rather more poignant when it's realized that such pleas would have been a common occurrence where Dawson came from. He could joke about it, thankful that he'd got out of the slums.

Although Dawson's work was now of a greater breadth and higher quality than in his first period of over-exposure, he still stood the risk of confusing the audience and overstaying his welcome. 'It was a positive move by Duncan to get Alan and Ray up,' argues Vernon Lawrence, 'and it was a positive move for him to try his hand at sitcom, which he did exceptionally well, but there was a lot of irritation about him doing the drama, because that confused his audience and confused everybody. It certainly blurred because you were doing cream here and cheese over here, and they landed up very close together. It wasn't particularly successful at that time.'[61] Ray Galton adds: 'With the *Dawson's Weekly*, it was a break in what he was doing and a lot of people preferred what he was doing to what we were doing with him. "Which Les Dawson are we watching?", I think, is the answer.'[62]

'Which Les Dawson are we reading?' would have been another question worth asking, for the comedian achieved a lifelong ambition in 1974 when the paperback publisher Sphere released his debut novel, *A Card for the Clubs*. Written in rare idle moments at home, in dressing rooms and hotel rooms when he first came to fame, the manuscript had been put away. Tidying the Bury bungalow before the move, Dawson's son Stuart stumbled across the sheaf of paper and was about to throw it up in the air to see the mess it would make, when Dawson retrieved it and decided, at last, to make something of the words he'd written.

For his initial foray into literature, Dawson had written about a subject he knew inside-out: the stratum of show business known as clubland, which included both the grottiest working men's clubs, where turns were expected to change into their stage clothes in the lavatory, and the far grander variety clubs, like Batley, which could afford acts as internationally revered as Louis Armstrong. The anti-hero of *A Card for the Clubs* was a comic by the name of Pete Warde, who worked the lower reaches of the clubland scene under the appallingly cheesy stage name of Joe King. At the start of the novel, his career seems permanently stalled. He cannot get any broadcasts or any decent live bookings. His stage suit is so old and threadbare, his agent tells him, 'every time a band plays the Lancers, your pants break into a gallop'.[63] The suit is matched by King/Warde's material, which is 'so old it's a wonder I don't pay death duties on my script'.[64] Worst of all, he is estranged from his wife Allison, who wishes that he would give up his dreams of making it in show business, for the sake of sanity and family life. Every cloud has a silver lining. Being estranged from Allison means that he doesn't have to face her mother, an 'overweight wombat' who wishes that he would give up breathing.[65] As much as he loves his wife, Warde is unable to resist any reasonable offers from women he meets on the road. Dancers, singers, landladies, members of the audience. Warde is on a sexual Cook's tour of the north.

What passes for Warde's career reaches a new low at Gawkesworth

Reform Club, where he dies the death on stage and the concert secretary informs him: 'Tha's worst act we've 'ad 'ere since club opened. Tha'd better get off afore't treasurer docks a pound or tow [*sic*] ... tha wilt never bleedin' well cum here again ... I've seen better turns int' Manchester eye hospital.'[66] To add insult to injury, one of the punters has smeared the word 'SHIT' in the dirt on Warde's car bonnet, and 'MORE SHIT' in the smuts on the boot. He takes his £8 earnings to a professionals' hang-out called the Front Cloth Club, where he bumps into Al Friday, a comedian who had been a big name but had fallen from grace. Nonetheless, Friday has in his pocket some new material that he lets Warde look over, and a date for a BBC audition that might revive his career. Unfortunately, over-indulgence leads Friday to collapse as he's leaving the club, and Warde swipes the script. Hearing that Friday has been taken to hospital, Warde decides to take Friday's place at the BBC audition. It goes badly, but the stolen material works on stage and Warde's bookings start to improve. Until, that is, Friday's associates beat Warde to a pulp. He carries on using the gags, but finds the responses increasingly muted, and realizes that everywhere he goes, Friday has been there a little before, wowing them with the same script. At the end of a disastrous week in Stockton-on-Tees, he ditches the script and starts telling them the truth about his life. 'Thank you ladies and gentlemen for your kind applause ... I'm very grateful, because if success breeds success ... then it looks as if I'm on the pill ... you should have seen my engagement book, the pages are so blank and white, you get snow blindness looking through it.'[67] The self-deprecation gets big laughs, so Warde ditches the stolen gags and builds a new routine around his history of dismal failure, to great acclaim.

Eventually, he finds himself on the same bill as Friday, who has been fulfilling a series of overseas engagements. Warde realizes that Friday thinks he will still be using the purloined funnies, and allows the older comedian to enjoy a moment's complacency. Instead, Friday 'dies', while Warde knocks the audience bandy with his new style. Friday slinks away, utterly humiliated. Soon, Warde is earning £100 a week, a figure reported dutifully in the *Manchester Evening News*, as a result of which his hated mother-in-law comes to plead with him to return to Allison. Seeing her for the venal old bag she is, he does so, but determines to show his mother-in-law who's boss.

Television fame follows, in the form of a series called *Pub Night*, recorded at licensed premises up and down the British Isles and hosted by Warde. The rough and ready atmosphere of the show makes it a hit, but the problems begin when a new, trendy producer insists on doing each show live, and introducing topical guests. On the first show of the new regime, a thinly veiled Kenneth Tynan figure, named, none too subtly, Peregrine Gaynor, refers to a controversial film of his, featuring 'nuns fucking', and brings down the ire of the press and other self-appointed moral guardians on the television company. Warde, who objected to the live transmission, is deemed blameless, but the neutered show – now recorded and studio-based – fails and, after a season at the London Palladium, Warde's career follows close behind. His home life falls apart too, with Allison pregnant and her apparently bed-ridden mother interrupting every private moment they try to steal. Eventually, Warde hires a nurse to look after both wife and mother-in-law, to say nothing of his sexual appetites. One night they are caught by Allison's mother, who, in her glee at exposing Warde, forgets that she's just revealed herself to be a conniving, lying old bag who was not incapacitated at all. Allison instructs Warde never again to tell her he loves her. She'll stay with him for the sake of the unborn child, but that's it. The pride of impending fatherhood is dimmed somewhat by news from one of his conquests that she is also expecting his child.

Having failed as a comic, Warde, with the encouragement of a record producer called Jim Casey, reinvents himself as a singer with a decent line in between-song comic patter, changing his performing name to the not much less cheesy Dino Warde. His debut record is an unexpected success, and audiences take to his act and to the sensational musicianship of his pianist Jess Hart. Warde is, for the second time, back on top and, when he catches Allison in bed with Hart, he feels the wheel has come full circle. It hasn't, not quite. He finds himself booked at Gawkesworth Reform Club, where only a few years before he had been given the bird and told by the concert secretary that he'd never be welcomed back. Fighting the instinct not to show up, Warde goes to Gawkesworth and finds that 'despite being tarted up, [it] was still the hole I remembered. The same mentally crippled committee, same cretinous audience'. Taking the stage to rapturous applause from the cretins, he gives them the exact same act that had gone down so badly on his last appearance, and ends up taking several curtain calls, after which he berates the committee, the audience and himself. 'For success, I sacrificed everything that was worth keeping hold of, and for this, I find myself back in this piss hole,' he tells them. He walks out, announcing that he'll write a book about his experiences, but that he first has something to tell his wife, something 'that might make her very happy'.[68]

It would be easy to assume that *A Card for the Clubs* is autobiographical. It certainly seems to be an attempt to settle a score with the upper echelons of an industry that kept Dawson at arm's length for so many years, and also to deal with the worst aspects of the lower levels of the same trade, where he had been stuck for a long time. Aspects of the novel undoubtedly spring directly from Dawson's own experiences, but it's fairer to say that Warde is a composite character, taking elements from other performers he knew and situations he had witnessed or heard of, and filtering them through Dawson's fertile imagination. The first and most obvious difference is between the wives of Dawson and his fictional creation. Allison Warde wishes that her husband would give up on his show business dreams. In contrast, Meg Dawson was endlessly supportive of Les and understanding of how much success would mean to him.

Dawson always worked under his real name whereas Warde adopts fake stage names. The fictional comedian also despises his audiences, describing them as 'Cro-Magna' [*sic*] and 'morons', and clearly regards himself as a cut above, despite his rotten material and his dependence on such people for a living. Dawson never looked down his nose at his audiences, knowing that they were mostly of the same solid working-class stock as himself. As Dec Cluskey recalled, before Dawson was famous he would sit in the audience himself, drinking and chatting until it was his turn to take the stage. He enjoyed being around people, and respected his audiences unless they took an irrational dislike to him. He wasn't above or below the odd dig at other comedians' fan bases, though. In the early nineties, Dawson spoke about Bernard Manning's followers in less than glowing terms. Coincidentally, Warde comes to national prominence as the host of a show called *Pub Night*, which bears some resemblance to the *Wheeltappers and Shunters Social Club*,[69] a variety show made by Granada and co-presented by Manning, which began in the same year as *A Card for the Clubs* was published.

Warde also despises his agent, 'a Manchester Jew, who's so crooked that the day he dies they'll have to screw him into his coffin ... a third-rate agent with delusions of grandeur ... so bald that the last time he went to a bowling alley, somebody put their fingers up his nose'.[70] In contrast, Dawson remained on good terms with Kevin McEntee, and had no obvious problems with Norman Murray or Murray's business partner, Anne Chudleigh. Another crucial difference between Warde and Dawson is that the former is a cheerful thief of bad gags, while his creator set great store by his originality.

Then there's the matter of the mother-in-law. Warde hates Allison's mother, with some justification, given her conniving, cruel, dishonest ways. Although Dawson did not always get on with Ada Plant, he maintained a considerable degree of respect for her. 'Our relationship had always been a mixed one,' he admitted, 'although strangely enough, of all the family, I think I probably understood her the best. She had ruled her brood according to her lights and her son and daughters were a credit to her vigilance. Despite the fact that I used her unmercifully as a basis for my act, and despite the fact that she often used to shake her fist under my nose ... she rather enjoyed the notoriety ... One night, she ... grabbed my arm and said, "Don't ever forget me when you do your 'turn'." I never have.'[71]

So much for the differences, but what of the similarities? Both Warde and Dawson have epiphanies with morose material; Dawson in Hull, Warde in Stockton. Warde becomes embroiled in gambling after an initial lucky run at a casino, followed by a longer very unlucky run. Dawson seems not to have become as addicted as Warde, but he refers in *A Clown Too Many* to 'the parties and the hangovers; the gambling and the guilt'.[72]

The main source of the guilt was, by Dawson's own admission, the fact that 'away from home … women flattered me and my head was turning'. Warde finds himself similarly tempted and succumbing frequently, while always professing his love for Allison. Did Dawson succumb? Questioned on the matter, he always played the modesty card. In 1975, a *TV Times* journalist wrote that 'Dawson still insists that he couldn't pull a ligament, let alone a woman', quoting the comedian as saying 'I'm the most unromantic lump of Northern suet. Yes, a woman did accost me once in South Shields, but she had a face like Red Rum.'[73] Later, in *A Clown Too Many*, he gives off more mixed signals. Recalling a fellow performer on a summer season whose 'aim in life appeared to be to make love to every woman in sight', Dawson confessed that he had 'often veered to that idea, but with a face and body like mine, it has to be pure fantasy, I'm afraid'.[74] He also observed that, while some view show business as 'a weekly orgy', he had 'been in the game many years, and I've yet to see an orgy'.

Weighing against these rueful protestations of reluctant innocence, Dawson notes elsewhere that as he became more famous, 'the tempo of my private life increased: clubs, late-night drinking, and I became obsessed with that most trite of dictums, "Wine, Women and Song"'.[75] Moreover, when he feared for the state of his marriage in the unwitting run-up to his first *This Is Your Life* appearance, he rationalized that he couldn't blame Meg for seeking comfort elsewhere, with him being 'away for weeks on end, no angel myself …'.[76] David Nobbs recalls one conversation at the YTV studios in Leeds, when the question of how Dawson planned to spend the evening brought an unexpected response:

Les said to me, 'I've got a date with an Israeli tank commander tonight. She's incredibly beautiful. I can't believe I'm going out with her.' The next day, I said, 'Les, how did it go?' He said, 'Well, David, you know my capacity to self-destruct and the way I'm drawn to failure like a moth to a flame. We had a very good dinner, we went back to the hotel, she took all her clothes off, I took all my clothes off. I'll never know what possessed me to mention the Golan Heights at that moment.' That's Les's wit. I don't know whether it was a true story. You couldn't tell.[77]

Nobbs is unsure whether the story of the failed seduction was real or an elaborate set-up for a gag. If it were true, though, why should it be a shock? Such behaviour is almost expected of touring musicians and forgiven by fans as part of the supposed rock-and-roll lifestyle. Frank Zappa's devotion to groupies was openly expressed, as was his genuine devotion to his wife and children. Whatever happened on tour was mere bedroom gymnastics. What really mattered was at home. And yet, family entertainers seem subject to a different moral code. As a disciple of Max Wall, Dawson would have been more aware than most of this curious double standard. Rockers are almost expected to be degenerate, while mainstream show business stars were (and still are, to a degree) expected to be wholesome. In reality, the temptations are identical, and the same can be said for so-called legitimate actors and film stars from the silent era up to the present day. In its own quiet way, *A Card for the Clubs* is a fictionalized *Hollywood Babylon* of clubland.

Its qualities were noted by Kenith Trodd, then working for the BBC drama department, who wanted to turn it into a *Play for Today*, with Colin Welland having shown interest in adapting the book for television. Trodd sent a memo to the contracts department on 21 February 1974, asking them to check the rights situation. Unfortunately, the project came to nothing, but it shows that Dawson was beginning to be taken seriously, and not just in the field of light entertainment.

His second novel, *The Spy Who Came ...*, was published in the autumn of 1976, and promoted with a round of bookshop appearances and a spot on *Parkinson*, where he conversed in erudite fashion with Lord Carnarvon, played out-of-tune piano (much to the delight of the backing band, particularly organist and leader Harry Stoneham, clearly visible in the background at his keyboard, rocking with laughter) and joked with the host about the length of time the fee took to arrive after his previous appearance on the show. 'Don't forget the cheque this time, as well,' Dawson instructed Parky, turning to shout into the interviewer's shoulder, 'It took seven weeks last time. Tell Billy Cotton.'[78] Dawson then turned back to the audience and announced, 'Seven weeks for nothing. You get nothing on this show, I tell you. He can't even afford a haircut. Have you seen the backing band? Come on. The whole thing is a mess.[79] Russell Harty for President.' At the mention of his friend and rival, a convulsed Parkinson aimed a mock-kick at his guest, who was, by this point, also giggling, and told the audience, 'He joins Jimmy Tarbuck on the blacklist.'

A Card for the Clubs was a slice of social realism, but *The Spy Who Came ...* was a far more freewheeling and surreal affair. At its centre is another down-at-heel club act, this time an impressionist known as Guy Fenner (real name: Percy Sidebottom). Fenner dreams both of attaining stardom and of not having to live with his bovine, pregnant wife, Rita, her shrill mother, Marion, and her constipated, noxiously flatulent father, Fred. During the course of the book, he manages to achieve both, but not in the way he intended. The main obstacle to stardom is the fact that his act stinks, almost as much as the outside privy after Fred's been in for one of his sessions. However, Fenner finds himself unwittingly involved in a Russian plot to relieve a German scientist's widow of the secret formula for extracting gold from sea water. Fenner's impersonation of Donald Duck, it transpires during a hospital radio interview heard by a Russian agent, sounds exactly like the deceased boffin, Dr Ernst Kitler. Consequently, he is enlisted by Russian agents posing as theatrical agents Mr Hampton and Mr Wick[80] to give a private show for Kitler's widow, who was entrusted with the information. Fenner's impersonation proves successful, and his problems only start when he mistakenly gives his paymasters the wrong piece of paper: Marion's laundry list. The Russians think the references to shirts and bed sheets are a fiendish code and send the slip of paper to Moscow for decryption. American operatives intercept the formula and realize that it is just a laundry list, and that Fenner must have double-crossed everyone. By a process of elimination, he is assumed to be in the pay of the Chinese and, from this point on, he becomes the two superpowers' most wanted man. Both agree to work together to eliminate him. Fenner reacts by hiding the formula in the one place no sane human being would dare to look: the inside of the toilet roll holder in Fred's malodorous domicile. Meanwhile, Elsa, a statuesque Russian operative, turns out to be a British agent called Ruth Weston, with whom Fenner begins a tempestuous and very physical affair in the safe house. Fenner's ineptitude as an impressionist is matched only by his cowardice, and he tries to avoid any confrontation with the enemy, but somehow manages to prevail accidentally when faced with the most fiendish opposition, becoming regarded as a feared and worthy adversary.

His show business career finally takes off, but only when he forgets his act and dries completely, remaining utterly silent. Thus elevated, Fenner is booked to appear on *The Golden Shot* with Bob Monkhouse, with the British assuming, correctly, that the presence of a live crossbow and Fenner in the same studio would prove irresistible to the enemy. When Fenner is ready to hand the formula over, he returns to the in-laws and finds that his foul father-in-law had discovered it in the tube, and, having run out of lavatory paper, had wiped his bum on the source of his son-in-law's misery and peril. 'I couldn't believe my ears,' Fenner commented. 'Men had died for that piece of paper, from Berlin, Leipzig, London, Leeds and Manchester ... Years of scientific research gone to cleanse a constipated old bleeder's backside ... Suddenly the whole idiotic situation struck me and I started to laugh.'[81]

Finally, Fenner is enlisted by the British secret services for one last mission, which is to see off an expected assassination attempt on

President Mah-Gumboil of the African state of Cannibala (an obvious send-up of Idi Amin), who is visiting London for the *Royal Variety Performance*. In entertainment terms, the show is a disaster, as Fenner loses his nerve, fails to stay silent and reverts to his rotten old act. The real purpose of his presence is, however, achieved, after which he is sent to an island near Trinidad called Wogo Wogo (a rare racially dubious gag for Dawson) for his own safety. The tropical idyll is broken when Rita, Marion and Fred are shipped out to join him, casting him into bitterness and gloom. Fortunately his mood lifts when he realizes that Ruth is with them, having volunteered to look after the clan, and the book ends with Fenner fairly confident that he'll be the one Ruth looks after most assiduously.

The Spy Who Came ... is a much more accomplished piece of work than *A Card for the Clubs*. Dawson had evidently learned a lot about structure and plot, for while *The Spy Who Came ...* is based on a ludicrous, improbable premise, everything is resolved in the end. Obviously, not having to obey the strictures of reality or plausibility helped, and it seems that Dawson was far more comfortable concocting Goonish flights of fancy from an earthy base than remaining unremittingly grim and bitter as he had in *A Card for the Clubs*. However far-fetched the book might be, there are, once again, several elements of autobiography present. Before becoming a performer, Fenner had been an insurance salesman and a Hoover representative and had sold a vacuum cleaner 'to a deaf mute who was on gas',[82] a story that Dawson later claimed really happened to him in his Hoover days. Meanwhile, when Fenner fails miserably at the Motor Show, also on the bill is an established comedian called Artie Cox, whose motoring jokes sound very familiar. 'My car is so old, it hasn't got a handbrake ... it's a pike staff,' Cox tells the Earls Court punters, adding that 'My wife is taking driving lessons ... Every time she goes on a main road, the cats' eyes squint.'[83] Dawson's love of a well-turned phrase is much in evidence. When Fenner is in hospital, what others would refer to merely as a plaster cast is a 'cocoon of gypsum'.[84] Also apparent is Dawson's catholic taste in books, with references to

A.A. Milne and abundant horror story clichés such as murderous butlers, as well as the obvious spy novel influences.

In between these longer fiction projects, Dawson was also in demand as a writer of features and short stories, for publications as diverse as *Punch* and *Penthouse*. In July 1976, he was commissioned by the *Daily Mirror* to contribute to its 'Star Story' strand, which ran fiction written by celebrities including Harry Secombe, Diana Dors, newscaster Gordon Honeycombe and pop mogul Jonathan King, ostensibly as holiday reading. Dawson's offering, 'The Humbling of Poddy', concerned Mr Merryweather Poddy, the self-important manager of the Hotel Splendide in Crouchmire-on-Sea. Poddy was a snob who made Basil Fawlty seem reasonable, given to confiscating books from guests if he thought they were unfit to be read in his establishment and known 'to gaze at his residents with the disdain of a boiled owl'.[85]

When a cloth-capped working-class guest from Bolton ventures to complain about the service, the trio of elderly female musicians stop playing and the room falls silent as everybody prepares for Poddy to humiliate the northern gent utterly. His complaint is that he can't eat the soup. Poddy opens fire on the complainant: 'How dare you, an ill-dressed clod, have the audacity to criticize the food? I might tell you that only last week the Princess Fiona of Hollandbach sat at this very table and waxed ecstatically about the food. And you, whose palate is no doubt conditioned to cod and chips from a newspaper, can sit there talking about our cuisine as though you had pretensions to a social caste. One can only assume, you insolent nonentity, that you are a near idiot with delusions of grandeur.'[86] Poddy is deflated completely when the man replies that the reason he can't eat the soup is because he hasn't been given a spoon. Ever after, Poddy can be brought to heel with a simple cry of 'spoons'.

Meanwhile, the November 1977 edition of *Penthouse* featured a curious piece by Dawson rejoicing in the honest, if not particularly creative, title: 'Accrington deck chair attendant mauled by deaf leopard while practising tuba in Congo rain forest'. It concerned 'a far-flung thespian cousin' of the comedian's called Dawson Flufflines-Skint, or

'Fluffit' to his friends. The highlight of Fluffit's career had been playing Lon Chaney's hump in *The Hunchback of Notre Dame*, so Dawson concentrated on the lowlights, which were many and various. During the Second World War, Fluffit was 'first off the landing craft during the Normandy invasion', not even waiting for it to leave Southampton.[87] After heavy editing, it might have made a decent monologue for Dawson in stand-up mode, but on the page, it's a fairly tortuous affair.

Throughout the mid-seventies, Dawson continued with his usual punishing run of live engagements in clubs and theatres, scheduled around his television, radio and writing commitments. In the summer of 1975, he was in Southport at the New Theatre with Irish singer Dana, and Bobby Bennett, a comedian best known for his appearances as one of the few adults on Yorkshire Television's *Junior Showtime*. Usually, the club and theatre audiences were of a higher class than the Cro-Magnons and morons of *A Card for the Clubs*. Sometimes, they were very high-flown indeed, as with the royal charity gala at C'esar's Palace in Luton. For one night only, on 1 December 1976, the Duke of Edinburgh took his place at a table usually groaning with chicken in baskets, and watched Dawson host an evening of entertainment featuring singing duo Peters and Lee. The event was televised six days later. Dawson's abiding memory of the evening was of what happened after the show. The comedian was already a firm favourite at Buckingham Palace, particularly with the Duke, and His Royal Highness made a point of singling out Dawson for a chat, jokily asking if he was still living in the north and commenting on how he'd enjoyed a black pudding he'd been given on a recent visit to Rochdale, which he'd had fried for breakfast. Dawson pointed out gently that the normal procedure was to boil a black pudding. Prince Philip remained adamant that frying was the correct way. 'From that moment on, I confess I forgot I was talking to a prince of the realm,' Dawson said later. 'I argued and, to his amusement, got hot under the collar about the flaming black puddings. Ashen-faced officials listened to the harangue in horror and the press were kept back as we went at it.'[88] It was a measure of the esteem in which Dawson was held that such a breach of etiquette became the basis of a lifelong in-joke between the Prince and the comedian.

The drought-hit summer of 1976 had been spent in Scarborough, again at the Floral Hall, where Dawson had worked with Bob Monkhouse six years earlier, but this time he was the headline act on a bill that included Bennett again and Scottish singer Kenneth McKellar. The production was reviewed favourably, as ever, with *The Stage* calling it a 'wonderful family holiday show'.[89] The value of this verdict is called into question, however, by Pete Warde in *A Card for the Clubs*, who suggested the trade paper erred towards kindness, saying, 'if you die on your feet, they'll dutifully report that you did well despite technical troubles'.[90] In fact, the Scarborough run exacerbated one of Dawson's periodic bouts of insecurity. 'The business wasn't bad,' he reported in his first autobiography, 'but I knew it could have been better ... and as the ratings for *Sez Les* sank, so did my spirits.'[91]

Dawson's tendency to blame himself when shows went badly, while others in show business have been known to blame everyone but themselves, was a recurring theme. Sometimes, the self-criticism was justified, but things were rarely as bad as he feared. The doubt felt by Dawson was not the usual self-doubt or lack of self-confidence displayed by some performers, so much as lack of faith in the public's reaction to the work. Dawson knew he was good at what he did and that he could only do his best. The imponderable was how it would go down with the audiences, and how tastes might change. Whatever the motivation, it was not a crippling malaise. Dawson fortified himself with strong drink and carried on as best he could.

CHAPTER 5

Farewell to Leeds

At the end of 1973, Alan Coren, writing in *The Times*, had been able to declare that Dawson was 'our most underrated comedian'.[1] Coren did not mean that he was unpopular. He was Yorkshire's star comedy performer, and, given YTV's status as one of the big five companies in the commercial television network, he was also one of ITV's leading names. The 1971 series of *Sez Les* had achieved a peak audience of 6.3 million and had, at times, been the third most popular programme on network television, whether ITV or BBC. By the summer 1974 run, the show was regularly achieving over 6 million viewers, tying with *Coronation Street* in the ratings and beating the BBC's most popular comedy programme, *The Two Ronnies*. What Coren was referring to was respect and cachet. Plenty of people watched Dawson, but, to begin with, not enough realized quite how good he was. By 1976, though, he was starting to get the recognition that Coren felt he deserved. The work that Dawson did at Yorkshire Television between 1973 and 1975 was often of very high quality, and more varied than previously. Although the quantity and breadth of the work had confused and alienated some of his audience, it had signalled to the business that Dawson was versatile, and, with nearly a decade in the limelight, he had longevity going for him too. The BBC had the variety output of Morecambe and Wise and the sketch comedy contribution of Dick Emery. ITV had Les Dawson, and he could hold his own against both acts.

Strangely, Yorkshire were the ones who seemed to appreciate this least, seemingly taking their star turn for granted. He was part of the furniture, having been around from the regional broadcaster's earliest days, and having outlasted those who brought him to the Kirkstall Road studios in the first place by a considerable margin. Dawson and his managers felt that it was time to move on after *Holiday With Strings* and *The Loner*, but had been persuaded to stay by Duncan Wood. The result was more *Sez Les*, first in the form of four hour-long specials transmitted in the early part of 1976, then with a series of six half-hour shows – by now more a pure sketch format than a variety production – at the end of the year. However, when the obligatory Christmas show came around, Dawson 'felt stale', and was informed by agent Norman Murray that his paymasters agreed and would not be taking up the option on another contract. All that remained was a run of four specials under the banner *Dawson and Friends*, although audience tickets seen in shot in one of the programmes clearly show the title as *Sez Les*.

For these four last Yorkshire shows, all signs of staleness had gone. They sparkle, and are arguably the peak of his television output. 'I had the confidence and the experience behind me to tackle anything that came along,' Dawson wrote in *A Clown Too Many*. 'I felt that at last, the little man had found himself.'[2] Whereas the musical elements sometimes jarred with the comedy in the earlier *Sez Les* shows, these specials incorporate the music brilliantly. In each show, a different top orchestra was in service: Don Lusher's Ted Heath band; the Geraldo Orchestra under Ivor Raymonde; Jack Parnell's orchestra taking a break from supplying the music to just about every show to come out of ATV's studios at Elstree; and, of course, Les's old mate Syd Lawrence – with Dawson's opening monologue delivered standing in the crook of a concert grand, the band's pianist noodling discreetly in the background.

The best of the run is the last, a freewheeling hour that begins with Dawson singing a snatch of 'My Way' and trying to put a ciga-rette between his lips and light it in a cool and nonchalant manner. Nonchalance is outstripped by incompetence, as he drops the contents of the packet on the floor and almost burns his eyebrows off. The burst of song is a prelude to a homily on being true to yourself and doing it your way even when all seems lost. The unlikely idea of Dawson giving a pep talk is soon torpedoed, as a tale of woe unfolds:

> Two years ago, I went through such a period of desolation … I played one theatre and the silence I endured throughout the whole of my act was so intense, the mere shifting of a cough lozenge from one molar to another reverberated like a musket volley. Nothing went right. I invested a lot of money in a company that made ladies' bonnets, and then the Government cancelled Easter. But I maintained dignity. I tried to bend frozen turkeys into the shape of a boomerang then I used to cross them with kangaroos. The idea was to produce a bird you could stuff from the outside. It didn't work. All I got was an omelette you couldn't throw away.[3]

The line about stuffing gets a good laugh. The second punchline brings the house down. The line doesn't actually quite make sense, even filtered through the mangled logic of such genetic modification, turkey eggs not being particularly renowned as a delicacy. It's possible that he meant to say chicken, rather than turkey. However, the confidence of the delivery and the concept of a rebounding omelette are enough to cast aside any such minor quibbles, at least in the eyes of that audience in YTV Studio 4. As show openings go, it's one of the most assured and gleeful of Dawson's television career. Behind him, the band are laughing heartily at the tales of the wife's mother suffering an accident at work ('Apparently a hot rivet had dropped down her drawers and she fell off the oil rig') and the wife leaving Dawson to care for their three children ('One of each') while she invades Poland, to say nothing of a doctor so old-fashioned he lances boils on horseback. Dawson says he dealt with his problems his way, and that, in time, his wife came back, her mother came back, and everything returned to normal. 'At that moment in time, a new feeling came over me that I'd never experienced before,' he concluded. 'Sick.'[4]

Announcing that the musicians are 'direct from a course of Grecian 2000', Dawson looks over at amused orchestra leader Don Lusher and bursts out laughing, taking a little while to regain his composure.

The star of the show is evidently having a ball. Dawson seizes on Lusher's surname, noting that it suggests 'an affinity with the grape', and states that the bandleader is 'standing from memory' and 'swaying like an aspen'. If these insults had been true, they wouldn't have been funny.

Throughout *Dawson and Friends*, jazz musician Humphrey Lyttelton appears as Sherlock Holmes to Dawson's Watson, and has a similar effect to John Cleese's tall, patrician presence in the earlier *Sez Les* shows. There were other similarities, more noticeable off-screen. 'We used to call them the Odd Couples, because Les hit it off immediately with John Cleese, and the great Lyttelton,' Barry Cryer observes. 'They hit it off straight away. Lyttelton loved Les Dawson. They were together immediately.'[5] Of course, this was not the first time that Dawson and Lyttelton had worked together, having both appeared on a Light Programme forces special from Germany in 1965. Lyttelton, a man of great wit, recognized a kindred spirit in Dawson. The downbeat style of Dawson's humour had a lot of parallels with the private jokes swapped by professional musicians on tour buses: only the tales of the worst humiliations are remembered, because they make the better stories. So, musicians tended to take to Dawson as one of their own.

Another recurring presence in *Dawson and Friends* was Willie Rushton, playing a German hot-air balloonist wearing the obligatory spiked helmet with predictably destructive consequences. With Humph, Cryer and Rushton on board, only Tim Brooke-Taylor and Graeme Garden would have been needed to make the series a full house for the participants of *I'm Sorry I Haven't A Clue*.

If Dawson had any last-minute doubts about leaving the company where he'd spent nine largely happy years, the wrap party for the series calmed them. 'There was a most insalubrious and inadequate little presentation ceremony for Les, when he was given, I think, a portrait of himself,' David Nobbs recalls. 'I'm pretty sure I can see him unwrapping it, and it was wrapped in newspaper. It was very inelegantly wrapped. And he said, "Thank you very much for this. I will stick it in the smallest room and every time I use it, I'll think of Yorkshire Television." It seemed a real shame that the relationship should end on such a note. It was a farewell. It was the most appallingly embarrassing thing.'[6] The warm send-off by the crews and the backstage staff, who gathered to toast Dawson and wish him well, singing a rewritten version of Gilbert O'Sullivan's song 'Clair', entitled 'Les', in his honour, made up for the management's insensitivity, but Dawson knew he needed to make the break. 'The sincerity of the lads brought me to the brink of tears as the emotion in the studio ran high: so many years ... some good, some, well, you can't win them all,' he said later, concluding that 'I needed to get away from the studios and start to reappraise my career'.[7]

In 1977, a top television comic leaving one network had two options: the other lot or retirement. Often, the move was seen in the press as a defection, a lucrative betrayal or a form of kidnapping, as happened when Thames 'snatched' Morecambe and Wise from the BBC in 1978. In Dawson's case, there was no such emotive brouhaha, probably because while the BBC were interested in giving him work, they were not inclined to snap him up with a lucrative contract. *The Stage* reported in June of that year, while *Dawson and Friends* was still running on ITV, that Dawson 'is going to work for the BBC, starting this week with a recording from Great Yarmouth of a BBC1 *Seaside Special* ... He has no long-term contract with the BBC, although an executive at the Television Centre says "We're talking about it".'[8]

There had been a jokey prelude to Dawson's move to the BBC at an awards ceremony at the Royal Albert Hall. Dawson was on the Yorkshire table with Vernon Lawrence, while on an adjacent table were a group of BBC executives, chief among them head of light entertainment Bill Cotton Jr. Lawrence recalls: 'I wrote on a serviette, "You can have us both for a hundred grand," folded it, put "Bill Cotton" on it and gave it to a waiter, who gave it to Bill. Who looked round, sent it back with "Thanks" and he'd crossed out one of the noughts.'[9] Lawrence also remembers the journey to Kensington that evening, with Dawson as an extremely fidgety car passenger, and their arrival:

He kept leaning over in the front seat all the time, fiddling. I said, 'What are you doing? Have you got fleas or something?' He was tearing YTV wardrobe labels off the socks he was wearing. When we got there, we were incredibly early, and he said, 'What shall we do?' I said, 'Let's get a drink,' so we walked off to find the bar, and we walked into this reception, which was Princess Anne's reception for the organizers. We just walked in, and because it was him, we were automatically accepted.[10]

In fact, the *Seaside Special* was not quite Dawson's first outing on BBC TV following his break from Yorkshire. On Saturday, 18 June, at 5.45 p.m., he appeared on BBC1's *Tell Me More*, a factual show for children hosted by Nanette Newman with help from Graeme Garden, talking about famous hoaxes; then he popped up again at 10.45 p.m. as a guest on *Make the Music Speak*, the first of a series starring the Scottish singer Lena Martell.[11] In his own words, 'I was on the box more than the test card'.[12] His presence on the Lena Martell show was down to the show's director – David Mallet. It was a big prestige network production for BBC Scotland and Mallet had gone all out to impress, telling the *Daily Mirror* that: 'The usual Northern chicken 'n' chips or scampi nightclub is unsuitable for TV. The ceilings, designed to retain heat, are too low and the lights are too dim. So we hired a large, empty hall, twice the size of the biggest TV studio in England, and turned it into a nightclub. We've recreated a glamorous club setting with a glass door and a black-and-white decor for Lena's cabaret.' Having built up an atmosphere of glamour, and dressed up the star of the show in BBC Scotland's finest gowns, who better than Dawson to deflate it? 'She says, "I'd like to introduce you to my guest" and Les Dawson comes on,' Mallet recalls. 'Lots of applause, he looks like that [a sideways glance] and he says, "It's the QE2". Les comes up from Manchester and calls her the QE2.'[13]

Recorded in a circus tent at Lowestoft (*The Stage* having confused its East Anglian resorts), the *Seaside Special* that heralded Dawson's transfer to the BBC also featured Dana, who had appeared in one of the *Dawson and Friends* shows barely a month before, and who also

The Dawson family: a composite picture of Julia, Leslie senior and Leslie junior, marking Leslie senior's wartime service in Egypt and Africa.

Thornton Street, Collyhurst, in 1934: Les Dawson's birthplace and his family's home for the first few years of his life.

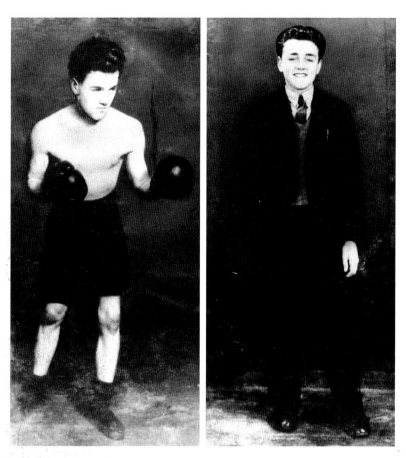

Portraits of the artist as a young man: Les Dawson the boxer and in his Sunday best.

Mess mates: Dawson and Army pals enjoying a beer or two.

Trooper Dawson of the Queen's Bays
defending the old country.

Someone to lean on: Dawson and friends
fooling about for the camera.

When Les met Meg: at the Hoover works dinner and dance in Sale, Cheshire, in 1959.

Les and Meg Dawson sign the register at St Thomas's, Crumpsall, on 25 June 1960.

A happy family: Meg, Stuart, Julie and Les Dawson, with Meg's mother, Ada Plant, *circa* 1970.

Mrs Cissie Braithwaite and Mrs Ada Shufflebotham, gossip girls.

At the Dawson Control nerve centre for *The Dawson Watch*, with a young Vicki Michelle on the far right.

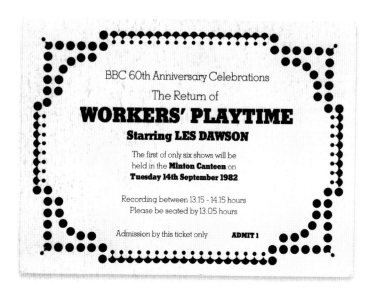

BBC 60th Anniversary Celebrations

The Return of

WORKERS' PLAYTIME
Starring LES DAWSON

The first of only six shows will be
held in the **Minton Canteen** on
Tuesday 14th September 1982

Recording between 13.15 - 14.15 hours
Please be seated by 13.05 hours

Admission by this ticket only   **ADMIT 1**

Dawson returns to his radio roots for the BBC's 60th anniversary in 1982 with a *Workers' Playtime*.

Launching an autumn and winter of light entertainment on BBC Television with *Hi-De-Hi*'s Ruth Madoc and Su Pollard on Blackpool beach in 1984.

Meanwhile, at the Grand Theatre, Blackpool, Les and company are packing them in for a record season.

Les marries the second Mrs Dawson, Tracy, at the White Church in Lytham St Annes in 1989. Bridesmaids include Pamela, who Les has his arm around, and, to the right of the picture, Julie.

Les at home with baby Charlotte in 1992.

An unusual co-star for *The Les Dawson Show*, BBC Television Centre, London in 1989.

Les Dawson as Morton Stanley in the ITV comedy-drama *Demob* in 1993.

knew Dawson well from working with him on stage. It was an important show for both of them, as it was her return to performing after serious throat trouble. The *Daily Mirror* reported that her singing had been pre-recorded in London to conserve her voice, doctors having rationed her to ten minutes' singing per day. Thankfully, on the night, both were able to relaunch their careers without much fanfare or incident.

When the BBC eventually made a full commitment to Dawson, it was for a series of six variety shows produced by John Ammonds. Although the title was *The Les Dawson Show*, he had a co-star in the form of Lulu, with whom he had worked extensively as a spot comic in the past. Perhaps surprisingly, Barry Cryer and David Nobbs were nowhere to be seen on the credit roller for the new show. 'When Les went off to the BBC, he did say all sorts of things. "See you at the BBC, lads",' recalls Nobbs. 'He thanked us for the brilliance of our stuff, the immense contribution that we'd given, how wonderful it had all been, and that was the last we heard from him. When we met him, he was as friendly as ever.'

While baffled and upset at the time, Nobbs has rationalized any traces of bitterness out of his assessment of the situation:

I don't think he was proactive about what people did for him. He made statements on the assumption that everybody would want to continue working with us. When they didn't, he was probably easily swayed by the view that he should do something different. And maybe that was right. Maybe we could only take our vision of Les to the BBC, and that vision had lasted a long time and maybe it was time that he did something else. He didn't want conflict. He wanted a peaceful ride, and to be funny. I don't think it was as unfair as all that. Why should Les stick his neck above the parapet and say, 'I want David and Barry'? At the time we took it a bit hard, and I'll tell you why we took it a bit hard, because Les had been so emotional and fulsome. I prefer now to think that he really meant it when he said it. I don't think there was any insincerity. The sincerity was tremendous.

If anything, Nobbs is sadder that he never got a chance to write anything for Dawson at Yorkshire outside sketch and variety shows. 'Even Alan Plater, as a writer, a great friend of mine, I didn't think he'd got Dawson fully first time, and why should he?' argues Nobbs. '[*The Loner*] didn't touch the heights of *The Beiderbecke Affair*, which is a gem in television from my point of view. We thought, well, we could have done it because we know Les, but they don't go to us.' The problem was one of perception. At YTV, Nobbs was seen as a broad comedy man, despite writing plays for other broadcasters:

I did a play for Granada, and somebody said to me, it might have been David Reynolds, 'We should be doing plays of yours like that.' Nobody took me seriously. We saw the drama department in the far corner of the room, Peter Willes and so on. Reggie [*The Fall and Rise of Reginald Perrin*] came along, and I was still doing the Les Dawson show during the first series of 'Reggie'. Not a whiff of interest from Yorkshire. The moment I left Yorkshire Television after Les left, the drama people started getting interested in me, and wanted me to do something. They no longer saw me as that man who sits in the corner with the comedy crowd. David Cunliffe took over and started commissioning me to do things.[14]

Vernon Lawrence concurs with Nobbs's analysis of why Cryer and Nobbs were jettisoned when Dawson moved to the BBC, and argues that Dawson either didn't realize the sway he had as the star of the show, or else he simply chose not to use it, for fear of upsetting anyone at the BBC, which itself caused inadvertent upset. 'He gave his absolute all [but] he was also a bit of a coward,' Lawrence suggests. 'A lot of them are cowards. [Harry] Secombe was a coward. Secombe didn't want confrontation. He'd walk a mile to get away from it, but the most generous man you could ever work with.'[15] Lawrence remembers a situation with a pair of guests on one Dawson show at YTV:

Norman Murray said, 'What about Hinge and Bracket?' And I thought, 'Yes, that's a good idea. That would balance everything out.' Anyway, at the end of the first day, I said, 'Is everyone happy?' We'd been through the sketches, we'd rehearsed whatever they were going to do, blocked it out, come back tomorrow. 'So, are you happy? Everything all right?' 'Yes, darling, everything's wonderful. Absolutely delightful, thank you. What time tomorrow?' That night, I got a phone call from Norman Murray. 'They're most unhappy. They don't like anything that's going on. They really don't like the material that's been provided.' Les could have been an instrumental person there. It was his show, the same agent, but he just backed off, just walked away, didn't want to know.[16]

Unfortunately, the loss of Cryer and Nobbs proved very harmful to the comedian's prospects. Not even the presence on the writing team of Morecambe and Wise's main scriptwriter, Eddie Braben, or the young former journalist David Renwick, on his way to great comedy-writing acclaim, was enough. One problem was that while the title was *The Les Dawson Show*, it was not his vehicle entirely, although the running joke that closed each show, with Dawson playing the piano in his usual fashion while Lulu knitted as the credits rolled, raised the odd smile. The fortnightly scheduling, with the established hit series *Mike Yarwood In Persons* appearing in the alternate weeks, helped highlight the cracks and invited unfavourable comparison with Yarwood's polished act. These new shows were fast-moving productions, going from Dawson's monologues to sketches to disco-influenced production numbers featuring Lulu and the Dougie Squires Dancers, but the quick pace accentuated rather than masked the problematic gear changes. The principle of sharing the burden was sound enough. David Mallet had known all along at Yorkshire that 'Les Dawson couldn't necessarily hold too long a sketch show'.[17] Indeed, in the early *Sez Les* shows, Syd Lawrence's band had, effectively, been a co-star. Lulu, however, was expected to join in the comedy as well, to be Dawson's main foil in sketches, and it didn't really work.

The first sketch of the run was a pre-titles quickie from Braben, with the pair in eighteenth-century costume, and Dawson offering to read his love poetry to Lulu. It turns out to be vulgar doggerel: 'It's a hell of a life in the Legion/The men roam the desert in tents/

I'd hate to be in the Legion/It's 300 miles to the gents'. After the cartoon titles, showing Dawson and Lulu as bill posters pasting up a billboard bearing the show's name, Dawson takes the floor with a monologue about how long it had been since he last worked for the BBC. 'I forget the exact date, but it was the year the Queen got married,' he explains. 'I remember turning to the producer at the time and saying, "I hope she'll be very very happy with Prince Albert.'"[18] A slightly overlong exchange with Lulu about Dawson's size, his mother-in-law and the wife's dog leads into a police station sketch written by Braben, where Dawson tries to report that the pet and the mother-in-law have gone missing, to a desk sergeant played by Glynn Edwards, better known as Dave the barman from *Minder*. When it emerges that the animal has been lost since 1947, the sergeant tells Dawson, 'The door's over there', receiving the reply, 'I don't want a door. I didn't come in for a door. I've got plenty of doors at home.' Sadly, the idea doesn't have far to go after this nice line, but takes an unconscionably long time to get there.

The real highlight of the show was a sketch in which Dawson played a zoo owner, reprimanding a keeper, played by David Jason, for his unfortunate tendency to stuff the animals. The name of the keeper, Thrimpson, gives away immediately that David Renwick was the author, and the quality of the writing apart, the sketch's appeal lay partly in the reversal of the normal casting. In so many of Dawson's other shows, he had played the irritant, while someone else, like Julian Orchard or John Cleese, played the authority figure. Here Dawson is the twitchy boss at his wits' end, and the compulsive taxidermist is portrayed superbly by David Jason. It seems likely that Dawson added to Renwick's handiwork when it came to the litany of animals that had succumbed to a kapok filling.

DAWSON: Thrimpson, how long have you worked as a keeper at this zoo?
THRIMPSON: Ooooh, er, it's four and a half weeks, sir.
DAWSON: Four and a half weeks, and in that time, you've managed to stuff nineteen lions, eight leopards, forty-five Masai giraffes, and the major part of the African wildlife reserve. Seventeen raccoons,

twenty-four New World monkeys, a Polynesian hermit crab and a hippopotamus. Why, Thrimpson?[19]

Dawson's pained, strained delivery is near-perfect, but it's the words that get the laughs, and the Polynesian hermit crab – a staple that Dawson liked to use as much as possible because of the rhythm and sound of the words, as well as the exotic nature of the creature – gets the biggest laugh of all.

The whole series was recorded between 19 October and 1 December 1977, well in advance of the first show's transmission on 21 January 1978, allowing Ammonds and his director Phil Bishop the luxury of swapping items between shows to create a more satisfactory order. For example, the aforementioned zookeeper sketch was recorded for show two, but put into show one, in place of another Renwick sketch called 'The Misfit', which was moved to show three. The reliance on Lulu as Dawson's comic foil was also lessened in later shows, with experienced comedy actress Jacqueline Clarke coming on board. Unfortunately, no amount of shuffling or recasting could disguise the show's fundamentally confused nature, and the critics were quick to pile in.

Reviewing the third of the run in the *Guardian*, Peter Fiddick wrote witheringly that 'when we weren't getting Lulu, the world's slimmest mother and home-catalogue saleswoman, doing Busby Berkeley routines with six slim friends, we got Les doing one joke ... exotically built up bits of rhetoric collapsing in a heap of tripe and the vernacular'.[20] As examples, Fiddick cited 'the sort of Robert Browning sketch ... with golden hair, starry eyes, and what have you got in your dress, pork pies? Or the one where Tchaikovsky can't get past the first chords of the piano concerto, discards "Raindrops Keep Falling on My Head", and finds the maid humming the Great Tune he's after.' Given that so much of Dawson's best material was precisely a combination of exotica, tripe and vernacular, Fiddick's problem seems odd, but all becomes clear in the end. The tripe was simply not of the standard Fiddick – an admirer – had come to expect from Dawson, whom he regarded as largely blameless. 'Considering that Les Dawson once went on the *Parkinson* show and had me almost helpless with mirth,' he concluded, 'somebody must have worked at doing this to him.'[21]

The reaction to the series, quite understandably, dismayed Dawson. 'It seemed that everything I tried to do was courted by disaster,' he wrote later, adding that Meg thought he should have stayed put at Yorkshire or given television a rest altogether.[22] Fortunately, the BBC kept faith and tried to find Dawson another vehicle. The answer came in the form of an anglicized version of an American show, *Alan King's Final Warning*. King was a Brooklyn-born Jew with a mastery of the elegant rant. He later became as known for his series *Inside the Comedy Mind*, in which he interviewed fellow performers, as for his own pioneering stand-up work. In the three *Final Warning* specials he made, he offered comedic tips for tackling the obstacles of modern life, such as bureaucracy. Transplanted to a studio at BBC Television Centre that was decked out to look like a computerized nerve centre and decorated with glamorous female assistants, *Final Warning* became *The Dawson Watch*.

The format successfully played on Dawson's comic persona of put-upon pessimist and realist everyman. Who better to explain the absurdities of authoritarianism to the viewer at home? Dawson was also lucky to be teamed with new, bright, sympathetic writers, including Terry Ravenscroft, who would become very close to the comedian. 'We were from the same part of the country,' Ravenscroft explains. 'He was born in Manchester, I was born maybe ten miles from Manchester. Same sort of working-class background. I started sending a few news items and sketches in to *The Two Ronnies*, and through that I got to know Ian Davidson, who was script editor. When they were looking for new writers for his new show, I was one that they picked out. *The Dawson Watch* was when I turned to writing full-time. I was still working in a factory at the time. The first commission I had really. I'd done everything else on spec before that.'[23]

Davidson paired Ravenscroft with another writer he'd been nurturing, Andy Hamilton, who had previously been submitting occasional gags for Barker and Corbett, and writing links for the comedienne Marti Caine on her BBC show. 'We got on really well from the outset,' Hamilton says of his writing partner, whom he had not met before. 'It felt good from day one. I think Ian Davidson thought that we'd work well together.' Hamilton was a first-generation university graduate from a working-class family, the educational landscape having changed considerably in the years since Dawson had been of student age. 'If he'd been born twenty years later, he would have gone to university and done all of those things,' Hamilton asserts. 'He read a lot. He had quite a wide base of reference. Probably wider than mine, to be honest.' Sometimes, though, Dawson's auto-didacticism would give him the wrong sense of a word's meaning. 'I would occasionally pick him up if he misused a long word,' recalls Hamilton. 'I was cocky enough to say, "Actually, Les, that's not quite right. That doesn't quite mean that." Les nicknamed me "Prof". He didn't use it relentlessly, but every so often, he'd say, "Prof has spoken." I was pretty young, so I must have looked pretty cocky in his eyes. Les was fine with me, and was encouraging, and he'd congratulate you if the material was good enough.'[24] Bob Monkhouse had noted the same tendency to slightly misuse a word, but observed that Dawson had often 'made it do the job he wants done', adding that 'what would normally be an inappropriate choice of word has less to do with Les's lack of formal education than with what he feels the word ought to mean'.[25] This is a typically perceptive remark by Monkhouse: Dawson was as much in love with the sound of words as with their meaning.

The job of producing *The Dawson Watch* was given to Peter Whitmore, very much a comedy man rather than a variety man, having produced *Dave Allen at Large* and the Terry Scott/June Whitfield situation comedy series *Happy Ever After*. 'Peter was very very BBC,' Ravenscroft notes. 'Very very correct. A nice man. If you looked at him, you'd say, "Yes, Wing Commander". He looked very much the RAF type. He had the moustache.'[26] Certainly he was a very safe pair of hands, but Whitmore was also a good judge of material and he knew the value of making his star stretch himself a little. 'He wasn't a John

Lloyd-type producer, part of the creative engine of the show, but what Peter had was that he was very professional and he had very good taste,' Hamilton adds. 'He knew the difference between good stuff and bad stuff. He knew the difference between lazy stuff and original, ambitious stuff, and, as far as he possibly could, he tried to steer Les towards doing something new.'[27]

The persona of *Watch*-era Dawson represented a development of the character who had battled big business to no avail in *The Loner*. This time, the little man had answers, as he explained how to deal with 'them'. For the purposes of the series, 'they' were the faceless bureaucrats, confidence tricksters, commission-takers and sundry authoritarians who conspired to make life complicated. Estate agents, bank managers, politicians, solicitors, car mechanics and next-door-neighbours were, in Dawson's eyes, all part of the problem not the solution.

The new team working with Dawson enjoyed their star's company and the performances they got on the studio floor, but, like Mallet, Lawrence, Cryer, Nobbs and the YTV family, sometimes found it hard to keep him at the required level of discipline in the run-up to each recording. 'Les was a bugger for not rehearsing,' Ravenscroft observes. 'You had to force him. As you know, with radio you don't have to do that. You go through the script once and then you stand there, with the script.'[28] As before, Dawson's enthusiasm for drink was noted, again because of his ability to imbibe heavily without apparent effect. 'Les liked a drink, but he wasn't a problem drinker,' Hamilton comments. 'He could hold his drink. The only thing was that it could affect his diction a bit. Peter Whitmore once asked, "Have you ever thought about trying, for once, just going out there and doing the show sober?" Les said, "What, and face them alone?" I think it was a W.C. Fields joke.'[29]

In the first *Dawson Watch* show, on the subject of property, Dawson is visibly uncomfortable reading from an autocue device on the front of the camera. He comes alive when conducting a straw poll among the audience, asking them where they live, seizing on one shout of

Weybridge for a discourse on snobs. He is finding his feet, but, even with this hesitant start, it's a format within which he can work well. In particular, the opening title sequences, depicting Dawson in various disguises as an unlikely snoop with a Minox spy camera – peering out from inside a pram or pretending to be a gorilla at the zoo – did a lot to set out the show for the viewer. During the first series, Dawson himself played only a small part in the sketches, illustrating various ludicrous situations, which were populated by comic actors like Michael Sharvell-Martin, whom Whitmore knew well from his supporting roles in *Dave Allen at Large*, and David Lodge, better known for his long association with Spike Milligan. However, when neighbours were required to intervene, it made sense for them to be Mrs Cissie Braithwaite and Mrs Ada Shufflebotham. When they enter near the end of the first show of the series, they receive a massive round of applause, showing how well established they were already in the viewers' affections. Ostensibly coming to introduce themselves to the new occupants of the house next door, their primary purposes are to nose ('I see they took the shag pile.' 'They had a lot of trouble with that cat.') and to alarm ('You'll be very happy here. If you're not psychic.').[30] When it came to supplying the old gossips with material, Dawson found a kindred spirit in Ravenscroft. 'It just seemed natural for me, because I knew these women. I'd grown up with them,' Ravenscroft explains. 'They used to stand on the front doorstep. They'd done the donkey stone on it. "Don't stand on that, I've just cleaned that." It isn't a step, you have to stride over it to get in. It was sacred. It was meat and drink to me, that was. I can't say they wrote themselves, because they were bloody hard work, some of them, but I was quite happy doing them, you know.'[31]

Cissie and Ada's conversation from the second show of the first *Dawson Watch* series, on transport, contains a couple of their best-remembered lines:

CISSIE: So you haven't decided then, where you're going for your holidays next year?

ADA: We've had a look through some brochures.

CISSIE: Leonard and I went to Greece last year.

ADA: Oh, Bert and I have been to Greece, with Wallace Arnold's Sunkissed Package Holiday and Inter-Continental Tours.

CISSIE: Oh really? Did you have the shish kebabs?

ADA: From the moment we arrived. All down that side.

CISSIE: Did you see the Acropolis?

ADA: See it? We were never off it. Our Bert were bent double. He's not been right for years, you know. There's no Vaseline over there you know.[32]

As had been the case on *Sez Les*, Dawson wrote his own monologues and much of the linking material, with other writers – largely Hamilton and Ravenscroft – supplying the sketches. Ravenscroft recalls that when Colin Bostock-Smith and Tom Magee-Englefield departed the writing team, Dawson observed, 'Well, that's got rid of four of the buggers.'[33] Some of the lines Dawson offered were a little familiar. In the third show of the first series, on the subject of finance, he said, 'Until I was fifteen, I thought knives and forks were jewellery', a joke that had been recounted by childhood friend Ken Cowx on Dawson's *This Is Your Life* eight years earlier. These were, however, leavened by new gags, like Dawson's assertion in the same routine that, as a child, 'Christmas dinner was always the same: Peruvian woodcock. It was a black pudding with a feather stuck in it,' and his claim that he could 'only remember being given one Christmas present by my father. It was a do-it-yourself electric train set. Turned out to be a roll of fuse wire and a platform ticket.'[34]

While the first series of *The Dawson Watch* helped restore the comedian's bankability in Corporation circles, in the view of the head writers, it still had a little way to go. The absence of the star from the bulk of the sketches was the biggest handicap, as Andy Hamilton explains:

We started the second series of *The Dawson Watch*, having learned the lessons of the first series, which were primarily that the sketches we wrote were funny on the page. One sketch we wrote had Terence

Alexander – very funny actor – briefing a client who was patently guilty. It was a very funny sketch. It did all right on the night, but all the sketches were penalized on the night because the audience would have been laughing a lot at Les, on his feet, being very funny, and then it would feel anti-climactic on the set, and you'd get a decent class of actor, but not great comedy actors maybe, doing these sketches. So, in the second series, Terry and I said 'Could Les be in the sketches as a sort of everyman?' Like a mini-sitcom. He could say, 'I experienced this myself, because I ended up in court,' and then you'd cut to the sketch and he'd be in court. For the first two shows, I think it was, Les learned his lines for the sketches and was pin-sharp, and was brilliant.[35]

Hamilton cites a sketch from the first show of the second series as a particular highlight, in which Dawson plays a barrister whose training appears to come mostly from television crime shows. With his thumbs in his lapels, he takes an age to speak. Asked by the judge to explain the delay, Dawson replies, 'I'm pausing for effect, m'lud. I've seen them use it to considerable advantage on *Crown Court*, particularly after the commercials. Apart from that, I appear to have my thumb stuck.' He then turns to the cross-examination. 'You are Arthur Harris, allegedly, and you were born on 18 February 1930,' he asserts, then asks, 'I assume you have witnesses to substantiate this claim?' When the reply comes in the negative, Harris explaining that his mother is no longer with us, Dawson seizes on it gleefully, and bellows 'Dead? How very convenient for you.' Following several other gambits to discredit the cross-examinee, including the suggestion that his birth certificate means nothing, being a potential forgery, Dawson says, 'I put it to you that your entire testimony is nothing but a tissue of mendacious calumnies. You have proven yourself to be a witness of total incredibility, an expert forger and a man who would not hesitate to stoop so low as to use as an alibi the memory of his poor dear departed mother. A scoundrel whose every words have been turned to the lie by irrefutable scientific proof. I ask you, could you believe a man such as this?'[36] The punchline is that Dawson is defending himself and that he has demolished his own witness, but the tag is almost irrelevant. The comedy is in the overblown theatrics of the cross-examination and the relish with which Dawson delivers phrases like 'mendacious calumnies'. Hamilton and Ravenscroft were right. Straight away, the second series was in a different class to its predecessor, and Dawson was on terrific form. It helped that the glamorous assistants were no longer quite so mute. A young Vicki Michelle, some years before *'Allo 'Allo*, made a good comic foil for Dawson's lecherous enquiries.

In preparing for the second series, however, the writers had some unwelcome and misguided advice from Dawson's management, which they felt they simply had to ignore:

> We had one meeting at the start of the second series where we watched an episode of the first series with Norman Murray sitting there. He had an unsettling sort of presence about him, I'd say. I just remember thinking, 'I've not really met anybody like this before.' We felt, me and Terry, that all of Norman's observations about the show were just completely wrong from a comic point of view. One of his main preoccupations was that he wanted Les to be warmer. He thought it was time for Les to move away from the droll he had been, the man who never smiled, but that was the secret of why he was so good. From a writer's point of view, to have someone with that defined personality was fantastic. We said, 'No, he should stay the same.'[37]

Dawson, perhaps uniquely for a big star at the start of a make-or-break TV series, chose not to get involved in these critical discussions. 'I don't know what Les felt. I think Les would just go with the flow,' says Hamilton. Dawson's willingness to go along with the consensus was an irritation in some ways, but a boon in others, Hamilton felt:

> Although it could frustrate you, it was an appealing side to his personality as well, because he was very low-maintenance. I was just starting out, so I didn't know that yet. I hadn't worked with other comedians, and I was a bit cocky and a bit pushy, so I was always trying to push for a bit more, but looking back, he was even-tempered, he was good around the

crew. He generated a good atmosphere. He was good fun to be around, so I think it's not that he didn't care, but he didn't agonize, and there's a lot to be said for that.[38]

Unfortunately, the discipline of the early second-series shows was not maintained. Hamilton recalls feeling that 'the first two or three shows were really strong', but then there came 'a sketch [in which] he'd been appearing as himself in an advert':

He was getting knocked about or soaked or something. It was a very slapsticky sketch, and he fell off his lines a bit. And that week it had been noticed that he'd been a lot later for rehearsals, he'd been out on the razz a lot more that week. So, we went into that show sensing that he wasn't firm on his cues. He fell off his lines on this sketch, and fell into a very funny stream-of-consciousness succession of jokes, and killed the audience stone dead. They just wet themselves. I remember, in the box, Peter Whitmore saying, 'Oh no', because he realized that Les had realized 'I don't have to learn this stuff. They love me. I'm Les Dawson.' So, for the rest of that series, Les was less assiduous about learning the material. Peter did try to say, 'You were great in those first shows', but the spell had been broken.[39]

In the sketch in question, in the third show of the second series, Dawson is playing the captain of a fishing smack in a commercial for sardines. He is standing on a mock-up of a boat that's being rocked violently by scene hands, getting drenched with buckets of water, attacked by inflatable sharks and besieged by pirates – and the director character in the sketch complains that Dawson needs to look more as though he's enjoying it. In the transmitted version of the sketch, Dawson's lines are few, so the stream of gags was purely for the benefit of the studio audience, but the writers and producer noticed the difference afterwards. 'The novelty had worn off a bit, I think,' Hamilton observes. 'To me, from a writer's point of view, it felt like an opportunity missed. As a performer, he thought it was fine.'[40]

The sketch had exploited the trait noted and loved by David Nobbs,

Barry Cryer and Vernon Lawrence: that Dawson would submit cheerfully to almost any amount of physical stress if he liked the idea and the gag demanded it. 'I think Les was pretty fearless, generally,' agrees Hamilton. 'A lot of people would be self-conscious, but he was happy to take his shirt off.' Hamilton remembers with amusement Dawson's ability to make himself look like a bodybuilder by sucking his stomach in, and the inevitable collapse back to pudgy reality when he had to breathe out. Dawson had also perfected a lovely bit of business, where he appeared to inflate himself simply by sticking his thumb in his mouth and blowing. Oddly, looking back at the recordings, Dawson's worst performance is on the previous show, on the subject of health. During his pieces to camera, he seems hesitant in his reading of the Autocue, despite having become steadily more fluent throughout the first series. There are also a number of fluffs left in the finished programme, including one where the last word of the written line 'Your average GP would strenuously deny that he discriminates in any way between his private and his National Health patients' comes out as 'payments'. Dawson corrects himself very quickly, and indeed the fluffed line almost works in its own right, but the show's star was clearly not quite himself that week.

The series did recover well, ending with a programme on entertainment, a word that Dawson explained in his opening monologue was 'a word formed from the Latin root "enter", which means "come in", and "tainment", which means "give us your money"'.[41] However, this particular *Dawson Watch* shows Dawson's tendency, identified by Hamilton, to rely on old, faithful material. During one link, he referred to playing Bottom in an American theatrical tour of *A Midsummer Night's Dream*: 'It was just accolade after accolade. In Chicago, they never let me walk anywhere. Every night, after the show, big fellers used to come backstage and say, "We've come to take the bum for a ride".'[42] A good line, but it had been in Dawson's stage repertoire as part of a longer routine about theatrical pretensions since at least the summer of 1970, when he used it in Scarborough. This final show of the second series also contains a playful reference to producer Peter

Whitmore. When Dawson asks glamorous assistant Sandra – played by Vicki Michelle – for some data on theatre closures, he invites her to a meeting that will further her career 'in a motel off the M4'. She replies that she's already committed after the show, going for a drink with 'Peter', who's been teaching her comic technique. 'Not with the Fulham Fondler?,' Dawson replies, amused that first names have been used. 'Oh, Peter is it? You bald viper. Peter, the inventor of the rubber casting couch. What does he know about comedy? He's been working on this show for weeks.'[43]

The final *Dawson Watch* was a Christmas special In 1980, in which the Desponds, a miserable husband and wife who repeated each other's sentences and groaned a lot, dispensed their strange idea of goodwill. Originally created for *Sez Les*, where Mrs Despond was played by Kathy Staff, the role was reprised in *Listen to Les* by Daphne Oxenford, who continued the part here. The writers relished the chance to create grim illogicality for the pair. 'They were great characters,' Andy Hamilton says, admitting, 'they were our favourite ones.'[44] Asked what they thought of the festive season, the Desponds replied:

MRS DESPOND: Christmas isn't what it used to be.

MR DESPOND: 'Tisn't what it used to be, no.

MRS DESPOND: Nowadays it's spoiled by all that … what's the word?

MR DESPOND: Fun. Christmas is for children.

MRS DESPOND: Yes, we only keep it up for the children.

MR DESPOND: Yes. [*Turns to wife*] We haven't got any children.

MRS DESPOND: We did try for a family.

MR DESPOND: Once.

MRS DESPOND: Made you tired, didn't it?

MR DESPOND: I nodded off halfway through.

MRS DESPOND: Mother loves Christmas.

MR DESPOND: Her mother loves Christmas.

MRS DESPOND: Last Christmas, when we had the little ones from next door around, Mother played hide-and-seek with them. We never did find where she hid them, did we?[45]

Dawson's loss of concentration during the second series was, perhaps, understandable given the fact that Meg had been diagnosed with breast cancer after the first series was completed. Up to this point, life in the Dawson household had been largely free of serious health problems, apart from one stroke of bad luck for eldest daughter Julie, who had sustained an eye injury while playing with Stuart. The two kids had dismembered an old annual to use the book's jacket as a folder. A bit of healthy sibling rivalry led to a struggle for control of the jacket, ending with the book's corner whacking Julie in the eye, which left her sight permanently impaired. None of the Dawson clan could be described as sickly, so the sudden change in Meg, who complained of being constantly tired and noted the presence of a lump in her breast, was all the more noticeable. 'She had shown me her dimpled breast (I was 15 at the time) when she picked me up from school (knowing I wanted to be a nurse, she trusted me),' explains daughter Julie, 'I had seen a patient with something similar on the ward at Blackpool Victoria where I was doing Social Service work through school and I urged her to see the GP that night. She was admitted and had the radical mastectomy within four days of that appointment. Knowing it had gone gave her hope that she would survive. Had it been left, without operating, I believe she would have died much sooner because she would have thought it was too late.'[46]

Even though the diagnosis was as prompt as it could have been, it was devastating. 'Our world collapsed at the utterance of those most dreadful words,' Dawson wrote later, admitting that the experience made him think twice about the jokes he'd told at the expense of a wife who bore no resemblance to Meg. 'Remember all the wisecracks, Dawson?' he asked himself. 'The ones directed at her in all those sleazy dumps ... "Take my wife ... please. I'm not saying she's ugly, but when she went to see a horror film the audience thought she was making a personal appearance."'[47] Dawson knew better than anyone that without Meg's support in the hard times, he would probably have given up his dreams of becoming a professional comedian.

A similar moment of reflection had struck him while his real mother-in-law, Ada Plant, had still been alive. He had told her that he would drop the mother-in-law jokes from his act if she found them offensive. Her response surprised him. 'She wanted to be sure I'd continue making jokes about her after she'd gone. In fact, she bloody well instructed me to keep them going,' he told Paul Callan of the *Daily Mirror* in 1977, the year after Ada died.[48] As well as having Ada's unstinting support, Dawson valued the backing of Meg's father too. The streak of steel running through Meg that had kept the household running smoothly with or without Les's presence came directly from Ada, Dawson knew

The whole family pulled together to keep the household going while Meg was preparing for and recovering from her mastectomy, with Dawson praising his three children, Julie, Stuart and Pamela, for 'demonstrating an inner strength that I did not possess'.[49] As Meg's recovery began, Dawson felt able to return to work gradually. He was helped by Peter Whitmore arranging to have rehearsals for the first show of the new run to be moved up to the Clifton Arms Hotel in Lytham, so that Dawson could go home to Meg and family at the end of each working day.

Perhaps the need to distract himself with work and the reduced travel commitments helped account for his polished performance at the start of the second series. Certainly, when in London, there was a temptation to drink and carouse, which the return to London-based rehearsals after show one put squarely in Dawson's lap. One such occasion – 'a hard and long night with Billy Connolly' – stuck with Dawson. In reality, it was far more than just a night: 'We finished up at about nine in the morning at a record company's party. We'd been at it for over twenty-four hours and if I had breathed on anyone they would have been arrested. I staggered into the bright light of day with eyes full of grit and a mouth coated like a chicken run.'[50] Dawson claimed that he collapsed in a back street, near some vagrants, one of whom he recognized as a former bill-topping variety comedian, and that the experience taught him to rein in his drinking just enough so that he was its master, not its slave.

*

While *The Dawson Watch* was ongoing, Dawson had kept up his run of guest appearances on other shows. One of the highlights was a spot on Shirley Bassey's BBC1 variety show, recorded on 27 and 28 March 1979, but not transmitted until 10 November. Producer Stewart Morris had been an admirer of Dawson for many years, using him whenever he could find an excuse. Setting the comedian's miserablism against the glamour of Bassey was a juxtaposition that Morris repeated gleefully over the years and, judging from the recordings, one that the girl from Tiger Bay genuinely relished. Bassey and Dawson had worked together before, as she had guested on a 1972 edition of *Sez Les*, but her contact with Dawson on that occasion had been limited to his introduction.

Bassey had and has a reputation for being a diva, once punching Morris over a minor disagreement at an early-morning location shoot, but her affection and respect for Dawson always seemed to override any hauteur. 'He used to send her up unmercifully, and would burst the bubble,' explains Lydia Vine, Stewart Morris's long-serving production assistant. 'I don't know now, because I haven't worked with her for a long time, but she could be temperamental. He was the only one who could burst the bubble. They had an enormous amount of affection. They weren't friends, but when they worked together, I don't think she would have dared to play up with him, because he would have sent her up.'[51]

Dawson's cheek manifested itself offstage as well as on. Vine recalls a story told to her by scriptwriter Paul Alexander: 'Paul can remember Les hammering on her door, saying, "Will you shut up? There are people trying to sleep here." He wasn't being serious, but nobody else could do that.' On the 1979 show, Bassey introduces Dawson, to much audience amusement, as 'one of the country's finest classical pianists'. Dawson takes control straight away by pretending to mistake Bassey for Vera Lynn, then launches into a typically atonal version of 'Side by Side'. Soon, he is joined by Bassey, at which he stops playing, looks disdainfully at her and says, 'I thought I told you to stay in the truck.' The star of the show, normally the embodiment of cool professionalism, is corpsing very obviously as she tries to inform Dawson that his fan club has arrived and that the members have parked their tandem. Bassey asks Dawson why he's so glum, at which he launches into a monologue of woe, with Bassey struggling to keep her mascara from running as she cries with genuine laughter:

> DAWSON: Well, I'm glad you noticed that I'm not my usual ebullient self. I never slept a wink last night, Shirley. I kept getting this hideous recurrent nightmare that the mother-in-law was chasing me with a crocodile on a lead down the banks of the Nile. I was wearing nothing but a pith helmet and Gannex spats. I could smell the hot rancid breath on the back of my neck. I could hear those great jaws snapping in anger. I could almost see those great yellow eyes full of primeval hatred devouring me.
>
> BASSEY: Oh, that's terrible.
>
> DAWSON: That's nothing. Wait till I tell you about the crocodile.[52]

Not everybody appreciated Dawson's good humour, however, as Hamilton discovered when he and Ravenscroft found themselves at Quaglino's restaurant in London for an edition of the Radio 2 programme *Medium Dry Sherrin*. They were there to help promote a spin-off book from the satirical radio comedy *The News Huddlines,* for which they both wrote. Dawson was also booked as a guest, alongside the actress Joan Collins. Dawson, as was his wont, sent Collins up very gently, but was met with a sense of humour failure and Hamilton remembers that a decidedly frosty atmosphere fell on the show. Ravenscroft is adamant that 'it wasn't in a malicious way, but this is what he does, isn't it?',[53] but nonetheless Hamilton recalls that fulsome apologies were made in the direction of Collins by Sherrin, the host. Danny Greenstone, who co-produced the show with Dawson's early advocate, Bobby Jaye, remembers that:

> Les simply went into his stand-up routine whenever he could get a word in edgeways, which, when Joan hogged the microphone, was not that often. Still, every chance he got he would adapt a mother-in-law gag and turn it towards Joan, who – obviously having spent a long

time away from our shores (at that time) – misread his gentle sniping and being personal. She was not exactly fresh from divorcing Anthony Newley (another of my great heroes) at that time, but I think she still took what she deemed to be personal slights as, well, personal slights. They weren't.[54]

Greenstone also recalls that 'we finished the evening with Les at the piano doing his usual gorgeous atonal unharmonic unrhythmic serenading – and Joan misunderstood that as well, remarking, "How can they let him play live on air?"'

After a third *Dawson Watch* series and final Christmas special in 1980, Dawson's BBC reputation was strong enough for light entertainment bosses to consider letting him loose once again on a traditional variety show of his own. Although it would retain the prosaic title of his initial BBC outing, the co-hosting idea was dropped. By this time, Dawson's old friend John Ammonds had left the BBC to follow Eric Morecambe and Ernie Wise to the London ITV contractor Thames, but Dawson's new producer was very much part of the same family, having been Ammonds's successor on *The Morecambe and Wise Show*. Dawson knew of Ernest Maxin's reputation and admired his work, a feeling that was fully reciprocated, so when they first met there was very little need for formalities, as Maxin relates:

I went with my wife Leigh [Madison, the actress] to see him in a cabaret performance, I think somewhere in Essex. He was a big star by then. I felt that here was a man that was quite unique purely because of his physical picture and how the voice, that gruff, growly voice fitted that physical picture. He'd heard of me, and when I went to see him at the end of the show, he said, 'Hello, love.' I said, 'Do you realize that you've called me "love", and we've never met before?' He said, 'Don't worry, love, I'm not a bit like that. I like the look of your missus, though.' I said to him, 'How would you like to work with me?' He said, 'I promise not to call you "love" if I work with you.' I said, 'So would you like to work with me?' and he said, 'Yes.'[55]

In some ways, Dawson and Ernest Maxin were opposites. One from north Manchester, the other from east London. One a heavy drinker, the other a teetotaller. The comedian inclined to run to fat and disinclined to exercise, the producer a former dancer with plenty of get up and go. However, in this case, opposites proved very attractive to each other, and the pair became firm friends. Dawson recognized the producer's care and professionalism from the off, and appreciated that Maxin's visual sense would complement and offset his own verbosity perfectly.

As usual, the easy-going Dawson did not assert himself with any grand concept for the show. It was down to Maxin and the writers to come up with the overall framework, into which Dawson would insert his personality and his own material. Maxin was asked by senior colleagues how he planned to differentiate the show from Dawson's previous programmes.

> I said, 'You've got to have entirely different people in it, but what he does need is that he shouldn't have the responsibility of carrying the whole show on his own shoulders, with a few variety acts in it. It's old hat now, doing that thing, and unless you're at the seaside or in the theatre, you've lost 50 per cent of the atmosphere. We've got to have a speciality attraction that will help him, that will be funny in itself, and in type will appeal to the same kind of people that like Les Dawson.'[56]

Maxin's solution for the first show, a May bank holiday special, and the series of six shows that followed in January and February 1982, was a troupe of talented youngsters that he named Kids International. Maxin had noted with concern the race riots in Brixton and, remembering his own experiences as a young Jewish boy in east London in the thirties, wanted to do what he could to promote understanding between races:

> I decided to get a United Nations of children together between the ages of six and eleven. I wanted about thirty. So I auditioned a thousand children of all different races, within the Home Counties radius. There was

a classical boy pianist, a black boy, and I taught him to play jazz. There was a little black boy who was cute, he was eight and a half, I taught him to dance like Sammy Davis and Fred Astaire. We had Japanese, Arab children. Israeli children, Chinese, Indian – a complete cross-section. I had vocal arrangements done for them that were adult, and the orchestrations were done as if it were for adults.

Some of the children were also paired with Dawson for comic routines. Maxin remembers one exchange in particular: 'One of them was outstanding, a little black boy, tap dancer. I said, "I want to add him in just one of the shows, and you say to him, 'You're a great dancer, do you think I could be able to dance like that?' This is the humour I want between you and him. He says to you, 'Yes, of course you'll be able to dance like me,' and then he looks at the camera and says, 'I should live so long.'" Les liked that. It got a big laugh.'[57]

In another routine, Dawson attempted to communicate with an Asian girl in various comic Chinese and Japanese accents. Finally he gives up and asks which part of the east she hails from. The answer is East Grinstead. The various accents used and the references to Japanese car manufacturers almost certainly wouldn't pass muster in a comedy show now, but, however misguided, the intent is harmless. Also, the child clearly outsmarts the foolish adult. This was a recurring theme in Dawson's one-to-ones with the children. He tells the aforementioned piano prodigy to watch and learn, only to be played off the stool by the young lad. As the boy plays a classical piece with great dexterity, Dawson stomps around, miming golf swings, grimacing and toying with the idea of shutting the lid on the precocious one's fingers.

One aspect of the new show that gave Dawson enormous pleasure came courtesy of the visual effects department at Television Centre, a semi-autonomous enclave of clever, resourceful individuals within the BBC who made the impossible happen on a routine basis. In the fifties, the department's founders, Bernard Wilkie and Jack Kine, had created convincing and frightening space monsters for the

Quatermass serials. In the eighties, visual effects designer Tony Oxley, who had created both the Tardis control console for *Doctor Who* and the Doctor's robotic dog, K9, found himself befriended by the Mancunian comedian. Dawson regarded Oxley as a 'wild-haired genius', and together they devised a remotely controlled prop piano that could move of its own accord and collapse to order. It was first seen by viewers in a pre-titles quickie on that May bank holiday special in 1981. Dawson took the stage and announced that he was to play Grieg's piano concerto. Before he could play a note, the legs of the piano stool splayed very slowly beneath him, bringing him to chin height with the keyboard.

In terms of the writing team, Andy Hamilton had moved on. 'It just sounded a bit less interesting,' Hamilton explains. 'It turned into a bit more of a shiny floor show. I think I went off to do *Not the Nine O'Clock News*, and as that show grew, I became more preoccupied with that.' Hamilton also recalls that his new project was the inspiration for 'the only negative thing I ever heard Les say'. The day after the first edition, Hamilton remembered 'him saying to me "What are they trying to prove?" At the time, I think I was a little bit hurt, because I wanted him to say, "I really liked the show", but looking back, I can see completely why he might have said that. I haven't looked at it, but I suspect that if you look at episode one of *Not the Nine O'Clock News*, like a lot of episode ones of new sketch shows that are meant to be breaking new ground, we were probably trying a bit too hard.'[58]

Terry Ravenscroft, while being a valued contributor of material to *Not The Nine O'Clock News*, felt he could do both comfortably, and so remained Dawson's trusted collaborator. For *The Dawson Watch*, Hamilton and Ravenscroft had had an office at Television Centre. Now, more often, Ravenscroft would visit Dawson at home. 'He used to sit there at his big desk in Lytham, in his office, writing away. That's how he usually was when I turned up,' Ravenscroft says. 'I think he'd have liked to do that all the time, but, as you know, you don't become a millionaire writing books. The big money for Les was in TV and the spin-offs from it, but he enjoyed writing.'[59]

The first show under Maxin's control was loosely themed as a look back at a fictional Dawson family tree ('which turned out to be a stunted willow') containing a plethora of down-at-heel performers, including one who had trouble learning his lines. His solution was to have them written in Braille in his tights, 'so he could really feel the part'.[60] Another of Dawson's claimed forebears was the Flamenco singer Cosmo Ramonov, aka Smallpiece, Argentine chart-topper of 1928. Cosmo was then seen in action, singing, while a male and female dancer gyrate sensuously in front of him. All of this proved too much for the celebrated lecher, who collapsed and had to be dragged off stage by several members of Kids International.

During that first programme, Dawson also spoke of the influence his musically inclined mother had on his career, reprising the 'hold my beer while I fetch me banjo' from his 1967 *Opportunity Knocks* appearance. The grotesque image he paints of his mother and the reality of his great love for the selfless Julia illustrates how wrong it would be to regard Dawson's jokes about women as misogyny. The women in Dawson's comedy are cartoonish: part McGill postcard, part *Beano*; half carrying rolling pins, the other half carrying their virtues in front of them. Other comedians have peddled material underpinned by genuine, heartfelt, truly meant hate and tried to dismiss it as 'just a joke'. Dawson had no time for hate. Resignation required less effort and had a greater chance of guaranteeing a quiet life. As it was, the banjo line was a prelude to the return of Cissie and Ada, with Ada, for the duration of the sketch, set in a forties pub, acting as Dawson's mother.

CISSIE: Talking of good for nothings, how old's your youngest now, love?

ADA: Our Leslie? Our Leslie's fifteen, bless him. Oooh, he has shot up this last couple of years, bless him. He leaves school this summer.

CISSIE: Oooh, he'll soon be matriculating. [ADA *looks away*]

ADA: I think he is already, judging by the bags under his eyes.

CISSIE: What's he taking, chuck?

ADA: Well, there's some stuff you can put in his tea.

...

CISSIE: What particular occupation have you got in mind for him, chuck?

ADA: Our Leslie? [*Leans in*] I thought that nosy cat from Number 3 was in. I wouldn't tell another living soul this.

CISSIE: Oh well, my lips are sealed.

ADA: I know that, chuck. The theatre, probably. I thought that would shake you. You know, it's not widely known round here that when I was younger I was something of a performer myself.

CISSIE: You know, I never knew you had any experience on the boards.

ADA: Yes, once, but I got backache and my husband got splinters in his knees.

CISSIE: What I meant to say was that I had no idea you'd ever been a thespian.

ADA: [*bristling*] Oooh, I never was.[61]

At the mention of thespians, Ada turns suddenly, and her hat falls off. Dawson looks off-camera, most likely to see if anyone's signalling a retake or coming to retrieve the headgear, while struggling not to burst out laughing. Later on in the sketch, the ever-professional Barraclough appears to be on the brink of corpsing, at Ada's mention of offering Leslie's singing teacher 'a cup of Bovril and a Devonshire split'. A later Cissie and Ada sketch was to see the pair in a travel agent's, planning a holiday. Maxin's production forte being visual, he felt there was something lacking:

They'd written quite a good script, but there was nothing I found at rehearsals in it that Les could get visually funny, without saying a word. Those things were more important than words. We were going through this script, and it was very humorous, but there was nothing for him to get the misunderstanding, [so] he'd look 'What's he saying?' So they're sitting talking about where they're going, doing a European tour, going to Poland, Austria, a few countries. So I said to Roy Barraclough, 'Say

"And we'll be on the Po for about five days."' Les never forgot that. It was a wonderful feeling.[62]

In rehearsal, Dawson, Barraclough and Maxin explored every permutation of the Po innuendo, with Dawson reduced to hysterics. On-screen, it made for a brief but effective exchange:

CISSIE: Look at Rome for instance, we could go on a river cruise. We could go on the Po.

ADA [*gurning and looking horrified*]: I'm not going all that way for that. We had one, but our Fred chipped the rim.[63]

Another branch of the stunted willow that was Dawson's fictional showbiz family was Uncle Zebediah, who performed magic under the stage name "the Great Pillock'. He was 'perhaps best known for his disappearing ferret down the front of the trousers trick', Dawson explained, adding that in that very same year, 'he won the yodelling championship'. The preamble is followed by a speechless vignette featuring Dawson as an inept magician, whose skills extend no further than making a fan out of the playing cards in his hand and grinning inanely, dropping his props, while a bird that is supposed to be hidden in his tailcoat keeps popping its head out. Known for his verbosity, Dawson could also be a superb visual comic, as he is here. However, in later shows, Uncle Zebediah would acquire a voice, all rasping sibilants – each 's' a raspberry – and a surname, which was Twine. As Dawson explained it, Twine was 'a sort of failed variety act who was a drunk ... some of my contemporaries suggested that the character was an extension of myself'.[64]

With a red nose indicating an overenthusiasm for the grape, his collar flying away and many of his teeth blacked out, Twine quickly became a favourite character for both Dawson and Ravenscroft. 'Zebediah Twine was Frank Randle,' notes Ravenscroft of the influence at work. 'There was a connection here and I've only just thought of it. Frank Randle's real name was Twist. Twist and Twine.'[65] In one 1983 show, Twine attempted 'the difficult feat of swallowing a great sword'. The sword, he informed the audience, in a hail of projected saliva, would 'go down the epiglottis, to the colonic canal'. He would be dicing with danger: 'one mistake on my part, and I will be shish-kebabbed'. Choosing to sit on a chair to do the trick, Twine finds himself pinned to the seat (achieved by fake swords and a couple of fairly obvious edits).[66]

Aside from broadcasting, Dawson had always been able to rely on cabaret and club appearances, as well as the guaranteed offers of summer season and pantomime work. By the second half of the seventies, however, the live side of the industry had changed. Even Batley Variety Club, the flagship of clubland, had suffered, closing in 1978 to make way for a discotheque called Crumpet. Fortunately, many of the gaps in Dawson's schedule left by the decline of clubland were filled with corporate and after-dinner gigs, which he admitted were a 'godsend'.[67] In *Les Dawson's Secret Notebooks*, published in 2007, the opening for one of these conference performances is featured, headed 'Movenpic [*sic*] Script'. Dawson begins with his trademark self-deprecation, telling the crowd that 'if it's true that applause indeed be music to an artist's ears then all I've heard just lateley [*sic*] is "Silent Night"', and admitting that once when he walked offstage, he was 'booked for loitering'.[68] This prelude would have set him up perfectly for the serious after-dinner sport of wittily insulting the company's senior executives, much to the delight of the lower orders.

Christmas 1980 saw Dawson at the Empire, Liverpool in *Babes in the Wood*, moving down south to the Richmond Theatre the following festive season, for a run of *Aladdin* with Arthur Askey, Rula Lenska, Christopher Timothy and Bernard Bresslaw. The booking was a particularly sad and notable one for Dawson. For one thing, Askey was clearly ailing, and had to drop out of the pantomime midway through the run. 'It seemed strange to pass his dressing room, empty now, not hearing that well-known cry which he always gave me: "Hello, Playmate"', Dawson observed. Askey's withdrawal was, however, overshadowed by the arrival, towards the end of rehearsals, of terrible news from Lytham. Meg had cancer again, this time in the spine.

Dawson missed two performances, one on Christmas Eve so he could be at home with Meg and the family, and another on Boxing Day, when bad weather prevented him from returning down south. The press picked up on Dawson's absences early in the New Year, and elicited a partial explanation from the comedian. 'Meg had an operation on her breast last year. And when she fell ill, we thought "Oh no, it's back again",' Dawson told the *Daily Express*. He admitted that he had taken to drinking a bottle of Scotch a day and asking 'How could I go on cracking jokes under these circumstances? It wasn't a case of "the show must go on" for me, mate.' All was true thus far, but Dawson told a small lie to put journalists off the scent, stating that 'we have now been told that it was nerve trouble. Everything is OK again.'[69]

Everything wasn't OK again. The cancer was back in a different place, and Meg was very seriously ill, but Dawson was sure that if the press had known the full story, 'they would have created a circus out of it'.[70] The comedian had a generally good relationship with journalists, and he knew the value of being available for a quote, particularly during the silly season, thanks to the expert advice of freelance PR man George Bartram. Up to his death in 1989, Bartram helped many major entertainers keep their names in the press by supplying their thoughts on issues of the day to the papers, sometimes direct from the stars themselves, sometimes ghostwritten for them by Bartram. As such, the tabloids of the seventies and eighties were rich in filler stories lent undeserved gravitas by a line or two from Dawson, playing the publicity game. However, the experiences of some of his show business peers had proved to him how quickly the inhabitants of Fleet Street could turn on a tame comic when they scented a juicy story. With Meg unwell, the last thing anyone needed was to be doorstepped by reporters, hence the diversion.

The first sign of Meg's illness came at the Water Rats' ball in November 1981 at the Grosvenor House Hotel. Meg had excused herself during the cabaret, citing back pain, and returned to their room. Having put her to bed, Dawson returned to the party, unalarmed by the mild ailment. At first, the pain was diagnosed as sciatica, and so Dawson began work on the panto. Then came the revised diagnosis. 'Although I had often put my career before the home, never once had I ceased to love that little lady who had shared so much pain with me,' Dawson said in 1985.[71] Meg had been strong for him throughout their marriage, pushing him forward and giving him confidence. It was now his turn to be strong for Meg.

CHAPTER 6

Hitler was my mother-in-law

Meg's illness began the worst period of Dawson's life, a time in which he questioned very seriously everything that he thought he knew about religion, ethics, medicine and life in general. However, it was also the richest period for Dawson as a writer, rather than as a comedian who sometimes wrote. Between 1982 and 1984, Dawson published three books – a novel, a compendium of puns and a volume on his beloved Lancashire – as well as taking part in two documentaries where he showed more of the real man behind the comic persona. He also took on a regular humorous column for the Blackpool *Gazette*. With a BBC1 series each January, this awful time was also, arguably, the most varied and interesting phase of his career. The image of the sad clown/tortured soul is a seductive one, and some have been tempted to apply it to Dawson, with his morose onstage manner and his contemplative nature offstage, to say nothing of the personal tragedy he went through with Meg. 'There is this current obsession with the dark side,' Alan Plater observed. 'Shirley [Rubinstein, Plater's wife] took a call a couple of years back from someone setting up a series: would I like to do an episode for this series? What was said to Shirley on the telephone was "We thought it would be a chance for Alan to get in touch with his dark side." Hysterics. "He hasn't got one."'[1] Indeed, when Barry Cryer was interviewed for a documentary on Dawson, he was asked whether there was a Les Dawson nobody ever saw. With impeccable logic, he replied that if there had been, nobody would have seen it. This telling exchange was left out of the final cut.

Dawson had a dark side, but it was questing and questioning rather than depressive. His early diaries contain references to futility and pointlessness, and his inability to break through into show business for most of the sixties certainly got him down, but once he had made it, Dawson tended towards melancholia and sentimentality rather than anything that can be described as depression. What seemed to sadden him most was the selfish, uncaring or unkind behaviour of others. A favourite story of Dawson's was of the South Wales club gig that never happened because of a serious pit accident. Returning to his digs, he conversed with the blind husband of his landlady. When he asked the blind man what, in his opinion, could be done 'to improve the lot of humanity', the reply was simple. 'Be kind.'[2] Dawson remembered those words when he encountered a tycoon with strong views on how to deal with strikers and foreigners ('shoot a few of the buggers') at a charity luncheon. Dawson repeated the blind man's mantra, to the utter bafflement of his hosts, one of whom was reported to have 'muttered something about "bloody show-business people"'.

Dawson drank heavily for most of his life, but the only obvious ramifications were to do with his physical health. As scriptwriter Andy Hamilton recalls:

> Les could hold his drink, and it didn't seem to affect his morale adversely. There were other comedians who would drink, and when they sobered up, this massive juggernaut of a depression would come steaming in. Compared to many comedians, he was one of the least self-obsessed performers. He was social, as well. He was genuinely social. A lot of comedians you'd write for would waver between being social one minute and staring out of the window the next. I don't remember Les ever being moody. I ended up writing for a lot of comedians, and Les was the least needy, the least insecure, the most comfortable inside his own skin of all of them. I was just starting out, so I didn't know that yet.[3]

The question of where a man of such obvious humanity and warmth sat on the political spectrum was answered by the *Daily Mirror* at the time of the 1979 General Election. This was a period of considerable political and industrial unrest, and many long-time Labour loyalists were beginning to question their allegiance to the party. Asked how he was planning to vote, working-class-lad-made-good Dawson confessed that he would 'vote Conservative though with mixed feelings about Mrs Thatcher. She can be bloody stubborn, which is not always a good thing'. This was in contrast to his friend Billy Connolly, who plumped for Labour, observing that he could 'sympathize with Mrs Thatcher when she wants to cut taxes, but on the other hand I don't want to invade Poland'.[4] Dawson's choice at the ballot box seems to sit uneasily with his assertion that 'today we tend to close our doors on the show we call life, and we are the lonely rooms in cities that are dying for the want of a community more interested in people than possessions ... Granite towers house people who now have no contact with their neighbours; children cannot mix, and therefore lose the sense of companionship and tolerance.'[5] After all, it was Mrs Thatcher who declared to *Woman's Own* magazine in 1987 that 'there is no such thing as Society. There are individual men and women and there are families.'[6] Why would someone of working-class stock, who set such store by community, vote for a party and a leader that refused to acknowledge society's existence, still less its importance?

The answer would seem to be that the Conservatives' espousal of low direct taxation appealed to a self-made man and a high earner. Unlike some of his contemporaries, he was no Tory tub-thumper. On a 1981 BBC show, he allowed himself a mild dig against the incumbent administration when discussing the magic act of his fictitious uncle Zebediah. 'In the 1930s, he perfected a new slant on the old vanishing cabinet, and overnight made the entire Government disappear,' said Dawson, before looking heavenward and begging, 'Come back, for God's sake.'[7] Although Dawson made a lot of money, he also let a lot of it out of his hands, or as he put it in one edition of *The Dawson Watch*: 'They say that money talks. All it's ever said to me was "Goodbye".'[8] He admitted that he took a lot of work that he didn't necessarily want to take because he needed the cash. Talking of one long-running TV gig, about which he had grave reservations as to his suitability, he said 'yes' initially because 'The income tax had yet again denuded me of the filthy, and I have never been much of a saver.'[9] In particular, calls to do TV advertisements were always welcomed as they represented a big payout for a day's work. He recalled one for Glow Worm boilers involving a 'pink padded one-piece suit with a bulb on the arse end, which lit up', causing the crew at Shepperton Studios to burst out laughing as one every time the bulb illuminated, ruining numerous takes. Dawson salvaged the exercise by delivering part of the sales spiel in purest Robb Wilton. Such an affront to Dawson's dignity was bearable, because 'the money was a godsend, [as] HM Inspector of Taxes was still delving into my linen for every groat he could steal'.[10]

While many other stars of his stature had financial advisers and investments, Dawson's approach to the money he earned was endearingly old-fashioned and clearly a hangover from his upbringing. Vernon Lawrence explains: 'I think it was either Norman Murray or Anne Chudleigh who told me that when the money came in, he got the cheque, he used to go to the bank and divide it up, and drive around Blackpool and Southport to all the local building societies. It was liberally spread in building societies. A bit there, bit there, bit there. Apparently, he was a building society man. Not gilts, not shares.'[11]

The first show in a series of six for BBC1 was broadcast on 30 January 1982, but all recording had been completed by early December, just before Meg's diagnosis. Although he could ill-afford to refuse work, Dawson scaled down his professional commitments for the rest of the year so he could spend more time at home with his wife and children. 'I had time in mid-1982 to enjoy family life and to see the children mature into their teens,' he said later, underlining his admission that he wished he'd been around more earlier in their development. The time he spent at home had always been treasured by all concerned, particularly the Friday evening ritual of tea from the chippy, eaten at the kitchen table, with the whole family spending a couple of hours talking about the preceding week and what they had done with it.[12]

At home, Dawson was a very different creature to the one who, on tour, did much to improve brewery and distillery profitability. When back in Lytham with the family, his favoured drink was tea, and the kettle was rarely given the chance to cool down. Eldest daughter

Julie's husband, Jon, then just a friend, recalls sitting with Dawson one night, drinking tea and discussing a multitude of subjects in fascinating depth and detail until 5 a.m., when he dragged himself away reluctantly as he had work later that morning. It was a happy house, full of warmth, where the occupants talked to each other a lot and laughed a great deal. Meg's illness dulled the happiness, but the warmth remained, along with much of the laughter. Once, when both Meg and Les were bed-bound with various illnesses, they found themselves watching the US historical drama *The Blue and the Gray* on television. Meg made a comment on Gregory Peck's portrayal of Benjamin Disraeli. When it was pointed out that Peck was playing Abraham Lincoln, Meg explained that both Lincoln and Disraeli 'had the same hat', at which she and Dawson both laughed uproariously.

One result of Dawson's housebound period was *The Malady Lingers On*, the first inkling of which came when it was mentioned in a *Daily Mirror* preview of his new TV show in January 1982. At that time, the working title was *The Book of Outrageous Puns*.[13] Throughout his career, one of Dawson's signature joke styles was to take a song lyric and work backwards from it, weaving a ludicrous tale that ends with the lyric, transformed into nothing more than a sequence of dreadful puns, left standing as the punchline. It was a development of what Frank Muir and Denis Norden had been doing for years with phrases or sayings on the radio panel game *My Word*, but with one important difference. The Muir and Norden stories often had an air of plausibility up until the reveal, whereas the Dawson jokes were clearly ludicrous and surreal from the off. In both cases, the audience became complicit, like passengers on a roller coaster ratcheting slowly up an incline, all anticipating the freewheeling drop after the peak.

For example, the Marlene Dietrich classic 'Falling In Love Again', with the line 'Falling in love again, what am I to do? What am I to do? I can't help it', became the basis for a rambling fantasy about a female baker that Dawson claimed to have met while on National Service in Germany. The poor woman had trouble with her loaves, which failed to rise due to an infestation of mice in the water supply. The suggested remedy was a pit of talcum powder in the water conduit, but the baker found herself unable to reach the pit to replenish the powder. Seeking solace in the bottle, she was heard to croon to herself 'Failing in loaves again, water mice to dough, water mice to dough, I can't talc pit'.[14]

The Malady Lingers On is full of such constructions, which work better spoken than written. For a man who hoped to be a great writer, it must have been an unsatisfying endeavour, but, with his usual work on hold due to Meg's illness, the mental exercise and the money would undoubtedly have been welcome, with Dawson dipping into his notebooks, and assembling a few of his favourites.

Dawson's third novel, also published in 1982, is far more reward-ing. The working title had been *Hitler Was My Mother-in-Law*, but this was changed on the book's hardback publication to *The Amy Pluckett Letters* 'because someone at the Robson publishing house wanted a more erudite title and a flop was spawned'.[15] Erudition apart, another objection might have been that the title gave away a fundamental detail of the book's gleefully absurd plot. As with his previous novels, the narrator was a comedian, but this time his name was Les Dawson. The story purported to stem from a series of letters written to Dawson by a demented fan, one Amy Pluckett of Miresea-on-Crouch. In her correspondence, she detailed information given to her by Sir Peregrine Oswald Potts-Belching, whom she had met when they were both institutionalized, about two German servants employed by his father just after the Second World War. The pair – a cook called Frau Gruber and her daughter Greta – were noted for their resemblance to Adolf Hitler and Eva Braun, with good reason, for that was exactly who Sir Henry Potts-Belching had rescued unwittingly from 'the burning ashes in Berlin … in return for a promise of money from a Swiss bank account, and the daughter's willingness to share his bed'.[16] From the Potts-Belching ancestral seat, Hawsbortem Towers in Ruff-on-the-Ole, Dorset, Hitler planned to activate a sleeper force of his former troops and rewrite the ending of the war. Meanwhile, Sir Henry had married his effete son Peregrine off to Greta, hence the title of the book.

Dawson has a great deal of fun with the establishment of the

Fourth Reich and its eventual thwarting, particularly when he introduces an elderly female assassin in the employ of the British government, who poses as Peregrine's Auntie Maude in order to get close to Hitler's sleeper forces and neutralize them. Unfortunately, she ends up in league with Hitler when he goes on a killing spree himself, where all of the victims are left as dummies, stuffed with kapok. In this way, several major entertainers meet grisly ends.

However, the greatest point of interest is the stand-off between Hitler and the police that occurs after a car chase through West London:

> We [Hitler, Auntie Maude and Sir Peregrine] roared past the Shepherd's Bush Common, narrowly avoiding several police cars in the process, and Maude then skidded the car into a narrow alley way that lay at the side of the Shepherd's Bush Empire ... Hitler ... dragged me onto the stage. The audience, or what there was of them (I found out later that business that week had been so bad, somebody had shot a stag in the balcony), started to laugh as the deranged dictator and I stood blinking in the spotlights. Hitler screamed 'Shut up you pigs' and the audience roared. I glanced down at the orchestra pit and saw that Aunt Maude was busy butchering the band.
>
> Adolf started walking up and down the stage, oblivious to the hordes of policemen hovering in the wings. He sang a German drinking song and the crowd joined in – it was a catchy tune and I couldn't resist warbling a snatch myself. Aunt Maude had finished stuffing the flute player with cotton wool balls, and she accompanied us on the piano. Hitler, flushed with success, broke into 'Lili Marlene' and the whole theatre joined in, including [secret service agent] Rodney [Barton] and his men. 'Take your clothes off, mein liebe' shouted Adolf, and I began to do my strip routine ... It brought the house down. As the last few bars of 'Lili Marlene' died away, Maude grabbed my left hand, Adolf the right one, and we leapt off the stage and down the centre aisle, closely pursued by Barton, policemen, and four theatrical agents waving commission sheets.[17]

From there, Hitler heads into central London and attempts to escape in a rocket disguised as Nelson's Column. The take-off fails and the Column lands in the Serpentine, killing Hitler. The date given for the incident is April 1956, at which time Dawson was about to make his humiliating retreat from London, as a result of Max Wall's fall from grace. By desecrating a much-loved monument, Dawson was almost certainly settling an old score with the city. The business in the variety theatre underlines his intent in no uncertain terms. The Shepherd's Bush Empire, built in 1903 to the designs of architect Frank Matcham, had, in 1953, become the BBC Television Theatre. And in the reality of 1956, it had been the scene of Dawson's dashed hopes, when Edmund Hockridge decided to break the strike and appear on *The Max Wall Show*. In the parallel universe occupied by Sir Peregrine Potts-Belching, the Empire had remained a variety theatre. What better way to stick two fingers up at the old pile than to have Adolf Hitler appearing there and being a success?

It was *Les Dawson's Lancashire*, published in 1983, that showed Dawson's real strength as a writer. He could write novels, as *A Card for the Clubs* and *The Spy Who Came* ... proved, but he was at his best over shorter distances, whether as a writer of short stories or essays, which he had done throughout his career for magazines as varied as *Punch* and *Penthouse*. Freed of the constraints of plot, he brought his considerable talents of perception and description to bear on subjects close to his heart, and *Les Dawson's Lancashire* is written with wit, love and pride. Lancashire, he argues, is 'the pivot for discussion ... when one talks of the North of England'. What of the other counties? 'Oh, I admit that Yorkshire does exist,' he says, 'but it's such a job to change your money into Leeds currency, and in any case who in their right mind honestly wants to go to Ripon? ... No, let Yorkshire act as ballast and thank the Lord for the Pennine Chain.'[18] Meanwhile, Cheshire is snobby, with fish and chips in briefcases, red cabbage ordered through Interflora and pubs whose barmaids' noses are 'so high in the air, their nostrils look like sunglasses'. The county does, however, have the virtue of shielding Lancashire from the Midlands. In other hands, this might sound like defensive, territorial and petty nonsense. With Dawson, who spent many happy years working in Leeds, it's merely good-natured ribbing.

To Dawson, 'describing Lancashire is like attempting to draw a portrait of a face seen only once – where to begin?' Officially, the tour begins in Liverpool (the definition of Lancashire being the historic county, not the modern administrative area), but not before the author has paid a brief visit to the Manchester of his youth, recollecting the 'warmth and comradeship in adversity', the beers ('Boddingtons, Chester's Bitter, otherwise known as "Lunatic Broth", Threlfall's Ales and Swales's. Eeh, tha's nowt to touch it.'), the Whit Walks ('long processions of faith down Oldham Street. Little kids marching proudly in new shoes', with bystanders sucking lemons to make the bandsmen's mouths dry), and art galleries that 'make the Louvre look like a junk shop'.[19]

In Liverpool, Dawson notes the deleterious effect had by developers and planners over the years. 'Modern Development … ripped the heart out of a truly noble city leaving gaunt concrete fingers and wastelands to the people of the night, muggers and defrocked VAT men.' Fortunately, what remains is the native humour and love of expressive language. 'The average Liverpudlian possesses the uncanny ability of being able to put a string of improbable words together and in so doing produce a verbal painting,' Dawson argues, offering the example of an acquaintance who had been rehoused from the slums of the Dingle to the smarter Kirby. The new house was, in the words of the Scouser, 'small … it's really a vampire's haversack'.[20]

The contrast between Lytham St Anne's, where Dawson lived, and nearby Blackpool, where he spent so much time working, is well drawn. St Anne's-on-Sea is, he says, 'a dowager who refuses to come to terms with anything remotely modern … still tea dances and lavender and swooning maidens in odd gazebos'.[21] Blackpool, meanwhile, is 'often dirty, always vulgar … a gaily painted harlot'.[22] Dawson passes no judgement on which is better, as he clearly loves both equally. He notes the airs and graces put on by St Anne's, 'an air of pretentiousness that often spoils what can be a very dignified resort', but observes that if you 'smile at it all ... soon you fall under the magic of the place'. Meanwhile, 'Lytham [Lytham St Anne's comprises two separate settlements that have come to be regarded as one] is delightful and charming, and any dreaded town planner who yearns to change it should be very carefully minced.'[23] Approaching Blackpool from Lytham, the first port of call is the Pleasure Beach, with 'machines to throw you up into the sky, machines that hurtle you into black tunnels, machines that attempt to tear your tripes into shreds', all attracting 'heated children ... lost children and over-excited children ... open-mouthed girls sat in booths, thrilling to the words of a Romany palmist ... young men in tight trousering who thrust out genitalia in the hope of securing a scented conquest on the night-time sands ... old couples putting coins into whirring machines ... young couples holding wet crying bundles ... Everyone comes to the Pleasure Beach'.[24]

Next comes the Tower, at the summit of which 'the wind bludgeons you and robs you of breath', the price that must be paid for the view. Rather contrarily, Dawson asserts that 'the spectacle of Blackpool seen from above is an anti-climax, less compelling than the real-life uproar at ground level'. Further up the coast, Dawson is a little unsure what to make of Morecambe, 'where even the sea looks shifty'.[25]

Les Dawson's Lancashire is part evocative travelogue, part flight of fancy. Every description of a real place or practice is balanced elsewhere by a Dawsonian invention, with made-up customs being a particularly rich seam. For example, the Lancashire Shuttle Dance sounds like a plausible enough product of the cotton mills, a shuttle being a vital part of the looms used to weave the cloth. Until, that is, Dawson outlines the exact nature of the dance. 'It is a simple reel and a joy to watch,' he explains. 'Two pairs stand in line and shove a ferret up a vicar's kilt, and when he yodels "Mammy" in Dutch, three of you stand with your back to the traffic and wallpaper each other's legs.'[26] Some of the material is recognizable, either from Dawson's act, or from 'The Dawson Slant', his series of humorous articles for the Blackpool *Gazette*. A section about Lancashire breaking off and forming a republic had begun in Dawson's newspaper column as a (fictional) description of the (real) town of Garstang (between Preston and Lancaster) declaring home rule and becoming a walled community. Dawson applies this to the whole of Lancashire in his book, outlining a plan suggested by a mad scientist to 'a conference of left-wing mindreaders that Lancashire should be jacked up 24 feet in the air and supported on rubber washers'.[27] Other proposals included Oldham Town Hall becoming a 'permissive launderette and bridge club'. Despite some of the material being borrowed from Dawson's repository, none of it seems crowbarred in, as it occasionally could, and it all hangs together very well. Aided by sympathetic illustrations by John Ireland, *Les Dawson's Lancashire* is probably the best of all the comedian's written works, with one foot in reality and the other in his inimitable fantasy world.

The Lancashire book had been inspired by a call from Peter Lee-Wright at BBC Television's Community Programmes Unit. He wanted to make a documentary for a new series called *Comic Roots*, in which Roy Hudd, Irene Handl and *Hi-De-Hi* star Paul Shane revisited the places where they had spent their formative years. Lee-Wright found many performers sceptical of the whole idea. 'Thirty years ago,' he explains, 'the culture of celebrity self-exposure was only in its infancy and, as I found when charged with setting up this series for BBC1, comics were particularly fearful that such exposure would destroy their method and mystique, like the Wizard of Oz having his curtain drawn back.' Although Dawson was receptive to the idea from the start, Lee-Wright knew of his subject's literary ambitions and worked out 'that the clincher would be to offer Les a separate contract as the writer of the show – unlike all the others, who were simply contracted to perform and with whom we evolved scripts through conversation. Les relished the prospect of writing his own life and his script formed the basis of the *Comic Roots* [documentary].'[28]

The programme was shot over a two-week period in the summer of 1981, with Dawson returning to Collyhurst to document what remained of his birthplace, which wasn't a great deal. At the time of production, the district was in the midst of rebuilding and regeneration, with the thirties flats that had replaced the old back-to-backs themselves being replaced with new houses. Dawson also took Lee-Wright and team to Blackpool, identifying it as the place that Mancunian families and their urchins would always head for, given a bit of free time and half a chance.

The finished programme opens with a Dawson narration over library shots of Manchester before the terraced houses were bull-dozed, including some from Denis Mitchell's 1959 BBC documentary *Morning in the Streets*. The commentary is Dawson in full wordsmith mode:

> Grimy hunched warehouses severing the skyline with dissipated pro-files, that lurch above narrow tenements gazing eyeless onto litter-pitted streets. Garish pools of pallid illumination retching from the open maws of public houses, twisting to freedom in wreaths of tobacco smoke. Red trams trundling down the road, escorting handcarts and dray horses. Shrieking children playing in the gutters, ignoring the reproof of the black-clad nuns scurrying by. Collyhurst in the 1930s.[29]

Interestingly, not all of the opening monologue was bespoke. Some of the same phrases had already appeared during a monologue in the opening show of Dawson's first disastrous BBC series in 1978, in which he ran down his old neighbourhood: 'We lived in a pretty filthy area. In fact, gypsies used to come round with clothes pegs made of soap. What an area. Grimy hunched warehouses severing the skyline with dissipated profiles. Soot-bearded tenements gazing eyeless onto litter-pitted streets. Garish bingo halls retching pools of pallid illumination onto dog-fouled-cobbles.'[30] The main point of interest is not the reuse of the lines, but the fact that he uses them successfully to convey two conflicting impressions of a place. In the original version, the location described is grim and squalid, while in *Comic Roots*, the place seems to be warmer and more inviting, the warehouses having somehow acquired a rough-hewn beauty.

At the core of the film are Dawson's encounters with people

connected with the area, including Mary Bertenshaw, who had written a book about the Collyhurst of her youth. Standing on the building site where her street had once been, Dawson listened rapt as she explained the layout to him. 'We lived at 87 here, so about there was Mrs Morley, and she was very, very stout,' Bertenshaw related. 'Of course we had no lobbies, and everybody used to sit on the steps during the very warm weather. Mrs Morley used to sit there and when the organist came round, she told him to put it on number four so I could dance and all of the policemen were on the corner, clapping.'[31] Dawson asked if the Mission was still standing, prompting Bertenshaw to speak of 'the magic lantern at the Mission. We thought it was so lovely. There were no films with noise to them, music, talking or anything. So, these coloured films. The magic lantern was actually magic to us kids, you know. All holy pictures. It was the only holiness some of us ever saw. I never went to church.' Gently ribbing Bertenshaw for having 'an air of Satanism', Dawson admitted that he never went to church either 'in case you had to put something in the collection box'. Seeing the Gay Street Mission still there, Dawson told Bertenshaw that its name has 'a different connotation today' and pulled a camp face.

Dawson was similarly delighted by local historian Mary Turner, who bemoaned the loss of the back-to-back houses. When she admitted that the true back-to-backs had no toilet facilities, Dawson pressed her on the issue, and she explained that some had pails that were emptied by the 'night-soil men', but others just went on the railway. Dawson was very amused by the memory and muses on what might happen if an express were to come past suddenly. He is even more amused when Turner adds that the Collyhurst ordure was collected 'to sell to the farmers in the lush greenery of Ardwick', once a village, but now very much part of the Mancunian sprawl.

While he wore a three-piece suit, complete with watch chain, for his return to the streets of Collyhurst, Dawson donned a sweatshirt for a trip to the Fox in Blackley, a pub run by his childhood friend John Donnelly. Dawson asked Donnelly why Collyhurst seemed to breed boxers. Both had been reluctant pugilists themselves, with Donnelly admitting to being known by the nickname 'Canvas Mat', due to the amount of time he spent in proximity to it during fights. 'The simple reason was that it was a hard area ... the escape route [from poverty] was boxing,' he explains, adding that his own experience of childhood penury had included going to school in odd shoes and cutting the arms off discarded jerseys to make socks. Those days continued to exercise a strong influence over Dawson, Donnelly noted. 'When I see you on the telly,' he told his old mate, 'I think to myself you're living your childhood again, because the people you take off are my mum and dad and your mum and dad, people from Collyhurst.'[32]

To follow this thread, Dawson visited a cotton mill to speak to the female workers, one of whose habits featured heavily in Ada Shufflebotham's repertoire. 'It was a common spectacle to see lines of women, dressed in clogs and coloured pinafores, trudging to the cotton mill,' he explained. 'For a pittance, they would toil all day at the belt-driven looms ... the noise of the massive machinery deafening, and pummelling the senses. Women being women, they found a way that they could beat the infernal racket and have a conversation with each other. It was very simple, they used to mouth the words.'[33]

Surrounded by millworkers, he concentrates on one of the seniors, Minnie, who would have been working there for fifty-four years that coming October – since 1927. Dawson demonstrated a little of his own Ada-style mouthing, and asked her if she could tell what 'he was saying'. Minnie couldn't, but the fault was his, she said, as he was barely opening his mouth. The value of lip-reading in these close-knit communities was considerable, Dawson argued, with old dears in pubs choosing their seats very carefully so every mouth and its movements could be seen. 'Hence the fact that nothing was sacred in the community where those old girls were,' he observed, adding that 'keeping a secret was about as easy as getting [prominent missing Nazi] Martin Bormann on *This is your Life*'.

The second half of the documentary was focused on Blackpool, where children from the ragged school would go for half-day trips, with the first child to spot the Tower receiving a prize of tuppence.

To illustrate this feat, Dawson was shown delivering his piece to camera in a field full of cows some distance from the Tower, ending on a shot zooming into the monument. Back in the deprived thirties, the children would make a beeline for the sea, many of them in home-knitted swimming costumes. 'Fine in theory, until you got in the water,' Dawson observed, paddling with a knotted hankie on his head, noting that 'the damned things used to stretch about six foot from your backside and held you back. It was a common sight to see hordes of little kids with bare bottoms thrashing around like minnows.'[34]

As the millworkers were to the Manchester segment of the documentary, the famed Blackpool landladies were to the second part, described by Dawson as 'majestic triangular females who could put the fear of God into you'. Taking tea with several of them, he guffawed heartily at the tale of one family who began the week having the best of everything, but soon ran out of money. The punchline – 'When it got to Friday, they were on bananas' – found particular favour with the comedian, probably because it sounds like something he'd have come up with himself. He asked whether the old Jimmy James joke about paying extra for 'use of cruet', a three-word construction that manages to be funny and economical, had any basis in truth, and the landladies replied in the affirmative.

The programme closed with a Cissie and Ada sketch, in which they played landladies. Shot in an understated style on 16mm film, without the contribution of a studio audience, it works beautifully. Cissie's guest house was packed to the rafters, while Ada was experiencing lean times. 'I must know, have you put that "No Vacancies" sign up because you're full or just to give me the hump?' enquired Ada, bemused by the lack of custom, particularly as she has gone to considerable efforts with the decoration. 'Of course, I've got a big muriel [*sic*] on the wall,' she informed Cissie. 'It came from Woolco, beautiful thing. It's the "Death of Lysander" in Dulux. You can see every wound.' The '"Death of Lysander" in Dulux' line would be reused in one of Dawson's 1982 BBC1 shows, which was transmitted eight months before *Comic Roots*, but this is its original usage. The effectiveness of the naturalistic setting and his new director's approach were a delight to Dawson. 'Les was a joy and he enjoyed the space I gave him to work in,' says Lee-Wright. 'He tried to get me to give up documentary to shoot his next series, telling me stories of heavy-handed light entertainment directors who trimmed pauses and other aspects of his humour they didn't understand. It was a tempting offer, but I didn't take it.'[35] The often-passive Dawson must have liked Lee-Wright, to assert himself in such a way, but the approach is consistent with Dawson's basic desire to be taken seriously. On the basis of this one experiment, a series exploiting Dawson's various characters in naturalistic settings could, potentially, have been one of his crowning achievements and years ahead of trends in television comedy, but the idea was never pursued.

The nostalgia in this *Comic Roots* is far from sentimental. For all the good that those days held, life had improved immeasurably for almost everyone. Mill girl Minnie says they're 'more happier [*sic*] now … we used to get fined threepence for a flaw … they used to put the list up with all your wages on, and first one you'd be going looking at how much somebody had, how much they'd been fined'. Harry Jordan, the creator of a news sheet for Harpurhey residents, told Dawson that 'I like these days. I wouldn't like the old days back', adding that 'I'd like the people back'.[36] Dawson was an engaging presenter of this type of documentary, his good cheer tending to bring the best out of his interviewees and his colleagues. Peter Lee-Wright recalls: 'Where some comics reserve their humour for performance, and can be quite morose company, Les was always enjoying a laugh, not just in meeting his adoring public – like the mill ladies from whom he got his silent mouthing, but also on the road. Stopped at a roadside Little Chef en route to Blackpool, he and I would trade puns until the crew groaned for relief.'[37] That Little Chef stop made a vital contribution to the programme, apart from feeding the entourage. At one point, Dawson is seen riding an open-top tram, enjoying an item of confectionery. 'He insisted on having the child's meal, and on getting the complimentary lolly, to which he was not entitled because he hadn't cleared his plate. He can be seen sucking it on the tram.' His glee in receiving the lolly shows that, in adulthood, he remained that ragged schoolboy hoping to get tuppence for spotting the Tower.

On transmission, the final sequence of the programme caused a mild controversy. 'The beach sequence, with which I finished the film, was one of the more hysterical days on a very enjoyable shoot,' Lee-Wright recalls:

> Les was nervous of animals, as the sequence with the cows reveals, but did not shy at my suggestion that he took a donkey ride on the sands. The donkey however did not take kindly to this large load, and bolted, with only the cameraman, Paul Berriff, fit and focused enough to stay with him. I and the rest of my crew collapsed in stitches. We all thought this a great conclusion to the film, but animal rights people in the audience thought otherwise. The editor of the *Radio Times* invited me to respond to the many letters of complaint and, only then, did I discover that the then County Borough of Blackpool had – despite the minor matter of a world war raging at the time – in 1942 introduced 'Regulations with Relation to Asses on the Foreshore', which forbade any person 'over sixteen years of age, or over eight stones in weight ... to ride any asses'. Guilty on both counts, I had to apologize.[38]

The comedian's first 'Dawson Slant' column for the Blackpool *Gazette* had appeared the week before *Comic Roots* went out on BBC1. In the first article, he adopted the mantle of fearless investigative reporter, setting himself up as a one-man Woodward and Bernstein of the Fylde Coast, and declaring that 'the world shall now know that two of the elephants in the zoo are battery-driven. I may eventually end up in a blocked culvert, but truth and the burning desire for money spur me on'.[39] In reality, the money a local newspaper could offer would have been meaningless to Dawson compared to the simple, priceless pleasure of being allowed to write whatever he liked and then having it published.

The investigative nose of that first column is, however, something of a red herring, as it turns out to be a deftly absurdist take on the conventions of local newspaper journalism, with its dutiful recording of the mundane and marvellous. The most obvious influence is that of J.B. Morton, who, as Beachcomber, wrote the 'By the Way' column in the *Daily Express* from 1924 to 1975. In particular, Dawson shared Morton's love of recurring characters, inhabitants of a parallel universe of their own creation. Among Morton's catalogue of grotesques was Captain Foulenough, a clubbable bounder whose unwelcome entrances at society occasions and monstrous whelk-stall debts made him notorious throughout the land. To the nation's gaiety, Beachcomber also contributed Justice Cocklecarrot and Dr Jan van Strabismus (Whom God Preserve) of Utrecht, inventor and eccentric.

Dawson built up a cast that included a Swiss-born scientist called Dr Helmut Clack, best known for blowing a fisherman's hat off with an explosive acorn, to say nothing of supplying faulty electric braces to US soldiers, and Roscoe Chip, an 'American draughtsman caught blowing eggs through his vest in Preston'. The Morton influence is at its most blatant when Chip is attacked in court by 'four red ladies with ginger beards', a clear reference to Justice Cocklecarrot's most celebrated trial, The Case of the Twelve Red-Bearded Dwarfs.[40] Meanwhile, the inventions of Clack – such as the expanding vest, gas-fired sandals for the flat-footed, musical socks for the shy, a collar-rotting substance used to lower the morale of a Panzer division by preventing them from wearing ties – echo some of the creations of van Strabismus, which included: 'a bottle with its neck in the middle ... false teeth for swordfish ... a hand-woven esparto grass egg-cosy which plays "Thora" when released from the egg ... [and] a cheese-anchor and a chivet for smearing radishes'.[41]

One of the recurring situations in 'The Dawson Slant' concerns the discovery of hidden deposits of vindaloo curry in the North Sea, and the political problems involved in making use of such a rich resource. 'The Indian high commissioner in Bradford has stated that if we exploit it, they will ban tins of Brown Windsor soup in New Delhi', Dawson reports in the first 'Slant', adding that it 'is easy to retrieve, all one has to do is wade out and suck it up through a length of conduit and drain fish droppings off it'. He notes that 'it's nice with a salad, and you can keep it in a hat'.[42] By week three, perhaps inspired by a combination of the Cod Wars and the Falklands War, the situation has become 'the North Sea Curry crisis', with India threatening to impose sanctions against the export of Eccles cakes. The news that chip shops are to sell North Sea curry leads to '300 Bengal poppadom fryers ... marching across Garstang burning every lamb chop in sight'.[43] After this, the curry thread is forgotten, as Garstang declares home rule, with General Catchpole Fogg taking charge of the Lancashire town from his headquarters in the local brewery. The plan comes adrift when the need to import foreign soldiers to keep order and repel invaders results in a shortage of food within the town walls. Finally, in November, Fogg reports 'that his brewery headquarters had run out of ale and the massed Cuban string orchestra was getting on his nerves'.[44]

As the year progressed, Meg's condition seemed to be improving, so Dawson began slowly returning to his normal line of work, but with the proviso that he wouldn't be away from home for too long. Consequently, he signed up to appear in pantomime at the Davenport Theatre, Stockport, and felt able to meet his Radio 2 commitments, recording the next run of *Listen to Les* in October. There was also a new BBC1 series to record at the end of the year, once again with Terry Ravenscroft and Ernest Maxin taking care of business. This time, however, Kids International were no longer on the bill. 'Norman Murray, who was Les's agent, said, "For the next series, we've got to take them out. They're getting too successful,"' Maxin recalls. 'I was getting letters into my office in dustbin liners. Thousands of them.'[45]

Nevertheless, the issue of how to alleviate pressure on the show's star remained. Dawson claimed the idea for the replacement was his own, eventually accepted reluctantly by Maxin and BBC TV head of variety Jim Moir. Maxin, however, recalls it differently:

> With comedy, he would get his big laughs and his characterizations, the mother-in-law and all that, but you've got to have something amusing

to keep that laughter there, so you don't have to build up every time. It's got to go along constantly, quicker and quicker, and at the end you pass the winning post. He said, 'Would it be good to have some girls in the show? I'm ugly, have something pretty around me.' I said, 'Females, yes, but you change the pace too much if you have pretty girls dancing, and you've got to start again, building. We've got to have something that keeps the laughter going, so that when you come back on, the viewers have still got a smile on their face. We'll have fat ladies.' Les said to me, 'I've got this woman that you want. She's up here in Blackpool. She's called Mo.' She came down to see me and she did her dancing. She said, 'Look, I can do the dancing up on the toes.' It was him thinking of her that got her into what we called the Roly Polys.[46]

Mo Moreland was well known in the tight-knit Blackpool entertainment community. The resort would play host to visiting stars, but many good professionals took up residence there and worked extensively in the hotels and cabarets. The best of them were known to and respected by all of the visiting pros, and the act that Moreland had with her husband, billed as 'The Mighty Atom and Roy', was one of these highly regarded turns. The call to work with her friend on his BBC1 show was not Moreland's first national television exposure, as she had appeared in a 1974 *Sez Les*, as well as appearing with Roy in the second edition of LWT's *Game for a Laugh* in 1981.

Finding the other dancers was less of a breeze. Maxin and Dawson both agreed that it would have been easy, distasteful and cruel to get cheap laughs out of the Roly Polys, by choosing the most inept dancers they could find. Consequently, the key was to confound the audience's expectations. After the initial amusement at the sight of seven older women, all comfortably proportioned, taking the stage in place of lithe young lovelies, the joke would be that they were excellent dancers. 'Not grotesque. Seaside postcards were what I had in mind,' Maxin outlines, adding that 'they had to have talent'. Unfortunately, many of those who auditioned didn't and others were merely clumsy. Indeed, one hopeful's dentures flew out in mid-performance.

Finally, when seven experienced dancers – the aforementioned Mo Moreland, plus Audrey Leybourne, Marie Ashton, Thea Macintyre, Ann Stephanie, Sue Cadman and Bea Aston[47] – had been found, the Roly Polys made their big entrance. They tapped their way across BBC1 on 15 January 1983, and were an instant hit, with their burlesquing of the sort of formation routine that the Tiller Girls had featured on *Sunday Night at the London Palladium* in the fifties. The basic idea wasn't new. A proto-Roly Polys act called the Glamazons had appeared in *Hancock's 43 Minutes*, the 1957 Christmas edition of *Hancock's Half Hour*, which took the form of a down-at-heel variety show. The originality of Dawson and Maxin's approach was that their dancing ladies weren't the butt of the joke.

When Dawson came to work on his next BBC series towards the end of 1983, it was without Maxin's guidance. 'I loved working with him,' Maxin explains. 'When he heard that I was leaving, the first thing he said was, "Have I done something wrong?" I said, "No." He said, "Well, why are you leaving me?" I said, "Well, it's a rule that we have to leave at 60. I'm very sorry, but they can't make an exception for me. It would be wrong." He said, "Will you do my theatre shows, then? You're not 60." I said, "I'll be 60 this year." He said, "Can't they make an exception?"'[48] Dawson was far from happy with his replacement, describing him in *A Clown Too Many* as having 'no sense of humour, in fact he had to make an appointment to see a joke'.[49] Discretion being the better part of valour, Dawson chose not to identify the producer by name. Maxin's successor was in fact Robin Nash, an experienced producer of light entertainment, best known for his work in situation comedy and his years overseeing *Top of the Pops*, as well as the only person to hold the executive positions of head of comedy and head of variety at BBC Television. Is it really possible that such a man could be devoid of humour? Terry Ravenscroft tends to side with Dawson, recalling something Nash said to him once. 'He'd been to see *The Graduate*,' says Ravenscroft. 'Everybody told him how good it was. He went along one afternoon to see it, and, because it was in the afternoon, there weren't that many people there. He said, "I couldn't see that it was funny."'

He was later enticed to go and see it again, this time at a well-attended screening. 'He said, "We went in the evening and they were laughing away. That's why I didn't think it was funny. I couldn't hear anybody laughing." He told this story to Andy and myself, and I couldn't believe that this had come from the head of comedy. The head of comedy needed a studio audience to tell if something was funny.'[50]

Whatever the disagreements between star and producer, the Nash-produced 1984 run successfully continued the formula established by Maxin, but it would be Dawson's last big TV variety show for some time. During that year, Meg's condition took a turn for the worse yet again. Her cancer had returned to her spine, making movement difficult and painful. Initially, a pair of walking sticks helped her mobility, but increasingly she was bed-bound. With Julie training to become a nurse in Nottingham, Dawson became a house-husband, caring for his wife and looking after Stuart and Pamela as much as he could. The full extent of Meg's illness became apparent to Dawson on a visit to Christie's Hospital in Manchester, where Meg received most of her treatment. The specialist told them that the situation was under control, but, in Dawson's version of events, he passed an ante-room on his way back from the gents, and saw Meg's specialist looking at X-rays and shaking his head ruefully. 'I wanted to shout out to him "What have you seen in those damned pictures?" But of course I didn't,' Dawson said later. 'I knew with a sickening certainty that the cancer had spread and that she was going to die ... I lit a cigarette and plunged into a trough of self-pity. Yes, I was thinking of myself, because my mind refused to believe that my partner of nearly 25 years was going to leave me alone ... I caught the eye of the specialist, and I knew that he was aware that the truth was now shared.'[51]

Dawson's immediate reaction was to drown his sorrows in drink, as he had before. 'I went on a two-day drinking session, but that just dulled it for a bit. I soon learned that was a mug's game,' he told the *Daily Mirror's* show business editor Hilary Bonner – a trusted friend as well as a journalist – in 1986.[52] For a while, Meg rallied and 'seemed stronger'. The only positive aspect of this awful situation was that it 'created a close feeling of unity with the children and myself and the in-laws'. Any distance that might have lingered from his years on tour dissipated. As James Casey observed of Meg, 'She looked after him, and she ruled him with a rod of iron, which is what he needed.'[53] When she could, Meg still ran the show, but when illness prevented her from doing so, the reunified family developed a self-sufficient mode, due in no small part to Julie, Stuart and Pamela. 'They were great kids,' Casey adds. 'It was a lovely family altogether. One of my happy memories is Les and all that to do with him.'

As much as Dawson was needed by his family, he also had to think seriously about his work. In spare moments at home, he had begun research on a serious novel. Meanwhile, the summer season of 1983 had seen him take a touring show to several resorts that couldn't sustain a single show for a full summer run, including Hastings, Lowestoft and Westcliff-on-Sea. The Roly Polys accompanied Dawson on this excursion, as did violinist Francis Van Dyke, with whom Dawson had worked a decade earlier on *Sez Les*. When the *Lowestoft Journal* trailed Dawson's three-night stint at the Sparrow's Nest Theatre, that was also the rough vintage of the publicity shot the paper used. However, with Dawson being unwilling to venture far from Lytham, such a tour was impossible in 1984. The ideal solution was a season in Blackpool itself, and so, on 28 June, Dawson, the Roly Polys, Roy Barraclough and supporting cast opened at the Frank Matcham-designed Grand Theatre, then celebrating its ninetieth year, in *Laugh With Les*. The run was a big hit, averaging 97 per cent capacity audiences.

Television was another matter entirely, with little option but to keep going to BBC Television Centre in London. 'Doing another variety series for the BBC which would entail weeks away from home was out of the question,' he realized. 'I informed the BBC that the way things were, I would have to bow out. Obviously, I was bitterly disappointed at the way my career had ground to a halt, but that was that.'[54] The timing of Dawson's announcement was fortuitous. The quiz show *Blankety Blank* had been running on BBC1 since January 1979, with Irish-born Radio 2 breakfast presenter Terry Wogan as host. It was the sort of programme hated by the BBC Governors, but loved by audiences. Alan Boyd, the producer who launched the show, was promised a bottle of champagne by then BBC1 controller Bill Cotton Jr if the show reached 10 million viewers. After a few weeks, Cotton called Boyd in and pointed to a brace of bottles of fizz, marking ratings of 20 million. The appeal of the show wasn't in the game itself, which was silly and frequently innuendo-laden, nor in the prizes that were on offer, as these tended to be, frankly, rubbish. It was in the interaction between the host and the contestants, who guessed the missing word or 'blank' in a sentence, and hoped that the panel of six celebrities sitting opposite would choose the same word, propelling them into the prize-winning Super Match Game.

Early in 1984, with plans afoot to give Wogan a thrice-weekly chat show on BBC1, the host stepped down from *Blankety Blank*, creating a vacancy. In Dawson, the BBC had a star who they wanted to keep in the family, but who could not commit to a series of variety shows, with each half-hour requiring at least a week of rehearsal. Game shows, on the other hand, can be made on a production-line basis. 'We would make two *Blankety Blanks* in a day, four in a weekend,' explains Alan Boyd, who had moved to LWT by the time Dawson took over the show, but whose influence was such that on a return visit he noticed that the basic camera scripts he had drawn up when he started the show were still in use.[55] The result was that *Blankety Blank* allowed Dawson to fill two half-hours of primetime BBC1 with a day's work, compared to the two solid weeks his own show would have taken to achieve the same air time, meaning that he could spend more time at home with the family. It was still hard work. Dawson described it as 'punishing but possible', leaving Lytham early on a Saturday morning to tape two shows, then returning in the early hours of Sunday. On top of the relative convenience, *Blankety Blank* was perfect for a man who loved conversation and who worked best with minimal preparation.

Everything seemed to add up, but Dawson was less sure of the new venture's potential. Wogan, he rationalized, 'possesses everything I haven't got: good looks and charm', asking how could he, 'a dumpy, craggy-faced comic, hope to take over from such a man?' He knew the precedents for new hosts taking over popular and long-running game shows were not good. The example at the forefront of his mind was *The Golden Shot*, on which he had appeared as a guest several times. When ATV sacked Bob Monkhouse in 1972 for an innocent, but ostensibly inappropriate friendship with an executive of a company in a position to supply prizes to the show, he was replaced by former *Sunday Night at the London Palladium* host Norman Vaughan, who took to the role, in Monkhouse's own memorable phrase, 'like a cat to water'.[56] Vaughan's successor, stand-up comedian Charlie Williams, fared no better, having none of the technical ability required to marshal contestants and guests on a show as tightly formatted as *The Golden Shot*.

Blankety Blank was a different proposition, however. It was a much looser show, with plenty of space for Dawson to just be himself, reacting to the guests and contestants, as well as sending up the cheapjack prizes. When Wogan was in charge, the meeting of the contestants was a brisk, business-like affair. Dawson spent longer talking to them, usually finding something in their name, interests or home town that inspired a terrible pun. The panellists were often caught in the crossfire. On one edition, a case of wine was offered as a prize, at a time when ITV game shows could run to a small family car. Dawson turned to panellist Henry Kelly, who was expected to come up with a missing word for the contestant, and instructed: 'Follow that, Kelly. You know how much that wine is? Fifteen shillings a gallon.'[57] Dawson also loved the story of the old woman from Tamworth who was sent home with a body-building kit. Stanley Appel, who took over as producer of *Blankety Blank* in January 1985, offers further insight into the prize policy:

> The prizes were purely a joke. They were never anything. One particular week, I remember, we had this car in the studio and the prize was the glass roof. It looked fantastic, with this car in the studio, but that's all it was. We just tried things like that to be outrageous, because we

didn't have the money to do expensive prizes and weren't allowed to. Commercial could, we couldn't. Ours was a holiday. We had to pay for them. I had a buyer and he had to buy everything. A lot of the things were on hire, because until the thing was won, we didn't need it.[58]

Nobody went away empty-handed, though. Even losers went home with the infamous *Blankety Blank* chequebook and pen, a silver-plated statuette marking the contestant's participation. It was seen very much as a booby prize, and both Wogan and Dawson sent it up something rotten, but it was far from valueless. 'Ironically, the *Blankety Blank* chequebook costs about £80 to make and is worth more than some of the prizes,' noted Marcus Plantin, who had been the show's producer when Dawson took over, in a 1985 newspaper article on quiz games.[59]

Dawson alluded to his trepidation about taking over in his opening chat on the first show. 'This is the first time I've hosted a quiz show,' he told the audience in the studio and at home, 'and quite frankly, I feel about as comfortable as a lame turkey sat on a pile of Paxo listening to Christmas carols.'[60] He went on to get in a dig at the ubiquity of his predecessor, instructing 'any viewers, wherever they lay, who may be watching this debacle tonight, please don't fiddle with your controls on the set. Just because Terry Wogan isn't here, it doesn't mean your set's broke. So all I shall say is I will do my best, Terry, to keep this show on the high level of asininity you have created.' Wogan used to use a thin stick microphone, which Kenny Everett delighted in bending every time he appeared on the panel. Dawson had taken the stage with the microphone, and in a symbolic act, ended his opening monologue by snapping it in half. From that point on, Dawson owned the show.

Part of the formula was a strict layout when it came to the panellists, who were arranged in two rows of three. 'The comedian was always down centre, the pretty girl was always on camera left at the bottom, another comedian was upstairs at the top,' Appel explains. For example, on the Christmas 1984 edition, the top row began with chat show host Russell Harty, then *Hi-De-Hi* actress Ruth Madoc in the middle and actor Derek Nimmo on the end. Downstairs, it ran female-male-female, with actress Suzanne Danielle, comedian Ken Dodd and actress Lorraine Chase filling the seats. One celebrity could usually be relied upon to produce daft answers, which no contestant had a hope of matching.

The key, however, was Dawson himself, or more precisely his gregarious nature and conspicuous lack of enemies in show business. 'He knew everybody,' Appel explains. 'The only other person who was like that, nothing at all to do with this, was the late Marti Caine. Very down-to-earth lady. They'd come up from the bottom, through the clubs.'[61] As well as having the celebrities on his side, he also had the audience with him, having done the show's warm-up himself.

With *Blankety Blank* underway and the rest of the week being spent at home with the family, writing again shot up the agenda. Dawson returned to a novel he had been working on for some time, and enthused Elm Tree Books with the idea of publishing it. This time, it would not be a gritty slice of clubland life or a surreal farce, but a grim, futuristic story of a dystopian society, in which all order had collapsed. The publisher accepted on condition that Dawson also write his memoirs for them. *A Clown Too Many* emerged first, in the autumn of 1985, and was well received. Reviewing it for the *Observer*, Paul Bailey called it 'a melancholy affair on the whole, despite some joyously funny passages'. He noted that 'Dawson clearly wrote his book himself, as the frequent over-writing indicates: "ghosts" don't go in for that', but concluded that it was 'several cuts above the average showbiz autobiography, and should be read for the picture it provides of the dying variety theatres'.[62]

The story of *A Time Before Genesis* – published in March 1986 with a cover that bears more than a passing resemblance to the distinctive jacket designs of Len Deighton's novels, and benefiting from a shared set of initials – begins in a fictional vision of the mid-nineties, where order and decency have collapsed. The turning point had been the 'insane miners' strike' of 1984 from which 'Britain never recovered',[63] the strike having destroyed whole communities and resulted in armed police intervening in all subsequent disputes. By the end of the eighties, the Conservative Government had fallen and been replaced by an 'ultra left-wing' administration led by the Socialist Union Movement Party. The pursuit of a slim physique at all costs meant that 'drug abuse became the norm',[64] with diet pills leading people on to other stimulants and resulting in an increase in robberies to feed the addictions. The Socialist Union Government had stopped the production of new money and abolished private property, 'so only people who had saved in earlier times used currency instead of barter'. The Royal Family were on the run and venereal disease was 'a bigger killer than cancer'. Entertainment had changed, too, now consisting largely of live sex shows, while comedians were routinely imprisoned:

> One popular cabaret comedian told a joke about the size of his wife. The entertainer was reported by a member of a watch group who went around monitoring such oral abuse, and the comedian was imprisoned for six months. Justice made no sense anymore. A man who raped and killed a young girl had little to fear from the courts, but a man who struck a government official could expect the death penalty. One could only hope with fervour that in the not too distant future, Mankind would come to his senses before the whole human race stumbled into the abyss of total anarchy.[65]

Although a little confused and simplistic, Dawson's dystopian vision seems consistent with his own political outlook. It counsels against extremism, while acknowledging how the policies of a Conservative administration such as the one he had voted unenthusiastically for in 1979 could provoke such action. He also finds room for a broadside against the 'ignorant, sniping ... national press'.

At the centre of the narrative, trying to make sense of this mean, awful world, is David Gates, formerly an investigative journalist on a national newspaper. Gates is cast out into the wilderness after trying to find an alternative explanation for the death of John F. Kennedy, having been told that the assassination had been the work of a single

US Government operative known as Roman, a shadowy figure present in the background of pictures as far back as the presidency of Woodrow Wilson but who seems never to age.

Fortunately, Gates is rescued from an alcoholic decline by a friend and former colleague, John Mason, who offers him a job on a local paper in Huddersfield. On arrival, Gates tells his full story to Mason, who produces a picture of Adolf Hitler and Martin Bormann. Gates is horrified. Bormann is clearly the man he saw in his source's pictures, identified as Roman. Mason, it transpires, heads a resistance movement called the Crusaders, who have been assembled to 'find the disease that was stifling Mankind into the abyss of eventual decay'.[66]

Gates is contacted by a vicar with the suggestion that he should read a children's book called *Fairies in the Garden*, by H.V. Potter. The book proves elusive. Library copies disappear, and Manchester Central Library suffers a fire in the section where the book is held. Potter, it emerges, was the founder of the Crusaders, and his apparently innocent novel contains vital codes explaining what he has discovered about Roman and what he represents.

Domestically, Gates is thrown into turmoil when he discovers his wife, Anna, is having a lesbian affair with a neighbour. On discovering them in bed together, he notices 'two angry marks on her neck, like small punctures'.[67]

Gates is given a dossier compiled by a Tibetan monk, explaining how the Earth came to be populated. According to the dossier, the planet had been created as 'a space vehicle of vast proportions'[68] by an 'alien life force from a galaxy far into the reaches of the infinite'. Man was also created by the aliens as 'a machine ... the result of genetic engineering ... capable of living with only half his vital organs'.[69] The machine's main purpose was to provide energy from which the alien creators would feed.

The problems for the alien masters apparently began when 'the Man-machine' began to think for himself. One product of this thought was the creation of a belief system, which, having been created as basically compassionate creatures, was predominantly geared towards goodness. To regain control, the aliens created a countervailing force, namely evil, with numerous temptations and a figurehead in the immortal form of Lucifer. In the world of 1995, as outlined at the start of the novel, evil is triumphing, and the mysterious Roman is at the centre of it. The puncture marks in Anna Gates's neck show where a serum had been administered, creating a state of 'near immortality' in exchange for breaking 'down the virtues of compassion, self-discipline and conscience, and the latent aberrations that every human being carries in the darker recesses of his nature rise in strength to the forefront'.[70] This, then, is a battle for the hearts and minds of the human race.

Finally, Gates locates a copy of *Fairies in the Garden*, and deciphers the code in its text. It reveals that Potter's son Daniel is the Second Coming – and that it is he who will bring the Principle of Goodness back to Earth. Daniel Potter, it emerges, has been sent to a monastic school near Glastonbury. In 1998, Daniel Potter meets Roman, the modern embodiment of Lucifer, who is struck down by God from on high. Unfortunately, the triumph of the Principle of Goodness comes too late to save humanity. Nobody has the ability or inclination to return to agrarian ways, so the crops die, and so do most of the remaining humans. Daniel Potter, Jesus himself, gives up and becomes a Buddhist. At the end of the book, the apparently abandoned, uninhabited planet Earth is discovered by aliens, who find it to be a mirror image of a planet in their own universe. High in the mountains, however, they find fur-clad primitives and cave-dwellers. Mankind has gone back to the beginning.

In some senses, the way the book ends is consistent with Dawson's comic outlook. There is no happy ending, just a bleak, resigned punch-line with a faint trace of hope. *A Time Before Genesis* is a confused, confusing book, but it is also interesting and intriguing. Dawson himself was all too aware that he was inviting ridicule by letting the world see his 'serious' novel. 'I was more than a bit apprehensive as to how it would be received,' he wrote in 1992, 'for after all we do tend to put people in boxes, do we not, and therefore could a comedian writing a serious work be taken seriously?'[71] It is clear from the way Dawson talks about *A Time Before Genesis* that it was something he was compelled to write, almost as a test of his understanding of belief and the world. *The Times'* reviewer called the prose style 'laborious ... like Dennis Wheatley on speed', but had to admit that the book was 'oddly compelling',[72] while a *Guardian* journalist said it was 'an ambitious piece of work worthy of serious consideration, even though his prose style betrays the unevenness of a dilettante'.[73]

There are many anomalies and inconsistencies in Dawson's alternative history of the universe. Not least of these is the question of who, if the belief system is created by man himself, appoints the new Messiah? However, it is the product of serious thought, and that it would have benefited from a bit more should not detract from Dawson's achievement in seeing it through. 'I've taken a lot of half-baked ideas and tried to give them credence,' he told the *Guardian* on the book's publication. This admission is what separates Dawson from the usual conspiracy theorists, notable for their fanatical belief in the ludicrous and improbable. But he nonetheless counsels against dismissing such absurdities out of hand, trying to make a sort of sense of them. 'I had done two years' research and studied the Bible and a translation of the Koran before writing a word,' he explained later. 'Philosophy kept me burning the midnight oil, and paranormal theories I devoured like food.'[74]

The gestation of *A Time Before Genesis* was, in reality, longer than that intense two years of research. He had mentioned his interests in religion and the possibility of extra-terrestrial life in a 1978 interview for Radio 4's *Woman's Hour*. Meanwhile, the paranormal had held particular interest for him since the days in the bungalow in Bury, with its benign presence. 'I am sure it doesn't all end with death,' he told the *Daily Mirror*'s Hilary Bonner in September 1986. 'I am not conventionally religious, but I really believe you do go on.'[75]During Meg's final illness, the thought that he might not be losing her completely will have come as comfort in those last months. After Meg's death, he noted numerous occasions when he felt her spirit was speaking to him. In particular, the house frequently smelled of freesias, her favourite flower, despite none being present.

As if Meg's illness wasn't enough to contend with, Dawson's own health became a matter for concern in February 1985. Since taking up golf during the 1977 Blackpool summer season, he had been an enthusiastic, if by his own admission undistinguished, amateur player. 'I have spent so much time in bunkers, I suffer from sandfly fever, but at least it's a nice stroll when I do play,' he admitted.[76] Family members suggest that this was no false modesty, and that he was precisely as useless a golfer as he claimed to be. Many show business golf enthusiasts had taken to organizing their own Golf Classic tournaments in aid of charity, and Dawson was not to be left out. It was during a lunchtime meeting at the Royal Lytham and St Anne's Golf Club to organize his tournament that he first noticed that all was not well. Following several pints of lager, he visited the lavatory, but was unable to urinate. By the time he reached home, he was experiencing serious pains in the stomach and kidneys. His GP diagnosed a swollen prostate gland and referred him to the Royal Preston Hospital for an operation to remove it. The operation was a success, but by the time it was completed, major damage had already been done to Dawson's kidneys, which began to fail, placing his life in the balance. He was moved into intensive care, with Meg being told his chances of pulling through were no better than 50/50.

Dawson's hospitalization could not be kept from the press, as it had occurred in the middle of recordings for *Blankety Blank*, and word soon got out that the host had missed a recording date. Interestingly, the edition that aired while Dawson was in intensive care showed him sparring with fellow Mancunian comic Bernard Manning, with whom he endured a spiky relationship. On 25 February, the *Daily Mirror* reported that Dawson was in intensive care, and was 'not responding to treatment'.[77] It was a big story, made bigger by the fact that the previous year had been a bad one for comedy. On 15 April 1984, Tommy Cooper had suffered a massive heart attack and died during his act on LWT's Sunday night variety spectacular *Live from Her Majesty's*. Just over a month later, on 28 May 1984, Eric Morecambe had died in similar circumstances, following a performance at the Roses Theatre in Tewkesbury. The *Daily Express* responded to news of 'the seemingly indestructible' Dawson's condition with an article describing him as 'the latest casualty', which ruminated on the stress of being a comedian and the tendency of many big names to overwork themselves. Ernie Wise observed to the *Express*'s Elizabeth Grice that 'the bigger your reputation, the harder the going gets, the deeper the stresses of live performances', adding that 'Bob Hope survives with a team of writers. We try to do a lot of it ourselves.'[78]

In Dawson's case, he hadn't been too good at looking after his health. Vernon Lawrence notes that the comic's main forms of exercise were lifting a glass to his lips or a lighter to his cigarette. Dawson himself often made a joke of it, referring to his morning exercises being 'up one, two, three, down, one, two, three, then the other eyelid'. His diet was another cause for alarm. In *Les Dawson's Lancashire* he had written lovingly of black puddings and chip butties, and his shape suggested a great deal of experience in tasting both. This time, fortunately, his luck held and, after three days in intensive care, his condition began to improve. And while this frightening period didn't make him reform his habits, the incident did give him pause for thought in one important area. 'The answer to the question "Have all the things I've done been worth the effort?" came in the shape of sacks and sacks of mail from the public,' he observed, proudly.[79] 'Goodwill cards, get well cards, fruit, flowers filled the hospital to overflowing ... Show business opened its heart and the affection brought tears to my eyes ... Yes, everything I had done had been worth it. I never knew how many lives had touched mine throughout the years.' Dawson was not an insecure or needy individual, but even he liked to be appreciated.

He would need as much kindness as he could get over the following year, as Meg's condition worsened. In November 1984, Dawson had been elected King Rat, the highest position in the Grand Order of Water Rats, which meant that he would preside over the following year's Grand Ball. Achieving the position meant a lot to him, and attending the 1985 Grand Ball as King Rat should have been one of the happiest nights of his life. Instead, it was an evening of mixed emotions, with Meg unable to walk and attending only with the aid of a wheelchair. 'As I wheeled Meg across the floor, the entire audience rose to its feet and the applause was deafening,' he wrote some years later. 'I could feel the love in that room all directed to my wife, a brave and well-respected lady. Stars like Michael Caine, Michael Crawford, Warren Mitchell and Robert Powell to name but a few, surrounded her, and she held court with radiant dignity.'[80]

The loss of mobility hit Meg hard, but her stoicism meant few realized the full extent of her anguish. Dawson's old friend and radio producer Jim Casey remembers a conversation he had with her: 'She said it had started in her legs. "I hope it's not the cancer, Jim, because I like dancing." She wouldn't tell anybody. I remember ringing her up shortly before then, and saying, "Hi, Meg, how are you?" "Fine." "No, Meg, it's Jim, how are you?" "Not so good, but I don't want bloody people being sorry for me."'[81] Meg's incapacity meant that her bed was moved downstairs at Garth House, and Dawson bought a Nissan Prairie with an electric lift installed so that Meg could be transported without leaving her wheelchair. 'At least I could take her out either for a spin in the countryside or along the promenade, or for her favourite pursuit – shopping,' Dawson said later. 'The van gave her a renewed interest and it was money well spent.'[82]

As spring 1986 approached, Meg's condition took a final turn for the worse. She told Dawson of blurred vision, and a visit to a specialist confirmed that the cancer had spread, this time affecting her eyes, and that it was now just a matter of time. After clearing the decks profes-sionally and cancelling all engagements, Dawson had the horrible job of telling his children that their mother had only a few weeks to live. 'Slowly, before our eyes, Meg began to fade from us,' he wrote in 1992. 'She looked so tiny and childlike as she lay in the bed, now unseeing, waiting to go. Occasionally she would rally but then she would sink again.'[83] Meg suggested, selflessly, that Dawson should get out of the house a bit more, so he took to visiting the St Anne's District Club, an all-male bastion of dominoes and drinking, each Friday, before ending with a nightcap at the St Ives Hotel, which stayed open later. Even as weak as she was by this point, she remained recognizably Meg, as Jim Casey recalls: 'Right towards the end, I went over to see him, and she was in bed, in her last illness. I said, "Give her my love." He said, "She wants to see you. You have to go in." So I went in and she said, "Has he given you a cup of tea? No? Tell him to get the kettle on." I said, "You see, Meg, if you're not doing it, he's useless." That was the last time I ever saw her, and it was lovely.'[84]

Finally, on the morning of 15 April 1986, Pamela, who often slept in the same room as her mother to keep a watchful eye, called to the other members of the family. Meg's breathing had changed and it soon became clear that she was fading fast. 'Julie took one look at Meg and the nurse in her knew,' Dawson later told Hilary Bonner of the *Daily Mirror*. "She's going, Dad," she said. Meg had been bad for a few days before, hallucinating, going back into childhood ... Two nights before she died I was holding her hand and the kids were all round me and she suddenly cried out: "You're pulling me back. You're pulling me back." Whether she meant I was pulling her back from death I will never know.'[85] Dawson recorded later that when the end came, 'the kids were marvellous' and that it was he 'who ran from the study blinded by tears'.[86] Dawson's partner, the one who had supported him through thick and thin for over twenty-five years, was lost to him. As his agent Norman Murray said at the time, 'There wouldn't be a Les Dawson as we know him today if it hadn't been for her.'[87]

Meg's funeral was attended by family and friends, many from within show business. Con Cluskey of the Bachelors recalls that the sombre occasion was:

> the first time I ever had a straight conversation with Frank Carson ...
> We all went to the funeral, then back to the hotel for a drink afterwards.
> Frank started his usual, and I said, 'Frank, for goodness' sake, we've
> known each other since 1957, when we were both young kids in the

business. Can we not have a straight conversation about the children and the wife?' So we're having a nice, interesting conversation for about five minutes, and then somebody else joins the conversation, and he turns to the new person, and he's off again.[88]

In the immediate aftermath of Meg's death, Dawson didn't feel he could face the outside world, and chose to stay home much of the time. Recordings of *Blankety Blank* were put on hold until May, but it was reported that his act would be different on his return. A 'close friend' had told the *News of the World* that while 'Les is determined to get back to work as soon as possible ... there won't be any more wife jokes. He treasured her more than anything in the world, so he won't be able to joke about her.'[89] The identity of this 'close friend' is unknown, but as Murray was the only other person quoted in the story, he is the most obvious candidate, particularly as writers like Andy Hamilton had noted Murray's tendency to tell them what sort of material Dawson did and didn't appreciate, often contradicted by the sort of material Dawson told.

As Dawson began to reintegrate into society, friends observed that 'there isn't a night goes by that he doesn't mention her by name, wistfully suggesting how much she would have enjoyed the occasion or get-together'.[90] Apart from losing his companion, becoming a widower with a family to look after meant that Dawson found himself learning how to run a household, with a little expert advice from outside. 'Old ladies keep coming up to me to say how sorry they are,' *The People* reported him as saying, five months after Meg's death, 'then they tell me what I should be buying, which things are bargains and which things have been on the shelf for a long time.'[91] *The People*'s article was a source of some discomfort for Dawson. He had agreed to talk exclusively to the *Daily Mirror*, or more precisely, his friend, the paper's show business editor, Hilary Bonner. In exchange for exclusivity, he had arranged for the paper to make a donation of £25,000 to Christie's Hospital for equipment. *The People*'s story, which appeared eight days before Bonner's double-page splash, was a 'spoiler' compiled from cuttings and what Dawson had thought would be a promotional chat for his books. It surprised Dawson that *The People* could act in this way towards a sister publication, but as it did not affect the donation to Christie's, he let it pass.

Dawson's professional re-emergence began with the resumption of the *Blankety Blank* recordings in May. The 1985 series of *Listen to Les* had been the comedian's last. Jim Casey had already retired from the BBC, but returned as a freelance to produce the last couple of runs at Dawson's insistence, one of the occasions when the star knew his bargaining power and used it, as Casey explains:

> When I retired [in 1982, Michael] Green was the boss then in Manchester. He said, 'We want another series of Les, of course, but we've got a producer who's got no work, so what we want to do is, you can write it, but he'll produce it.' I said, 'OK.' I went to see Les and he said no. 'No bugger's going to get on your back. You've done it all. Sod 'em. Tell them you don't want to do it.' I went home to my wife and said, 'I'm going to lose twelve bloody scripts.' Anyway, I went to see Green and I said that the situation was that he wouldn't do it unless I produced it. He said, 'OK, you produce it.' I was horrified. I thought I was going to lose all those scripts, but Les wasn't going to do it without me.[92]

Unfortunately, the BBC was changing, and with Casey's departure from the full-time staff there began a dismantling of BBC North's radio comedy production infrastructure. 'When I left, within about eighteen months, they didn't have a light entertainment department in Manchester,' Casey continues. 'I remember ringing up to speak to someone and them saying, "We don't have a light entertainment department." So I said, "Anybody who produces for Radio 2." They said, "No, we haven't got anybody."' Perhaps most indicative of what was going on had been the announcement, in early 1986, that the Corporation was selling the Playhouse theatre in Hulme, where so many of Dawson's shows had been recorded. The vacating of the much-loved venue was marked by a gala show written and produced by Casey's colleague Mike Craig, entitled *Farewell to the Playhouse*, recorded on 15 June and transmitted on Radio 2 on August Bank Holiday Monday. Dawson was the penultimate act on the broadcast version, and was in fine form, adapting some old favourites to fit the occasion:

> How dare they close this place, when you think of the great names that have appeared here. People like Gladys Allsop, the Jenny Lind of Ripley. She used to sing 'Nearer My God to Thee' and do a striptease in a bucket of ferrets. One night I was here with her, and she lost one of her ferrets in the bucket, but she had a hell of a smile on her face. One name comes through the mist of nostalgia, which we must never be allowed to forget. I refer, of course, to Seth Bottlecrud, the first man to discover that people who ate prunes were never late for work. He did write some wonderful songs and here are just a few of them: [*Plays piano and sings*] 'There was a young man from Bombay, who sailed to China one day. He was strapped to the tiller with a sex-starved gorilla, and China's a bloody long way.' Can we forget? 'My Auntie Fanny by mistake put senna pods in the currant cake, and the only advice that we could give was skip to the loo my darling.'[93]

This rendition is followed by the suggestion that the Playhouse should be closed with a singalong, which brings a murmur of amused recognition. The audience knows what's coming, as Dawson tears into his usual discordant reading of 'Side by Side', followed by an equally off-key attack on 'For Me and My Gal'. Perhaps mercifully for the building's dignity, the final music to be heard came not from Dawson, but from the Beverley Sisters, who closed the show.

Dawson's return to broadcasting was followed by a summer season at the Grand in Blackpool. Instead of his usual variety show, he had returned to theatre, starring in Ray Cooney's *Run For Your Wife*, alongside Eric Sykes and Peter Goodwright, with the production moving on to Nottingham and Manchester after the summer run ended. Cooney, known for his view that most stand-up comedians didn't have the skills for farce, admitted that Dawson was, in the right role, an exception. 'They are used to getting up themselves as entertainers and unused to relating to other characters,' Cooney told *The Stage*. 'In farce, it is essential for the actors to work with one another very closely . . . The character in *Run For Your Wife*, a silly buffoon originally played by Bernard Cribbins and now being taken in the West End by Roy Hudd, sits quite well on Les Dawson. The particular part lends itself to interpretation by a comic, providing he is a sufficiently good actor.'[94] So-called straight acting would become increasingly important to Dawson over the next few years, but for the rest of 1986 and early 1987 it was back to the Alexandra Theatre in Birmingham for a season of *Babes in the Wood* with John Nettles, by now a firm friend, and Ruth Madoc.

In contemporary press reports, Dawson was still very much the grieving widower. Indeed, in September 1986, an article in *The People* had reported him as saying 'I know my name will always be linked with women. People are fiends for whispers. But I will never marry again.'[95] In this case, however, the 'whispering fiends' were onto something.

CHAPTER 7

Run for your wife

The St Ives hotel in Lytham St Anne's had become one of Les Dawson's favoured drinking establishments during Meg's final illness, and was the venue chosen for her wake. It was a regular haunt of Blackpool show business folk because of its out-of-the-way location and late bar opening. For many, however, there was another attraction working behind the bar. 'Her name was Tracy and her smile always made me feel good,' Dawson wrote later. 'She really was a stunner, and all the male customers would try to flirt with her.'[1] In his second volume of autobiography, *No Tears for the Clown*, Dawson admits at the outset that he has omitted specific dates 'because I didn't want my autobiography to read like a diary',[2] so the exact chronology of events is vague. However, in September 1987, a *Daily Mirror* interview with Dawson reported that he 'had first met Tracey [*sic*] almost five years ago' and that she 'became a family friend'.[3]

However long they had known each other, when he announced to the press that he would remain a widower and denied links with any women, Dawson was being dishonest. Tracy had already moved into Garth House in August 1986. This fact is at odds with the 'official' version, later codified in Dawson's second volume of autobiography, which suggests the move happened eighteen months after Meg's death, nor four months.

According to Dawson's version, he had acknowledged quickly that 'it was no good kidding myself, I was drawn to Tracy'.[4] He said later that '[I] kept telling myself that it was the company that gathered there that was the attraction' and that 'it was a break for me to get out of the house where the memories still hung like ghostly curtains'. In the summer after Meg's death he was busy performing at the Grand, but felt 'desperately lonely'. The situation he found himself in was far from straightforward. For one thing, there was the perception of indecent haste. For another, Tracy Roper was twenty years younger than him. For yet another, she was married, albeit unhappily, as a helpful colleague told Dawson, with children, Richard and Samantha. 'The girl had a personality that kept me spellbound,' Dawson rationalized, 'but she was another man's wife, and there was no way that I intended to make matters worse for her and her children, even supposing she might welcome my advances, which I doubted very much.'5 Finally, there was the fact that anything he did would be of enormous interest to the tabloids. At first, he was far from frank with his children about the matter, admitting to 'a certain cowardice' and noted that when he did tell Julie, Stuart and Pamela, they 'remained more than a little wary of her ... it was to take the children a long time to come to grips with their father falling for another woman'.

Initially, he resolved to remove himself from the eye of the storm, and began drinking in other local establishments. He did not see Tracy again until some time later, when he attended a charity event at the St Ives connected with fund-raising for a scanner for Blackpool Victoria Hospital. Quietly, Dawson had been heavily involved with the appeal, and had put in many appearances locally, knowing his presence helped inspire donors to dig a little deeper. Normally he turned up in casual gear, but, on the off-chance of seeing Tracy, he put on a suit, and 'took longer under the shower than normal – shaved myself more closely than usual ... What a silly old fool!'6

As it turned out, she was off duty, so Dawson got stuck into the Scotch with zeal. A couple of hours later, as he was making his exit, refreshed, there she was, expressing concern about his drink-sodden state. When Dawson lent his weight to these local fund-raisers, he went by taxi so he could have a drink or several without worrying about losing his driving licence. After re-encountering each other, Tracy offered to drive Dawson to the various scanner appeal events, and during those journeys they found themselves talking openly in a manner that wouldn't have been possible in the hotel bar. Dawson talked over his feelings for Tracy with Roly Poly Mo Moreland, who told him that it would not be disrespectful to Meg to want to find happiness with someone new.

For a year from August 1986, information about Dawson's association with Tracy had been strictly need-to-know, but the first public inkling that there was a new woman in his life came after the ball in September 1987 at Manchester's Piccadilly Hotel to mark Hollywood star Howard Keel's charity golf tournament. Dawson had taken Tracy as his guest, no longer caring who knew about her. The following morning, as an afterthought to a report about a fire scare at the hotel that saw Keel descending fourteen flights of stairs 'clutching just a decanter of whisky', the *Daily Mirror* noted that Dawson had 'caused a stir by taking a mystery girl to the gala. The *Blankety Blank* compère, who lost his wife 18 months ago, danced with her into the early hours'.[7]

If Dawson had been alarmed by the press interest in Meg's cancer, this would pale in comparison to the frenzy that greeted the emergence of his relationship with the woman who seemed likely to become the second Mrs Dawson. On 22 September, she was merely a 'mystery blonde'. On 23 September, she was named as Tracy Roper, and her estranged husband, Richard Roper, had begun talking to the newspapers, suggesting that Dawson had been the cause of his marriage break-up. Under the headline 'Les Dawson stole my wife', Roper was quoted by the *Sun* as saying 'My Tracey's [*sic*] walked out on me and our lovely kids. Now all sorts of people are telling me they've seen her with Les.' The report went on to say that Roper had suspected his wife of having an affair for six months before the split, alleging that it would not have been the first time, and that 'she kept coming home at four and five in the morning ... Often she was drunk'.[8]

While the *Sun* had access to Tracy's ex-husband, the *Star* was in contact with her sister-in-law, Pat Brown, who was reported as saying that Tracy 'was always talking non-stop about Les Dawson, bragging how he used to come into the hotel and talk to her' and adding that she 'was always the sort of woman who was turned on by famous people and lots of money'. Twisting the knife further, Brown noted that 'Tracy managed to get front-row seats to see Les in his summer show last year ... I remember thinking at the time "I wonder what she has done to get those seats."'[9]

Later, the tabloids got wind of the fact that Dawson and Tracy's pet names for each other were 'Lumpy' and 'Poo', and made much of this detail. The comedian was used to tabloid reporters turning up on his doorstep asking impertinent questions, but Tracy wasn't, and the experience scared the living daylights out of her. Exasperated, Dawson told one hack that a marriage date would be announced as soon as possible.

Once the intention to marry had been announced, the story withered, helped by Richard Roper retracting his suggestion that Dawson had stolen Tracy, telling the *Daily Mirror* on 25 September that 'I don't know why I did it, except that I was just so terribly hurt'.[10] He suggested that he had been taking a lot of ribbing from his friends about his ex-wife's involvement with the comedian. In the following day's edition, it was reported that Dawson and Roper had met and shaken hands. Furthermore, Roper had offered to give his ex-wife away. Dawson said that it had been 'really good now to sit down with Richard man to man and sort everything out', while on Roper's offer, Tracy said only, 'We will think about that'.[11]

The low point of this whole period came on 24 September with a headline that Dawson said 'really made me consider homicide ... "Spiritualist says Carry on Bonking, Les".' The offending article had appeared in the *Daily Star*, at the time going through a period of particularly low standards under editor Michael Gabbert, who had been seconded from the sex-and-sensationalism weekly, the *Sunday Sport*. The *Sport* had built a reputation for printing ludicrous and implausible stories about London buses being spotted on the surface of the moon, so, in relative terms, a table-tapper would have been regarded by Gabbert as a copper-bottomed source. The article relayed Meg's supposed message via medium Meryllyn Seddon: 'He is the sort of person who needs a woman as an earthly companion. Naturally I feel sorry for the girl's husband, but I know the magnetism that Les has.'[12] The *Guardian*'s leader writers noted this practice disapprovingly, commenting that 'in terms of chequebook journalism, the dead come cheap'.[13] Dawson himself was sympathetic to spiritualism, and objected only to the manner of the story's presentation. 'Along with this garbage was a photograph of Meg's grave,' he noted. 'The maudlin caption, supposedly spoken from beyond the grave, was so uncharacteristic of Meg that it was beyond belief – and beneath contempt.'[14] In fact, the headline was subtly different to Dawson's recollection. The front page said, 'Carry on Les! Amazing message from his dead wife', while the continuation of the story on pages four and five bore the legend, 'Wife Meg tells Les from beyond the grave it's all right to Bonkety-Bonk!'[15] To make matters even worse, the following day the *Star* quoted Dawson as having said to its reporters, 'Thanks a million for standing by me. A lot of distasteful stuff has appeared in other papers',[16] when Dawson thought the *Star*'s approach the most distasteful of all. The line was completely fabricated, along with all of the quotes supposedly given to the newspaper by Dawson's children.

Between 1984 and 1987, Dawson's television work was confined solely to *Blankety Blank*, with *The Les Dawson Show* put on hold. When his eponymous variety show returned for a Christmas special at the end of 1987, it felt like a comeback, but this was anything but a new, invigorated Dawson. The presence of David Nobbs and Barry Cryer among the writers in the *Radio Times* credits should have been a clue. The linking material was original, but most of the sketches were very recognizable, several being remounts of *Sez Les* successes. The show began with a set full of dancers gyrating on an opulent, tiered set, then the star made his entrance and, declaring himself unable to negotiate the many stairs, asked for a sketch to be put on while he made his way down. The sketch in question featured Peter Goodwright as a mithering patient with a very minor injury, with Dawson as a GP with practically every limb in plaster. It was a good, effective sketch, particularly with Dawson's galumphing attempts to move around the surgery while the patient refuses to lift a finger, but then it had been a good, effective sketch over a decade earlier, with Roy Barraclough as the patient. Dawson's closing monologue had also appeared previously, in *Dawson and Friends* ten years earlier. In its day, with no repeats or video releases to remind viewers of the original outings for these routines, the repetitions weren't a problem. It is only in retrospect that Dawson is seen to be treading water more obviously than at any other time in his career.

One of the all-new contributions to the show found Cissie and Ada in a nightclub, sampling cocktails and watching a male stripper, who turns out to be Ada's husband Bert. Another featured Dawson as the world's unlikeliest personal trainer, trying to whip Mo Moreland into shape, a skit memorable primarily for Dawson's *Gym'll Fix It* T-shirt. The highlight of the show by some distance was a sketch set in a restaurant, featuring Patrick Mower as Dr Jekyll, sometime Goodie Graeme Garden as an imperious maitre d' and Dawson as a hapless waiter. Mower keeps turning into Mr Hyde when Dawson approaches, causing him to drop food and scream in shock, but, naturally, when Garden comes to inspect the trouble, he has returned to normal, leaving Dawson to take the blame for any commotion. Hyde smashes the first bottle of wine over Dawson's head. When a second bottle is brought, Dawson does it to himself to save Hyde the bother. Also delightful, if not particularly funny, is an item featuring four pianists at white grand pianos, with Dawson joining them in white tie and tails. For once, he plays straight, and the only comic relief comes when his piano walks off after him at the end of the scene, another triumph from the BBC visual effects department.

After this one-off, it was back to *Blankety Blank*, with another series of the game show to record for autumn transmission. One important difference between Meg and Tracy made itself apparent immediately. Whereas Meg had been a stay-at-home wife, disinclined to join her husband in the show business social whirl, Tracy was to be Dawson's constant companion on and off duty, both as partner and personal assistant-cum-dresser, helping keep him organized.

'Meg was old-fashioned, and when they got married, he was nothing,' outlines Stanley Appel. 'Tracy always came to the studio. She loved the showbiz. She really did. She really loved it. She loved coming to the Centre. She was so caring with him, she really was. There was a genuine love for him.'[17]

As well as the television commitments, there was a summer booking at the Opera House in Blackpool, sharing comic duties with friend and fellow Blackpool resident Frank Carson. Having been told that it would be a lavish production, Dawson was unperturbed to see only six dancers on the first day of rehearsals. Asking director Stewart Morris, his old BBC friend and supporter, who was on a busman's holiday from television, when the rest of the troupe would be turning up, he was alarmed to hear that this *was* the troupe. Dawson was worried about filling a stage 'so vast you could service two Boeing 747s on the apron of it and still have room to build some bungalows – and a day-care centre as well' with only six dancers.[18] However, as the eighteen-week season got underway, the emptiness of the stage concerned him far less than the emptiness of the 2,920-seat auditorium. Ticket sales were uninspiring, and although the company gave their best, the profits were scant. Dawson began to doubt his ability to top any bill, and retreated into his usual solace of heavy drinking.

Midway through the season, Dawson suffered what he thought was an attack of bad indigestion, perhaps unsurprisingly, given his enthusiastic patronage of the Scotch bottle over the previous few weeks. Tracy put her foot down and insisted he see a doctor. The next thing he knew, he was in Blackpool Victoria Hospital, surrounded by family. He had suffered a mild heart attack, and would be unable to return to the show. As Blackpool seasons tended to be longer than in other seaside resorts, with many of the shows continuing through October and into November to cover the famed Illuminations, the Krankies and Jimmy Cricket were free to come in and fill Dawson's shoes once their own season in Scarborough had ended. The official line was to deny that Dawson had suffered a heart attack, but the message from the medical staff was clear. Dawson had to take it easier than he had been doing.

Less drink, healthier eating, no smoking and, crucially, a less punishing work schedule. His scheduled panto season in Stewart Morris's production of *Aladdin* at the Bristol Hippodrome had to go ahead with Gary Wilmot taking his star billing and Gordon Peters taking Dawson's role as Widow Twankey. All the years of forgoing sleep and grabbing a pie and a pint between shows in lieu of a balanced meal had caught up with him. For kidney failure to be followed by heart trouble was an indication to the funny man that comedy could have a serious effect on his health. Perhaps those ambulance-chasing tabloid articles on the stress of being a performer weren't so wrong after all?

Dawson was also having to contend with the stress of changes in his profession. The mid-eighties had been one of the most turbulent in the history of British comedy, and various forces conspired to end the dominance of the old-style sketch and variety shows in which Dawson excelled. Shortage of money was one factor, as a properly lavish variety show required a sizeable budget. The reduced circumstances that had meant the Blackpool show could run to only six dancers were affecting the whole entertainment industry. Dawson had weathered the changing fashions better than many comics of his generation, but as the eighties progressed, even big names were not immune from budget cuts. As the economics of the business started to shift, so did Dawson's fortunes. Clubland was now almost non-existent. Summer work was no longer guaranteed, as seaside theatres closed down or shortened their seasons.

Dawson was well aware of his role in his own creative stagnation, relying on the same canon of material for so long. Naturally, he made a joke of it, informing his live audiences that 'My act is so old, I get fan mail from Aesop',[19] but it is clear from his later writings that he realized it to be a genuine problem, and acknowledged that he needed to update his act.

In the late seventies, younger performers had reacted against the stereotypes employed by some of their elders. Sexism and racism were off-limits, except as objects of ridicule, satire and contempt. The epicentre of this so-called 'alternative comedy' movement was the

Comedy Store club in London. Early in the venue's history, Dawson turned up and took advantage of the 'open mike' policy. In the words of alternative stalwart Jim Barclay, Dawson 'did fifteen minutes and was brilliant', with others admiring the way he could handle any audience. Dawson himself noted that some of the alternatives' material was 'bad' and that 'there's one or two on here who'd get murdered up north. But it's useful, because it's a place to fail, and no matter what type of comedian you want to be, you need the experience of failure.'[20]

With his mother-in-law and wife jokes, Dawson might have been seen as a prime target for the angry young men and women of the laughter business, but he did not view himself as such. Explaining his jokes about women to Helen Boaden for Radio 4's *Woman's Hour* in 1991, he said that it was:

> A defence mechanism, I suppose, because women generally are much better at controlling things than men are. 'The hand that rocks the cradle rules the world' is still a great axiom. Despite the fact that feminists say they're not getting a fair deal, women are still very powerful. They're always taking the central point. The mother-in-law is the centre of a family. With wives, men hide behind the air of bravado, which is basically a defence mechanism, I think. Clever creatures, women. Very clever.[21]

Boaden pressed the point that many women were put off by Dawson's jokes, perceiving them as derogatory, which the comedian dismissed as 'very silly ... the prerequisite of having intelligence is being able to laugh at yourselves'. It must also be acknowledged that neither the wife or mother-in-law characters depicted in Dawson's jokes were ever likely to pass an Olympic-standard hormone test. When Dawson died, Helen Lederer, part of that alternative comedy movement, wrote a warm tribute in the *Observer*, in which she accepted his explanation for the wife and mother-in-law jokes and said, 'I never met Les Dawson ... But I'd have liked to. I would have liked him. You can just tell, can't you? ... He was a pre-alternative to the alternatives.' Lederer was sure that Dawson's comedy was not rooted in misogyny, and suggested that if it had been, he wouldn't have been as funny as he was, asking, 'How many times do people laugh at the comedy of hate – where the comic is so full of venom the gags just disappear up their own venomous orifices?'[22] So, the alternatives were happy to let Dawson ply his trade, undisturbed, even respected from afar, but the fact that nobody paired him with any of the younger turns on television until near the end of his career represented a massive missed opportunity, both for Dawson and the younger comedians. It wouldn't have been impossible. Paul Jackson, the producer/director who spearheaded the alternative comedy revolution on BBC television with *The Young Ones* was also an experienced producer of the more traditional variety and comedy shows like *The Two Ronnies*. In general, though, the alternatives were BBC2 material, while Dawson was perceived as a mainstream BBC1 personality.

It was a source of some anguish to Dawson that, just as his personal happiness was on the up, his professional fortunes seemed to be heading into decline. As ever, though, quiet patches could be filled with writing, and when not required to perform, Dawson would take to his study and work on another book. Part of the joy was the freedom. 'I can't work to a routine – never could,' he told the *Radio Times* in 1989. 'I once met novelist Nicholas Monsarrat, who told me how he'd march into his study at 6 a.m. and work a nine-hour day. I could never do that.' Each morning after breakfast, Dawson would disappear to his room 'for an hour or so' in which he would 'prepare a few ideas, and somehow get a couple of thousand words down'.[23] The best of Dawson's latter-day literary offerings was a collection of essays entitled *Les Dawson Gives Up,* inspired directly by the instructions he had been given by medical professionals to cut back on all of his vices. On nutrition, he declared that:

> Chips, sausages, red meat, fried bacon will thicken my arteries until I finally expire clutching a slice of gammon in a disco. When I was a lad, eggs, milk and butter were prized for building a sturdy body ... Now I'm

told that they're bad for me, that they could shorten my lifespan, and I won't live to see my grandchildren get divorced ... Salads invariably form the basic ingredients of a diet. Lettuce and more bloody lettuce, tomatoes, cottage cheese and celery are sluiced down with grapefruit juice. Sugar is a bigger enemy than the Third Reich and so you use 'sweeteners' that were probably the by-product of chemical warfare ... Within a week, you're wearing National Health blinkers to stop you gazing into shop windows that sell pies and aromatic cooked meats.[24]

While most of the book is exaggerated for comic effect, some of the situations have their basis in fact. Dawson's suggestions on how to continue smoking surreptitiously while convincing loved ones that you've given up are elaborate and improbable but, in real life, Dawson secreted packets of fags around the house when told to stop smoking.

Rather less enjoyable were the trio of novels he produced for Robson Books: *Come Back with the Wind*; *Well Fared, My Lovely*; and *The Blade and the Passion*. Having tackled life, the universe and everything without once cracking wise in *A Time Before Genesis*, it was back to comedy with diminishing returns. The main problem with these late-period Dawson comic novels is that they forsake plot for punchlines. Earlier works like *Hitler Was My Mother-in-Law* and *The Spy Who Came ...* have their own admittedly demented internal logic, and the jokes are deployed in the service of telling the story. In his final three novels, the story is all too often a slender excuse for the gags. The best of the three is *Well Fared, My Lovely*, published in 1991, a spoof of the hard-boiled Raymond Chandler style of detective story. It succeeds because Dawson had a strong working knowledge of the genre as a reader, and also because Chandler had himself been in the one-liner business.

As Dawson recuperated from his Blackpool collapse, he and Tracy began to plan an occasion that would, at least temporarily, banish any fears and concerns about his health: their wedding. The date was set at 6 May 1989, two days before Dawson's charity golf tournament at Royal Lytham, and the venue chosen was Lytham's architecturally outstanding United Reformed Church, known locally as 'the White Church'. Tracy favoured a quiet occasion, but Dawson was insistent on a proper big affair, even to the point of agreeing to wear white tie and tails, despite looking 'like a beached sperm whale in it'.[25] Entertainment for the 500 guests, including numerous celebrity friends, was, naturally, high on the agenda, and Dawson contacted Brian Fitzgerald, previously of the Northern Dance Orchestra and the comedian's former musical director from *Listen to Les*, to put together a band for the night. Unsurprisingly, the line-up was a virtual reunion of the NDO, including Dawson's old friend and benefactor Johnny Roadhouse on lead alto saxophone. 'He wanted us because we were all very friendly,' Roadhouse explained. 'It was his family. He never forgot. It was a good do.'[26]

Roadhouse's main memory of the day had nothing to do with the music, though. A friend had provided a vintage Rolls-Royce as a stylish mode of transport, but on the way to the reception, the car developed a problem. 'I've had a few vintage Rolls-Royces in my time, and this one was beautiful, but there was a driveway up to this place, and halfway up, it stopped,' Roadhouse recalled, 'and we all had to get out and push this bloody thing up to the wedding reception. We got him going again. That was a good start to the day, wasn't it?' One of the guests was Alan Hart, the *News of the World*'s Manchester-based correspondent, who relates that the happy couple 'retired at around 10 p.m., I recall, and I filed a few final words for the *News of the World* wedding story. I was relaxing at the bar at midnight with a couple of other guests when Les came down from his bridal suite to join us for drinks. He then spent two hours telling jokes to an audience of three, including the night barman.'[27]

After the Golf Classic and a honeymoon in Scotland, Dawson returned to work in earnest for the first time in nearly a year for an eight-week summer season at the Festival Theatre in Paignton, Devon, with Peter Goodwright and Dana. Once again, the company gave their all, but all too frequently to a half-empty house. Local theatre bosses were beginning to question the wisdom of putting on two big variety shows at both Torquay and Paignton, rather than concentrating on one big show.

In Dawson's television career, *Blankety Blank* was losing some of its appeal for viewers, although how much of this was down to the programme itself getting old and tired and how much was down to scheduling is open to question. Ever since Dawson had taken over in 1984, the show had been a staple of the Friday night BBC1 schedules, but when it returned for a new series in September 1989, it had been moved to 8 p.m. on Thursdays. On the up side, Dawson had been approached by Stewart Morris with a view to mounting a new series of *The Les Dawson Show*. Officially, Dawson was still under orders to take it easy, but the prospect of working with his old friend and reminding viewers that he was more than just a game show host proved irresistible. Morris was one of the Corporation's most experienced and innovative light entertainment directors, a former head of BBC TV variety and a man of withering sarcastic wit. He and Dawson had known each other for twenty years, and had worked together when Dawson guested on Morris-produced shows, and also on numerous stage productions. The comedian knew he would be in safe hands.

New writers – including Charlie Adams, Paul Alexander and Gavin Osbon – were enlisted for the show, but, as ever, Dawson penned his own monologues, and then dictated them to Morris's production assistant Lydia Vine, an experience he found slightly alarming, as Vine relates:

> I'd take it down in shorthand, which wasn't easy, and of course he'd stop and say, 'You're not laughing.' I'd say, 'You cannot laugh and take shorthand, because you'll lose it. I'm sorry.' 'Well, it's very off-putting just dictating it with nobody even chuckling.' I said, 'Well, my shorthand only has a lifespan of about ten minutes before I have to get it down.' I was concentrating tremendously hard with this eminent comedian doing his full bit down the phone to me. I could never be an audience as well as take it down.[28]

Working on a weekly show with Dawson, Vine noticed his tendency to recycle material, sometimes rather too quickly. 'I did occasionally have to say to him, "Les, you did that last week,"' Vine admits. 'He'd say, "They'll never notice."'

The infusion of new blood did the revived series a power of good. Also, much to Dawson's delight, the budget allowed for a twenty-five-piece orchestra in vision behind him, under the direction of John Coleman, who had worked with Dawson on his first BBC series. Large troupes of dancers were conspicuous by their absence, and the shows are all the better for this. This isn't to say that the shows were completely dance-free, as each contained a feature for Lia Malcolm and Wayne Eagling from the Royal Ballet. In fact, the 1989 run of *The Les Dawson Show* is quality all the way. Dawson seems happy and confident in his surroundings and with his noticeably fresher material, and the direction is, as expected, first-rate.

In the last show of the series, a running joke is set up at the start, with a crate on stage marked 'BBC ACCOUNTS DEPT'. The crate shakes and monstrous noises are to be heard from within, but each guest is required to leave the stage via the crate to collect their fee. As the credits roll, Dawson walks off, and the punchline to the crate joke is revealed, with the door opening slightly, and a live penguin emerging. The delightful surrealism of this pay-off is underlined by the way the penguin appears to respond to the audience's applause. The guests included *All Creatures Great and Small* star and old panto colleague Christopher Timothy, in a good sketch where Timothy purports to be a down-at-heel acting tutor working from a sparsely furnished garret just up the stairs from an Asian foot masseur and 'Fi Fi – French lessons'. Late for his session due to being waylaid by Fi Fi, Dawson, in full Rathbone Mole outfit, is informed by his teacher that he is not the only luminary to call in that day:

TIMOTHY: You've just missed Roger Moore, you know.
DAWSON: Roger Moore? You give acting lessons to Roger Moore?
TIMOTHY: Indeed I do.

DAWSON: Right, I'm off.

TIMOTHY: Pray, tarry a while. As we say in the theatre, the secret of a good performance is restraint.

DAWSON: What a strange utterance. That's precisely what Fi Fi said when she chained me to the floorboards … Just a minute, hold fast, sirrah, I sincerely hope you're not one of those out-of-work actor laddies, who'll take the money and run?

TIMOTHY: How dare you. I'll have you know that my name in a script is like money in the bank.

DAWSON: Yes, I know, and it guarantees very little interest. I know of your work on the stage, Timothy, you've been in more turkeys than Paxo.

TIMOTHY: I've conquered the West End. You saw me, remember. *Underneath the Arches.*

DAWSON: Was it you I tripped over?

TIMOTHY: Do you wish to continue with these lessons or do you not?

DAWSON: What do I have to do?

TIMOTHY: I need to see if you have the rudiments.

DAWSON: I didn't think I had to have a medical.[29]

Unfortunately, the series was not a ratings success and, once again, scheduling is likely to have been the culprit. It was decided to halt the run of *Blankety Blank* for six weeks, to make way for the variety shows, then resume the quiz series, with enough programmes already recorded to last into March 1990. The whole exercise had shades of Yorkshire Television's tendency to over-expose Dawson. On top of this, when watched over twenty years later, the variety shows come across as quintessential Saturday night viewing, rather than something to go out on a Thursday, straight after *EastEnders*. The option to make more was not picked up, and it's a great shame, as the only thing that makes the 1989 series uncomfortable viewing in retrospect is Dawson's apparent shortness of breath, particularly during the monologues. This worrying detail would become more noticeable over the following years.

The termination of *The Les Dawson Show* was not the end for the comedian's professional association with Stewart Morris, though. In 1987, BBC TV had revived the show that had brought Dawson to national prominence, this time with Bob Monkhouse presenting, under the title *Bob Says Opportunity Knocks*. When, in 1989, Monkhouse opted to take a lucrative offer from Central Television to host the revival of the US game show *The $64,000 Question*, it was decided that *'Opnox'* would continue, with Dawson taking over as host. If nothing else, it made for a nice publicity angle, an alumnus of the show coming back to host it over twenty years later. Sadly, it was a bad fit. Royston Mayoh, who had directed the show in the ABC Manchester days, had a clear idea of why it didn't work:

> The thing about *Opportunity Knocks* – and these were rules that were broken by their [the BBC's] version of it, first with Bob Monkhouse, and then with Les – the compère must not in any way, shape or form be a performer who can outperform anybody on that bill. Don't open with Les's stand-up. What chance has the comic on the bill got? Don't use the interview as a vehicle for comedy. That's what they did, and you mustn't do that. With *Opportunity Knocks*, you've got two shows running – the talent show and the interviews, which were a public service, where you're talking to the Mayor of Bradford, or the person who's dug the biggest hole. They missed that and they turned it into the Les Dawson show, and then by the side, *Opportunity Knocks*. Interviewing the comic before he goes on, it's rubbish. Don't break the image. If Les had been interviewed before he'd gone on, he couldn't have opened with the line about talking rubbish when you're nervous.[30]

Morris spent some considerable time and effort fending off helpful suggestions from Hughie Green about how to run the show. 'We paid him £5000 a week on the condition he didn't come near the studio,' Morris said in 2005. 'All he wanted to do was knock everything.'[31]

The series culminated in a live final, transmitted from Studio D at the BBC's Elstree centre, formerly the studios of Lew Grade's ATV, on 2 June 1990, won by singer Mark Rattray. Footage from the dress rehearsal held earlier in the afternoon shows Dawson overcoming his natural disinclination to rehearse and taking the work very seriously, making mental notes on what he was to do on the show itself, knowing live transmissions to be a high-stakes business. The transmission itself was a success, and a fragment of studio banter recorded just after the show came off-air gives an insight into the relationship between Dawson and Morris, and Morris's hopes for the future of the series. The recording begins with warm-up man Bobby Bragg telling Dawson that the producer is on his way:

DAWSON: He's out of his brains. Totally out of his brains. He's no right to produce. He couldn't produce a fart in a colander. No bloody right.

BRAGG: He's on his way. He's in the other gallery.

DAWSON: Have you seen the size of him? He'll have to come in a convoy.

BRAGG: Mr Stewart Morris.

DAWSON: Here's our Stewart Morris.

MORRIS: [*Putting his arm around Dawson*] Ladies and gentlemen, how about this incredible man? Pound-for-pound, I think we're the best value in television. I think to have taken over as he has and made this series what it is, you're brilliant. Thank you. Well done. [*Morris looks around for the teleprompter with his closing spiel*]

DAWSON: You don't even know your own bloody cameras do you? You're good at shouting from up there. [*Dawson points up towards gallery, smiling, then turns to orchestra and mimes a swaggering walk*]

MORRIS: I wish the audience could see what they're doing to me. On the teleprompter, they've put up a row of dots for me. Quite seriously, I'd like to thank the artists … it's an honour for us, and please God, may this show continue.[32]

Morris's wish was not granted. The show had been losing viewers under Bob Monkhouse, dropping from 11 million to 7 million during the course of the previous run, and Dawson's intervention had failed to arrest the decline. It soon became apparent that the *Blankety Blank* run that had ended on 12 March 1990 would also be the last, leaving Dawson without a regular outlet on national television for the first time in over a decade. 'Had some august figure at the BBC declared that Dawson was to be made redundant?' he wondered. 'Had I offended someone there? Never handling money well, I was not in a position to get out of the business; saving for a rainy day was never a favourite axiom of mine, and I viewed the future with apprehension.'[33] At the time, Dawson admitted to the *Daily Express* that '*Blankety Blank* needed resting' but seemed hurt by the fact that the BBC didn't 'seem to have any other plans for me at all'.[34] The professional problems were leavened by the pleasure of eldest daughter Julie's wedding in September 1990, at which he used his father-of-the-bride speech to 'roast' anyone in earshot, including many of the groom's relatives. Being Les, he got away with lines that might otherwise have caused mortal offence.

In fact, some people at the BBC did have exciting plans for Dawson. The call came from the drama department at the Corporation's Pebble Mill studios in Birmingham for Dawson to play the title role in a BBC2 production of the Argentinian political satire *La Nona*, written in the seventies by Roberto Cossa. Starring alongside Dawson were Jim Broadbent, Timothy Spall, Liz Smith, Sue Brown and a then almost unknown Jane Horrocks. Nona is the 100-year-old grandmother of a Buenos Aires family struggling to survive in times of great privation, and Dawson plays her as a cross between a South American cousin of Ada and the Grandma from Carl Giles's *Daily Express* cartoons. With very little money coming in and rampant inflation rendering any cash worthless almost immediately, everybody in the family has to make sacrifices – apart, that is, from Nona, who has a ravenous appetite that has to be fed. The dialogue spoken by Nona consists mostly of demands for foodstuffs, while the action of the play enters the realms of farce as the family try various ruses first to marry off the old crone and then to kill her off. The BBC production set the drama in 1982, at the time of the Falklands War. In fact, the play is an allegory. The family represents the Argentinian people, and La Nona is the military dictatorship that ruled over them, causing massive inflation and poverty. Keith Salmon was senior cameraman on the play, and he remembers that Dawson 'approached the job very professionally, was very pleasant to work with and showed little glimmers of humour from time to time during rehearsal ... Les must have been under quite a lot of pressure with such a distinguished cast around him ... [but he] rose to the occasion and gave a very good performance.'[35] The role involved a lot of eating or rather appearing to eat, at which Dawson had a great deal of practice and experience, but his attitude to rehearsal and recording is consistent with his approach to all so-called legitimate work. In comedy, he knew his abilities well enough to mess around. In drama, he felt like the apprentice rather than the master.

Pantomime remained a constant through the years of Dawson's fading fortunes at the BBC, often in partnership with John Nettles. Christmas 1989 had taken Dawson to the Empire in Sunderland for a season of *Jack and the Beanstalk* with Liverpudlian comedian Ted Robbins. Dawson had misgivings about the booking, knowing that Sunderland was 'not the easiest of venues to play', especially if you weren't from the north-east. Slim advance bookings seemed to underline his fears, and the show itself confirmed them. It wasn't, he said later, 'a bad pantomime, but it lacked ... glitter and imagination ... I got the feeling that the production had been conceived in a burning desire to see how cheaply it could be staged. Some of the scenery looked as if it had once graced a Second World War ENSA concert. The whole thing smacked of accountancy.'[36]

A story that has gained currency is that, during the run, Dawson had an unnerving experience in his dressing room. He never talked about what he was supposed to have seen, although his interest in the paranormal and the fact that Sid James had died while working at the same theatre have both been significant in its retelling. Thankfully, the following Christmas saw Dawson and Nettles in *Dick Whittington* at the Palace Theatre in Manchester, where success was almost guaranteed for one of the city's favoured sons. So it proved, with healthy bookings and a happy run.

Finally, in early 1991, came a call from the BBC, which had bought a new game show format called *Fast Friends* and decided Dawson was the man to present it. On the plus side, he would be reunited with his friend and *Blankety Blank* producer Stanley Appel. On the down side, the show was needlessly complex. It began with a stage containing two teams of twenty people. One had to choose the four friends most likely to answer questions correctly and increase their chance of winning the holiday star prize. Dawson described it as an American show that should have stayed in America. Crucially, it had been an American show that had never proceeded past the pilot stage in its homeland, and Dawson's experience on the series indicated why.

The show went from vague possibility to reality with what both host and producer regarded as indecent haste. 'What happened was that the show was given to me suddenly,' Appel reveals. 'They gave it to him, me as well, too quickly. "You're doing the show, you're in the studio in two weeks time." We knew nothing about it. It was very complicated. We had no time to plan anything. It was quite a difficult show for Les to remember all the different things, and we didn't have time to work out how the things would work. It was a total disaster.'[37]

The first show went out on Saturday, 30 March 1991, at 7 p.m., but by the third week of the series, Margaret Forwood of the *Daily Express* was already thinking it had outstayed its welcome. 'How Les Dawson's *Fast Friends* hangs on to its Saturday night slot is as big a mystery as what has happened to Les' hair,' she mused, alluding to the fact that the comedian's greying thatch was now a straw colour.[38] Forwood's view was prescient and the programme was moved to Friday nights from show eight onwards. The critics' misgivings about the show were clearly shared by Dawson himself, and not just retrospectively. There are moments on the recordings where the poor man has a look on his face that indicates he'd rather be somewhere, anywhere else. It was a duff format, but with a game show technician like Bob Monkhouse or Bruce Forsyth at the helm, it might have been saved from being a complete and utter waste of videotape. Dawson was not a technician. The joy of *Blankety Blank* was the minimalism of the game itself, leaving plenty of space for the host to stamp his personality on proceedings. *Fast Friends* was anything but minimalist, as Dawson himself acknowledged:

> Rehearsals were full of the sort of happy anticipation usually associated with a grave-robber's lunch break … and nothing went right. Behind me … was a sort of screen with a string of lights in a semi-circle over the top. The contestants sat slightly below me, divided into teams, and each team had to select a team leader, who then pranced on to the rostrum with me, one on each side. I now asked one of them to pick a member of his or her team to answer a question, while the string of lights above me clicked off the number of seconds it took the team member to answer. (Have you got it? Good, because I couldn't get the hang of the game, and tempers began to fray.)[39]

The amount of business to cover in a half-hour show was such that meeting each contestant consisted of a quick hello followed by a one-liner, whereas Dawson's interaction with the contestants had been one of the main selling points of *Blankety Blank*. Only occasionally did he allow himself a longer chat, as with a lady on one show who responds to his question about her profession with 'retired shop-keeper'. Dawson enquires as to whether it was a 'proper old shop', then the pair of them lapse into an impromptu and all too brief Cissie and Ada dialogue.

Dawson and Appel didn't need to wait for ratings to know that their show had tanked. Not even their combined professional experience could make it anything other than a car crash in weekly instalments. 'We returned home from Elstree after canning the series and I wanted to go into immediate hiding, but Tracy pulled me out of the coal cellar,' Dawson recalled. In *No Tears for the Clown*, the man who had made a virtue of failure gave the impression of feeling unwanted at this stage of his career, but it wasn't strictly true. He had to admit that he had been offered theatre work for summer 1991, not in a variety show, but at Bournemouth in the play *Boeing, Boeing*. However, Dawson didn't think he was right for the part on offer, so declined.

He was less willing to pass up on panto at the Wimbledon Theatre, where he was due to reprise the previous year's production of *Dick Whittington* with his friend John Nettles. The southern audiences were receptive and responsive, and all seemed to be going well until Saturday, 21 December, when Dawson began to complain of chest problems. On returning to their accommodation after the evening's show, Dawson collapsed. Tracy called a doctor, and Dawson was rushed to the Westminster Hospital's intensive care cardiac ward. After evasive action, the distinct possibility that Dawson might be mortally ill receded. The situation had been caused by a build-up of fluid on the lungs, putting pressure on his heart. Once again, Dawson was told to give up smoking, and to cut out his beloved Scotch in favour of a moderate intake of wine and beer. This time, for a change, he listened and complied, to a greater degree than ever before. The message had got through. There was no question of returning to the pantomime, into which Bernard Cribbins had stepped to fill some of the gap left by the ailing star.

Before the health scare, 1991 had been enlivened slightly by a spat with Bernard Manning. Both comedians were burly and Mancunian, but there the similarities ended, Dawson having gone down a self-consciously clean and inoffensive comedic path. Asked by a *Guardian* journalist what he made of his near-contemporary, Dawson had dismissed Manning's audience as 'gum-chewing morons who've got tattoos'. [40] It seems a curious outburst for a man whose motto was 'Be kind', but it sits very comfortably with Pete Warde's estimation in *A Card for the Clubs* of the crowds that gave him the bum's rush. It was a risky comment to make, though. Although Dawson might have felt safe admitting his reservations to a paper like the *Guardian*, he must have realized that it might be picked up and taken out of context by the tabloids. As it was, the only fallout happened in the pages of *The Stage*. Responding, Manning said:

> It doesn't bother me, as long as they don't get the wage packets mixed up! I have never looked upon him as a comic. He's mostly a dame in

pantomime ... It doesn't offend anyone, it's absolutely magic, my act. The proof of the pudding is in the eating. I drive a Rolls-Royce Silver Spirit. What does Les Dawson drive? It certainly won't be a Rolls Silver Spirit ... He grew up in the same neighbourhood as me and I don't think anybody knows him. I have got four LPs out, videos, Royal Command performances, Las Vegas, you name it I have done it. I don't think they have ever heard of Les Dawson in Las Vegas ... It's disgusting. Men are men and women are women and never the twain shall meet. If you've got to dress up as a woman to get laughs it's time to turn it in.[41]

For all the bravado, the writer of *The Stage*'s story noted that Manning was 'clearly stung'. Indeed, most of his criticisms of Dawson make very little sense. Manning performed once by royal command, as part of the cast of *The Comedians* at a London Palladium gala on 22 May 1972, but never figured in the bill of the annual *Royal Variety Performance*, unlike Dawson, who appeared three times at the big prestige show, in 1973, 1979 and 1987. Manning's Las Vegas achievement was not all that it was made out to be, either. Indeed, as Jonathan Margolis noted in his *Independent* obituary of Manning, 'it was only one afternoon appearance as part of a Granada documentary'.[42] To be fair, Manning did go down well that day and was offered further lucrative work in the US, but declined because of his commitments back home in Manchester.

Manning continued his offensive a year later when interviewed by Robert Chalmers for the *Observer*, who noted, with some alarm, that Manning's 'current act features a routine about the death of Les Dawson – an event which, Manning implies, may be imminent'. Chalmers asked Manning what he thought of Dawson's 'Be kind' motto, to which Manning replied, 'Yeah, well, he'll wind up fucking skint won't he ... He's not in my fucking league. He's third division. He dresses up as women.'[43]

Was there genuine bad blood between the two men, leading to this extraordinary exchange? Could there have been some event in their pre-fame history that turned them into bitter rivals? Possibly, but it's unlikely. The simple fact is that Manning insulted his peers largely for sport, and knocking Dawson had been part of his repertoire since at least the mid-eighties, when *The Stage* documented the fact in a review, which described Manning as:

> A man whose level of humour rarely rises above the belt, unless it's to dwell light-heartedly on the gallows he erects [*sic*] to poke fun at those no longer in a position to defend themselves.
>
> Starting with Arthur Askey he works through Leonard Rossiter, John Lennon, Judy Garland, Isabel Barnett [*sic*] – in fact anyone whose memory has hitherto been thought secure in the affections of the public – and onto a number of sacred cows who presumably would be well able to take care of themselves. The list is long and catholic (pun intentional), from the Pope, Billy Graham and Jess Yates to Dame Vera Lynn, Les Dawson and the Right Honourable Margaret Thatcher.[44]

Having been needled for so long, maybe it should have come as no surprise that Dawson did decide to react, finally, in that *Guardian* interview.

When keen to drum up a bit of publicity, Manning would insult a fellow comedian within earshot of a journalist, but many of the comedians he was harshest about were good friends. The gaff was blown somewhat in 1983 when fellow comedian and host of LWT's quiz game *Punchlines*, Lennie Bennett, told the *Daily Mirror* that 'I think [Bernard]'s been misguided by knocking his mates over the years … Off stage he's a real pussycat, and he should start showing his nice side to the paying public.'[45] Naturally, Manning responded by pointing out that Bennett had never taken part in a *Royal Variety Performance* or played America, but it seems that Bennett was on the money.

Manning's claim that Dawson was not in his league is a curious one. Dawson was a true original, whereas Manning's main selling point was his delivery of gags that anyone could tell, and frequently did. When it came to material, Manning was in the habit of receiving stolen goods. A story told by Barry Cryer underlines his approach to harvesting the gags:

There was a break-in at the Embassy Club one night. Bernard had gone, it was four o'clock in the morning or something. He was in bed, but they brought him back. Nothing gone. No money, no costumes, no booze. Nothing. One of the coppers ... there was a wall in the club, sounds weird now, whitewashed, and the copper asked 'why?'. Bernard would book a comic in his club and watch them, and nick jokes he liked, but he wrote on the wall with a pen, the odd word. Somebody had broken in, and whitewashed his jokes. Nobody was charged. The story went around the business: 'Somebody's whitewashed Bernard's fucking wall.'[46]

Patter apart, there were other obvious differences between the two comedians. While Dawson was a Tory voter in 1979, that was the year in which Manning became an abstainer after years of supporting the Labour party. The supposedly racist Manning was a man of left-wing sympathies, while the more tolerant Dawson favoured the Conservatives. Manning spent his entire married life in a modest semi-detached house in Harpurhey, near where he grew up, while Dawson, as soon as he could afford it, bought a big house in Lytham with a swimming pool. Manning avoided leaving Manchester for long periods of time, ideally coming straight home from gigs no matter where they were in the British Isles, and he never travelled abroad between his National Service and the Granada-sponsored visit to Las Vegas. Dawson relished a change of scenery, and displayed a penchant for expensive holidays, particularly as a source of material when they went wrong. Manning frequently railed against the sort of comedians who played golf. Dawson played golf, but, by his own admission, very badly. Dawson, after his run of money worries, was worth about £1.3m when he died, while Manning's estate was closer to £10m when he died in 2007. It's possible that Dawson made more than Manning and spent most of it, because Manning was far from extravagant. However, Manning was also a shrewd businessman who ran his own small chain of clubs, while Dawson always worked for others. Coming from greengrocery to the licensed trade in the fifties, Manning was shocked and delighted at the differences between the two forms of business. 'We went overnight from taking hundreds of pounds a week, to thousands,' Manning told his biographer Jonathan Margolis. 'And the beauty of the club business is there is no waste ... Bananas ripening, going yellow, then getting spotted, then they'd go black and they'd have to be thrown away. With beer, it lasts for months and months in a barrel. We couldn't believe it. With no waste, it's liquid gold.'[47] As obvious as the differences are, there were a number of parallels between the two men. The most obvious was size, although Dawson always carried his bulk more gracefully than Manning. Both comedians also held W.C. Fields in high regard, with friends of the young Manning recalling him 'laughing his head off' at Fields's work when it came to the local cinema. 'I love sarcastic comedy,' Manning told Margolis. Another was that both men lost their wives in 1986, Vera Manning succumbing to a heart attack.

Manning and Dawson reacted in different ways to their declining television fame. Dawson saw clearly that he had to adapt to a new market and a new audience in order to remain relevant and bankable, whereas when producers stopped calling Manning, he retreated to Harpurhey and ramped up the profane, offensive material that he knew would appeal to the core Embassy Club audience. The chance for Dawson to test himself in a new arena came in late September 1992, after a summer in Bournemouth in *Run For Your Wife*. He appeared on a BBC2 panel game called *The Brain Drain*, made by Hat Trick Productions, in which audience members put questions on burning topics of the day to a panel of comedians. The company was making many of the new wave of hit BBC2 and Channel 4 comedy shows, including *Have I Got News For You, Drop the Dead Donkey* and *Whose Line Is It Anyway?*, so for an old-school BBC1 comic to get the call to appear on one of their programmes was a vote of confidence. But a degree of cynicism was involved too. 'We weren't getting noticed quite enough, so you put Les Dawson on, and you get a bit of press for that,' explains the show's producer and co-creator Dan Patterson. 'To get Les Dawson was quite an exciting booking.'[48]

At first Dawson – looking and sounding healthier than he had for some time – seemed nervous, responding to host Jimmy Mulville's gently knocking introduction with a cry of 'Boom boom boom boom!' He soon settled in, though, and his response to the first question – 'Which subject would you like to see taught in schools? – produced gales of laughter and thunderous applause, after which he could do no wrong. To be fair, he didn't venture into uncharted territory to get the laugh, as his response – "A love of ecology' – is merely a pretext to present the young audience with a refurbished version of the monologue about the duck with breeding trouble first heard in *Listen to Les* seventeen years earlier. It doesn't matter, though, because the gag was paced brilliantly and, crucially, most of the punters had never heard it before. For comic effect, fellow panellist Angus Deayton kept a straight face and looked at his watch midway through Dawson's monologue, while Tony Hawks watched appreciatively, but Craig Ferguson, later to become a top US TV chat show host, and Jimmy Mulville were unable to suppress their genuine and uproarious guffaws of delight at Dawson's shtick.

Patterson was equally delighted: 'I remember bits where I was thinking, "This is a very funny man," and it was a younger audience for that show, but they still liked him. It was the first time I'd heard some of [Dawson's jokes]. He'd gone down well and I thought, "This guy's a very class act."' He was, however, slightly alarmed by the apparent change in Dawson's affable personality once the main part of the recording had been dealt with. 'I had to do pick-ups to make sure I wouldn't get stuck with really difficult edits, and he was giving me a really hard time over it in a jokey way, but I couldn't tell whether it was really jokey,' the producer explains. 'Usually I get abuse from people when I'm doing things, but it's clear that they're slightly pissed off, but they're joking. I couldn't tell with him whether he was absolutely pissed off or whether he was just playing the audience.' Given his lifelong aversion to overcooking the material, and the fact that he'd just come through what he felt to be a high-pressure gig unscathed, it's most likely that he just wanted to get to the bar. This final detail apart, Patterson went away favourably disposed to Dawson, and would undoubtedly have booked him again had the opportunity arisen: 'He was great, Les. It was a bit like Peter Cook, one of those people you feel privileged to work with. He was very bright. I liked him. It was just that last ten minutes of the recording where I was thinking, "I'm not sure whether he just hates me or is putting it on."'[49]

Dawson had met with the younger generation of comedians, and succeeded on his own terms. Admittedly, some of the material was well tested. When Dawson told Dave Lanning of the *TV Times* in 1967 that 'I'm no different. Neither is the act', he wasn't saying it to be self-deprecating. He had spent the previous ten years honing his material, and when he came to fame, he already had a sizeable core repertoire that he knew worked. Although he was always making notes and adding new jokes and situations over the years, many of the lines that had stood him in good stead during the years of struggle continued to give useful service until his death. One producer who had worked with Dawson and was given the job of compiling a tribute programme was surprised by the extent to which old favourites recurred. It was a tribute to Dawson's delivery and the affection in which he was held by audiences that he was able to make his oldest jokes sound fresh nearly every time. People either failed to notice the repetition, forgave it, or, perhaps most likely of all, welcomed it, greeting each one of the more venerable gags – 'I could tell the mother-in-law was coming to visit, because the mice were throwing themselves on the traps' or 'The wife's run off with the bloke next door. I do miss him' – as old friends.

Work uncertainty apart, the Dawson that had appeared on *The Brain Drain* was a very happy man indeed, as Tracy was in the final stages of pregnancy and the comedian was on the verge of becoming a father for the fourth time. Like Meg, Tracy Dawson had experienced miscarriages, so expert advice was sought, while Dawson feared that he would be the weak link in the chain due to his health issues. 'I had a weight problem,' he rationalized, 'I'd had a mild heart attack; I no longer had a prostate gland ... I was a heavy drinker and smoked like a kipper-curing shed.'[50] Mercifully, his fertility belied his condition, resulting in the birth at St Mary's in Manchester on Saturday, 3 October 1992, of a 5lb 6oz girl they named Charlotte Emily Lesley. Just as Tracy had become Dawson's constant companion, so the comedian was determined not to be an absentee father this time round. 'He was a devoted father. He doted on Charlotte,' Stanley Appel observes, but adds, 'He used to talk about Charlotte far more than his other children. I don't know if the other children resented it or not.'[51] To be fair, Appel wasn't around when Dawson's elder children were Charlotte's age, so he may well have been equally effusive about them at that time.

The acquisition of a stepmother had been problematic for Julie, Stuart and Pamela, not helped by their father's unwillingness to be open with them at the outset about the burgeoning relationship. He had worried that they would react badly and had tried to protect them from the truth, when they'd rather have known the situation from the start. His closer interest in the new child was not so much a question of greater love, rather a reflection of the changes in parental roles that had occurred in the intervening twenty years. Dawson wished he had spent more time at home in his elder children's formative years and was now making the most of the chance to be a hands-on father.

Although he had no current BBC commitments, the Corporation claimed him as their own in a trade advertisement after he won Variety Performer of the Year at the 1992 British Comedy Awards. His acceptance speech at the ceremony gave him a chance to remind younger producers in the audience of his abilities, although the producer of the event already knew him well, being Michael Hurll, who'd booked him on *Cilla* twenty-four years earlier. The award was a welcome fillip as he prepared to go into *Dick Whittington* at the Theatre Royal in Plymouth with his old friend Peter Goodwright. After the medical trouble that had caused him to pull out of pantomime the previous year, Dawson was pleased to be asked to do the show, and with his new-found enthusiasm for moderation and exercise was in a far better condition to perform than in previous years.

So it was that the run passed without incident, apart from the night that a mysterious figure walked on stage while Dawson was dressed as Britannia and interrupted his flow. The audience knew who the man was, the cast knew too. Only Dawson was incredulous when Michael Aspel indicated his red book and told Dawson that he was being 'Lifed' for the second time. 'Not me. What? Bloody hell,' he spluttered. The pantomime set was then redressed as the *This Is Your Life* set and Dawson returned in a suit, clearly mouthing 'Bastards' with a slightly shell-shocked twinkle in his eye at Goodwright and fellow cast member Patrick Mower, who had both been keeping the big secret. Baby Charlotte is present at the start of the show, but is soon taken away to sleep by a nanny. The look of concern as Dawson clearly fears he won't get a chance to kiss her goodnight is very affecting.

As, in their way, were the tributes from friends and colleagues, most of them mock-insulting. John Nettles, detained in Stratford, regretted that he couldn't 'be there to lend a cultured gloss to the vulgar proceedings', while Bruce Forsyth – also on tape, in an empty studio ('I hope business is better in Plymouth') – told Dawson, 'If ever I do a piano duet with you, our friendship may have to end.' Speaking from Budapest, Rula Lenska and Dennis Waterman wished Dawson the best, with Waterman reminding his then-wife that 'You've worked with him twice. He's tried to ruin my career hundreds of times.'

It was only natural that Roy Barraclough should break his commitments to be there in person, and he remembered the early days of the Cissie and Ada characters. 'He'd long been an admirer of Norman Evans, as indeed I was,' Barraclough related. 'In those days we used to pre-record loads of sketches without an audience, and you had to hang around for a long time, and people used to get bored, so Les used to amuse all the crew and the technicians and go into this routine, and I joined in.' The anecdote is followed by the pair lapsing into gossip with a discussion about a local spiritualist:

> CISSIE: Mrs Scattergood, she gets all the spirits through her. They come through her weegee.
> ADA: Does she ever get cramp?

Not many of the guests from Dawson's first *Life* had survived the intervening twenty-one years, but Betty Lawrence, his friend and mentor from the fifties London interlude, was present, at which Dawson became genuinely very emotional. Rather lighter in tone was the story of the Duke of Edinburgh and the black puddings, which Dawson was prevailed upon to relate. This was followed by a shot of a communication on Buckingham Palace notepaper saying simply 'Fried!!!, Philip'.[52]

Once Plymouth had been dealt with, it was back to Lytham for writing and bringing up baby. There were dates here and there, such as after-dinner speeches and the odd TV booking as a guest, including appearances on *Aspel and Company* and *Surprise Surprise*. Both shows were made at London Weekend Television, where producers looked to Dawson for the next programme in the prestigious *An Audience With ...* series, a show in which a celebrity keeps a gathering of his or her peers entertained by answering their scripted questions. If all went well, there was a distinct possibility that Dawson might be called upon to cross the river from the BBC and join LWT at the South Bank studios on a more permanent basis.

The comedian had also been enlisted to play a vaudeville comic called Morton Stanley in the Griff Rhys-Jones/Martin Clunes period comedy-drama *Demob*, which had been shot through the spring of 1993. His performance showed a maturity and sense of pace that had eluded him all too often in previous dramatic roles. No lines were garbled this time, and he captured the seediness of the character beautifully, with more than a nod to his hero Bill Fields. It seemed that, although it had taken time to recover from the *Fast Friends* debacle, Dawson was still known in the industry as a man who could deliver, and it appeared that his career would be going in some new and interesting directions. In addition, there were always calls to appear on chat shows and to do guest spots on light entertainment productions. What turned out to be Dawson's last TV interview, on LWT's *Aspel and Company*, with Michael Aspel and alongside fellow piano torturer Jerry Lee Lewis, was transmitted on Saturday, 22 May 1993. Around the same time, he had also recorded an appearance on Cilla Black's *Surprise Surprise*.

Most pleasing of all, though, was the call from Dr Anthony Clare to appear on *In the Psychiatrist's Chair* for Radio 4. Dawson appreciated the way that Clare took him seriously, without being humourless. For his part, Clare had a penchant for befriending comedians – he had become close to Spike Milligan and co-wrote a book on depression with the former Goon – and was fascinated and delighted with the self-educated and deep-thinking Dawson. After the recording, in Manchester, Clare asked if Dawson would come to Dublin to talk to his students about humour, and he agreed readily. The two men parted as friends.

Dawson never did get to Dublin, and *An Audience With Les Dawson* was never made. On 10 June 1993, a week after the radio recording, the comedian was back in Manchester for a medical check-up, as a prelude to trying for another child. As ever, Tracy was with him. While waiting in a cubicle to be seen, he asked her if she could go and get him a newspaper to read. When she returned, her husband was dead, felled by a massive heart attack. He was 62 years old.

Tabloid journalists had joked with Dawson that they were waiting for him to pop his clogs so they could run their pre-prepared 'Last of the Comic Dinosaurs' headlines, but the response to Dawson's demise was unusually respectful. The production team that had been slated to make *An Audience with Les Dawson* refocused and began work on a tribute to the comic, to be hosted by Roy Barraclough. Meanwhile, BBC1's tribute *The Last Laugh* went out on 5 July 1993, consisting of an introduction from Ken Dodd with some clips, then an edited repeat of the 1984 *Favourite Things* documentary. Dawson's appearance on *In the Psychiatrist's Chair* was broadcast by Radio 4 in September, with *Demob* following in October. The LWT tribute was transmitted over Christmas 1993. Once the annual articles remembering that year's deceased had been written, it might have been expected that the name of Les Dawson would fade into a happy half-memory. Instead, he continues to loom large, two decades on.

CHAPTER 8

Post-Dawsonism

On 24 February 1994, family, friends and fans of Les Dawson gathered in Westminster Abbey to pay tribute to a great comedian. Dr Anthony Clare described him as 'an anti-depressant with no side-effects', while actor Edward Woodward noted the greats – dead and alive – who were present in the Abbey. 'We have Edward the Confessor and we have Bruce Forsyth, Robert Browning and Chaucer, not to mention Bobby Davro,' Woodward joked, in the bathetic manner of his chum. Woodward's wife, Michele Dotrice, read an extract from *A Time Before Genesis*, and Mo Moreland and Roy Barraclough also spoke of their departed colleague and friend. Tracy sat in the pews with 16-month-old Charlotte, who did not yet fully comprehend the waves of affection that were filling the room or the fact that they had been inspired by her late father.

From the moment he took part in *Opportunity Knocks* in 1967, Les Dawson was popular. He achieved more than most slum children could ever wish for, but he would have loved to have been taken seriously too. It's impossible to escape the feeling that, if he'd lived a little longer, maybe a decade, he would have finally been given the full respect he was due. Perhaps sadder is the distinct possibility that he might have got that serious recognition during his foreshortened lifetime had he chosen some of his projects more carefully. In retrospect, taking him away from ITV to the BBC in 1977 may have been a mistake. The experimentation of the YTV years was absent during his time at the BBC, when, for many, he was merely a variety comic, albeit an excellent one, and a reluctant, if idiosyncratically brilliant, game show host. Dawson should have found time for that stage version of

The Loner, and should have collaborated far more with Alan Plater, a dramatist who understood him fully. Meanwhile, it is a shame that David Nobbs was commissioned to write nothing but sketches for Dawson. All of these are missed opportunities that might have helped redefine Les Dawson in the way he would have wanted.

Only when the Corporation appeared to have no immediate use for Dawson did he begin to challenge and stretch himself again. Not that the fault is wholly down to BBC pigeonholing. Dawson was often happy to take the path of least resistance as long as it paid well. If he'd stood up for himself a bit more and told Norman Murray and Anne Chudleigh what he would and wouldn't do, it might have been a different matter, but then if he'd spoken up like that, he wouldn't have been easy-going Les, loved by all of his colleagues.

It has to be questioned whether Murray and Chudleigh fully understood their client, or what made him quite so appealing to audiences, a point underlined by Mark Tinkler. While researching material for the LWT tribute show, Tinkler had found a documentary made by the Open University called *Mussolini With Knickers*, all about the phenomenon of the mother-in-law in comedy. Dawson had been interviewed, and Tinkler thought it would make an ideal excerpt. He was told that it would not:

> What came back was that the tape had been shown to Anne Chudleigh, Les's management, which was also the same as Michael Barrymore. They had said that Les had stopped doing mother-in-law jokes years before and wanted the whole section taken out. My protests that he had done mum-in-law jokes just a few days before he died fell on deaf ears because LWT did not want to annoy the management of Michael Barrymore, a VERY big TV fish at that time.[1]

For much of Dawson's career, the constraints of the entertainment industry made it difficult for a comedian to diversify. 'In fact, it's a wonder that he could point to such a variety of achievements. These days it's common for comedians also to be published novelists and straight actors, so he would be in less of a unique position. In the modern world of entertainment, where the year zero of alternative comedy is almost ancient history itself, many older comics have been re-evaluated. It took a single appearance on *Have I Got News For You* in 1994 to change the public's perception of Bob Monkhouse. After years of game shows, he unleashed on TV the comedy brain that he had reserved for his live audiences and won over a younger audience that had been happy to dismiss him before. By the time he died in 2003, he was widely recognized as a skilled stand-up comedian and creator of humorous material. A bright, self-aware man like Dawson could have pulled off a similar reinvention, and would have been in his element in the comedy arena of the twenty-first century. 'If Les was living today, he'd be resident on *QI*,' Royston Mayoh argues, convincingly. 'He and Stephen Fry would be in bed together, if you know what I mean. They've both got the same fascination with that wonderful turn of phrase.'[2]

All of these possibilities have to remain 'what ifs', but there's no question that the name of Les Dawson still inspires huge recognition, awareness and affection. His shows are rarely repeated, but the DVDs of his Yorkshire Television productions have sold well, and stand in contrast to the single, paltry commercially available compilation of his BBC work. Whenever a newspaper story features mothers-in-law, nagging wives or jokes about either (and the subject is a hardy perennial space-filler), the picture editor's first impulse is to reach for a shot of Les as Ada.[3]

Modern television exhibits a sometimes morbid fascination with entertainment's past, and Dawson has been covered extensively, if not always too well, by documentaries. In 1997, well-respected light entertainment producer/historian/biographer John Fisher chose Dawson as the subject for one of his Channel 4 *Heroes of Comedy* shows, part of a long-running series of affectionate, rounded, well-constructed portraits, always notable for their thoughtfully chosen clips and high standard of interviewees. In 2001, ITV's *The Unforgettable ...* series paid warm tribute to Dawson, though the programme was unsatisfyingly short. Then, in 2004, Yorkshire Television produced *Les Dawson's*

Lost Diaries for Channel 4, choosing to dwell on a dark side to Dawson's personality that was completely absent in real life, the false impression causing much anguish to family members who had agreed to participate.

One of the most notable tributes to Dawson came from a younger north-western comedian, Johnny Vegas, who co-wrote and starred in a Radio 4 *Afternoon Play* entitled 'Chequebook and Pen', which was broadcast in December 2010. Using Dawson's takeover of *Blankety Blank* from Terry Wogan as the starting point, Vegas and collaborator Andrew Lynch wove a tale of chicanery, rivalry, cock-up, coincidence and managerial ineptitude, at the centre of which, Dawson – played by Vegas – remained innocent and non-plussed. The result was so much better, more interesting and funnier than the usual run of biographical dramas about beloved comedians.

The books Dawson wrote are now out of print, and *A Time Before Genesis* has become particularly collectable. In 2007, his widow Tracy added to the bibliography with a compilation of notes, jottings and script extracts from his personal files, under the title *Les Dawson's Secret Notebooks*, overseen by Dawson's old publisher, Jeremy Robson. In 2010, the Blackpool *Gazette* produced a book of the 'Dawson Slant' columns from the early eighties, garlanded with pictures of Les from the newspaper's archives. For better or worse, Tracy continues to be a source of tabloid interest, while daughter Charlotte, now a young woman, is trying to forge a career as an actress, model and presenter, making it to the finals of the Miss Manchester title in June 2011. In contrast, Dawson's three eldest children stay out of the public eye quite happily, having made lives and careers outside show business. In some ways, this reflects the different outlook of each of Dawson's wives, Meg being down to earth and focused on home life, while Tracy was always keen to be part of the social whirl. However, it's also a reflection of the changing attitudes of youth, with modern media encouraging celebrity as a viable career option. Doubtless Dawson would have been as proud of the adult Charlotte as he was of Julie, Stuart and Pamela, but he would almost certainly have taken his youngest girl aside and made her fully aware of the pitfalls of fame.

When, in 2008, Tracy Dawson finally succeeded in having her late husband commemorated with a statue in Lytham St Anne's, the unveiling of the monument by Tracy, Mo Moreland and Charlotte was carried live on BBC1's early-evening magazine programme, *The One Show*. It seemed that the only absentees from the well-attended occasion were Julie, Stuart and Pamela Dawson, who felt their father would not have wanted to be commemorated this way. 'We support the idea of a lasting tribute, but feel Dad would have got more joy from more than one project benefiting from the money,' said their press statement,[4] although the newspapers were quick to wonder whether it wasn't more down to the cool relations between the children of his first marriage and Tracy, which had prevailed since the comedian's funeral. In fact, Julie was at the unveiling, with her husband Jon and their daughter Megann. No official invitation had been issued, so they came as private individuals and stayed well in the background. The causes of any family disagreements remain firmly private, although the press have, over the years, emulated Cissie and Ada in their gossip and speculation about legacies and wills.

Dawson's real legacy is his body of work, and the attitude that shone through it, summed up in two simple words. Be kind.

NOTES AND REFERENCES

CHAPTER 1: *'Slumps don't bother me. I was a failure during the boom'*

1 He would break the record officially on 5 February 1931, reaching 245.73 mph.
2 Les Dawson, *Les Dawson's Lancashire* (Elm Tree Books, London, 1983), pp.11–12.
3 'Tailor made for laughs' by Nancy Banks-Smith, *Guardian*, 3 August 1982, p.9.
4 Les Dawson, *A Clown Too Many* (Elm Tree Books, London, 1985), p.4.
5 Manchester *Guardian*, 2 February 1931, p.1.
6 'Progress in slum clearance: Sir Hilton Young on his critics', *The Times*, 19 October 1934, p.9.
7 Albert Hunt, 'Look back in laughter', *Radio Times*, 31 July–6 August 1982, p.12.
8 Dawson, *A Clown Too Many*, pp.ix–x.
9 *Morning in the Streets* (BBC Television, tx: 25 March 1959).
10 'Fascist rally at Manchester', *The Times*, 1 October 1934, p.14.
11 Dawson, *A Clown Too Many*, p.7.
12 'Fascist rally at Manchester', *The Times*, 1 October 1934, p.14.
13 Dawson, *A Clown Too Many*, p.6.
14 Anthony Clare, *In the Psychiatrist's Chair II* (William Heinemann, London, 1995), p.88.
15 Ibid.
16 168 Moston Lane is not listed in the 1942 *Kelly's Directory*, and there is no house of that number in the road now. So the second move might have been one of necessity, following bomb damage or similar. Dawson mentions in *A Clown Too Many* that he and his mother had to vacate one house because of an unexploded bomb in the back garden.
17 Clare, *In the Psychiatrist's Chair II*, p.87.
18 Although registration of stillbirths was and is required, that register is, perhaps understandably, not available for public scrutiny.
19 Clare, *In the Psychiatrist's Chair II*, pp.87–8.
20 Dawson, *A Clown Too Many*, p.5.
21 *This Is Your Life* (Thames Television, tx: 22 December 1971).

22 Dawson, *A Clown Too Many*, p.46.

23 Ibid., p.5.

24 Author's interview with David Nobbs, 22 June 2009.

25 Dawson, *A Clown Too Many*, p.6.

26 Ibid., pp.9–10.

27 Ibid., p.10.

28 Newsreel footage: *Pathetone Parade of 1941*, released 1941.

29 *Parkinson* (BBC1, tx: 16 November 1974).

30 Mike Craig, *Look Back With Laughter*, Volume 2 (Mike Craig, Altrincham, 2001), pp.37–38.

31 Newsreel footage: *Pathetone Weekly 376*, released 7 June 1937.

32 Author's interview with James Casey, 17 June 2009.

33 Hutton Conyers, named after a North Yorkshire village, was played by various performers, including Roy Castle, while Bretton Woods was always portrayed by James's nephew Jack Casey, better known as Eli Woods.

34 James Casey recreates 'The Chipster' with Roy Hudd and Eli Woods in Halls of Fame: Sunderland Empire (BBC1, tx: 18 December 1984).

35 Ibid.

36 Mike Craig, *Look Back With Laughter*, Volume 1 (Mike Craig, Altrincham, 1996), p.48.

37 Ibid., p.33.

38 Author's interview with Barry Cryer, 15 September 2010.

39 Author's interview with James Casey, 17 June 2009.

40 Dawson, *A Clown Too Many*, p.11.

41 Dawson, *A Clown Too Many*, pp.8–9.

42 Clare, *In the Psychiatrist's Chair II*, p.92.

43 Ibid., p.97.

44 Ibid., p.89.

45 Dawson, *A Clown Too Many*, p.12.

46 Ibid.

47 *Les Dawson's Lost Diaries* (Yorkshire Television, tx: 3 April 2004).

48 Author's interview with Andy Hamilton, 15 September 2009.

49 Clare, *In the Psychiatrist's Chair II*, p.88.

50 Dawson, *A Clown Too Many*, p.13.

51 Clare, *In the Psychiatrist's Chair II*, p.91.

52 Dawson, *A Clown Too Many*, p.14.

53 Clare, *In the Psychiatrist's Chair II*, p.91.

54 Dawson, *A Clown Too Many*, p.16.

55 Ibid.

56 Ibid., p.20.

57 Ibid., p.25.

58 Ibid., p.26.

59 *Les Dawson's Lost Diaries* (Yorkshire Television, tx: 3 April 2004).

60 Bob Monkhouse, *Over the Limit: My Secret Diaries 1993–1998* (Century, London, 1998), p.221.

61 This is not intended to cast doubt on whether Dawson read the original stories. I have read them myself several times and still had to check that the bassoon reference was not present.

62 'Profile: Master of the belly laugh', *Observer*, 24 December 1989, p.11.

63 Dawson, *A Clown Too Many*, p.28.

64 *Les Dawson's Lost Diaries* (Yorkshire Television, tx: 3 April 2004).

65 Dawson, *A Clown Too Many*, p.28.

66 Which, all evidence suggests, is exactly what they did.

67 *Les Dawson's Lost Diaries* (Yorkshire Television, tx: 3 April 2004)

68 Dawson, *Les Dawson's Lancashire*, p.104.

69 Author's interview with Royston Mayoh, 27 February 2009.

70 Audition notes by John Ammonds and Jimmy Lelliott, 17 August 1954, in BBC Written Archives Centre, file N18/2443/1, Artists: Les Dawson: 1956–1965.

71 'Calls for next week', *The Stage*, 13 October 1955, p.2.

72 Dawson, *A Clown Too Many*, p.33.

73 Ibid.

74 Clare, *In the Psychiatrist's Chair II*, pp.93–4.

75 Dawson, *A Clown Too Many*, pp.105–106.

76 Clare, *In the Psychiatrist's Chair II*, pp.103–4.

77 Dawson, *A Clown Too Many*, p.32.

78 Ibid., p.57.

79 Ibid., p.34.

80 Ibid., p.40.

81 'Sir Ian wins, fights on', *Daily Express*, 17 February 1956, p.1.

82 *Les Dawson's Lost Diaries* (Yorkshire Television, tx: 3 April 2004).

83 *Favourite Things* (BBC2, tx: 10 March 1985).

84 *Les Dawson's Lost Diaries* (Yorkshire Television, tx: 3 April 2004).

85 Ibid.

86 Dawson, *A Clown Too Many*, p.42.

87 *Les Dawson's Lost Diaries* (Yorkshire Television, tx: 3 April 2004).

88 Ibid.

89 King popularized the song 'Give Me the Moonlight' and acted as a mentor to the young Frankie Vaughan.

90 Dawson, *A Clown Too Many*, p.48.

91 *Parkinson* (BBC1, tx: 16 November 1974).

92 Author's interview with Alan Plater, 25 February 2009.

93 *Les Dawson's Lost Diaries* (Yorkshire Television, tx: 3 April 2004).

94 Dawson, *A Clown Too Many*, p.50.

95 Monkhouse, *Over the Limit*, p.223.

96 Author's interview with Alan Plater, 25 February 2009.

97 Tracy Dawson (ed.), *Les Dawson's Secret Notebooks* (JR Books, London, 2007), p.142.

98 Dawson, *A Clown Too Many*, p.51.

99 Ibid., p.63.

100 Dawson, *A Clown Too Many*, pp.51–2.

101 Ibid., p.53.

102 *This Is Your Life* (Thames Television, tx: 22 December 1971).

103 Dawson, *A Clown Too Many*, p.61.

104 Ibid., p.61.

105 Ibid., p.58.

CHAPTER 2: A *Plant in the audience*

1 Les Dawson, *A Clown Too Many* (Elm Tree Books, London, 1985), p.71.

2 Paul Callan, 'The sad secret of success behind Les Dawson's jokes', *Daily Mirror*, 5 January 1977, p.19.

3 Audition notes by Peter Pilbeam and Geoff Lawrence, 8 February 1961, in BBC Written Archives Centre, file N18/2443/1, Artists: Les Dawson: 1956–1965.

4 Author's interview with Peter Pilbeam, 22 August 2009.

5 Author's interview with James Casey, 17 June 2009.

6 Dawson, *A Clown Too Many*, p.105.

7 Author's interview with Johnny Roadhouse, 28 February 2009.

8 'Club Corner: Northern favourites claim TV chance', *The Stage*, 21 June 1962, p.4.

9 Author's interview with Royston Mayoh, 27 February 2009.

10 Author's interview with Johnny Roadhouse, 28 February 2009.

11 Author's interview with Dec and Con Cluskey, 20 June 2009.

12 'Hackett and Dawson get their own show', *The Stage*, 12 March 1964, p.9.

13 In *A Clown Too Many*, Dawson dates this engagement as happening in 1960, but Cotton's only Manchester dates that year were at the Ardwick Hippodrome. Cotton's Band Show was at the Opera House for a week from 31 May 1965, with Dawson, Jack Beckitt and his friends, Pat Hatton and Peggy, The Rexanos, Gilbert and Partner, and Cotton's regular associates Alan Breeze and Kathie Kay.

14 Dawson, *A Clown Too Many*, p.78.

15 Ibid., p.79.

16 Author's correspondence with Johnny Ball, 13 December 2010.

17 Letter from Bobby Jaye to Les Dawson, 5 October 1965, in BBC Written Archives Centre, file N18/2443/1, Artists: Les Dawson: 1956–1965.

18 Memo from Denis Morris to Roy Rich, 15 October 1965, in BBC Written Archives Centre, file N18/2443/1, Artists: Les Dawson: 1956–1965.

19 'A date with Doonican', *The Stage*, 12 August 1965, p.26.

20 'Unknown Jim rocks Palladium', *Daily Mirror*, 28 October 1963, p.2.

21 Author's interview with Royston Mayoh, 27 February 2009.

22 Ibid.

23 The real title is 'Pavane pour une infante défunte'.

24 Dawson, *A Clown Too Many*, p.91.

25 Ibid.

26 Author's interview with Royston Mayoh, 27 February 2009.

27 Ibid.

28 Dave Lanning, 'Lanning at Large meets the happy "failure"', *TV Times* (northern edition), 29 July–4 August 1967, p.11.

29 This had been the show's title in 1964 and 1965, but from 1966 it was called *The Blackpool Show*. The old title seems to have remained in internal use at ABC.

30 Author's interview with Royston Mayoh, 27 February 2009.

31 Dawson, *A Clown Too Many*, p.109.

32 Ibid., p.111.

33 Author's interview with Royston Mayoh, 27 February 2009.

34 George Melly, 'Television: In a country garden', *Observer*, 6 August 1967, p.16.

35 Author's correspondence with Johnny Ball, 13 December 2010.

36 Letter to Les Dawson from John Law, 9 October 1967, in BBC Written Archives Centre, file TVART4: Les Dawson.

37 Author's interview with John Ammonds, 14 April 2005.

38 Author's interview with Lydia Vine, 10 February 2010.

39 Ibid.

40 An obese, monocled character comedian and actor best known for playing pompous old fools.

41 *Lulu's Back In Town* (BBC1, tx: 11 June 1968).

42 Author's interview with James Casey, 17 June 2009.

43 Martin Jackson, 'TV and radio', *Daily Express*, 26 April 1968, p.13.

44 Author's interview with John Ammonds, 14 April 2005.

45 Ibid.

46 Four of the nine 1968 *Comedy Playhouse* shows – *View by Appointment* (or *Wink to Me Only* as it became for the series) starring Hugh Paddick and Beryl Reid, *Wild Wild Women* starring Barbara Windsor, *B&B* starring Bernard Braden and Barbara Kelly, and the Irish family sitcom *Me Mammy* – were developed further. Only *Me Mammy* ran for more than one series, notching up twenty-one episodes in three runs between 1969 and 1971.

47 Angela Moreton, 'Fails to ignite and be funny', *The Stage*, 2 May 1968, p.12.

48 Author's interview with John Ammonds, 14 April 2005.

49 Always credited on-screen as G.B. Lupino.

50 Dawson, *A Clown Too Many*, p.139.

51 Author's interview with John Ammonds, 14 April 2005.

52 Sidney Vaucez, 'Beside the seaside '68', *The Stage*, 15 August 1968, p.9.

53 Author's interview with Con and Dec Cluskey, 20 June 2009.

54 'Christmas Shows', *The Stage*, 9 January 1969, p.27.

55 Author's interview with Con and Dec Cluskey, 20 June 2009. Con Cluskey recalls that the antics left the piano lid broken.

56 Dawson made three appearances on *The Val Doonican Show* in the relevant time frame: 12 October, 9 November and 7 December 1968.

57 Author's interview with John Duncan, 4 November 2004.

58 Dawson, *A Clown Too Many*, p.126.

CHAPTER 3: *We don't take any notice of what Les sez*

1 Author's interview with David Nobbs, 22 June 2009.

2 Author's interview with David Mallet, 3 February 2010.

3 Ibid.

4 Ibid.

5 Sheila Tracy, *Talking Swing: The British Big Bands* (Mainstream, Edinburgh, 1997), p.158.

6 Tracy Dawson (ed.), *Les Dawson's Secret Notebooks* (JR Books, London, 2007), p.161.

7 Ron Boyle, 'Review: *Sez Les* – ITV', *Daily Express*, 1 May 1969, p.16.

8 Author's interview with David Mallet, 3 February 2010.

9 *TV Times*, 26 April–2 May 1969, p.11.

10 *TV Times*, 10 May–16 May 1969.

11 *TV Times*, 3 May–9 May 1969.

12 Author's interview with Barry Cryer, 15 September 2010.

13 *Jokers Wild* (Yorkshire Television, tx: 29 September 1971).

14 Author's interview with Barry Cryer, 15 September 2010.

15 Graham Chapman, *A Liar's Autobiography: Volume VI* (Methuen, London, 1980 – paperback edition, Magnum, London, 1981), p.136.

16 *It's Lulu* (BBC1, tx: 25 July 1970).

17 Author's interview with David Mallet, 3 February 2010.

18 *It's Lulu* (BBC1, tx: 25 July 1970).

19 Bob Monkhouse, *Over the Limit: My Secret Diaries 1993–1998* (Century, London, 1998), p.219.

20 Private recording of *The Golden Show*, Floral Hall, Scarborough, 10 September 1970.

21 Ibid.

22 *The Golden Shot* (ATV, tx: 22 August 1971), from camera script in author's collection.

23 Ibid.

24 Author's interview with David Nobbs, 22 June 2009.

25 Author's interview with David Mallet, 3 February 2010.

26 Ibid.

27 *Sez Les*, series 3 show 1 (Yorkshire Television, tx: 16 August 1971).

28 *Sez Les*, series 4 show 1 (Yorkshire Television, tx: 20 January 1972)

29 Author's interview with David Mallet, 3 February 2010.

30 'All is forgiven, sez Mr Botibol', *Daily Mirror*, 22 August 1972, p.4.

31 The sound dips very obviously on the DVD release of these shows.

32 'All is forgiven, sez Mr Botibol', *Daily Mirror*, 22 August 1972, p.4.

33 Author's interview with David Mallet, 3 February 2010.

34 *Sez Les*, series 5 show 1 (Yorkshire Television, tx: 29 July 1972).

35 Ibid.

36 Ibid.

37 Ibid.

38 *Sez Les*, series 8 show 7 (Yorkshire Television, tx: 8 March 1974).

39 *Sez Les*, series 5 show 2 (Yorkshire Television, tx: 5 August 1972).

40 Ibid.

41 'Christmas Shows', *The Stage*, 11 January 1973, p.21.

42 'Blackpool Shows', *The Stage*, 19 August 1971, p.8.

43 Ibid.

44 James Hartley, 'Lines from Lancashire', *The Stage*, 5 August 1971, p.4.

45 Les Dawson, *A Clown Too Many* (Elm Tree Books, London, 1985), p.142.

46 Author's interview with David Mallet, 3 February 2010.

47 Author's interview with David Nobbs, 22 June 2009.

48 Ibid.

49 Author's interview with James Casey, 17 June 2009.

50 Gillian Reynolds, 'This week's radio', *Guardian*, 26 October 1968, p.7.

51 Author's interview with James Casey, 17 June 2009.

52 Ibid.

53 Russell Davies (ed.), *The Kenneth Williams Diaries* (HarperCollins, London, 1994), p.383.

54 Dawson, *A Clown Too Many*, p.122.

55 Ibid., p.124.

56 Ibid., p.122.

57 Author's interview with Royston Mayoh, 27 February 2009.

58 Ibid.

59 Author's correspondence with Fergie Maynard, 9 September 2010.

60 Dawson, *A Clown Too Many*, p.146.

61 Ibid., p.131.

62 Ibid., p.126.

63 Author's interview with Vernon Lawrence, 20 May 2009.

64 Author's interview with David Mallet, 3 February 2010.

65 Author's interview with David Nobbs, 22 June 2009.

66 Ibid.

67 Roy Hudd with Philip Hindin, *Roy Hudd's Cavalcade of Variety Acts* (Robson Books, London, 1997), p.32.

68 Author's interview with Barry Cryer, 15 September 2010.

69 *Sez Les*, series 7 show 2 (Yorkshire Television, tx: 4 August 1973).

70 Author's interview with David Mallet, 3 February 2010.

71 Author's correspondence with Fergie Maynard, 9 September 2010.

72 Author's interview with Barry Cryer, 15 September 2010.

73 Ibid.

74 *Sez Les*, series 8 show 4 (Yorkshire Television, tx: 15 February 1974).

75 Author's interview with David Nobbs, 22 June 2009.

76 Ibid.

77 Ibid.

78 Author's interview with Barry Cryer, 15 September 2010.

79 Author's interview with David Nobbs, 22 June 2009.

80 Author's interview with Vernon Lawrence, 20 May 2009.

81 Author's interview with David Nobbs, 22 June 2009.

82 Author's interview with David Mallet, 3 February 2010.

CHAPTER 4: *Les is more*

1 Les Dawson, *A Clown Too Many* (Elm Tree Books, London, 1985), pp.148–9.

2 *Royal Variety Performance* (ATV, tx: 2 December 1973).

3 Ibid.

4 'In An 18th Century Drawing Room' was the title of a jazzed-up 1930s adaptation of the original theme by avant-garde American composer and electronic music pioneer Raymond Scott. Dawson's preference for this title suggests a familiarity with Scott's work.

5 Author's correspondence with Gary Husband, 25 June 2008.

6 Dawson, *A Clown Too Many*, p.151

7 Author's interview with John Duncan, 4 November 2004.

8 Author's interview with David Nobbs, 22 June 2009.

9 Author's interview with John Duncan, 4 November 2004.

10 Dawson, *A Clown Too Many*, p.127.

11 Duncan had seen Eric Chappell's original play *The Banana Box* and taken a TV option on it, encouraging Chappell to reshape the narrative into sitcom form, but he left YTV before it reached the pilot stage.

12 Author's interview with David Mallet, 3 February 2010.

13 Ibid.

14 *Sez Les*, series 8 show 7 (Yorkshire Television, tx: 8 March 1974).

15 Author's interview with David Mallet, 3 February 2010.

16 Author's interview with David Nobbs, 22 June 2009.

17 *Sounds Like Les Dawson* (Yorkshire Television, tx: 4 December 1974).

18 Author's interview with David Nobbs, 22 June 2009.

19 *Sounds Like Les Dawson* (Yorkshire Television, tx: 4 December 1974).

20 Author's interview with Vernon Lawrence, 20 May 2009.

21 Author's interview with David Nobbs, 22 June 2009.

22 Ibid.

23 *Les Dawson's Christmas Box* (Yorkshire Television, tx: 21 December 1974)

24 Author's interview with Barry Cryer, 15 September 2010.

25 Author's interview with Lyn Took, 7 October 2009.

26 *Parkinson* (BBC1, tx: 16 November 1974).

27 Author's interview with James Casey, 17 June 2009.

28 Ibid.

29 *Listen to Les* (BBC Radio 2, tx: 28 December 1980).

30 Author's interview with James Casey, 17 June 2009.

31 *Listen to Les* (BBC Radio 2, tx: 22 June 1975).

32 *Listen to Les* (BBC Radio 2, tx: 18 November 1979)

33 Dawson, *A Clown Too Many*, p.94.

34 Author's interview with James Casey, 17 June 2009.

35 Author's interview with David Mallet, 3 February 2010.

36 Author's interview with Ray Galton and Alan Simpson, 7 December 2009.

37 Ibid.

38 *Holiday With Strings* (Yorkshire Television, tx: 26 August 1974).

39 Author's interview with Ray Galton and Alan Simpson, 7 December 2009.

40 *Holiday With Strings* (Yorkshire Television, tx: 26 August 1974).

41 Author's interview with Ray Galton and Alan Simpson, 7 December 2009.

42 Author's interview with David Nobbs, 22 June 2009.

43 Leonard Buckley, 'TV Review: *Holiday With Strings*', *The Times*, 27 August 1974, p.8.

44 *Dawson's Electric Cinema* (Yorkshire Television, tx: 3 April 1975).

45 Author's interview with David Nobbs, 22 June 2009.

46 Author's interview with Alan Plater, 25 February 2009.

47 Ibid.

48 Ibid.

49 *The Loner: Dawson's Complaint* (Yorkshire Television, tx: 7 May 1975).

50 Author's interview with Alan Plater, 25 February 2009.

51 *The Loner: Dawson's Connection* (Yorkshire Television, tx: 14 May 1975)

52 *The Loner: Dawson's Encounter* (Yorkshire Television, tx: 21 May 1975)

53 Author's interview with Alan Plater, 25 February 2009.

54 *Dawson's Weekly: Les Miserables* (Yorkshire Television, tx: 12 June 1975).

55 *The Fall and Rise of Reginald Perrin*, series 2 show 3 (BBC1, tx: 5 October 1977)

56 Author's interview with Ray Galton and Alan Simpson, 7 December 2009.

57 The Barraclough character asks, 'Did you vote Gay Lib?', and Dawson replies, 'No, I voted Jeremy Thorpe, Miserable Lib.' Four years later, this joke would

acquire further layers of meaning, when Thorpe's homosexual affair with male model Norman Scott came out into the open.

58 Dawson, *A Clown Too Many*, p.14.

59 Lesley Salisbury, 'The Les Dawson removal show', *TV Times*, 3–9 May 1975, pp.2–3.

60 Ibid.

61 Author's interview with Vernon Lawrence, 20 May 2009.

62 Author's interview with Ray Galton and Alan Simpson, 7 December 2009.

63 Les Dawson, *A Card for the Clubs* (Sphere Books, London, 1974), p.38.

64 Ibid., p.8.

65 Ibid.

66 Ibid., p.10.

67 Ibid, p.51.

68 Ibid., p.144.

69 The main inspiration, however, seems to have been Associated-Rediffusion's sixties pub-based variety show, *Stars and Garters*.

70 Dawson, *A Card for the Clubs*, pp.8 and 15.

71 Dawson, *A Clown Too Many*, pp.166–167.

72 Ibid., p.128.

73 Alix Coleman, 'Inside TV: Cheerfully resisting life's stings and arrows', *TV Times*, 7–13 June 1975, pp.23–4.

74 Dawson, *A Clown Too Many*, p.120.

75 Ibid., p.132.

76 Ibid., p.143.

77 Author's interview with David Nobbs, 22 June 2009.

78 *Parkinson* (BBC1, tx: 30 October 1976).

79 Throughout the routine, bandleader Harry Stoneham is visible in the background, convulsed with laughter.

80 Hampton Wick being a slang term for the penis, as well as one stop on from Kingston on the train line to Shepperton in London's western suburbs.

81 Les Dawson, *The Spy Who Came...* (Star Books, London, 1976), p.116.

82 Ibid., p.10.

83 Ibid., p.73.

84 Ibid., p.88.

85 Les Dawson, 'The Humbling of Poddy', *Daily Mirror*, 19 July 1976, p.18.

86 Ibid.

87 Les Dawson, 'Accrington deck chair attendant mauled by deaf leopard while practising tuba in Congo rain forest', *Penthouse*, vol. 12, no. 8, pp.60–2.

88 Dawson, *A Clown Too Many*, p.170.

89 'Summer Shows', *The Stage*, 19 August 1976, p.62.

90 Dawson, *A Card for the Clubs*, p.36.

91 Ibid., p.132.

CHAPTER 5: *Farewell to Leeds*

1 Alan Coren, 'That's entertainment!', *The Times*, 24 December 1973, p.19.

2 Les Dawson, *A Clown Too Many* (Elm Tree Books, London, 1985), p.179.

3 *Dawson and Friends*, show 4 (Yorkshire Television, tx: 29 June 1977).

4 Ibid.

5 Author's interview with Barry Cryer, 15 September 2010.

6 Author's interview with David Nobbs, 22 June 2009.

7 Dawson, *A Clown Too Many*, p.178.

8 'Nowhere left an artist can "die"', *The Stage*, 16 June 1977, p.13.

9 Author's interview with Vernon Lawrence, 20 May 2009.

10 Ibid.

11 By a fluke of scheduling, he was also to be seen at 6.45 p.m. on ITV as a panel-list in the quiz show *Celebrity Squares*.

12 Dawson, *A Clown Too Many*, p.179.

13 Author's interview with David Mallet, 3 February 2010.

14 Author's interview with David Nobbs, 22 June 2009.

15 Author's interview with Vernon Lawrence, 20 May 2009.

16 Ibid.

17 Author's interview with David Mallet, 3 February 2010.

18 *The Les Dawson Show*, series 1 show 1 (BBC1, tx: 21 January 1978).

19 Ibid.

20 Peter Fiddick, 'Television: Les Dawson', *Guardian*, 20 February 1978, p.8.

21 Ibid.

22 Dawson, *A Clown Too Many*, p.180.

23 Author's interview with Terry Ravenscroft, 6 December 2009.

24 Author's interview with Andy Hamilton, 15 September 2009.

25 Bob Monkhouse, *Over the Limit: My Secret Diaries 1993–1998* (Century, London, 1998), p.220.

26 Author's interview with Terry Ravenscroft, 6 December 2009.

27 Author's interview with Andy Hamilton, 15 September 2009.

28 Author's interview with Terry Ravenscroft, 6 December 2009.

29 Author's interview with Andy Hamilton, 15 September 2009.

30 *The Dawson Watch*, series 1 show 1 (BBC1, tx: 23 February 1979).

31 Author's interview with Terry Ravenscroft, 6 December 2009.

32 *The Dawson Watch*, series 1 show 2 (BBC1, tx: 2 March 1979).

33 *Les Dawson's Cissie and Ada* by Terry Ravenscroft (Kindle eBook – Razzamatazz Publications, 2011)

34 *The Dawson Watch*, series 1 show 3 (BBC1, tx: 16 March 1979).

35 Author's interview with Andy Hamilton, 15 September 2009.

36 *The Dawson Watch*, series 2 show 1 (BBC1, tx: 22 November 1979).

37 Author's interview with Andy Hamilton, 15 September 2009.

38 Ibid.
39 Ibid.
40 Ibid.
41 *The Dawson Watch*, series 2 show 6 (BBC1, tx: 27 December 1979).
42 Ibid.
43 Ibid.
44 Author's interview with Andy Hamilton, 15 September 2009.
45 *The Dawson Watch*, Christmas special (BBC1, tx: 27 December 1980).
46 Author's correspondence with Julie Ryder, 20 September 2011.
47 Dawson, *A Clown Too Many*, pp.188–9.
48 Paul Callan, 'The sad secret of success behind Les Dawson's jokes', *Daily Mirror*, 5 January 1977, p.19.
49 Dawson, *A Clown Too Many*, p.188.
50 Dawson, *A Clown Too Many*, p.172.
51 Author's interview with Lydia Vine, 10 February 2010.
52 *Shirley Bassey*, series 2 show 4 (BBC1, tx: 10 November 1979).
53 Author's interview with Terry Ravenscroft, 6 December 2009.
54 Author's correspondence with Danny Greenstone, 17 January 2011.
55 Author's interview with Ernest Maxin, 24 June 2009.
56 Ibid.
57 Ibid.
58 Author's interview with Andy Hamilton, 15 September 2009.
59 Author's interview with Terry Ravenscroft, 6 December 2009.
60 *The Les Dawson Show*, special (BBC1, tx: 25 May 1981).
61 Ibid.
62 Author's interview with Ernest Maxin, 24 June 2009.
63 *The Les Dawson Show*, series 3 show 4 (BBC1, tx: 20 February 1982).
64 Dawson, *A Clown Too Many*, p.200.
65 Author's interview with Terry Ravenscroft, 6 December 2009. Twist was not actually Randle's real name, but Arthur Twist was one of the stage names adopted by Arthur Hughes before he became famous as Randle.
66 *The Les Dawson Show*, series 3 show 2 (BBC1, tx: 22 January 1983).
67 Dawson, *A Clown Too Many*, p.195.
68 Tracy Dawson (ed.), *Les Dawson's Secret Notebooks* (JR Books, London, 2007), p.133.
69 Sydney Brennan, 'Why comic Les took to the bottle', *Daily Express*, 4 January 1982, p.3.
70 Dawson, *A Clown Too Many*, p.197.
71 Ibid., p.196.

CHAPTER 6: *Hitler was my mother-in-law*

1 Author's interview with Alan Plater, 25 February 2009.
2 Les Dawson, *A Clown Too Many* (Elm Tree Books, London, 1985), p.168.
3 Author's interview with Andy Hamilton, 15 September 2009.
4 Alasdair Buchan, 'What the stars foretell', *Daily Mirror*, 21 April 1979, p.9.
5 Dawson, *A Clown Too Many*, p.ix.
6 'Sayings of the Week', *Observer*, 1 November 1987, p.11.
7 *The Les Dawson Show* – special (BBC1, tx: 25 May 1981).
8 *The Dawson Watch*, series 1 show 3 (BBC1, tx: 16 March 1979).
9 Dawson, *A Clown Too Many*, p.205.
10 Ibid., p.187.
11 Author's interview with Vernon Lawrence, 20 May 2009.
12 Dawson favoured steak-and-kidney pudding, chips and peas, while the rest of the family opted for fish.
13 Or, as the *Mirror*'s clumsy typesetters had it, *The Boob of Outrageous Puns*. Cosmo would have approved.
14 Les Dawson, *The Malady Lingers On* (Arrow Books, London, 1982), p.31.
15 Dawson, *A Clown Too Many*, p.204 – the novel's original title was restored when it emerged in paperback.
16 Les Dawson, *Hitler Was My Mother-in-Law* (Arrow Books, London, 1985), p.12.
17 Ibid., p.98.
18 Les Dawson, *Les Dawson's Lancashire* (Elm Tree Books, London, 1983), p.10.
19 Ibid., p.12.
20 Ibid., p.19.
21 Ibid., p.32.
22 Ibid., p.36.
23 Ibid., p.30.
24 Ibid., pp.36–7.
25 Ibid., p.42.
26 Ibid., p.24.
27 Ibid., p.59.
28 Author's correspondence with Peter Lee-Wright, 6 February 2011.
29 Comic Roots: *Les Dawson's Lancashire* (BBC1, tx: 2 August 1982).
30 *The Les Dawson Show*, series 1 show 1 (BBC1, tx: 21 January 1978).
31 Comic Roots: *Les Dawson's Lancashire* (BBC1, tx: 2 August 1982).
32 Ibid.
33 Ibid.
34 Ibid.
35 Author's correspondence with Peter Lee-Wright, 6 February 2011.
36 Comic Roots: *Les Dawson's Lancashire* (BBC1, tx: 2 August 1982).
37 Author's correspondence with Peter Lee-Wright, 6 February 2011.

38 Ibid.

39 Les Dawson, 'The Dawson Slant', *Gazette*, 29 July 1982, in Steve Singleton (ed.), *The Dawson Slant* (*The Gazette*, Blackpool, 2008), p.6.

40 Morton's account of this bizarre affair appeared first in the *Daily Express* in 1937, but was collected and reprinted in *The Best of Beachcomber*, edited by Michael Frayn.

41 Michael Frayn (ed.), *The Best of Beachcomber* (William Heinemann, London, 1963), pp.26–7.

42 Les Dawson, 'The Dawson Slant', *Gazette*, 29 July 1982, in Steve Singleton (ed.), *The Dawson Slant*, p.6.

43 Les Dawson, 'The Dawson Slant', *Gazette*, 26 August 1982, in Steve Singleton (ed.), *The Dawson Slant*, p.23.

44 Les Dawson, 'The Dawson Slant', *Gazette*, 11 November 1982, in Steve Singleton (ed.), *The Dawson Slant*, p.60.

45 Author's interview with Ernest Maxin, 9 November 2005.

46 Ibid.

47 Aston was to return to her native Australia shortly after the group made its TV debut.

48 Author's interview with Ernest Maxin, 24 June 2009.

49 Les Dawson, *A Clown Too Many*, p.203.

50 Author's interview with Terry Ravenscroft, 6 December 2009.

51 Les Dawson, *No Tears for the Clown* (Robson Books, London, 1992), p.6.

52 Hilary Bonner, 'My Darling Meg by Les Dawson, part 1', *Daily Mirror*, 15 September 1986, pp.14–15.

53 Author's interview with James Casey, 17 June 2009.

54 Les Dawson, *A Clown Too Many*, p.204.

55 Author's interview with Alan Boyd, 3 August 2005.

56 Bob Monkhouse, *Crying With Laughter* (Arrow, London, 1994), p.263.

57 *Blankety Blank*, series 12 show 5 (BBC1, tx: 5 October 1989).

58 Author's interview with Stanley Appel, 13 October 2009.

59 Jenny Rees, 'Big game bonanza', *Daily Express*, 18 February 1985, p.13.

60 *Blankety Blank*, series 7 show 1 (BBC1, tx: 7 September 1984).

61 Author's interview with Stanley Appel, 13 October 2009.

62 Paul Bailey, 'India-rubber grimaces', *Observer*, 1 December 1985, p.21.

63 Les Dawson, *A Time Before Genesis* (Elm Tree Books, London, 1985), p.10.

64 Ibid., p.9.

65 Ibid., p.12.

66 Ibid., p.47.

67 Ibid., p.38.

68 Ibid., p.112.

69 Ibid., p.114.

70 Ibid., p.75.

71 Dawson, *No Tears for the Clown*, p.21.

72 Tom Hutchinson, 'Review: *A Time Before Genesis*', *The Times*, 24 April 1986.

73 Nick Smurthwaite, 'The Les majesty', *Guardian*, 13 March 1986, p.12.

74 Dawson, *No Tears for the Clown*, p.22.

75 Hilary Bonner, 'My Darling Meg by Les Dawson, part 3', *Daily Mirror*, 17 September 1986, p.21.

76 Dawson, *A Clown Too Many*, p.179.

77 Maurice Chesworth, 'Fears for Les', *Daily Mirror*, 25 February 1985, p.1.

78 Elizabeth Grice, 'When it's no joke being a funny man', *Daily Express*, 26 February 1985, p.9.

79 Dawson, *A Clown Too Many*, p.210.

80 Dawson, *No Tears for the Clown*, p.20.

81 Author's interview with James Casey, 17 June 2009.

82 Dawson, *No Tears for the Clown*, p.21.

83 Ibid., p.38.

84 Author's interview with James Casey, 17 June 2009.

85 Hilary Bonner, 'My Darling Meg by Les Dawson, part 1', *Daily Mirror*, 15 September 1986, pp.14—15.

86 Dawson, *No Tears for the Clown*, p.41.

87 Ivan Waterman, 'Tragic Les cuts out the wife jokes', *News of the World*, 20 April 1986, p.13.

88 Author's interview with Con and Dec Cluskey, 20 June 2009.

89 Ivan Waterman, 'Tragic Les cuts out the wife jokes', *News of the World*, 20 April 1986, p.13.

90 John Smith, 'Life without my brave lass by Les Dawson', *People*, 7 September 1986, pp.8—9.

91 Ibid.

92 Author's interview with James Casey, 17 June 2009.

93 *Farewell to the Playhouse* (BBC Radio 2, tx: 4 August 1986).

94 Tony Barrow, 'The serious art of falling flat on your face', *The Stage*, 9 October 1986, p.9.

95 John Smith, 'Life without my brave lass by Les Dawson', *People*, 7 September 1986, pp.8—9.

CHAPTER 7: *Run for your wife*

1 Les Dawson, *No Tears for the Clown* (Robson Books, London, 1992), p.11.

2 Ibid., p.vi.

3 Hilary Bonner, 'My Meg would bless us', *Daily Mirror*, 24 September 1987, pp.4—5.

4 Dawson, *No Tears for the Clown*, p.51.

5 Ibid., p.55.

6 Ibid., p.57.

7 'Dallas star's escape', *Daily Mirror*, 22 September 1987, p.7.

8 Gordon Broome and Dick Saxty, 'Les Dawson stole my wife', *Sun*, 23 September 1987, pp.1 and 3.

9 John Mahoney, 'My sis is Les Dawson's bit o' stuff', *Daily Star*, 23 September 1987, p.2.

10 Hilary Bonner, 'Forgive Me!', *Daily Mirror*, 25 September 1987, p.7.

11 Hilary Bonner, 'I'll give my wife away to Les', *Daily Mirror*, 26 September 1987, p.7.

12 *Daily Star*, quoted in 'Medium is the message', *Guardian*, 26 September 1987, p.16.

13 'Medium is the message', *Guardian*, 26 September 1987, p.16.

14 Dawson, *No Tears for the Clown*, p.80.

15 John Mahoney and David Graham, 'Carry on Les!', *Daily Star*, 24 September 1987, pp.1, 4 and 5.

16 John Mahoney, 'Wait for it, Les!', *Daily Star*, 25 September 1987, p.15.

17 Author's interview with Stanley Appel, 13 October 2009.

18 Dawson, *No Tears for the Clown*, p.104.

19 Ibid., p.93.

20 William Cook, *The Comedy Store: The club that changed British comedy* (Little, Brown, London, 2001), p.71.

21 *Woman's Hour* (BBC Radio 4, tx: 4 January 1991).

22 Helen Lederer, 'Funny man who had the last laugh', *Observer*, 13 June 1993, p.22.

23 William Greaves, 'My Kind of Day', *Radio Times*, 4–10 November 1989, p.122.

24 Les Dawson, *Les Dawson Gives Up* (Papermac, London, 1989), pp.29 and 31.

25 Ibid., p.118.

26 Author's interview with Johnny Roadhouse, 28 February 2009.

27 Author's correspondence with Alan Hart, 9 October 2009.

28 Author's interview with Lydia Vine, 10 February 2010.

29 *The Les Dawson Show*, series 5 show 6 (BBC1, tx: 23 November 1989).

30 Author's interview with Royston Mayoh, 27 February 2009.

31 Author's interview with Stewart Morris, 1 April 2005.

32 Private recording of post-show banter after *Opportunity Knocks*, live final (BBC1, tx: 2 June 1990).

33 Dawson, *No Tears for the Clown*, p.131.

34 'Les is *Blankety Blank*ed out', *Daily Express*, 28 September 1990, p.5.

35 Author's correspondence with Keith Salmon, 30 September 2010.

36 Dawson, *No Tears for the Clown*, p.133.

37 Author's interview with Stanley Appel, 13 October 2009.

38 'Pick of the Week' by Margaret Forwood, *Daily Express*, 13 April 1991, p.28.

39 Dawson, *No Tears for the Clown*, p.148.

40 Stephen Moss, 'The language of laughter', *Guardian*, 17 October 1991, p.25.

41 'Comic heavyweights in a war of words', *The Stage*, 24 October 1991, p.3.

42 Jonathan Margolis, 'Obituary: Bernard Manning – Stand-up comedian who countered accusations of racism with the claim that his act was "just jokes"', *Independent*, 19 June 2007, taken from online edition.

43 Robert Chalmers, 'Portrait of a bigot', *Observer* magazine, 8 November 1992, p.39.

44 Eric Braun, 'Gallows humour', *The Stage*, 9 May 1985, p.5.

45 Tom Merrin, 'Punchlines land below the belt', *Daily Mirror*, 23 June 1983, p.7.

46 Author's interview with Barry Cryer, 15 September 2010.

47 Jonathan Margolis, *Bernard Manning* (Orion, London, 1996), pp.75–6.

48 Author's interview with Dan Patterson, 25 August 2010.

49 Ibid.

50 Dawson, *No Tears for the Clown*, p.169.

51 Author's interview with Stanley Appel, 13 October 2009.

52 *This Is Your Life* (BBC1, tx: 23 December 1992).

CHAPTER 8: *Post-Dawsonism*

1 Author's correspondence with Mark Tinkler, 2 December 2009.

2 Author's interview with Royston Mayoh, 27 February 2009.

3 A list of examples would need a book of its own, but take Jane Warren, 'Curse of the mother-in-war', *Daily Express*, 26 February 2010, pp.24–5, as a fairly typical offering.

4 David Collins, 'Blankety blanked', *Daily Mirror*, 25 October 2008, p.33.

APPENDICES

APPENDIX I: LIVE WORK

The following is an extensive, but not exhaustive list of Les Dawson's live engagements from 1964 to the end of his career, gleaned largely from listings in *The Stage*.

1964

June: Cavendish Club, Sheffield – with Marty Wilde. June: Wetherell's, Sunderland – with Marty Wilde. September: Lyceum Cabaret Club, Bradford – with the Overlanders and Jacqueline Ward. September: City Varieties, Leeds – with Johnny Moxham, Paul Fox and Ann, Diane, Geddes Bros, Sally Ford and Tuesday Child.

1965

Summer season: Palace Coliseum, Isle of Man – *Date with Doonican*, with Val Doonican, Jackie Trent, the Jones Boys, Don Dwight, the Rudy Ammon 5, Dollies and the Fox-Miller Dancers. May/June (one week): Opera House, Manchester – *Billy Cotton Band Show*, with Alan Breeze, Kathie Kay, Pat Hatton and Peggy, the Rexanos, Gilbert and Partner, Ellis Jackson, Jack Beckitt and his Friends.

1966

May–June: Lancashire and Cheshire Clubs. May: Sporting Club, Rhyl. September: Kingsway Casino, Southport – also billed: Les Chants, Jan Panter, Nelson Firth Girls, Jimmie Lauria, Gordon Staples Trio.

1967

Summer season: Central Pier, Blackpool. August: Regent Variety Club, Langley Green – with Gary Miller, Miss Peggi, Regent Lovelies, Ken James, and Eric Burton at the organ. September: Kingsway Casino, Southport – with Toni Eden, the Gordon Staples Quintet, Davy Williams and Charles Smitton. September: Coventry Theatre, Coventry – with the Shadows, Ray Fell, Morton Fraser's Harmonica Gang, Glenn Weston, Pat and Olivia, and the Betty Smith Quintet. November: New 77 Club, Brierfield – also billed: Bert Weedon, Mike and Sonya, Leslie Lewis, Ramoni Brothers and Paul Baker. November: Starlight Club, Blackburn – also billed: Dubliners, Bert Weedon, Erik and Juel, Des Owen, Paul Baker.

1968

February: Kon-Tiki Club, Wakefield – with Jackie Day, Martin Dale and the Phil Langton Trio. April: Mersey Hotel, Didsbury – with Angela Heaton. May: Carlton Club, Chesterfield – also billed: Jeri Benton, Del Derrick, Dennis Day Trio and Joy. Summer season: Central Pier, Blackpool – *Star Show '68*, with Ray Martine, Solomon King and Don Partridge. Christmas: Grand

Theatre, Leeds – *Bachelors Show*, with the Bachelors, Norman Collier and Arthur Worsley.

1969

January: Opera House, Manchester – *Bachelors Show*, with the Bachelors. Christmas: Gaumont, Doncaster – *Mother Goose*, with the Rockin' Berries.

1970

Summer season: Floral Hall, Scarborough – *The Golden Show*, with Bob Monkhouse, Ronnie Hilton, Jane Fyffe, the Mistins, the Voyagers, Golden Girls, Will Fyffe Jr and his Orchestra. Sunday nights in summer: Middleton Sands, Lancashire.
December: La Dolce Vita, Birmingham – with Isabel Duncan and Joe Benjamin. Christmas: Grand Theatre, Leeds – *Babes in the Wood*.

1971

April: Club Fiesta, Stockton. May: Wakefield Theatre Club – also billed: Audrey Jeans, Rockinghams, Maxello, Ballet Montmartre, Martin Dale. May (7 shows): Various venues for Teesside Social Clubs and Phillips Brothers Enterprises. May: Webbington Country Club, Weston-Super-Mare – with Susan Richards. Summer season: Queen's Theatre, Blackpool – *The Queen's Show*, with Dora Bryan, Ronnie Hilton, Lennie Bennett, Alister Jons, Helena Garron, the Mistins, Jimmy Currie's Waltzing Waters, Bel Canto Singers, Queen's Dancers, and Queen's Orchestra conducted by Morris McLean. September: ABC Theatre, Blackpool – *Midnight Matinee* for local charities and the Variety Artists' Benevolent Fund. September: Queen's Theatre, Blackpool – *Midnight Matinee* for the Mayor of Blackpool's memorial fund (tribute to murdered police officer). November: Talk of the Midlands, Derby – *The Les Dawson Show*, with Ron Cooper Band and Ricki Disoni (B Lowndes Entertainments).

Christmas: Alexandra Theatre, Birmingham – *Robinson Crusoe*, with New World, Jack Tripp, Allister Bain, Allen Christie, Michael Cotterill, Cox Twins, Emerson and Jayne, Helena Garron, Pat Lancaster, Heather McConachie, Miles Twins, Arthur Tolcher and Alexandra Dancers.

1972

April: Club Fiesta, Stockton – with Sam and Samantha, and Judy Moxon. August: Golden Garter, Wythenshawe – with Jenny Maynard and Looking Glass. Summer season: Pier, Skegness – *Don't Tell the Wife*.
Christmas: Grand Theatre, Leeds – *Goody Two Shoes*, with Ronnie Hilton, Peter Goodwright, Brian Marshall, Don Smoothey, and Paul and Peta Page's Puppets.

1973

Royal Variety Performance

1974

April: Jollee's, Stoke – *Les Dawson and Joan Regan Show*. September: Talk of the Midlands, Derby – with Billy Hall, Judy Jones, Penny Cress, Bob Taggart Band.
November: C'esar's Palace, Luton – with Keeley Ford. December: Oasis, Rotherham – Gala reopening night with Tony Hatch and Jackie Trent, hosted by Len Marten.

1975

Summer season: Southport – with Dana and Bobby Bennett.

1976

May: Double Diamond, Caerphilly – with Julie Thursday and Dennis Bullen Sextet. May: Park Hall, Charnock Richard – with Mike Gannon, the Dot, the Geoff Moore Sound. Summer season: Floral Hall, Scarborough – *Holiday Showtime* with Kenneth McKellar, Dougie Squires' Second Generation, Cool Breeze, Bobby Bennett, Jumping Jack.

Live work

1977

March: Trocadero, Bulkington. Summer season: ABC Theatre, Blackpool – with Bobby Bennett. September: Belle Vue, Manchester – *National Club Show*, with Colin Crompton and Dame Vera Lynn.

1978

March: Caesar's Palace, Luton – with Elaine Carole, Gerry Brooke, Geoff Walker Orchestra, Sonia Montego, Communications. April: Wakefield Theatre Club – with Martin Dale and Junior Jansen. April: Night Out, Birmingham – with Juniper Green. Summer season: Spa Theatre, Bridlington – with Janet Brown, Stu Francis, Tammy Jones, Dougie Squires' Second Generation, the Sunshine Girls, the Wychwoods, the Kids Krazy Kar and the Edwin Harper Theatre Orchestra. Christmas: Alhambra Theatre, Bradford – *Babes in the Wood*, with Peter Goodwright, Tammy Jones, Roy Barraclough, Eli Woods, Patrick Newell.

1979

April: Bermuda – with Valentine. May–June: Wakefield Theatre Club – with John Milner and Samantha Sinclaire. June: Blazers, Wigan – with Dave Blakele. Summer season: Wellington Pier, Great Yarmouth – One-night Sunday show. Christmas: Hippodrome, Birmingham.

1980

February: King's, Great Barr – *Water Rats Ball*, with Bonnie Langford, Nigel Hopkins and Pat Mooney. August: Pavilion, Bournemouth – Two Sunday shows. Christmas: Empire, Liverpool – *Babes in the Wood*.

1981

Summer season: Spa Theatre, Bridlington. Christmas: Richmond Theatre, London – *Aladdin*, with Arthur Askey, Rula Lenska, Christopher Timothy, Bernard Bresslaw.

1982

May: Night Out, Birmingham – with Glyn Jones and Lips. July: Southport Theatre. Christmas: Davenport Theatre, Stockport – *Jack and the Beanstalk*, with Lenny Windsor.

1983

May: Night Out, Birmingham – with Jay and Bonnie Diamond. July: Cliffs Pavilion, Westcliff-on-Sea. August: Spa, Felixstowe; Winter Gardens, Margate; Sparrow's Nest, Lowestoft – with the Roly Polys, Jade and Francis Van Dyke, and Lenny Windsor on early billings. Christmas: Grand Theatre, Wolverhampton – *Cinderella*, with Michael Barrymore.

1984

November: Night Out, Birmingham.

1985

February: Blazers, Windsor. September: Marlowe Theatre, Canterbury – Grand Order of Water Rats charity gala night with Roy Hudd and Bernie Winters. Christmas: Palace Theatre, Manchester – *Babes in the Wood*, with John Nettles, Ruth Madoc, John Noakes, Mark Curry, the Roly Polys.

1986

Christmas: Alexandra Theatre, Birmingham – *Babes in the Wood*, with John Nettles and Ruth Madoc.

1987

February: Blazers, Windsor – with Katie Budd, Del Derrick and Geoff Walker Orchestra. Autumn tour: Norwich, Dartford, Darlington and Blackpool – *Run For Your Wife*. Christmas: Mayflower Theatre, Southampton – *Babes in the Wood*, with John Nettles, the Roly Polys, Aiden J. Harvey, Allan Stewart, Pepe's Pop Party and Ann Sidney.

1988
Summer season: Opera House, Blackpool –
with Frank Carson, Keith Harris and Orville,
and the Roly Polys.
Christmas: Hippodrome, Bristol – *Aladdin*
(Dawson pulled out because he was
recovering from a heart attack, and was
replaced by Gary Wilmot).

1989
Summer season: Festival, Paignton –
with Dana, the Roly Polys, Gary Lovini,
Peter Goodwright and Dawson Dancers
choreographed by Rosita Yarboy.
Christmas: Empire, Sunderland – *Jack and
the Beanstalk*, with Ted Robbins, Rose-Marie
and Dooby Duck.

1990
Summer season tour – *Run For Your Wife*.
October: Savvas, Usk – with Helen Jayne.

Christmas: Palace Theatre, Manchester –
Dick Whittington, with John Nettles, the
Roly Polys, Mark Walker, Dooby Duck and
his Disco friends, Ann Sidney, Richard and
Lara Jarmain, Claire Rimmer and Buckley
School of Dance.

1991
Christmas: Wimbledon Theatre, Wimbledon
– *Dick Whittington*, with John Nettles, the
Roly Polys and Rula Lenska (Dawson was
taken ill and replaced by Bernard Cribbins).

1992
Summer season: Pier Theatre, Bournemouth
– *Run For Your Wife*, with Peter Goodwright.
Christmas: Theatre Royal, Plymouth – *Dick
Whittington*, with Peter Goodwright, Ellis
Ward, Michele Dotrice, Dooby Duck and his
Disco Friends, Patrick Mower, Richard and
Lara Jarmain, and Denise Douglas.

APPENDIX II: BROADCASTS

The following is, again, an extensive, but not exhaustive, listing of Les Dawson's broadcast
appearances. Where a show is known to survive in the broadcaster's archive, this is
indicated. Some extra editions of *Listen to Les* are known to survive in the BBC radio
comedy department's own archive, but details of exactly which editions are unavailable at
the time of publication. Where an ITV show is marked as 'networked', this means that it was
shown by all regions, but not necessarily at the same time or on the same day.

Radio work

LP: BBC Light Programme
HS: BBC Home Service
HS(N): BBC North of England Home Service
R1/2: BBC Radio 1 and 2 combined
R2: BBC Radio 2
R3: BBC Radio 3
R4: BBC Radio 4
R4(N): BBC Radio 4 (northern
  transmitters only)

Spots and guest appearances

1961
Aim at the Top – 16 March 1961, HS(N),
19.00–19.30. Recorded: 26 February 1961,
20.15–21.00, Studio 1, Broadcasting House,
Piccadilly, Manchester. Producer: Bill
Scott-Coomber. Fee: 10 guineas (£10 and
10 shillings).
Midday Music Hall – 17 April 1961, LP,
12.31–13.31. Recorded: 26 March 1961,
19.45–21.15, Playhouse Theatre, Hulme,
Manchester. Taking part: Roger Moffat
(host), Derek Roy, Janie Marden, Mike and

Bernie Winters, Harry Hayward, Avril Angers, the Gaunt Brothers, Paul Andrews, L.D., the Crescendos, the BBC Northern Dance Orchestra directed by Tommy Watt. Producer: Bill Scott-Coomber. Fee: 10 guineas.

....

1962

Blackpool Night – 5 August 1962, LP, 18.30–19.30. Recorded: 31 July 1962, 14.45–16.15, Jubilee Theatre, Sheppard Street, Blackpool. Taking part: Jack Watson (host), Arthur Haynes and Nicholas Parsons, Joe 'Mr Piano' Henderson, Jimmy Gay, Sheila Buxton, L.D., the Four Ramblers, Edmund Hockridge, Reginald Dixon, the BBC Northern Dance Orchestra directed by Bernard Herrmann. Producer: James Casey. Fee: 10 guineas. Repeated: 10 August, HS (not South and West or Welsh), 19.00–19.30.

....

1963

Music Hall – 25 March 1963, LP, 12.31–13.30. Recorded: 17 March 1963, 20.00–21.30, Playhouse Theatre, Hulme, Manchester. Taking part: Roger Moffat (host), Charlie Chester, Dennis Lotis, Tommy Reilly, George Martin, Jackie Allen and Barbara, Doreen Hume, L.D., the Peter Crawford Trio, the BBC Northern Dance Orchestra directed by Bernard Herrmann. Producer: James Casey. Fee: 10 guineas.

Blackpool Night – 30 June 1963, LP, 18.31–19.30. Recorded: 20 June 1963, 14.45–16.15, Jubilee Theatre, Sheppard Street, Blackpool. Taking part: Jack Watson (host), Ted Ray, David Hughes, Jack Storey, Joe Henderson, Miki and Griff, L.D., the Hedley Ward Trio, the BBC Northern Dance Orchestra directed by Bernard Herrmann. Producer: James Casey. Fee: 10 guineas.

A Night at the Music Hall – 8 July 1963, LP, 19.31–20.00. Recorded: 23 June 1963, 20.45–21.30, Garrick Playhouse, Barrington Road, Altrincham. *Radio Times* billing: 'Your Chairman, Bill Scott-Coomber introduces

Mr. Charlie Chester – Speak to Charlie, Mr. Alf Edwards – the versatile virtuoso, Mr. Les Dawson – mirth at the piano, Miss Marjorie Jones – the Wirral nightingale, and the Gentlemen of the Pit Orchestra, conducted by Mr. Morris McLean.' Producer: Peter Pilbeam. Fee: 10 guineas.

Music Hall – 14 October 1963, LP, 12.31–13.30. Recorded: 29 September 1963, 20.00–21.30, Playhouse Theatre, Hulme, Manchester. Taking part: David Hamilton (host), Jewel and Warriss, Joe 'Mr Piano' Henderson, Harry Bailey, Norman George, Elaine Hewitt, L.D., the Jeridale Three, the BBC Northern Dance Orchestra directed by Bernard Herrmann. Producer: James Casey (listed in *Radio Times* as Geoff Lawrence). Fee: 10 guineas.

Visiting Time – 24 December 1963, HS(N), 18.35–19.30. Recorded: 20 November 1963, 18.15–19.45, Nurses' Home, Manchester Royal Infirmary, Oxford Road, Manchester. Producer: Peter Pilbeam. Fee: 15 guineas, to cover script and compering duties.

....

1964

Variety Parade – 7 January 1964, HS(N), 19.00–19.30. Recorded: 6 January 1964, 20.00–21.00, Playhouse Theatre, Hulme, Manchester. Producer: Geoff Lawrence. Fee: 10 guineas.

Workers' Playtime – 13 February 1964, LP, 12.31–13.00. Transmitted live from William E. Cary Ltd (spring manufacturers), Red Bank, Manchester 4. Taking part: Roger Moffat (host), Peter Goodwright, Rosemary Squires, L.D., the Hedley Ward Trio, accompaniment by the Harry Hayward Trio. Producer: James Casey. Fee: 10 guineas.

Variety Parade – 17 March 1964, HS(N), 19.00–19.30. Recorded: 2 March 1964, 20.00–21.00, Playhouse Theatre, Hulme, Manchester. Producer: Geoff Lawrence. Fee: 10 guineas.

The Ray Fell Show – 23 March 1964, HS(N),

19.00–19.30. Recorded: 9 March 1964, 20.00–20.45, Playhouse Theatre, Hulme, Manchester. Producer: Geoff Lawrence. Fee: 10 guineas.

Music Hall – 6 April 1964, LP, 12.31–13.30. Recorded: 22 March 1964, 20.00–21.30, Playhouse Theatre, Hulme, Manchester. Taking part: Ken Dodd, Ian Wallace, Joe 'Mr Piano' Henderson, Billy Dainty, Julie Jones, Gordon Glenn, L.D., the Morgan-James Duo, the BBC Northern Dance Orchestra directed by Bernard Herrmann. Producer: John Wilcox. Fee: 10 guineas.

Blackpool Night – 19 July 1964, LP, 18.30–19.30. Recorded: 25 June 1964, 14.45–16.15, Jubilee Theatre, Sheppard Street, Blackpool. Taking part: Jack Watson (host), Dick Emery, the Kaye Sisters, Harry Bailey, Mrs Mills, Pat O'Hare, L.D., the Morgan-James Duo, Reginald Dixon, the BBC Northern Dance Orchestra directed by Bernard Herrmann. Producer: James Casey. Fee: 15 guineas plus expenses. Edited repeat: 24 July 1964, HS (not Scottish or Welsh), 19.00–19.30.

Blackpool Night – 6 September 1964, LP, 18.30–19.30. Recorded: 20 August 1964, 14.45–16.15, Jubilee Theatre, Sheppard Street, Blackpool. Taking part: Jack Watson (host), Ken Dodd, Rosemary Squires, L.D., Clive Lythgoe, Pat O'Hare, Reg Thompson, the Morgan-James Duo, Reginald Dixon, the BBC Northern Dance Orchestra directed by Bob Miller. Producer: James Casey. Fee: 15 guineas plus return Manchester–Blackpool rail fare. Edited repeat: 11 September 1964, HS (not Scottish or Welsh), 19.00–19.30.

A Night at the Music Hall – 14 September 1964, LP, 20.40–21.20. Recorded: 26 July 1964, 19.15–20.15, Garrick Playhouse, Barrington Road, Altrincham. *Radio Times* billing: 'Your chairman Mr. Bill Scott-Coomber introduces Mr. Ken Platt – I won't take my coat off, Herr Julius Nehring – Master of the Xylophone, Mr.

Jack Watson – Memories and Monologues, the Gladstone Harmony Four – Waiting for a Song, Mr. Les Dawson – Dispensing Doom and Despair, and the Gentlemen of the Pit Orchestra conducted by Mr. Morris McLean.' Producer: Peter Pilbeam. Fee: 15 guineas.

Workers' Playtime – 22 September 1964, LP, 12.31–13.00. Transmitted live from the Metal Box Co., Southcoates Works, St John's Grove, Southcoates Lane, Hull. Taking part: Roger Moffat (host), Cyril Fletcher, Rosemary Squires, L.D., the Brooks, accompanied by the Harry Hayward Trio. Producer: John Wilcox. Fee: 15 guineas.

Comedy Parade – 1 October 1964, LP, 20.00–20.30. Recorded: 16 August 1964, 20.00–20.45, Playhouse Theatre, Hulme, Manchester. *Radio Times* billing: 'Ray Fell and Les Dawson are *Going Places* with the Barry Sisters, Doris Rogers, the BBC Northern Dance Orchestra conducted by Johnny Spence.' Writers: James Casey and Frank Roscoe. Producer: James Casey. Fee: 21 guineas.

Startime – 19 October 1964, LP, 12.31– 13.30. Recorded: 20 September 1964, 20.00–20.45, Playhouse Theatre, Hulme, Manchester. Taking part: Roger Moffat (host), Ken Dodd, the Barry Sisters, Norman George, L.D., Myrna Rose, Mike Yarwood, the Brooks, the BBC Northern Dance Orchestra directed by Bernard Herrmann. Producer: Geoff Lawrence. Fee: 15 guineas.

....

1965

Startime – 15 March 1965, LP, 13.00–14.00. Recorded: 14 February 1965, 20.00–21.30, Playhouse Theatre, Hulme, Manchester. Taking part: Roger Moffat (host), Ted Ray, Joan Regan, Bert Weedon, L.D., John Hauxvell, Freddie Davies, the Morgan-James Duo, and the BBC Northern Dance Orchestra directed by Bernard Herrmann. Producer: James Casey. Fee: 20 guineas.

Air Break – 22 March 1965, HS(N),

19.00–19.30. Recorded: 17 March 1965, 20.00–21.00, Playhouse Theatre, Hulme, Manchester. Producer: Geoff Lawrence. Fee: 10 guineas.

Light Up the Night – 3 April 1965, LP, 19.30–21.00. Recorded: 28 March 1965, 19.30–21.30, Camden Theatre, London. Taking part: Don Arrol (host), Peter Goodwright, 'Mrs Shufflewick', L.D., Craig Douglas, Anita Harris, Andy Cole, the Adam Singers, Ronnie Price and his Quartet, Johnny Pearson at the piano, the Galaxy Orchestra conducted by Paul Fenoulhet. Writer: Denis Goodwin. Producers: John Browell and Richard Willcox. Fee: 20 guineas plus £2 18s night allowance and return Manchester–London rail fare (£5).

Light Up the Night – 17 April 1965, LP, 19.30–21.00. Recorded: 11 April 1965, 19.30–21.30, Camden Theatre, London. Taking part: Don Arrol (host), Dick Bentley, June Whitfield, Fred Gaunt, L.D., Sheila Buxton, Anita Harris, Andy Cole, the Adam Singers, Ronnie Price and his Quartet, and Malcolm Lockyer at the piano and conducting the Galaxy Orchestra. Writer: Denis Goodwin. Producers: John Browell and Richard Willcox. Fee: 20 guineas plus £2 18s night allowance and return Manchester–London rail fare (£5).

Light Up the Night – 1 May 1965, LP, 19.30–21.00. Recorded: 25 April 1965, 19.30–21.30, Camden Theatre, London. Taking part: Don Arrol (host), Charlie Chester, Bill Kellie, L.D., Ronnie Hilton, Anita Harris, Andy Cole, the Adam Singers, Ronnie Price and his Quartet, and Malcolm Lockyer at the piano and conducting the Galaxy Orchestra. Writer: Denis Goodwin. Producers: John Browell and Richard Willcox. Fee: 20 guineas plus £2 18s night allowance and return Manchester–London rail fare (£5).

Light Up the Night – 29 May 1965, LP, 19.30–21.00. Recorded: 23 May 1965, 19.30–21.30, Camden Theatre, London. Taking part: Don

Arrol (host), Clive Dunn, Roy Hudd, L.D., the Swingle Singers, Anita Harris, Andy Cole, the Adam Singers, Ronnie Price and his Quartet, and Malcolm Lockyer at the piano and conducting the Galaxy Orchestra. Writer: Denis Goodwin. Producers: John Browell and Richard Willcox. Fee: 20 guineas plus £2 18s night allowance and return Manchester–London rail fare (£5).

Blackpool Night – 11 September 1965, LP, 19.30–20.30. Recorded: 17 August 1965, 14.45–16.15, Jubilee Theatre, Sheppard Street, Blackpool. Taking part: Jack Watson (host), Donald Peers, Bill Waddington, the Karl Denver Trio, L.D., Gordon Glenn, Barbara Kay, Terry Kaye, Reginald Dixon, and the BBC Northern Dance Orchestra directed by Bernard Herrmann. Producer: James Casey (listed in *Radio Times* as Geoff Lawrence). Fee: 20 guineas plus return Isle of Man–Blackpool air fare.

Home and Away – 6 November 1965, LP, 19.30–20.15. Recorded: 29 September 1965, Gütersloh, Germany. Taking part: Peter Goodwright (host), Elkie Brooks, Humphrey Lyttelton, L.D., the Ronnie Aldrich Quartet and the Migil 5. Writer: Dick Vosburgh. Producer: Bobby Jaye. Fee: 30 guineas plus 7 and a half guineas for British Forces Broadcasting Service transmission.

Home and Away – 20 November 1965, LP, 19.30–20.15. Recorded: 30 September 1965, Münster, Germany. Taking part: Peter Goodwright (host), Elkie Brooks, Humphrey Lyttelton, L.D., the Ronnie Aldrich Quartet, the Migil 5. Writer: Dick Vosburgh. Producer: Bobby Jaye. Fee: 30 guineas plus 7 and a half guineas for British Forces Broadcasting Service transmission.

1968

The Golden Parrot Club – 19 October 1968, R1/2, 19.35-20.30. Taking part: Freddie Davies, Vince Hill, L.D., Barbara Law, Nigel Hopkins, Spencer's Washboard Kings, Colin Edwynn, Barbara Mullaney and Fred Gaunt, the BBC Northern Dance Orchestra directed by Bernard Herrmann. Writers: Michael Craig, Lawrie Kinsley, Gary Knight. Producer: Geoff Lawrence.

....

1976
The Northern Comic – 15 May 1976, R3, 22.55–23.40. Archive listing: 'The Northern Comic – who is he, why is he? An investigative entertainment conducted by James Casey in conversation with Ken Dodd, with various contributors.' Taking part: Roy Castle, L.D., Ron McDonnell, Geoffrey Wheeler, Bill Spink, Dr. John Oldroyd, Lawrie Kinsley, Dennis Smith, Duggie Brown, Tony Dowling. Producer: James Casey. *A copy of this programme is kept in the broadcaster's archive.*

....

1977
Be My Guest – 20 November 1977, R2, 15.30–16.00. *Radio Times* billing: 'Les Dawson says Be My Guest and invites you to meet him at his home, to recall some not too serious moments in his life, and share some of his favourite music.' Producer: Phyllis Robinson.

....

1978
Windsor Davies Presents . . . the Multi-National Eisteddfod Show – 26 March 1978, R2, 22.02–22.30. Taking part: Windsor Davies, L.D., Bryan Carroll, Penny Lane, the Max Harris Orchestra. Writer: Peter Spence. Producer: Richard Willcox. *A copy of this programme is kept in the broadcaster's archive.*

Desert Island Discs – 8 April 1978, R4, 18.15–18.50. Producer: Derek Drescher. Repeated: 11 April 1978, R4, 12.20–12.55.

Woman's Hour – 7 July 1978, R4, 13.45–14.45. June Knox-Mawer interviews Les Dawson about his comedy, his books and why he stays in the north. *A copy of this interview excerpt is kept in the broadcaster's archive.*

1979
The Grumbleweeds Christmas Party – 26 December 1979, R2, 18.03–19.00. Taking part: The Grumbleweeds, L.D., Roy Castle, Mike Burton, Eddie Braben, Jacqueline Clarke, Daphne Oxenford, Alison Steadman, Eli Woods and Colin Edwynn. Producers: Mike Craig and James Casey.

....

1981
Variety Club – 13 October 1981, R2, 22.00–23.00. Taking part: L.D., Pat Mooney, Jacqui Scott, Kenny Martyn, Chester Harriott, Martin Dale (host). Musical director: Brian Fitzgerald. Producer: Mike Craig.

It Makes Me Laugh – 31 December 1981, R4, 18.30–18.55. *Radio Times* billing: 'Les Dawson invites you to join him in listening to some entertainers and comedians who make him laugh: including the voices of Jack Benny, Robb Wilton, Tony Hancock, Norman Evans, Gerard Hoffnung and W.C. Fields.' Producer: Phyllis Robinson.

....

1982
Laughalong with Les Dawson and Roy Castle – 3 May 1982, R2, 22.00–23.00. Taking part: L.D., Roy Castle, Eli Woods, Daphne Oxenford and Brian Fitzgerald and his orchestra. Writers: James Casey, Mike Craig, Lawrie Kinsley, Ron McDonnell. Producer: James Casey.

....

1983
Laughalong with Les Dawson and Roy Castle – 29 August 1983, R2, 13.00–14.00. Taking part: L.D., Roy Castle, Eli Woods, Daphne Oxenford and Brian Fitzgerald and his orchestra. Writers: James Casey, Ron McDonnell. Producer: James Casey.

Today 8 November – 1983, R4, 06.30–09.00. The cast of the *Royal Variety Performance*, including Les Dawson, talk about the show. *A copy of this item is kept in the broadcaster's archive.*

Laughalong with Les Dawson and Roy Castle – 28 December 1983, R2, 13.30–14.30. Taking part: L.D., Roy Castle, Eli Woods, Daphne Oxenford, and Brian Fitzgerald and his orchestra. Writers: James Casey, Ron McDonnell. Producer: James Casey.

Sport on 2 – 31 December 1983, R2, 13.30–18.00. Ian Darke speaks to Les Dawson about his interest in sport. *A copy of this interview excerpt is kept in the broadcaster's archive.*

1984

Talkabout Gardening – 22 July 1984, R4, 14.00–14.30. L.D takes Clay Jones around his garden at Lytham. Producer: Ken Ford.

1986

It's a Funny Business – 22 January 1986, R2, 22.00–22.30. Mike Craig interviews Les Dawson. Producer: Mike Craig.

Farewell to the Playhouse – 25 August 1986, R2, 13.05–14.00. Recorded: 15 June 1986, Playhouse Theatre, Hulme, Manchester. Taking part: Ray Moore, Ken Platt, Peter Goodwright, Geoffrey Wheeler, Cardew Robinson, Bill Waddington, Joe Gladwin, Kevin Kent, Alyn Ainsworth, Harry Worth, Norman George, David Hamilton, Ernie Wise, the Beverley Sisters, and the BBC Northern Dance Orchestra directed by Brian Fitzgerald. Writer/producer: Mike Craig. *A copy of this programme is kept in the broadcaster's archive.*

1990

Broadcasts for Schools: Whirligig – Tubby the Tuba – 26 February 1990, R4. Taking part: L.D. (narrator), BBC Concert Orchestra directed by Barry Wordsworth, Patrick Harrild (tuba soloist) and Rod Elms (piano). Producer: Brian Scott-Hughes. *A copy of this programme is kept in the broadcaster's archive.*

John Dunn – 2 November 1990, R2, 17.05–19.00. Les Dawson talks about his new novel, *Come Back with the Wind*. *A copy of this interview excerpt is kept in the broadcaster's archive.*

1991

Woman's Hour – 4 January 1991, R4, 14.00–15.00. L.D. talks to Helen Boaden about mother-in-law jokes. *A copy of this interview excerpt is kept in the broadcaster's archive.*

1993

In the Psychiatrist's Chair – 5 September 1993, R4, 12.15–12.55. (repeated 8 September 1993, 09.05–09.45) Professor Anthony Clare talks to L.D. A Michael Ember Associates production for the BBC. *A copy of this programme is kept in the broadcaster's archive.*

Starring vehicles

The Les Dawson Show

27 May 1968; R4(N), 12.25–12.55.

Les Dawson – Man of Fiction

26 February–2 April 1970; R4(N); Thursdays, 12.25 – 6 × 30 minutes.

Our Les

Series 1: 8 December 1971–26 January 1972; R1/2, Wednesdays, 20.02; 8 × 30 minutes. Recorded: Playhouse Theatre, Hulme, Manchester. Writer/producer: James Casey.

Series 2: 31 December 1972–25 February 1973; R2, Sundays, 14.30 (repeated Fridays, 20.02); 9 × 30 minutes. Recorded: Playhouse Theatre, Hulme, Manchester. Cast included: Colin Edwynn, David Mahlowe, Daphne Oxenford, Brian Trueman, Barbara Mullaney and Marlene Sidaway. Writer/producer: James Casey. *The third show (14 Jan. 1973) and final show (25 Feb. 1973) of this series are kept in the broadcaster's archive.*

Listen to Les

Series 1: R2, 7 July–25 August 1974; Sundays, 14.02 (repeated Saturdays, 19.02) – 9 × 30 minutes. Cast: L.D., Colin Edwynn, Daphne Oxenford. Musical director: Brian Fitzgerald. Writer/producer: James Casey. *The seventh show of this series (11 Aug. 1974) is kept in the broadcaster's archive.*

Series 2: R2, 8 June–27 July 1975; Sundays, 14.02 (repeated Saturdays, 19.02) – 8 × 30 minutes. Cast: L.D., Colin Edwynn, Daphne Oxenford. Musical director: Brian Fitzgerald. Writer/producer: James Casey *The third show of this series (22 June 1975) is kept in the broadcaster's archive.*

Series 3: R2, 17 October–5 December 1976; Sundays, 14.02 (repeated Saturdays, 19.02) – 8 × 30 minutes. Cast: L.D., Colin Edwynn, Daphne Oxenford. Musical director: Brian Fitzgerald (except first 3 shows, Brian Pendleton). Writer/producer: James Casey.

Series 4: R2, 7 August–25 September 1977; Sundays, 14.02 (repeated Saturdays, 19.02) – 8 × 30 minutes. Cast: L.D., Colin Edwynn, Daphne Oxenford. Musical director: Brian Fitzgerald. Writer/producer: James Casey.

Series 5: R2, 1 October –19 November 1978; Fridays, 22.30 – 8 × 30 minutes. Cast: L.D., Colin Edwynn, Daphne Oxenford. Musical director: Brian Fitzgerald. Writer/producer: James Casey.

Series 6: R2, 18 November 1979–6 January 1980; Sundays, 13.30 (repeated Fridays, 19.02) – 9 × 30 minutes. Cast: L.D., Colin Edwynn, Daphne Oxenford. Musical director: Brian Fitzgerald. Writer/producer: James Casey.

Series 7: R2, 7 December 1980–25 January 1981; Sundays, 13.32 (repeated Fridays, 22.02) – 9 × 30 minutes. Cast: L.D., Colin Edwynn, Daphne Oxenford. Musical director: Brian Fitzgerald. Writer/producer: James Casey.

Series 8: R2, 17 January–4 April 1982; Sundays, 13.30 (repeated Fridays, 22.02) 13 × 30 minutes. Cast: L.D., Colin Edwynn, Daphne Oxenford. Musical director: Brian

Fitzgerald. Writer/producer: James Casey.

Series 9: R2, 10 July–25 September 1983; Sundays, 13.30 (repeated Fridays, 22.00) – 13 × 30 minutes. Cast: L.D., Roy Barraclough, Colin Edwynn, Daphne Oxenford. Musical director: Brian Fitzgerald. Writer/producer: James Casey.

Series 10: R2, 20 January–24 March 1985; Sundays, 16.00 (repeated Fridays, 22.00) – 13 × 30 minutes. Cast: L.D., Eli Woods, Colin Edwynn, Daphne Oxenford. Musical director: Brian Fitzgerald. Writer/producer: James Casey *The first show of this series (20 Jan. 1985) is kept in the broadcaster's archive.*

Mike Yarwood in the Les Dawson Show
25 August 1975, R2, 13.02–14.00. Taking part: L.D., Mike Yarwood, Wilma Reading, the BBC Northern Radio Orchestra directed by Neil Richardson. Writers: Eric Davidson, James Casey. Producer: James Casey. *A copy of this programme is kept in the broadcaster's archive.*

Television work

ABC: ABC Television (ITV weekend company for the Midlands and North from 1956–68)

ATV: Associated Television (ITV weekend contractor for London from 1955–68, ITV weekday contractor for the Midlands, 1956–68, then ITV contractor for the Midlands from 1968–81)

YTV: Yorkshire Television (ITV contractor for Yorkshire from 1968–2002)

All programmes networked nationally unless otherwise indicated.

Spots and guest appearances

1962
Saturday Bandbox – 16 June 1962, ABC (not networked, shown only in the ABC Midlands and North regions), 19.25–20.10.

TV Times billing: 'A weekend blend of music and laughter, this week presenting another All Star Comedy Concert featuring music you might like to have missed from Jimmy Clitheroe, Norman Evans, Tessie O'Shea, the Three Monarchs, Les Dawson with others too humorous to mention, and the ABC Television Orchestra, directed by Bob Sharples.' Director: Kenneth Carter.

1963

Comedy Bandbox – 23 November 1963, ABC (not networked, shown only in ABC Midlands, ABC North, Anglia and TWW regions), 18.35–19.15. Taking part: Gerry and the Pacemakers, Clive Dunn, Des Lane, Syd and Max Harrison, Neville King, L.D.

1964

Two's a Crowd – 18 March 1964, BBC TV (North region only), 19.35–20.00. Recorded: 16 March 1964, BBC North region TV studio, Dickenson Road, Rusholme, Manchester (Programme as Broadcast sheet lists 'Facilities: Rusholme Cons. Club'.). Taking part: Johnny Hackett, L.D., Althea Lambert, the Harry Hayward Orchestra. Producer: James Casey. Editor: Geoff Lawrence.

1967

Opportunity Knocks! – 20 May 1967, ABC (networked), 18.20–19.00. *TV Times* billing: 'Opportunity Knocks! says Hughie Green. Have a competition with your neighbour and see who has forecast the winner for next week's show. Last week's winner, Les Dawson, Kay and Kim, the Glendoi Singers, Yvonne Marsh, the Rose Fletcher Pipe Band, Bob Sharples and the ABC Television Showband.' Producer: Milo Lewis. Director: Royston Mayoh.

The Blackpool Show – 30 July 1967, ABC (networked), 22.05–23.05. *TV Times* billing: 'Another comedy and music spectacular from the summer home of show business. From the stage of the ABC Theatre,

Blackpool. Dickie Henderson introduces the Shadows, Julie Rogers, the Peiro Brothers, Chris Kirby, Les Dawson, Irving Davies and the Blackpool Show Dancers. Bob Sharples with the ABC Television Showband. Staging by Irving Davies. Designer Harry Clark. Produced by Mark Stuart. ABC Weekend Network Production.' Taking part: Dickie Henderson (compère), the Shadows, Julie Rogers, Chris Kirby, the Periot Brothers, L.D., Irving Davies and the Blackpool Show Dancers. Musical director: Bob Sharples. Producer: Mark Stuart.

The Blackpool Show – 13 August 1967, ABC (networked), 22.05–23.05. Taking part: Dickie Henderson (compère), Frankie Vaughan with Basil Tait and the V Group, L.D., Tanya, Jenda Smaha, L.D., Irving Davies and the Blackpool Show Dancers. Musical director: Bob Sharples. Producer: Keith Beckett.

The Val Doonican Show – 7 October 1967, BBC1, 19.45–20.30. Transmitted live from the BBC Television Theatre. Taking part: Val Doonican, Cliff Richard, Rolf Harris, L.D. and the Gojos, with the Adam Singers directed by Cliff Adams. Musical director: Ken Thorne. Writers: Austin Steele, John Law, Val Doonican. Producer: John Ammonds.

Dee Time – 4 November 1967, BBC1, 18.00–18.45. Transmitted live from Studio G, BBC Television Studios, Lime Grove, London, W12. Taking part: Simon Dee, Len Marten, Colin Chapman, Michael Craig, Vince Hill, L.D., John Walker, Myrna Rose, Madeline Bell, the Scaffold, Juliet Morris. Musical director: Alyn Ainsworth. Vocal backing: the Ladybirds (Gloria George, Margaret Stredder, Ann Simmons). Producer: Terry Henebery.

Strictly for Laughs – 16 December 1967, ABC (not networked – ABC Midlands and North only), 23.05-23.35. Taking part: Kenneth Horne (chairman), June Murdoch, Norman Vaughan, Terry Hall, L.D. Writers: Brad Ashton, George Evans, Derek Collyer.

Programme associate: Len Marten.
Producer/director: Pat Johns

Mike and Bernie's Show – 30 December 1967,
ABC (networked), 18.15–19.00. Taking part:
Mike and Bernie Winters, L.D., Tanya the
Elephant, the New Vaudeville Band, Chris
Langford. Writers: Brad Ashton, George
Evans, Derek Collyer. Musical director: Bob
Sharples. Director: Tom Clegg. Producer:
Pat Johns.

1968

Mike and Bernie's Show – 13 January 1968,
ABC (networked), 18.15–19.00. Taking
part: Mike and Bernie Winters, L.D., the
Kaye Sisters, Malcolm Roberts, Los Zafiros,
Malcolm Roberts. Writers: Brad Ashton,
George Evans, Derek Collyer. Musical
director: Bob Sharples. Director: Tom Clegg.
Producer: Pat Johns.

Cilla – 13 February 1968, BBC1, 20.00–20.50.
Transmitted live from the BBC Television
Theatre. Taking part: Cilla Black, Frankie
Vaughan, Roy Hudd, Donovan, L.D., Irving
Davies Dancers, the Ladybirds. Musical
director: Harry Rabinowitz. Producer:
Michael Hurll. *A copy of this programme is
kept in the broadcaster's archive.*

The London Palladium Show – 10 March
1968, ATV (networked), 20.25–21.15.
Transmitted live from the London
Palladium. Taking part: Dickie Henderson
(compère), Tony Bennett, Buddy Rich and
his Orchestra, Dusty Springfield, L.D., Les
Farfardets. Musical director: Jack Parnell.
Producer: Colin Clews.

Show of the Week: Rolf Harris – 19 May
1968, BBC2, 20.35–21.35. Recorded studios
TC7 and TC8, BBC Television Centre,
London. Taking part: Rolf Harris, Dora
Bryan, Arthur Worsley, L.D. and the Paper
Dolls. Producer: Stewart Morris.

Lulu's Back in Town – 11 June 1968, BBC1,
21.05–21.30. Recorded: 1 May 1968. Taking
part: Lulu, L.D., the Everly Brothers, and the
Ladybirds (vocal backing). Musical director:

Peter Knight. Producer: John Ammonds.
*A copy of this programme is kept in the
broadcaster's archive.*

1969

Opportunity Knocks! – 10 November 1969,
Thames (networked), 18.45–19.30. Taking
part: Hughie Green (host), L.D., Dave
Swann, Monica Rose, the Chicago Soup
Queue (musical group from HMS *Hermes*).
Musical director: Bob Sharples. Producer/
director: Robert Fleming.

1970

Inside George Webley – 11 and 18 February
1970, YTV (networked), 22.30–23.00. L.D.
appears as Mr Marigold in two episodes of
Keith Waterhouse and Willis Hall's situation
comedy, starring Roy Kinnear. Director:
David Mallet. Producer: John Duncan.
*Copies of these shows are kept in the
broadcaster's archive.*

David Nixon's Magic Box – 13 April 1970,
Thames (networked), 18.45–19.30. Taking
part: David Nixon (host), L.D., Stubby
Kaye, Tony Riding. Writer: George Martin.
Producer/director: Robert Fleming.

It's Lulu – 25 July 1970, BBC1, 20.45–21.30.
Taking part: Lulu, L.D., Dudley Moore,
Mama Cass, Marmalade. Musical director:
Alyn Ainsworth. Writer: Eric Merriman.
Producers: Stewart Morris and Colin
Charman. *A copy of this programme is
kept in the broadcaster's archive.*

The Golden Shot – 2 August 1970, ATV
(networked), 16.45–17.30. Taking part:
Bob Monkhouse (host), Ronnie Hilton,
L.D., Stefanie Powers, Anne Aston. Writer:
Wally Malston. Producer/director: Mike
Lloyd. *A script for this show exists in the
Bob Monkhouse collection, maintained by
Kaleidoscope.*

A Gift For Gracie – 25 December 1970, YTV
(networked), 14.00–15.00. Taking part: The
Bachelors, Gracie Fields, Bruce Forsyth,
Harry Secombe, Mike and Bernie Winters,

Ted Ray, Arthur Askey, L.D., Sandy Powell, Patricia Ruanne, Lionel Blair. *TV Times* billing: 'Take a set sweeping the entire length of Yorkshire Television's largest studio (7,650 square feet); add an all-star line up, two top writers and a director who has been connected with some of television's leading shows and the result can only be a variety spectacular with a capital S. The set is made up of three levels to look like the entrance hall and grand staircase of an eighteenth-century mansion. It is here that Gracie's party takes place. With her guests – the Poole and Brook families, the Lionel Blair Dancers, the Mike Sammes Singers and butler Bruce Forsyth – she settles down to watch the Queen's Christmas message. But there are constant interruptions – interruptions, however, that become welcome surprises.' Writers: Mike Craig and Lawrie Kinsley. Director: Ian Fordyce. Executive producer: Jess Yates.

Holiday Star Time – 26 December 1970, LWT (networked), 18.45–20.00. Taking part: Maggie Fitzgibbon (host), L.D., Peter Cook, Thora Hird, Vincent Price, Arthur Lowe, Max Jaffa, Ted Ray, Reg Varney, the Bee Gees, Kenny Ball, Chris Barber and Acker Bilk. Writers: Peter Dulay, Barry Cryer, Peter Cook. Producer: David Bell. Executive producer: Terry Henebery. *A copy of this programme is kept in the broadcaster's archive.*

The Syd Lawrence Band Show – 31 December 1970, YTV (not networked – shown only in the YTV, HTV, Westward and Channel regions), 18.30–19.00. Taking part: Syd Lawrence Orchestra, L.D., Kevin Kent, the Skylarks. Director: David Mallet. Producer: John Duncan. *A copy of this programme is kept in the broadcaster's archive.*

1971

David Nixon's Magic Box – 18 January 1971, Thames (networked), 18.45–19.30. Taking

part: David Nixon (host), L.D., Anita Harris, Clifford Davis, Mr Cox and his Magic Lady. Writer: George Martin. Musical director: Ronnie Aldrich. Producer/director: Peter Frazer-Jones.

The Golden Shot – 31 January 1971, ATV (networked), 16.40–17.35. Taking part: Bob Monkhouse (host), L.D. Writer: Wally Malston. Producer/director: Mike Lloyd. *A script for this show exists in the Bob Monkhouse collection, maintained by Kaleidoscope.*

The Golden Shot – 22 August 1971, ATV (networked), 16.40–17.35. Taking part: Bob Monkhouse (host), L.D., Malcolm Roberts, Christine Holmes, Anne Aston, Jenny Lee-Wright. Writer: Wally Malston. Producer/director: Mike Lloyd. *A script for this show exists in the Bob Monkhouse collection, maintained by Kaleidoscope.*

David Nixon's Magic Box – 11 October 1971, Thames (networked), 18.40–19.30. Taking part: David Nixon (host), L.D., the Beverley Sisters, Tonny Van Dommelen and Alistair. Writers: David Nixon and George Martin. Musical director: Ronnie Aldrich. Director: Robert Reed. Producer: David Clark.

1972

The Golden Shot – 12 March 1972, ATV (networked), 16.45–17.35. Taking part: Norman Vaughan (host), L.D., Christie, Anne Aston, Jenny Hanley. Writers: Spike Mullins, Charles Hart. Director: Paul Stewart Laing. Producer: Les Cocks.

The Good Old Days – 16 March 1972, BBC1, 20.00–20.50. Taking part: Leonard Sachs (chairman), L.D., Sandie Shaw, Nigel Hopkins. Producer: Barney Colehan.

1973

Shut That Door – 28 March 1973, ATV (networked), 20.00–20.30. Taking part: Larry Grayson, Arthur Worsley, Linda Grant, L.D. Writers: Peter Dulay, Bryan Blackburn, Bernie Sharp. Musical director: Jack Parnell.

Producer/director: Colin Clews.

It's Lulu – 29 September 1973, BBC1, 19.15–20.00. Taking part: Lulu, L.D., Sergio Mendes and Brasil 77, Adrienne Posta, Roger Kitter, Paul Greenwood, Segment. Writers: Geoff Rowley, Andy Baker, Tony Hare. Musical director: Alyn Ainsworth. Executive producer: John Ammonds. Producer: Vernon Lawrence.

Omnibus: Laughter – Why We Laugh – 14 October 1973, BBC1, 22.15–23.05. *Radio Times* billing: 'We all know that we do laugh, but the reasons why we laugh are often puzzling. In tonight's Omnibus, Barry Took, who earns his living laughter-making, tries out his ideas on an invited audience and is joined by John Cleese, Les Dawson and Peter Black for a discussion on the subject. Examples of what makes us laugh include: Buster Keaton in *Steamboat Bill Junior*, *Traffic* by Jacques Tati, *Rowan and Martin's Laugh-In, But Seriously – It's Sheila Hancock, Look – Mike Yarwood, Monty Python's Flying Circus* and Norman Chappell.' Producer: Vernon Lawrence.

Stars on Sunday – 4 November 1973, YTV (networked), 19.00–19.25. Taking part: James Mason, L.D., Kiri te Kanawa, the Beverley Sisters, Kamahl, 400 York Celebration Choir directed by John Warburton, the Doncaster Wheatsheaf Girls' Choir, the massed bands and choirs of the Salvation Army, the young ladies of *Stars on Sunday*. Musical director: John Barker. Director: Len Lurcuck. Executive producer: Jess Yates.

The Glories of Christmas – 25 December 1973, YTV (networked), 14.00-15.00. Taking part: Roy Barraclough, John Bluthal, Alan Browning, Dora Bryan, Patrick Cargill, Diana Coupland, L.D., Arthur English, Harry Fowler, Gerald Harper, Kathleen Harrison, Melvyn Hayes, James Hayter, Gordon Honeycombe, John Laurie, Alfred Marks, Penny Meredith, Bob Monkhouse, Stephen Murray, Patrick Newell, Patricia Phoenix,

Patrick Troughton, Freddie Trueman, Richard Todd, Gorden Kaye, Timothy Spall, Princess Grace of Monaco, The Bachelors, Janet Baker, Margaret Barron, The Beverley Sisters, Igor Gridneff, Trevor Lawson, Kenneth McKellar, Ludmila Nova, Colin Prince, Rostal and Schaefer, Patricia Ruanna, Richard Tucker, Francis Van Dyke, Huddersfield Choral Society, Wheatsheaf Girls' Choir. Producer/director: Len Lurcuck. *A copy of this programme is kept in the broadcaster's archive.*

1974

Second House – 30 March 1974, BBC2, 21.40–23.10. Introduced by Melvyn Bragg. *Radio Times* billing: '*Never give a sucker an even break* – the catchphrase of the great W.C. Fields, comic genius anti-hero, whose splendidly idiosyncratic views on politics, big business, marriage, babies and alcohol are legendary. For *Second House*, comedian Les Dawson, himself a W.C. Fields devotee, presents a collection of hitherto unpublished letters, speeches and sketches from Fields's "intended autobiography", due to be published in April.' Assistant editor: Tony Staveacre. Editor: Bill Morton. *A copy of this programme is kept in the broadcaster's archive.*

Stars on Sunday – 9 June 1974, YTV (networked), 19.00–19.25. Taking part: James Mason, L.D., Moira Anderson, Frank Ifield, Bobby Bennett, Rhosllanerchrugog Orpheus Male Voice Choir conducted by John Glyn Williams, the Massed Bands and Songsters of the Salvation Army conducted by Major Leslie Condon, the young ladies of *Stars on Sunday*. Director: Ian Bolt. Producer: Peter Max-Wilson.

The Best of Les Dawson – 15 June 1974, YTV/Tyne-Tees/Scottish only, 20.00–20.30.

Parkinson – 16 November 1974, BBC1, 23.25–00.25. Taking part: Michael Parkinson (host), L.D., Nettie Bainbridge, Eva Von Rueber-Staier, Twiggy. Musical director:

Harry Stoneham. Director: Colin Strong. Producer: Roger Ordish. *A copy of this programme is kept in the broadcaster's archive.*

1975

Cinema – 4 July 1975, Granada (networked), 22.30–23.00. *TV Times* billing: 'Les Dawson on W.C. Fields. Universal have recently undertaken the production of the biographic film *W.C. Fields*, with Rod Steiger in the title role. In this edition of *Cinema* comedian Les Dawson looks at the career of W.C. Fields, and with the help of film clips, examines some of the master's "subtly executed jocosities".' Director: Mike Becker. Producer: Arthur Taylor. *A copy of this programme is kept in the broadcaster's archive.*

1976

The Good Old Days – 19 February 1976, BBC1, 21.25–22.10. Taking part: Leonard Sachs (chairman), L.D., Peggy Mount, Larry Parker, Chantal and Dumont, Jeannie Harris, the Jan Madd Magic Show, members of the Players' Theatre company. Musical director: Bernard Herrmann. Producer: Barney Colehan. *A copy of this programme is kept in the broadcaster's archive.*

Summer Night Out – 7 July 1976, YTV (networked) 20.00–21.00. Recorded at Batley Variety Club. Taking part: L.D. (host), Kenneth McKellar, Paco Pena, Warren Mitchell, Rod Hull and Emu, Dougie Squires' Second Generation, Kristine, the Mike Sammes Singers. Musical director: Peter Husband. Producer/director: Vernon Lawrence. *A copy of this programme is kept in the broadcaster's archive.*

Parkinson – 30 October 1976, BBC1, 23.00–00.00. Taking part: Michael Parkinson (host), L.D., Lord Carnarvon, Tom Paxton. Musical director: Harry Stoneham. Director: Colin Strong. Producer: Richard Drewett. *A copy of this programme is kept in the broadcaster's archive.*

A Royal Club Night – 7 December 1976, BBC2, 21.30–22.15. Recorded at Cæsar's Palace, Luton, in aid of the Entertainment Artists' Benevolent Fund and the Bowles Mountaineering Outdoor Pursuits Centre. Taking part: L.D. (host), Nana Mouskouri, Larry Parker, Charlie Smithers, Jerry Brooke, Peter Gordeno and his dancers. Television production: Michael Hurll.

1977

Celebrity Squares – 12 February 1977, ATV (networked), 18.15–19.00. Taking part: Bob Monkhouse (host), Colin Baker, Gemma Craven, L.D., Sandra Dickinson, John Inman, Libby Morris, Arthur Mullard, William Rushton, Terry Scott. Director: Paul Stewart Laing. *A copy of this programme is kept in the broadcaster's archive.*

Celebrity Squares – 26 February 1977, ATV (networked), 18.15–19.00. Taking part: Bob Monkhouse (host), Dickie Davies, Les Dawson, Julie Ege, Vince Hill, Henry McGee, Barbara Mitchell, Arthur Mullard, Jean Rook, William Rushton. Director: Christopher Tookey. *A copy of this programme is kept in the broadcaster's archive.*

The Good Old Days – 17 February 1977, BBC1, 21.25–22.10. Taking part: Leonard Sachs (chairman), L.D., the King's Singers, Patsy Gilland, Peter Gale, Dinardi, Les Renees, members of the Players Theatre company. Musical director: Bernard Herrmann. Producer: Barney Colehan. *A copy of this programme is kept in the broadcaster's archive.*

Celebrity Squares – 19 March 1977, ATV (networked), 18.15–19.00. Taking part: Bob Monkhouse (host), L.D., Don Maclean, Lorna Luft, Ron Moody, Joe Brown, Jean Rook, George Roper, Willie Rushton, Barbara Windsor. Additional material: Jeremy Beadle. Director: Paul Stewart Laing. *A domestic off-air video recording of the*

show is retained by Kaleidoscope as part of
the Bob Monkhouse archive.
Celebrity Squares – 9 April 1977, ATV
(networked), 18.15–19.00. Taking part: Bob
Monkhouse (host), L.D., Nerys Hughes,
Frank Carson, Jean Rook, Willie Rushton,
Ted Moult, Roy Hudd, Katie Boyle, Arthur
Mullard. Additional material: Ian Messiter,
Jeremy Beadle. Director: Paul Stewart Laing.
*A copy of this programme is kept in the
broadcaster's archive.*
Celebrity Squares – 23 April 1977, ATV
(networked) 18.15–19.00. Taking part:
Bob Monkhouse (host), L.D., Julie Ege,
Dickie Davies, Les Dawson, Roy Hudd,
Arthur Mullard, Madeline Bell, Henry
McGee, John Conteh, Willie Rushton.
Additional material: Ian Messiter, Jeremy
Beadle. Director: Paul Stewart Laing.
*A partial audio recording of the studio
session for this programme is retained by
Kaleidoscope as part of the Bob Monkhouse
archive.*
The Royal Windsor Big Top Show – 29 May
1977, BBC1, 19.15–21.45. Recorded at Billy
Smart's Big Top in Home Park, Windsor,
in the presence of HM the Queen and
HRH the Duke of Edinburgh, in aid of the
Queen's Silver Jubilee Appeal. Taking part:
Bruce Forsyth (host), Ronnie Corbett, L.D.,
Barry Humphries, Elton John, New Edition,
Olivia Newton-John, Leo Sayer, Eric Sykes,
Mike Yarwood, Yasmin Smart, Alan Alan,
the Boichanovi Troupe, the Castors, the
Flying Terrells, Judy Murton, the Roberts
Brothers Elephants, Arthur Scott and his
sea lions, the Veterans. Writer: Barry Cryer.
Musical directors: Ken Griffin and Ronnie
Hazlehurst. Variety associate producer:
James Moir. Producer: Michael Hurll.
*A copy of this programme is kept in the
broadcaster's archive.*
Celebrity Squares – 4 June 1977, ATV
(networked), 18.15–19.00. Taking part:
Bob Monkhouse (host), Tony Adams,
Christopher Beeny, Ray Alan and Lord

Charles, Katie Boyle, Pat Coombs, L.D.,
Michele Dotrice, Dickie Henderson,
Willie Rushton. Additional material: Ian
Messiter, Jeremy Beadle, Garry Chambers.
Director: Christopher Tookey. *An audio
recording of this programme is retained by
Kaleidoscope as part of the Bob Monkhouse
archive.*
Night of 100 Stars – 5 June 1977, LWT
(networked), 19.15-21.45. Taking part:
Gordon Jackson, Moira Anderson, John
Clements, John Dankworth, Stéphane
Grappelli, Glenda Jackson, Cleo Laine,
John Mills, Kenneth More, Merle Park,
Beryl Reid, Martin Shaw, Lewis Collins,
Edward Woodward, Barbara Windsor,
Simon Williams, Kenneth Williams, John
Williams, Richard Todd, Talk of The Town
Girls, Elaine Stritch, John Standing, Leonard
Sachs, Denis Quilley, Brian Rix, Helen Ryan,
Nyree Dawn Porter, Jack Parnell, David
Nixon, the cast of *Oh Mr Porter*, Derek
Nimmo, Ron Moody, Aimi MacDonald,
Jessie Matthews, Patrick Allen, Ambrosian
Opera Chorus, Kenny Ball, Amanda Barrie,
Bernard Bresslaw, Wendy Craig, L.D., Charlie
Drake, Wayne Eagling, English National
Opera, Geraint Evans, Frank Finlay, Liz
Fraser, John Gielgud, Richard Goolden, Diz
Disley Trio, Wendy Hiller, Alan Howard,
Rod Hull and Emu, John Inman, 'Irene'
Company, Jimmy Jewel, Penelope Keith,
Felicity Kendal, Dinsdale Landen, Danny
La Rue, Hugh Lloyd, Humphrey Lyttelton.
Producer/director: Jon Scoffield. *A copy of
the programme is kept in the broadcaster's
archive.*
Tell Me More – 18 June 1977, BBC1, 17.40–
18.10. Taking part: Nanette Newman,
Graeme Garden, L.D., the Tommy Whittle
Quintet, Jacquie Sullivan. Producers: Johnny
Downes and Roger Ordish. *A copy of this
programme is kept in the broadcaster's
archive.*
Celebrity Squares – 18 June 1977, ATV
(networked), 18.45–19.30. Taking part: Bob

Monkhouse (host), L.D., Faith Brown, Joe Brown, Jacquie-Ann Carr, Dickie Davies, Dickie Henderson, Mollie Sugden, Freddie Trueman, Willie Rushton. Additional material: Jeremy Beadle, Ian Messiter, Garry Chambers. Director: Christopher Tookey. *An audio recording of this show is retained by Kaleidoscope as part of the Bob Monkhouse archive.*

Make the Music Speak – 18 June 1977, BBC1, 22.45–23.30. Taking part: Lena Martell, L.D., Brotherhood of Man, the Tony Mansell Singers, the Scottish Radio Orchestra directed by Brian Fahey. Director: David Mallet. Producer: Iain Macfadyen. *A copy of this programme is kept in the broadcaster's archive.*

Seaside Special – 2 July 1977, BBC1, 20.00–20.50. Recorded at the Gerry Cottle's Circus Big Top, Lowestoft. Taking part: L.D., Dana, Bernie Clifton, Brother Lees, Stuart Gillies, David Hamilton, New Edition. Musical director: Ronnie Hazlehurst. *A copy of this programme is kept in the broadcaster's archive.*

Pro Celebrity Snooker – 12 September 1977, YTV (not networked – shown only in YTV, LWT, ATV Midlands and Anglia regions), 22.30–23.15. Taking part: Fred Dinenage (host), Ted Lowe (commentator), Dennis Taylor, Graham Miles, L.D., Kenny Lynch. Director: Geoff Hall. *A copy of this programme is kept in the broadcaster's archive.*

Network: Profile of a Stand-Up Comedian – Frank Carson – 1 October 1977, BBC1, 23.40–00.10. Contains sequence with L.D. *A copy of this show is kept in the broadcaster's archive.*

Pro Celebrity Snooker – 3 October 1977, YTV (not networked – shown only in YTV, LWT, ATV Midlands and Anglia regions), 22.30–23.15. Taking part: Fred Dinenage (host), Ted Lowe (commentator), Cliff Thorburn, Graham Miles, Frazer Hines, L.D. Director: Geoff Hall. *A copy of this programme is*

kept in the broadcaster's archive.

Des O'Connor Tonight – 17 October 1977, BBC2, 20.10–21.00. Taking part: Des O'Connor, Marvin Hamlisch, Diana Trask, L.D. Programme associate: Neil Shand. Musical director: Colin Keyes. Producer: James Moir. *A copy of this programme is kept in the broadcaster's archive.*

1978

The Good Old Days – 31 January 1978, BBC1, 20.10–22.10. Taking part: Leonard Sachs (chairman), L.D., Lorna Luft, Stephanie Voss, Bryan Burdon and company, Jacqueline Clarke, Peter Reeves, Bill Drysdale and Chrissie Cartwright, Valente-Valente, members of the Players Theatre company. Musical director: Bernard Herrmann. Producer: Barney Colehan. *A copy of this programme is kept in the broadcaster's archive.*

Miss Yorkshire Television 1978 – 26 August 1978, YTV (not networked). Taking part: Bob Warman (host), L.D., Tammy Jones, Barbara Law, Phil Argent, Councillor Norman Atha. Director: Burt Budin. *A copy of this programme is kept in the broadcaster's archive.*

Multi-Coloured Swap Shop – 18 November 1978, BBC1, 09.30–12.15. Taking part: Noel Edmonds (host), Maggie Philbin, Keith Chegwin, John Craven, L.D., Graham Dangerfield. Producer: Crispin Evans. Editor: Rosemary Gill.

Word for Word – 20 November 1978, BBC2, 22.20–22.50. Taking part: Robert Robinson, Vicky Payne, L.D. Director: Martin L. Bell. Producer: Antony Rouse. *A copy of this programme is kept in the broadcaster's archive.*

Parkinson at the Pantomime – 25 December 1978, BBC1, 22.30–23.35. *Radio Times* billing: 'Michael Parkinson, with his special guest Arthur Askey, explores the curious crazy world of this unique seasonal entertainment, with demonstration from some of its greatest performers, including Kings of Slapstick – Charlie Cairoli and Company; There's nothing like a Dame – Les Dawson; Following in Father's footsteps – Lauri Lupino Lane; With a farmyard surprise – Little and Large; the Prince of Principal Boys – Pat Kirkwood; Presenting a watery diversion – Stan Stennett; also featuring Roy Barraclough, George Truzzi and the Harry Stoneham Show Band.' Director: Ian Hamilton. Producer: John Fisher. *A copy of this programme is kept in the broadcaster's archive.*

1979

Saturday Night at the Mill – 3 March 1979, BBC1, 23.00–23.50. Taking part: L.D., Virginia McKenna, Tony Lewis and the Roberts Brothers Circus, Kenny Ball and his Jazzmen. Director: Roy Norton. Producer: Roy Ronnie. *A copy of this programme is kept in the broadcaster's archive.*

The Good Old Days – 24 April 1979, BBC1, 20.10–21.00. Taking part: Leonard Sachs (chairman), L.D., Sweet Substitute, Peter Hudson, Joan Merrigan, Paul Rhodes, Julia Sutton, Eleanor McCready, Ralph Heid, Eve 'n' Alan and the Players Theatre company. Musical director: Bernard Herrmann. Producer: Barney Colehan. *A copy of this programme is kept in the broadcaster's archive.*

Seaside Special – 18 August 1979, BBC1, 20.10–21.00. Taking part: L.D., Roy Barraclough, the Krankies, the Dooleys, Berni Flint, Dollar, Stu Francis, New Edition, the Maggie Stredder singers. Producer: Michael Hurll. *A copy of this programme is kept in the broadcaster's archive.*

Larry Grayson's Generation Game – 15 September 1979, BBC1, 18.35–19.30. Taking part: Larry Grayson, Isla St Clair, L.D., David Hamilton. Director: K Paul Jackson. Producer: Alan Boyd. *A copy of this programme is kept in the broadcaster's archive.*

Junior That's Life – 6 October 1979, BBC1, 17.35–18.15. Taking part: Esther Rantzen, Paul Heiney, Chris Serle, L.D., Shaun Ley, Toby Robertson. Director: Peter Chafer. Producer: Patricia Houlihan. *A copy of this programme is kept in the broadcaster's archive.*

Shirley Bassey – 10 November 1979, BBC1, 20.15–21.00. Taking part: Shirley Bassey, L.D., the Nolan Sisters, Third World. Musical director: Arthur Greenslade. Producer: Stewart Morris. *A copy of this programme is kept in the broadcaster's archive.*

Sykes – 16 November 1979, BBC1, 19.30–20.05. Taking part: Eric Sykes, Hattie Jacques, L.D., Henry McGee. Writer: Eric Sykes. Producer: Roger Race. *A copy of this programme is kept in the broadcaster's archive.*

Mainstream – 18 December 1979, BBC2, 22.15–22.45. Arts programme containing a feature in which L.D. discussed the history of pantomime. *A copy of this programme is kept in the broadcaster's archive.*

Boxing Night at the Mill – 26 December 1979, BBC1, 22.35–23.25. Taking part: L.D., Kenny Ball and his Jazzmen, Dana. Director: Roy Norton. Producer: Roy Ronnie. *A copy of this programme is kept in the broadcaster's archive.*

1980

The Val Doonican Music Show – 5 April 1980, BBC1, 19.50–20.35. Taking part: Val Doonican, L.D., Nana Mouskouri, Roy Clarke. Producer: Yvonne Littlewood. *A copy of this programme is kept in the broadcaster's archive.*

Lena – 4 June 1980, BBC1, 20.30–21.00. Taking part: Lena Zavaroni, L.D., the Nolans. Producer: Stewart Morris. *A copy of this programme is kept in the broadcaster's archive.*

Larry Grayson's Generation Game – 4 October 1980, BBC1, 18.40–1935. Taking part: Larry Grayson, Isla St Clair, L.D.,

Bernie Clifton, Anita Harris, Percy Thrower, Duncan Goodhew, Tony Blackburn. Producer: Marcus Plantin. *A copy of this programme is kept in the broadcaster's archive.*

Blankety Blank – 13 November 1980, BBC1, 19.55–20.30. Taking part: Terry Wogan (host), L.D., Henry Cooper, Isla Blair, Brian Murphy, Beryl Reid and Isla St Clair. Director: Alan Boyd. Producer: Stanley Appel. *A copy of this programme is kept in the broadcaster's archive.*

Children in Need – 21 November 1980, BBC1, 18.50–00.40.

Nationwide – 3 December 1980, BBC1, 17.55–18.45. Mike Neville interviews L.D. on an appeal for the donation of Christmas presents for the disadvantaged.

Des O'Connor Tonight – 8 December 1980, BBC2, 20.10–21.00. Taking part: Des O'Connor, L.D., Kelly Monteith. Producer: Brian Penders. *A copy of this programme is kept in the broadcaster's archive.*

Blankety Blank – 26 December 1980, BBC1, 18.45–19.25. Taking part: Terry Wogan (host), Roy Hudd, L.D., Beryl Reid, Patrick Moore, Rula Lenska, Madeline Smith, Katie Boyle, Shirley Anne Field, Jimmy Tarbuck, Sandra Dickinson, Windsor Davies and David Hamilton. Director: Stanley Appel. Producer: Marcus Plantin.

1981

That's Life – 26 April, 10 May, 24 May and 7 June, BBC, mostly 21.30–22.15. Taking part: Esther Rantzen, Paul Heiney, Chris Serle, Cyril Fletcher, L.D. (judging the National Laughter Contest). Director: Bob Marsland. Producer: Ron Neil. *Copies of these programmes are kept in the broadcaster's archive.*

Summertime Special – 12 September 1981, BBC1, 20.00–20.50. Taking part: Bernie Clifton, Dana, L.D., Jay and Bonnie Diamond, the Trio Dymek, Jeep and the A Team. Producer: Stewart Morris.

A copy of this programme is kept in the broadcaster's archive.

Mussolini With Knickers – 18 October 1981, BBC2, 21.10–21.35. Radio Times billing: 'His mother-in-law has provided Les Dawson and us with an endless supply of laughs. Les reveals why she is not only an inspirational source for his humour, but is necessary for the very continuation of life as we know it. Professor Laurie Taylor extends this look at a family stereotype by asking writer and broadcaster Benny Green and cartoonist Posy Simmonds of the *Guardian* why we need family figures for family fun.' Producer: Suzanne Campbell-Jones. A BBC Open University production.

1982

Parkinson –

16 January 1982, BBC1, 22.55–23.55. Taking part: Michael Parkinson, Cleo Laine, Barbara Castle, L.D. Producers: Gill Stribling-Wright and Graham Lindsay. Executive producer: John Fisher. *A copy of this programme is kept in the broadcaster's archive.*

The Variety Club Awards – 3 February 1982, BBC1, 19.25–20.10. Les Dawson wins BBC radio personality award. Producer: Ken Griffin. *A copy of this programme is kept in the broadcaster's archive.*

Looks Familiar – 10 May 1982, Thames (networked), 22.45–23.15. Taking part: Denis Norden, L.D., Eric Sykes, Arthur Marshall. *A copy of this programme is kept in the broadcaster's archive.*

A National Salute: Falklands War Gala – 18 July 1982, LWT (networked), 19.45–21.00 and 21.25–23.00. **Recorded at the Coliseum, London.** Taking part: Adam Ant, Michael Aspel, Ronnie Corbett, Leslie Crowther, Billy Dainty, L.D., English National Opera, Jill Gascoigne, Robert Hardy, Anita Harris, Dickie Henderson, Dame Vera Lynn, Alfred Marks, Dame

Anna Neagle, Sir Laurence Olivier, Danny la Rue, Sir Harry Secombe, Alvin Stardust, Jimmy Tarbuck, Twiggy. Director: Alan Boyd. Producer: David Bell. *A copy of this programme is kept in the broadcaster's archive.*

Summertime Special – 24 July 1982, BBC1, 20.35–21.20. Taking part: L.D. (host), the Anderson Sisters, Dollar, Roger Kitter, Nicole and Rudolf Reyes. Producer: Stewart Morris. *A copy of this programme is kept in the broadcaster's archive.*

Comic Roots – 2 August 1982, BBC1, 18.50–19.25. Documentary about Les Dawson's childhood, filmed in Manchester and Blackpool. Producer: Peter Lee-Wright. *A copy of this programme is kept in the broadcaster's archive.*

It's a Knockout: the Knockout Championship 1982 – 6 August 1982, BBC1, 19.30–20.30. Les Dawson presents a trophy. *A copy of this programme is kept in the broadcaster's archive.*

Looks Familiar – 16 September 1982, Thames (networked), 19.00–19.30. Taking part: Denis Norden, L.D., Eric Sykes, Pat Kirkwood. Producer/director: David Clark. *A copy of this programme is kept in the broadcaster's archive.*

Crackerjack – 5 November 1982, BBC1, 16.55–17.35. Taking part: Stu Francis, Leigh Miles, Julie Dorne Brown, Keith Harris, Amanda Jones, Teddy Peiro and Patricio. Writer: Mike Radford. Director: John Bishop. Producer: Paul Ciani. *A copy of this programme is kept in the broadcaster's archive.*

Lena – 14 December 1982, BBC1, 19.40–20.10. Taking part: Lena Zavaroni, L.D., Janet Brown. Producer: Stewart Morris. *A copy of this programme is kept in the broadcaster's archive.*

The Funny Side of Christmas – 27 December 1982, BBC1, 20.05–21.25. A light-hearted look at the festive season through the eyes of favourite comedy characters and personalities. Introduced by Frank Muir. Contains a specially recorded Cissie and Ada sketch, directed by Ernest Maxin. Producer: Robin Nash. *A copy of this programme is kept in the broadcaster's archive.*

1983

Wogan – 2 April 1983, BBC1, 21.40–22.25. Taking part: Terry Wogan (host), L.D., Eamonn Andrews, Jerry Lee Lewis. Director: Stanley Appel. Producer: Marcus Plantin. *A copy of this programme is kept in the broadcaster's archive.*

The Good Old Days – 4 September 1983, BBC1, 21.00–21.55. Taking part: Leonard Sachs (chairman), L.D., Bernie Clifton, Lorna Dallas, Peter Skellern. Producer: Barney Colehan. *A copy of this programme is kept in the broadcaster's archive.*

The Late Late Breakfast Show – 17 September 1983, BBC1, 18.20–19.05. Taking part: Noel Edmonds, L.D., Murray Walker. Producer: Michael Hurll. *A copy of this programme is kept in the broadcaster's archive.*

Breakfast Time – 19 September 1983, BBC1, 06.30–09.00. Taking part: Nick Ross, Selina Scott, L.D., Boy George. *A copy of L.D.'s interview segment is kept in the broadcaster's archive.*

Calendar – 20 September 1983, YTV (regional, not networked), 18.00–18.30. Les Dawson appears on the regional news show, talking about his new book, *Les Dawson's Lancashire. A copy of this programme is kept in the broadcaster's archive.*

The Royal Variety Performance – 13 November 1983, LWT (networked), 19.15–22.00. Taking part: Gene Kelly (host), L.D., Bonnie Langford, Wayne Sleep, Grace Kennedy, Tick and Tock, Diana Moran, Twiggy, George Carl, the Royal Ballet, Anthony Dow Ballet. Director: Alan

Boyd. Producer: David Bell. *A copy of this programme is kept in the broadcaster's archive.*

Show Business – 18 November 1983, BBC1, 18.55–19.20. Taking part: Mike Smith, Sally James, Jean Seberg, Anneka Rice, Tom Brook, L.D., Robert Redford, Ringo Starr, Engelbert Humperdinck, Marvin Hamlisch, Peter Stringfellow. Director: Bruce Thompson. Producer: Allan Kassell. *A copy of this programme is kept in the broadcaster's archive.*

Crackerjack – 16 December 1983, BBC1, 17.00–17.40. Taking part: Stu Francis, Julie Dorne Brown, Sara Hollamby, L.D., Chas and Dave, Bartschelly, Modern Romance, Acromaniacs, Suzi Quatro, Mark Robertson, the Great Soprendo, Basil Brush and Dexy's Midnight Runners. Director: David Taylor. Producer: Paul Ciani. *A copy of this programme is kept in the broadcaster's archive.*

1984

Pebble Mill at One – 10 January 1984, BBC1, 13.00–13.45. Taking part: Marian Foster, Paul Coia, Donny Macleod, L.D., Maureen Green, Teresa Brewer. Director: Chris Wright. Producer: Steve Weddle. Editor: Peter Hercombe. *A copy of this programme is kept in the broadcaster's archive.*

Sixty Minutes – 12 April 1984, BBC1, 17.40–18.40. Report from Blackpool on a tram race, featuring L.D. *A copy of this item is kept in the broadcaster's archive.*

The Saturday Picture Show – 21 April 1984, BBC1, 08.45–10.45. Maggie Philbin interviews L.D. *A copy of this item is kept in the broadcaster's archive.*

The Main Attraction – 25 August 1984, BBC1, 20.15–21.00. Taking part: L.D., Randy Crawford, Philippe Genty, Bobby Knutt, Wayne Dobson, Bobby Davro, Shakin' Stevens, Vicki Brown, the Roly Polys. Producer: Stanley Appel. Executive producer: Stewart Morris. *A copy of this*

programme is kept in the broadcaster's archive.

1985

Wogan – 30 August 1985, BBC1, 19.00–19.40. Taking part: Terry Wogan, Joanna Lumley, Mel Gibson, L.D., Roy Kinnear, Mike Winters, Gloria Gaynor. Director: Michael Leggo. Producer: Roger Ordish. Series producer: Frances Whitaker. *A copy of this programme is kept in the broadcaster's archive.*

Wogan with Selina Scott – 7 October 1985, BBC1, 19.00–19.40. Taking part: Selina Scott (host), L.D., Prue Leith, Graham Smith, Alain Prost. Director: Kevin Bishop. Producer: Frances Whitaker. *A copy of this programme is kept in the broadcaster's archive.*

Wogan – 20 December 1985, BBC1, 19.00–19.40. Taking part: Terry Wogan (host), L.D., Judi Dench, Aled Jones. *A copy of this programme is kept in the broadcaster's archive.*

1986

The Bob Monkhouse Show – 27 January 1986, BBC2, 21.30–22.10. Taking part: Bob Monkhouse (host), L.D., The Roly Polys, Jim Carrey. Musical director: Harry Stoneham. Director: David Taylor. Producer: John Fisher. *A copy of this programme is kept in the broadcaster's archive*

Aspel and Company – 15 March 1986, LWT (networked), 22.00–22.45. Taking part: Michael Aspel (host), L.D., Paul Nicholas, Anneka Rice. Director: Ian Hamilton. Producer Gill Stribling-Wright. *A copy of this programme is kept in the broadcaster's archive.*

Breakfast Time – 22 December 1986, BBC1, 07.00–08.40. Tony Butler interviews L.D. on the subject of the pantomime dame. *A copy of this item is kept in the broadcaster's archive.*

A Question of Sport – 23 December 1986,

BBC1, 20.00–20.30. Taking part: David Coleman (host), Bill Beaumont, Emlyn Hughes, L.D., Leslie Grantham, Leo Sayer, Su Pollard, Shirley Strong, Clive Lloyd. Director: Mick Dempsey. Producer: Mike Adley. *A copy of this programme is kept in the broadcaster's archive.*

What the Butler Saw – 23 August 1986, BBC1, 21.10–21.20. L.D., in various character guises, presents a preview of the forthcoming season of entertainment on BBC1. Writer: Geoff Lister. Producer: Vicki Marriott. *A copy of this programme is kept in the broadcaster's archive.*

1987

Bygones Special: Top of the Town – Blackpool Tower – 12 March 1987, Anglia (regional, not networked), 19.00–19.30. Taking part: Lord Delfont, L.D., Harry Wallasey, Phil Kelsall, Eric Redfern, Peter Jay. *A copy of this programme is kept in the broadcaster's archive.*

Disney Time – 31 August 1987, BBC1, 18.15–19.00. Presenter: L.D. Producer: Richard Evans. *A copy of this programme is kept in the broadcaster's archive.*

Royal Variety Performance – 29 November 1987, LWT (networked), 19.15–20.45 and 21.00–22.00. Taking part: Michael Barrymore, Shirley Bassey, Sarah Brightman, Cannon and Ball, George Carl, Rosemary Clooney, Bobby Davro, L.D., Dudu Fisher, Five Star, Stephen Fry and Hugh Laurie, James Galway, Dolores Gray, Hale and Pace, Tom Jones, Eartha Kitt, The cast of *Les Miserables,* Johnny Logan, Kenny Lynch and Jimmy Tarbuck, Jessica Martin, Hilary O'Neil, The Roly Polys, Sir Harry Secombe, Allan Stewart, Mel Torme and George Shearing, Gary Wilmot, Bernie Winters, Mike Yarwood. Director: Alasdair Macmillan. Producer: David Bell. *A copy of this programme is kept in the broadcaster's archive.*

1988

Wogan – 29 August 1988, BBC1, 19.00–19.40. From the North Pier, Blackpool. Taking part: Terry Wogan, L.D., Val Doonican, the Roly Polys, Doris Thompson, Norman Barrett, Gina Jefferson, Joan Moxley, Elsie Vipont, Claude and Edith Hatton, Doris Barlow. Director: Tom Corcoran. Producer: Jon Plowman. Series producer: Peter Weil. *A copy of this programme is kept in the broadcaster's archive.*

1989

Wogan – 17 February 1989, BBC1, 19.00–19.35. Taking part: Terry Wogan (host), L.D., Tracey Roper, Jackie Mason, Joe Longthorne. Director: Tom Corcoran. Producer: Jane O'Brien. Series producer: Peter Estall. *A copy of this programme is kept in the broadcaster's archive.*

Daytime Live – 30 October 1989, BBC1, 12.00–12.55. Taking part: Sue Cook, Tina Baker, Andy Craig, L.D., Delia Smith, Elaine Paige, Bernard Cribbins, John Barrowman. *A copy of this programme is kept in the broadcaster's archive.*

Wogan – 3 November 1989, BBC1, 19.00–19.30. Taking part: Terry Wogan (host), L.D., Louise Plowright, Rosalind Plowright. Director: John Burrowes. Producer: Graham Owens. Series producer: Peter Estall. *A copy of this programme is kept in the broadcaster's archive.*
networked – shown in LWT and Channel regions only), 17.35–18.30. Taking part: Gloria Hunniford (host), L.D., Chubby Checker, Jane Russell, Jenny Seagrove. Director: Nick Vaughan-Barratt. Producer: Graham Stuart. *A copy of this programme is kept in the broadcaster's archive.*

Open Air – 10 November 1989, BBC1, 11.00–12.00. Taking part: Jayne Irving, Gloria Hunniford, L.D., Simon Weston, Ruth Mott, Elaine Lipworth. Producer: Roger Wilkes. *A copy of this programme is kept in the broadcaster's archive.*

1990

Wogan – 26 October 1990, BBC1, 19.00–
19.30. Taking part: Terry Wogan (host), L.D.,
Paula Yates, Lisa Stansfield. Director: Tom
Corcoran. Producer: Jane O'Brien.

Going Live – 3 November 1990, BBC1, 09.00–
12.12. Taking part: Sarah Greene, Phillip
Schofield, L.D., Noel Edmonds, Trevor Neal,
Simon Hickson, Andy Albeck, Danny McCall,
Breathe. Director: Julia Knowles. Editor:
Chris Bellinger. *A copy of this programme is
kept in the broadcaster's archive.*

1991

Wogan – 11 October 1991, BBC1, 19.00–19.35.
Taking part: Terry Wogan (host), L.D., Frank
Bruno, Naomi Campbell, Roberta Flack,
Maxi Priest. Director: John L Spencer.
Producer: Natalie Elsey. *A copy of this
programme is kept in the broadcaster's
archive.*

Pebble Mill – 17 October 1991, BBC1,
12.20–12.55. Taking part: Alan Titchmarsh
(host), L.D., Alison Moyet, Gary Glitter,
Michael Windsor, Henry Corden. Director:
Katie Wright. Producer: Pamela Creed.
*A copy of this programme is kept in the
broadcaster's archive.*

Performance: Nona – 19 October 1991, BBC2,
21.30–22.55. Cast: L.D., Jim Broadbent,
Timothy Spall, Liz Smith, Jane Horrocks,
Maurice Denham, Susan Brown. Writer:
Roberto Cossa. Adapted by Michael
Hastings. Producer/director: Simon Curtis.
*A copy of this programme is kept in the
broadcaster's archive.*

Noel's Christmas Presents – 25 December
1991, BBC1, 10.45–11.45. Taking part: Noel
Edmonds (host), L.D., John Nettles, Michael
Ball. Director: Bill Morton. Producer:
Michael Leggo. *A copy of this programme is
kept in the broadcaster's archive.*

1992

The Brain Drain – 26 September 1992, BBC2,
22.05–22.35. Taking part: Jimmy Mulville

(host), Tony Hawks, Craig Ferguson, Angus
Deayton, L.D. Director: Sue Judd. Producer:
Dan Patterson. A Hat Trick production for
BBC TV. *A copy of this programme is kept
in the broadcaster's archive.*

Friday Night with Wogan – 6 November
1992, BBC1, 22.20–23.00. Taking part:
Terry Wogan (host), L.D., Jennifer Saunders,
Donna Tartt, Cher. Director: John Burrowes.
Producer: Jane O'Brien. Executive producer:
Peter Estall. *A copy of this programme is
kept in the broadcaster's archive.*

Good Morning with Anne and Nick –
9 November 1992, BBC1, 10.30–12.15.
Anne Diamond and Nick Owen interview
Les and Tracy Dawson, with Charlotte.
Editor: Mike Hollingsworth. *A copy of this
programme is kept in the broadcaster's
archive.*

This Morning – 27 November 1992, Granada
(networked), 10.35–12.10. Richard Madeley
and Judy Finnigan interview L.D. and Tracy
Dawson about Charlotte. *A copy of this
programme is kept in the broadcaster's
archive.*

1993

Classic Coronation Street – 3 January 1993,
Granada (networked), 18.15–19.15. Taking
part: Judy Finnigan (presenter), L.D.
Director: Royston Mayoh. Producer: Mark
Wells. *A copy of this programme is kept in
the broadcaster's archive.*

Bruce's Guest Night – 17 May 1993, BBC1,
20.00–20.30. Taking part: Bruce Forsyth,
L.D., Luther Vandross, Frank Oz with Miss
Piggy. Director: John L Spencer. Producer:
Kevin Bishop. *A copy of this programme is
kept in the broadcaster's archive.*

Aspel and Company – 23 May 1993, LWT
(networked), 22.00–22.45. Taking part:
Michael Aspel, L.D., Jerry Lee Lewis, Bea
Arthur. Director: Alasdair Macmillan.
Producer: Lorna Dickinson. *A copy of this
programme is kept in the broadcaster's
archive.*

Surprise Surprise – 4 July 1993, LWT
(networked), 20.00–21.00. Taking part:
Cilla Black, Bob Carolgees, L.D., Ian Botham,
Bella Emberg, Jonathan Morris. Director:
John Gorman. Series Producer: Michael
Hurll. Producer: Colman Hutchinson.
*A copy of this programme is kept in the
broadcaster's archive.*

Demob – ITV (networked) 15 October,
29 October and 19 November 1993, 21.00–
22.00. L.D. appeared as Morton Stanley
in parts 1, 3 and 6 of this comedy drama,
starring Griff Rhys Jones, Martin Clunes
and Samantha Janus. Director: Robert
Knights. Producer: Adrian Bate. A TalkBack
production for Yorkshire Television. *Copies
of all programmes in this series are kept in
the broadcaster's archive.*

Starring vehicles and regular appearances

Comedy Playhouse: State of the Union
26 April 1968, BBC1, 20.20–20.50.
Recorded: 31 March 1968, Studio TC4, BBC
Television Centre, London, W12. Cast: L.D.,
Patsy Rowlands. Writer: Ronnie Taylor.
Producer: John Ammonds.

International Cabaret
29 November 1968–3 January 1969,
BBC2 – 5 × 40 minutes, 1 × 45 minutes;
Fridays, 20.25 (except 27 December, 20.50).
Recorded at the Talk of the Town, London.
Compère: L.D. Taking part:
• 29 Nov. (recorded 29 Oct.): Nana
Mouskouri, Robert Harbin, Malcolm
Roberts, Les Curibas.
• 6 Dec. (recorded 10 Nov.): Marian
Montgomery, Potassy, Duo Milik, Brenda
Arnau.
• 13 Dec. (recorded 20 Oct.): Enrico Macias
and Company, Judy Ginn and Jim, the
Alfreros, Finn Jon.
• 20 Dec. (recorded 3 Nov.): Eartha Kitt, Flight

Four, the D'Amores, Vincent Zarra, Claude
Richard and Stella.
• 27 Dec. (recorded 24 Nov.): Kenneth
McKellar, Marvyn Roy, Susan Maughan,
Senor Wences, Los Trianas, the Mike
Sammes Singers.
• 3 Jan. (recorded 8 Dec.): Dickie Henderson,
Jackie Trent, Tony Hatch, Silvan, Ravic and
Babs.
Musical director: Ronnie Hazlehurst (show
1), Dennis Wilson (show 2), Alyn Ainsworth
(shows 3–6).
Vocal backing: the Ladybirds. Script: Bob
Andrews and Austin Steele. Producer: G.B.
Lupino.

Jokers Wild
All TX data is for the Yorkshire Television
region.
Barry Cryer is chairman for the entire run,
except for four shows in series 3.
Series 1: 9 July–12 November 1969 –
19 × 30 minutes; Mondays, 19.00. L.D. is in
14 of the 19 shows.
• 9 July, 16 July, 23 July, 24 Sept.:
David Nixon, L.D., Ray Martine, Ted Ray,
Don Maclean, Bobby Pattinson.
• 30 July: Ted Ray, Charlie Chester, Ken Earle,
L.D., Ray Martine, Kenneth Cantor.
• 6 Aug.: Charlie Chester, L.D., Ray Martine,
Ted Ray, Lennie Bennett, Paul Andrews.
• 13 Aug.: Ted Ray, Charlie Chester, Ken Earle,
L.D., Ray Martine, Kenneth Cantor.
• 1 Oct.: Jimmy Edwards, L.D., Ray Martine,
Ted Ray, Bobby Dennis, Bobby Pattinson.
• 8 Oct., 15 Oct., 22 Oct., 29 Oct.: Ted Rogers,
Ted Ray, Ray Martine, Lennie Bennett, L.D.,
Ken Earle.
• 5 Nov., 12 Nov.: Ted Ray, Ted Rogers,
Ray Cameron, Norman Collier, L.D., Ray
Martine.
*Copies of all 14 of L.D.'s transmitted
appearances from this series are kept in
the broadcaster's archive.*
Series 2: 30 March–11 November 1970
– 32 × 30 minutes; Mondays, 18.15.

- 30 Mar., 6 Apr.: Stubby Kaye, L.D., Arthur Askey, Ray Martine, Ted Ray, Clive Dunn.
- 13 Apr., 20 Apr.: Arthur Askey, Ted Ray, L.D., Ray Martine, Lance Percival, Joe Baker.
- 27 Apr., 4 May: L.D., Ray Martine, Arthur Askey, Ted Ray, Ray Fell, Jack Douglas.
- 11 May, 18 May, 25 May: Ted Rogers, Ted Ray, Ray Martine, L.D., Arthur Askey, Graham Stark.
- 10 June: Ted Ray, Ray Martine, Kenneth Connor, L.D., Arthur Askey, Arthur Worsley.
- 17 June, 24 June: Eric Sykes, Ray Martine, Alfred Marks, Clive Dunn, Arthur Askey, L.D.
- 1 July, 8 July: Stanley Unwin, Alfred Marks, L.D., Arthur Askey, Ted Ray, Ray Martine.
- 15 July, 22 July, 29 July: Ray Martine, Ted Ray, Arthur Askey, Fred Emney, Warren Mitchell, L.D.
- 5 Aug., 12 Aug., 19 Aug., 26 Aug.: Arthur Askey, Ted Ray, Harry Fowler, Deryck Guyler, L.D., Ray Martine.
- 2 Sept., 9 Sept.: Patrick Cargill, L.D., Ted Ray, Arthur Askey, Ray Martine, Clive Dunn.
- 16 Sept., 23 Sept.: Joe Brown, Ray Martine, Ted Ray, Arthur Askey, Bernard Bresslaw, L.D.
- 30 Sept., 7 Oct.: Jack Douglas, L.D., Ted Ray, Arthur Askey, Ray Martine, Johnny Hackett.
- 14 Oct., 21 Oct.: Ted Ray, Arthur Askey, L.D., Ray Martine, Billy Dainty, Joe Brown.
- 28 Oct.: Arthur Askey, Ted Ray, David Nixon, Ray Martine, L.D., Ray Cameron.
- 4 Nov., 11 Nov.: Ray Martine, Lonnie Donegan, Ted Ray, Arthur Askey, David Nixon, L.D.

Director: Mike Bevan. Producer: David Mallet. *Copies of all programmes in this series are kept in the broadcaster's archive.*

Series 3: 19 May–10 November 1971 – 26 × 30 minutes; Wednesdays, 19.00. L.D. is in 24 of the 26 shows.

- 19 May, 9 June, 30 June: Jack Douglas, Ray Martine, Sid James, L.D., Ted Ray, Clive Dunn.
- 26 May, 2 June: Jack Douglas, John Cleese, L.D., Clement Freud, Ted Ray, Ray Martine.
- 16 June, 23 June: Dick Bentley, Jack Douglas, L.D., Ray Martine, Ted Ray, Deryck Guyler.
- 7 July, 28 July: Ray Martine, L.D., Ted Ray, Joe Brown, Clive Dunn, John Le Mesurier.
- 14 July, 4 Aug.: Jimmy Jewel, Clive Dunn, L.D., Ray Martine, Ted Ray, Clement Freud.
- 21 July, 11 Aug.: Ray Martine, Ted Ray, L.D., Clive Dunn, John Cleese, Roy Kinnear.
- 18 Aug., 25 Aug.: Michael Bentine (chairman), David Nixon, Albie Keen, Ray Martine, L.D., John Cleese, Mike Hope.
- 1 Sept., 8 Sept.: Michael Bentine (chairman), L.D., Ray Martine, Ted Ray, Lennie Bennett, John Cleese, David Nixon.
- 15 Sept., 22 Sept.: Ted Ray, Ray Martine, John Cleese, Ray Cameron, L.D., Clement Freud.
- 29 Sept., 6 Oct.: Harry H. Corbett, Fred Emney, Ted Ray, Ray Martine, L.D., Bryan Marshall.
- 27 Oct., 3 Nov., 10 Nov.. Arthur Askey, Ray Martine, Joe Baker, L.D., John Cleese, Ted Rogers.

Director (some shows): Mike Bevan. Producer: David Mallet. *Copies of all programmes in this series are kept in the broadcaster's archive.*

Series 4: 17 May–26 July 1972 – 11 × 30 minutes; Wednesdays, 19.00. L.D. is in 9 of the 11 shows.

- 17 May, 24 May: Roy Kinnear, L.D., Jack Douglas, Freddie Starr, Warren Mitchell, Norman Collier.
- 31 May: L.D., Warren Mitchell, Clive Dunn, Jack Douglas, Norman Collier.
- 7 June, 14 June: Norman Collier, Bob Monkhouse, L.D., Warren Mitchell, Jack Smethurst, Lonnie Donegan.
- 21 June: L.D., Bob Monkhouse, Warren Mitchell, Clive Dunn, Jack Smethurst, Norman Collier.
- 28 June: Bob Monkhouse, Tim Brooke-Taylor, L.D., Jack Smethurst, Warren Mitchell, Clive Dunn.
- 5 July, 12 July: Tony Brandon, Alfred Marks, Norman Collier, L.D., Bob Monkhouse.

Producer/director: David Millard.
Copies of all programmes in this series are kept in the broadcaster's archive.

Series 5: 19 October 1972–11 January 1973 – 13 × 30 minutes; Thursdays, 13.00. L.D. is in 12 of the 13 shows.

• 19 Oct., 26 Oct.: L.D., Peter Goodwright, Jack Smethurst, Clive Dunn, Alfred Marks, Tim Brooke-Taylor.

• 2 Nov.: L.D., Bob Monkhouse, Clive Dunn, Jack Douglas, Warren Mitchell, Norman Collier.

• 9 Nov., 7 Dec., 14 Dec., 28 Dec.: Ray Cameron, Milo O'Shea, L.D., Tim Brooke-Taylor, Peter Goodwright, Lennie Bennett.

• 16 Nov., 23 Nov.: L.D., Clive Dunn, Jack Smethurst, Alfred Marks, Peter Goodwright, Tim Brooke-Taylor.

• 30 Nov.: Alfred Marks, L.D., Tony Brandon, Bob Monkhouse, Warren Mitchell, Norman Collier.

• 4 Jan., 11 Jan.: Diana Dors, Audrey Jeans, Aimi McDonald, L.D., Alfred Marks, Jack Smethurst.

Producer/director: David Millard. *Copies of all programmes in this series are kept in the broadcaster's archive.*

Special: *All the Jokers – Full House!*: 26 December 1972, 17.15–18.15 – 1 × 60 minutes. Taking part: Barry Cryer, L.D., Norman Collier, Peter Goodwright, Thora Hird, Jenny Lee-Wright, Brian Marshall, Billy Dainty, Keith Harris, Clodagh Rodgers, Chic Murray, Alfred Marks, Aimi McDonald, Diana Dors, the Syd Lawrence Orchestra and Roy Hudd. Writers: Barry Cryer, Brad Ashton. Producers: Bill Hitchcock, Peter Dulay. Director: David Mallet. *A copy of this programme is kept in the broadcaster's archive.*

Series 6: 17 May 1973–20 May 1974 – 43 × 30 minutes; Thursdays, 13.00. L.D. is in 28 of the 43 shows.

• 17 May, 31 May, 5 July, 12 July, 19 July, 26 July 1973: Chic Murray, L.D., Jack Douglas, John Junkin, Michael Aspel, Lennie Bennett.

• 7 June, 2 Aug., 9 Aug. 1973: L.D., Paul Melba, Frank Carson, Chic Murray, Michael Bentine, Michael Robbins.

• 30 Aug., 13 Sept. 1973: L.D., Peter Goodwright, Richard Wattis, Ken Earle, Norman Collier, Lennie Bennett.

• 19 Nov., 26 Nov., 2 Dec. 1973, 21 Jan. 1974: L.D., Michael Aspel, Peter Murray, Tony Cawley, Warren Mitchell, Clive Dunn.

• 31 Dec. 1973: David Nixon, Peter Goodwright, Clive Dunn, Norman Collier, L.D., Norman Vaughan.

• 7 Jan., 28 Jan., 11 Mar. 1974: L.D., Tim Brooke-Taylor, Michael Aspel, Warren Mitchell, Davy Kaye, Lennie Bennett.

• 4 Feb., 18 Mar. 1974: Bob Todd, Johnny Hackett, Jon Pertwee, Chic Murray, Leslie Crowther, Lance Percival.

• 25 Feb., 4 Mar., 25 Mar. 1974: Chic Murray, L.D., Alfred Marks, Stu Francis, Stan Stennett, Ken Earle.

• 22 Mar., 13 May 1974: Ted Ray, Warren Mitchell, Don Maclean, Alfred Marks, Mike Newman, Peter Murray.

• 29 Mar. 1974: Alfred Marks, Jon Pertwee, Ray Cameron, Norman Vaughan, Lennie Bennett, John Junkin.

• 1 Apr., 29 Apr., 3 June, 10 June, 24 June 1974: Diana Dors, Jack Douglas, June Whitfield, Tony Cawley, John Junkin, Bryan Marshall.

• 8 Apr., 22 Apr., 6 May, 20 May 1974: Lennie Bennett, L.D., John Cleese, Mike Goddard, Michael Aspel, David Nixon.

Producer/director: David Millard. *Copies of all programmes in this series are kept in the broadcaster's archive.*

Series 7: 23 October–20 November 1974 – 5 × 30 minutes; Wednesdays, 15.55. L.D. is in 4 of the 5 shows. 23 Oct.: Roy Kinnear, Jack Douglas, Ray Martine, L.D., Frank Carson, Ray Alan. 30 Oct., 6 Nov., 13 Nov.: L.D., Michael Aspel, Peter Goodwright, Norman Collier, David Nixon, Stephen Lewis.

Producer/director: David Millard. *Copies of all programmes in this series are kept in the broadcaster's archive.*

Sez Les

All TX data is for the Thames/LWT region.

Series 1: All ITV regions except Scottish and Tyne-Tees, 30 April, 14–28 May, 11–18 June 1969 – 6 × 30 minutes; Wednesdays, 22.30 (except 30 Apr., 22.40). Regulars: L.D., Brian Murphy, Redvers Kyle, Syd Lawrence Orchestra, the Skylarks. Guests: 30 Apr.: La Compagnie André Tahon. 14 May: Roy Orbison and the Art Movement. 21 May: Georgie Fame. 28 May: No guest listed. 11 June: Cleo Laine, Sidonie Bond. 18 June: Alan Price and Friends. Musical director: Dave Lee. Writers: L.D., Barry Cryer, Peter Vincent, John Vincent. Director: David Mallet. Producer: John Duncan.

Series 2: All ITV regions, 10–17 September, 8–15 October, 5 November, 19 November 1969 – 6 × 30 minutes; Wednesdays, 22.30. Regulars: L.D., Brian Murphy, Redvers Kyle, Syd Lawrence Orchestra, the Skylarks. Guests: 10 Sept.: Carol Sloane, the Morgan James Duo. 17 Sept.: Maynard Ferguson, Terri Stevens. 8 Oct.: Dakota Staton, Linda Hoyle and Affinity. 15 Oct.: Roy Hudd. 5 Nov.: Salena Jones. 19 Nov.: Francoise Hardy. Musical director: Syd Lawrence. Director: David Mallet. Producer: John Duncan.

Series 3: All ITV regions, 16 August–6 September 1971 – 4 × 30 minutes; Mondays, 20.30 (except 30 Aug., 22.30). Regulars: L.D., Syd Lawrence Orchestra, the Skylarks, Kevin Kent. Guests: 16 Aug.: Manitas de Plata. 23 Aug.: Dana. 30 Aug.: John Cleese, Frank Ifield, Anita O'Day with the Stan Tracey Trio. 6 Sept.: John Cleese, Kathy Kirby, Georgie Fame and Alan Price. Producer/director: David Mallet. *Copies of all programmes in this series are kept in the broadcaster's archive.*

Series 4: All ITV regions, 13 January–17 February 1972 – 6 × 30 minutes; Thursdays, 21.00 (except 13 Jan., 20.45). Regulars: L.D., Syd Lawrence Orchestra, the Skylarks. 13 Jan.: Gilbert O'Sullivan. 20 Jan.: Kenneth Connor, the Bachelors. 27 Jan.: Shirley Bassey. 3 Feb.: Aimi McDonald. 10 Feb.: New World. 17 Feb.: Esther Marrow, Peter Noone. Producer/director: David Mallet. *Copies of all programmes in this series are kept in the broadcaster's archive.*

Series 5: All ITV regions, 29 July–9 September 1972 – 5 × 45 minutes, 2 × 40 minutes (26 Aug. and 9 Sept.); Saturdays, 17.45 (except 26 Aug., 17.50; 2 Sept., 17.55; 9 Sept., 18.00).Regulars: Damaris Hayman, Johnny Vyvyan, Roy Barraclough, Bartlett Mullins, Syd Lawrence Orchestra, Les Girls. Guests: 29 July: Aimi Macdonald, Labi Siffre, Middle of the Road, Richard Whiteley. 5 Aug.: Gilbert O'Sullivan, Johnny Nash, Jenny Lee Wright. 12 Aug.: Sandie Shaw, Daliah Lavi, Mac and Katie Kissoon. 19 Aug.: Roy Orbison, Aimi Macdonald, the Peddlers. 26 Aug.: Sandie Shaw, Dana, Bruce Ruffin, Brian Glover. 2 Sept.: Vicky Leandros, the Dallas Boys, Blue Mink. 9 Sept.: Gene Pitney, Aimi Macdonald, Design. Producer/director: David Mallet. *Copies of all shows in this series are kept in the broadcaster's archive.*

Series 6: *Les Sez*: All ITV regions, 30 September–4 December 1972 – 6 × 30 minutes; Mondays, 20.30. Regulars: Eli Woods, Roy Barraclough. Director: Bill Hitchcock. Producers: Bill Hitchcock and Peter Dulay. *Copies of all programmes in this series are kept in the broadcaster's archive.*

Series 7: All ITV regions, 28 July–8 September 1973 – 7 × 45 minutes; Saturdays, 18.35 (28 July–11 Aug.), then 17.15 (18 Aug.–8 Sept.). Regulars: Eli Woods, Roy Barraclough, the Syd Lawrence Orchestra. Guests: 28 July: Olivia Newton-John. 4 Aug.: Linda Lewis. 11 Aug.: The Clark Brothers, Blue Mink, Richard Whiteley. 18 Aug.: The Flirtations. 25 Aug.: Labi Siffre. 1 Sept.: Dana, Richard Whiteley. 8 Sept.: Olivia Newton-John. Director: David Mallet. Producer: Bill Hitchcock. *Copies of all* programmes in this series are kept in the broadcaster's archive.

Special: *That's Christmas Sez Les*: All ITV regions, 26 December 1973 – 1 × 60 minutes; Wednesday, 15.30. Taking part: David Essex, Lynsey de Paul, Slade, the Kessler Twins, Roy Barraclough, Jack Douglas, Clive Dunn, Ronnie Carroll, Eli Woods, the Syd Lawrence Orchestra and the Irving Davies dancers. Musical director: Johnny Pearson. Director: David Mallet. Producer: Bill Hitchcock. *A copy of this show is kept in the YTV archive*

Series 8: All ITV regions, 25 January–8 March 1974 – 7 × 30 minutes; Fridays, 20.30. Regulars: John Cleese, Roy Barraclough, Eli Woods. Guests: 25 Jan.: Ray Alan, Breakaways. 1 Feb.: Brenda Arnau, Deryck Guyler, Damaris Hayman. 8 Feb.: Francis Van Dyke. 15 Feb.: Kenny Ball and his Jazzmen, RSM Britton. 22 Feb.: Lynsey de Paul. 1 Mar.: Salena Jones. 8 Mar.: Neil Sedaka. Director: David Mallet. Producer: Bill Hitchcock. *Copies of all programmes in this series are kept in the broadcaster's archive.*

Series 9: All ITV regions, 28 June–9 August 1974 – 7 × 30 minutes; Fridays, 20.30. Regulars: John Cleese, Roy Barraclough. Guests: 28 June: Kenny Ball and his Jazzmen. 5 July: The Hollies. 12 July: Lynsey de Paul. 19 July: Lyn Paul, Mo Moreland also featured. 26 July: Clodagh Rodgers. 2 Aug.: Ian Anderson. 9 Aug.: Marian Montgomery. Producer/director: David Mallet. *Copies of all programmes in this series are kept in the broadcaster's archive.*

Special: *Sez Les Special*: All ITV regions, 2 January 1976 – 1 × 60 minutes; Friday, 21.00. Taking part: Roy Barraclough, Dana, Guys and Dolls, Henry Cooper, Cyril Smith. Producer/director: Vernon Lawrence. *A copy of this show is kept in the YTV archive.*

Series 10: *Sez Les Special*: All ITV regions, 25 February–10 March

1976 – 3 × 60 minutes; Fridays, 20.30. Regulars: Roy Barraclough, Kathy Staff. Guests: 25 Feb.: Kenneth McKellar, Caterina Valente, Roy Budd, Freddie Trueman. *Copies of all programmes in this series are kept in the broadcaster's archive.*

Series 11: All ITV regions, 19 October–6 December 1976 – 7 × 30 minutes; Mondays, 22.30 (except 19 Oct., Tuesday, 19.00). Regulars: John Cleese, Roy Barraclough, Julian Orchard, Kathy Staff, Norman Chappell. Guests: 19 Oct.: Michael Aspel. 25 Oct.: Jan Curry. 1 Nov.–6 Dec.: none listed. Writers: David Nobbs, Barry Cryer, L.D. (all shows), Alec Gerrard (shows 1, 3), Don Clayton (shows 2, 3, 5 and 6), John Hudson (shows 4 and 7), Peter Vincent (show 7). Producer/director: Vernon Lawrence. *Copies of all programmes in this series are kept in the broadcaster's archive.*
There were also Sez Les segments in the 1971, 1972 and 1973 All Star Comedy Carnival specials, of which 1972 and 1973 exist in full.

Holiday With Strings

YTV (networked), 26 August 1974, 20.00-20.35. Taking part: L.D., Patricia Hayes, Mollie Sugden, Frank Thornton, Roy Barraclough, Alec Bregonzi, Ernest Arnley, Ronnie Brody, Felix Bowness. Writers: Ray Galton, Alan Simpson. Producer/director: Duncan Wood. *A copy of the programme is kept in the broadcaster's archive.*

Sounds Like Les Dawson

Special, YTV (networked), Wednesday 4 December 1974, 20.00–21.00. Taking part: L.D., Olivia Newton-John, the Second Generation, Roy Barraclough, John Gower, Colin Prince. Writers: David Nobbs, Barry Cryer, L.D., Dick Vosburgh. Musical director: Peter Husband. Producer/director: Vernon Lawrence. *A copy of this programme is kept in the broadcaster's archive.*

Les Dawson's Christmas Box

Special, YTV (networked), Saturday
21 December 1974, 20.30–21.30.
Taking part: L.D., Roy Barraclough, Wanda
Ventham, John Cleese, Kenny Ball and his
Jazzmen, Gilbert O'Sullivan, the Second
Generation. Writers: Barry Cryer, David
Nobbs; additional material – Les Dawson,
Alec Gerrard, Eric Idle. Musical director:
Peter Husband. Producer/director: Vernon
Lawrence. *A copy of this programme is kept
in the broadcaster's archive.*
Special, YTV (networked), Friday
26 December 1975, 22.15–23.15.
Taking part: L.D., Roy Barraclough, the
King's Singers, Julian Orchard, Kenny Ball
and his Jazzmen. Writers: Barry Cryer,
David Nobbs, Peter Robinson, Les Dawson.
Musical director: Peter Husband. Producer/
director: Vernon Lawrence. *A copy of this
programme is kept in the broadcaster's
archive.*

Dawson's Electric Cinema

Special, YTV (networked), Thursday 3 April
1975, 21.00–22.00.
Taking part: L.D., Roy Barraclough, Stuart
Dawson. Writers: Barry Cryer, David
Nobbs. Producer/director: Ronnie Baxter.
*A copy of this programme is kept in the
broadcaster's archive.*

The Loner

YTV (networked), 7–21 May 1975 – 3 × 30
minutes; Wednesdays, 21.30.
• 7 May: 'Dawson's Complaint' – L.D., Cyril
Luckham, Brian Wilde, George Malpas,
Helen Rappaport.
• 14 May: 'Dawson's Connection' – L.D.,
Roy Kinnear, Fred Feast, Reginald Marsh,
Sharon Maughan, Ted Carroll, Peter Ellis,
Anthony Millan.
• 21 May: 'Dawson's Encounter' – L.D., Gillian
Raine, Anita Carey, Reginald Marsh.
Writer: Alan Plater. Director: James
Ormerod. Executive producer: Peter Willes.

*Copies of all programmes in this series are
kept in the broadcaster's archive.*

Dawson's Weekly

YTV (networked), 12 June–29 July 1975 –
7 × 30 minutes; Thursdays, 20.00, then,
from 8 July, Wednesdays, 21.30.
• 12 June: 'Les Miserables' – L.D., Roy
Barraclough, Hilda Fennemore, Campbell
Singer, Jack May, Jenny McCracken.
• 19 June: 'Where There's a Will' – L.D., Roy
Barraclough, Richard Vernon, Terence
Alexander, Peggy Ann Clifford, Kathy Staff,
John Sharp, Bert Palmer, Lesley North.
• 26 June: 'Stage-Struck' – L.D., Julian Orchard,
Josephine Tewson, Bernard Spear, Alan
Curtis, Pamela Manson, Michael Gover,
Tony Sympson, Damaris Hayman, John
Harvey.
• 3 July: 'Accident-Prone' – L.D., Roy
Barraclough, Richard Morant, Neil
McCarthy, Gordon Rollings, Georgina
Moon.
• 8 July: 'All Pools Day' – L.D., Roy
Barraclough, Patsy Rowlands, Avril Angers,
Felix Bowness.
• 22 July: 'The Clerical Error' – L.D., John Bird,
Ann Beach, Sharon Duce, George A Cooper.
• 29 July: 'Strangers in the Night' – L.D., Roy
Barraclough, Sue Lloyd, Kenny Lynch,
Edward Sinclair.
Writers: Ray Galton and Alan Simpson.
Producer/director: Vernon Lawrence.
*Copies of all programmes in this series are
kept in the broadcaster's archive.*

The Les Dawson Show

Special, YTV (networked), Wednesday
10 September 1975 – 20.00–21.00. Taking
part: L.D., Roy Barraclough, Cleo Laine,
Joan Sanderson. Writers: Barry Cryer,
David Nobbs. Director: Len Lurcuck.
Producer: Vernon Lawrence. *A copy of this
programme is kept in the broadcaster's
archive.*

Dawson and Friends

Specials, YTV (networked), 20 April–29 June 1977 – 4 × 60 minutes, Wednesdays, 20.00–21.00.

Regulars: L.D., Roy Barraclough, Norman Chappell, Kathy Staff, Julian Orchard, Humphrey Lyttelton, William Rushton. Guests:

· 20 Apr.: The Syd Lawrence Orchestra, Lulu, Guys and Dolls. 25 May: The Jack Parnell Orchestra, Dana, the Nolan Sisters.

· 15 June: The Geraldo Orchestra directed by Ivor Raymonde, Freddie Trueman, Susie Baker.

· 29 June: The Ted Heath Orchestra directed by Don Lusher, Moira Anderson, Hinge and Bracket, Susie Baker.

Writers: L.D., Barry Cryer, David Nobbs (all shows); plus Alec Gerard, John Hudson, Don Clayton, Bob Nicholson (show 2); Peter Vincent (show 3).

Director: Len Lurcuck. Producer: Vernon Lawrence. *Copies of all programmes in this series are kept in the broadcaster's archive.*

The Les Dawson Show (BBC)

Series 1: BBC1, 21 January–1 April 1978 – 6 × 30 minutes; Saturdays, fortnightly, various times between 20.30 and 20.45. Regulars: L.D., Lulu, the Dougie Squires Dancers. Guests: 21 Jan.: David Jason, Glynn Edwards. 4 Feb.: Royce Mills, Daphne Riggs. 18 Feb.: June Jago, Maureen Lane, Kenneth Watson. 4 Mar.: Claire Nielson. 18 Mar.: Jacqueline Clarke, Vicki Michelle, Ralph Watson. 1 Apr.: Raymond Mason, Claire Nielson, Michael Stainton.

Writers: L.D., David Renwick, Eddie Braben, Peter Robinson (all shows); plus Tom Magee-Englefield and Tony Hare (show 4); Peter Vincent, Dennis Berson and Garry Chambers (show 5); Mick Loftus (show 6). Musical director: Johnny Coleman. Producer: John Ammonds. Director: Phil Bishop. *Copies of all shows in this series are kept in the broadcaster's archive.*

Special: BBC1, 25 May 1981 – 1 × 45 minutes; Monday, 21.35. With: Kids International, Los Gauchos and Roy Barraclough. Writers: Terry Ravenscroft, Peter Vincent, Peter Robinson, Tony Hare, Ernest Maxin. Musical director: Alyn Ainsworth. Producer: Ernest Maxin. *Copies of all shows in this series are kept in the broadcaster's archive.*

Series 2: BBC1, 30 January–6 March 1982 – 4 × 30 minutes, 2 × 35 minutes; Saturdays, mostly 20.05. Regulars: L.D., Roy Barraclough, Kids International. Guests: 30 Jan.: Helen Gelzer. 6 Feb.: Lena Zavaroni. 6 Mar.: Denise Nolan. Writers: L.D., Terry Ravenscroft (all shows); Peter Robinson, Peter Vincent, Tony Hare (shows 1–5); Roy Barraclough (shows 1, 4 and 6); Ernest Maxin (show 6). Musical director: Alyn Ainsworth. Producer: Ernest Maxin. *Copies of all shows in this series are kept in the broadcaster's archive.*

Series 3: BBC1, 15 January–18 February 1983 – 6 × 35 minutes; Saturdays, mostly 20.20. Regulars: L.D., Roy Barraclough, the Roly Polys. Guests: 15 Jan.: Grace Kennedy. 22 Jan.: Karen Fell, Daphne Oxenford. 29 Jan.: Steve 'n' Bonnie, Eli Woods. 5 Feb.: Jade. 12 Feb.: Steve 'n' Bonnie, Eli Woods. 19 Feb.: The Andersons, Eli Woods. Writers: L.D., Terry Ravenscroft. Musical director: Alyn Ainsworth. Producer: Ernest Maxin. *Copies of all shows in this series are kept in the broadcaster's archive.*

Series 4: BBC1, 21 January–25 February 1984 – 6 × 30 minutes; Saturdays, mostly 20.05. Regulars: L.D., Roy Barraclough, the Roly Polys. Guests: 21 Jan.: Bertice Reading. 28 Jan.: Karen Kay, Colin Edwynn. 4 Feb.: Madeline Bell, Bryan Pringle, Eli Woods. 11 Feb.: Stephanie Lawrence, Diana King, Eli Woods. 18 Feb.: Gloria Hunniford, Vicki Michelle, Mick Walter. 25 Feb.: Eli Woods, Jenny Kenna, Jade, Bertice Reading. Writers: L.D., Terry Ravenscroft. Producer: Robin Nash. *Copies of all shows in this series are kept in the broadcaster's archive.*

Special: BBC1, 28 December 1987 – 19.40-20.30. Taking part: L.D., Roy Barraclough, Graeme Garden, Brian Godfrey, Peter Goodwright, Johnny More, Mo Moreland, Patrick Mower, Toni Palmer, Jane Marie Osborne and the Roly Polys. Writers: Barry Cryer, David Nobbs, Paul Minett, Brian Leveson. Musical director: Alyn Ainsworth. Producer: John Bishop. *A copy of this show is kept in the broadcaster's archive.*

Series 5: BBC1, 19 October–23 November 1989 – 6 × 30 minutes; Thursdays, 20.00. Regulars: L.D., Lia Malcolm. Guests: 19 Oct.: John Nettles, Elio Pace, Shirley Bassey. 26 Oct.: Leslie Grantham, Randy Crawford, Status Quo. 2 Nov.: Brian Blessed, David Essex. 9 Nov.: Dennis Waterman, Gerard Kenny, Elkie Brooks, the Roly Polys. 16 Nov.: Chas and Dave, Diamond and Layton, Evelyn Glennie, Rose Marie. 23 Nov.: Christopher Timothy, Leo Sayer, the Fairer Sax, Wayne Eagling. Writers: L.D., Charlie Adams, Paul Alexander, Gavin Osbon, Andy Walker. Musical director: John Coleman. Production: Stewart Morris. *Copies of all shows in this series are kept in the broadcaster's archive.*

Special: BBC1, 30 December 1989, 19.20–20.00. Taking part: L.D., Michael Ball, Marti Webb, John Williams, Stuart Anderson, Lia Malcolm, Michael Corder, Jay Jolley. Writers: L.D., Charlie Adams, Paul Alexander, Gavin Osbon. Production: Stewart Morris. *A copy of this programme is kept in the broadcaster's archive.*

....

The Dawson Watch

Series 1: BBC1, 23 February–6 April 1979 – 6 × 30 minutes; Fridays, 20.00. Taking part:
• 23 Feb.: 'Housing' – L.D., Roy Barraclough, Tim Barrett, Neville Barber, David Gooderson, Brian Jameson, Michael Sharvell-Martin, Gordon Peters, April Walker.
• 2 Mar.: 'Transport' – L.D., David Lodge, Andrew Sachs, Roy Barraclough, Sam Kelly, Derek Seaton, Johnny Wade, Johnny Ball, Roger Avon, Debbi Blythe, Mimi de Braie, Michael Chesden, Paddy Joyce.
• 16 Mar.: 'Finance' – L.D., Bill Pertwee, Tony Caunter, Gordon Peters, Roy Barraclough, Burt Kwouk, Derek Seaton, Peter Bland, Simon Barry, Debbi Blythe, Anthony Woodruff, Norman Atkyns, Michael Boothe, John Pennington, Brian Jameson.
• 23 Mar.: 'Leisure' – L.D., John Junkin, Patrick Newell, Roy Barraclough, Robert East, Brian Jameson, Ralph Watson, Debbi Blythe, Heather Beel, April Walker, Josephine Gordon, Vilma Hollingbery, Paul Luty, Larry Martyn, Carolyn Simmonds, Martin Carroll, Norman Hartley.
• 30 Mar.: 'Law' – L.D., Roy Barraclough, Donald Hewlett, David Battley, Tony Caunter, Jerold Wells, Roland McLeod, Neville Barber, Lindy Alexander.
• 6 Apr.: 'Family' – L.D., Roy Barraclough, David Battley, Carol Hawkins, Johnny Ball, Michael Knowles, Roland McLeod, John Pennington, Raymond Mason, Debbi Blythe, Stuart Sherwin, Colin McCormack, Ann Curthoys, Michael Halsey, Gordon Salkild, Marie Claire, Doreen Purchase, Dafydd Hywel.

Writers: L.D., Terry Ravenscroft, Andy Hamilton, Ian Davidson (all shows); plus Tom Magee-Englefield (show 1); Eric Geen (shows 2 and 3); Colin Bostock-Smith (show 3). Producer: Peter Whitmore. *Copies of all shows in this series are kept in the broadcaster's archive.*

Series 2: BBC1, 22 November–27 December 1979 – 6 × 30 minutes; Thursdays, 20.30. Regulars: L.D., Roy Barraclough, Daphne Oxenford, Vicki Michelle, Gordon Peters.
• 22 Nov.: 'Crime' – Neville Barber, Roger Avon, Stuart Sherwin, John Pennington, Tony McHale, David Rowlands, Jay Neill.
• 29 Nov.: 'Health' – Ian Lindsay, Stuart Sherwin, David Gooderson, Lindy Alexander, Kirsten Cooke, Christopher Lawrence.

- 6 Dec.: 'Media' – John Junkin, Peter Blake, Peter Bland, Brian Jameson, John Pennington, John Owens, Lindy Alexander, David McNally, Jay Neill.
- 13 Dec.: 'Education' – Jacqueline Clarke, David Rowlands, Bella Emberg, Judy Gridley, Tommy Barnett..
- 20 Dec.: 'Environment' – Peter Bland, Roy Holder, Michael Stainton.
- 27 Dec.: 'Entertainment' – Robin Parkinson, Michael Ripper, Rex Robinson, Jay Neill, Stuart Sherwin, Steve Veidor, Gordon Peters, Ivan Hunte

Writers: L.D., Terry Ravenscroft, Andy Hamilton. Producer: Peter Whitmore. *Copies of all shows in this series are kept in the broadcaster's archive.*

Series 3: BBC1, 17 October–28 November 1980 – 6 × 30 minutes; Fridays, 19.30. Taking part:

- 17 Oct.: 'Politics' – L.D., Michael Ripper, Daphne Oxenford, Neville Barber, Jeffrey Segal, Tony Millan, Dominic Letts.
- 24 Oct.: 'Culture' – L.D., Jay Neill, Roy Barraclough, Mike Lewin, Robin Parkinson, Barrie Gosney, Mike Lewin, Harry Fielder.
- 31 Oct.: 'Holidays' – L.D., Gordon Peters, Roy Barraclough, Peter Blake, Gordon Peters, Debbi Blythe, Michael Keating.
- 7 Nov.: 'Communications' – L.D., Daphne Oxenford, Roy Barraclough, Kirsten Cooke, George Sweeney, Robin Parkinson, Michael Stainton, John Pennington, Michael Sharvell-Martin.
- 14 Nov.: 'Love and marriage' – L.D., Vicki Michelle, Bella Emberg, Roy Barraclough, Peter Bland, Jay Neill, Kirsten Cooke, Gordon Peters, Claire Nielson, Michael Sharvell-Martin, Stella Tanner, Norman Hartley.
- 28 Nov.: 'The future' – L.D., Roy Barraclough, Raymond Witch, Michael Keating, Nicholas McArdle, Kit Thacker, Tim Barrett. Writers: L.D., Terry Ravenscroft, Andy Hamilton. Producer: Peter Whitmore. *Copies of all shows in this series are kept in the broadcaster's archive.*

Special: BBC1, 23 December 1980 – 1 × 30 minutes; Tuesday, 20.30. 'Christmas' – L.D., Daphne Oxenford, Roy Barraclough, Bella Emberg, Roger Avon, Neville Barber, Robin Parkinson, Gordon Peters, Michael Sharvell-Martin, April Walker, Lindy Benson, Ruth Burnett, Monica Teama. Writers: L.D., Terry Ravenscroft, Andy Hamilton. Producer: Peter Whitmore. *A copy of this show is kept in the broadcaster's archive.*

Blankety Blank

Series 7: BBC1, 7 September 1984–26 March 1985 – 24 × 35 minutes, 1 × 30 minutes; Fridays to 8 February 1985, mostly 18.55 (except 7 Sept., 19 Oct., 14 Dec. 1984, 19.00; 16 Nov., 7 Dec. 1984, 19.05; 23 Nov. 1984, 19.25); 25 December 1984, Tuesday, 17.30; then, from 19 February 1985, Tuesdays, 19.30. L.D. takes over as host. Taking part:

- 7 Sept. 1984: Lorraine Chase, Henry Cooper, Barry Cryer, Stacy Dorning, Sheila Ferguson, Tom O'Connor.
- 14 Sept. 1984: Janet Ellis, Roy Hudd, Karen Kay, Matthew Kelly, Ted Rogers, Lizzie Webb.
- 21 Sept. 1984: Dana, Janice Long, Johnny More, Wendy Richard, Danny La Rue, Chris Tarrant.
- 28 Sept. 1984: Dana, Windsor Davies, Bobby Davro, Sabina Franklyn, Don Maclean, Linda Nolan.
- 5 Oct. 1984: Lorraine Chase, Les Dennis, Sabina Franklyn, Dustin Gee, Kelly Monteith, Anneka Rice.
- 19 Oct. 1984: Geoff Capes, Lynsey de Paul, Jan Leeming, Don Maclean, Spike Milligan, Claire Rayner.
- 26 Oct. 1984: Lynsey de Paul, Sheila Ferguson, Johnny More, Anneka Rice, Jeff Stevenson, Dennis Waterman.
- 9 Nov. 1984: Keith Barron, Kirsten Cooke, Pat Coombs, John Junkin, Roy Kinnear, Wendy Richard.

- 16 Nov. 1984: Sandra Dickinson, Stu Francis, Cherry Gillespie, Paul Shane, Frank Thornton, Lizzie Webb.
- 23 Nov. 1984: Cheryl Baker, Keith Harris, Finola Hughes, Nicholas Lyndhurst, Mike Reid, Mollie Sugden.
- 30 Nov. 1984: Janet Brown, Roy Kinnear, Joanna Monro, Linda Nolan, Duncan Norvelle, Jon Pertwee.
- 7 Dec. 1984: Stan Boardman, Henry Kelly, Bonnie Larigford, Bertice Reading, Beryl Reid, Cyril Smith.
- 14 Dec. 1984: Jimmy Cricket, Bella Emberg, Sarah Greene, Mike Nolan, Duncan Norvelle, June Whitfield.
- 25 Dec. 1984: Lorraine Chase, Suzanne Danielle, Ken Dodd, Russell Harty, Ruth Madoc, Derek Nimmo.
- 11 Jan. 1985: Desmond Lynam, Faith Brown, Chris Serle, Sally James, Mike Reid, Pat Coombs.
- 18 Jan. 1985: Stan Boardman, Mollie Sugden, Paul Heiney, Tessa Wyatt, Gary Wilmot, Wendy Richard.
- 25 Jan. 1985: Dave Lee Travis, Liz Fraser, June Whitfield, Pete Murray, Roy Kinnear, Cherry Gillespie.
- 1 Feb. 1985: Roy Walker, Janet Brown, Fred Housego, Tessa Sanderson, Bobby Davro, Patricia Hayes.
- 8 Feb. 1985: Tony Blackburn, Sheila Ferguson, Nicholas Lyndhurst, Sabina Franklyn, William Rushton, Rula Lenska.
- 19 Feb. 1985: Barry Cryer, Bertice Reading, Guy Michelmore, Sharron Davies, David Copperfield, Anna Raeburn.
- 26 Feb. 1985: Ian McCaskill, Claire Rayner, David Jacobs, Wincey Willis, Bernard Manning, Aimi MacDonald.
- 5 Mar. 1985: Fred Feast, David Jacobs, Lesley Judd, Jonathan King, Claire Rayner, Wincey Willis.
- 12 Mar. 1985: Duncan Norvelle, Barbara Windsor, Chris Tarrant, Sarah Greene, Frank Carson, Leslie Ash.
- 19 Mar. 1985: Michael Barrymore, Sandra Dickinson, Nicholas Parsons, Emily Bolton, Rolf Harris, Sue Cook.
- 26 Mar. 1985: Jimmy Cricket, Bella Emberg, Sarah Greene, Mike Nolan, Duncan Norvelle, June Whitfield.
  Directors: David Taylor, Tony Newman.
  Producers: Marcus Plantin, John Bishop, Stanley Appel.

Series 8: BBC1, 6 September 1985– 21 March 1986 – 22 × 35 minutes; Fridays, mostly 19.40 (except 20 Sept. 1985, 3 Jan., 21 Mar. 1986, 19.35). L.D. hosts. Taking part:

- 6 Sept. 1985: Pat Coombs, David Jacobs, Roy Kinnear, Bonnie Langford, Aimi MacDonald, Dave Lee Travis.
- 13 Sept. 1985: Joe Brown, Billy Dainty, Dana, Tessa Sanderson, Kathy Staff, Chris Tarrant.
- 20 Sept. 1985: Tony Blackburn, Joyce Blair, Faith Brown, Norman Collier, Suzanne Dando, Nicholas Smith.
- 27 Sept. 1985: Madeline Bell, Henry Cooper, David Copperfield, John Junkin, Ruth Madoc, Madeline Smith.
- 4 Oct. 1985: Fern Britton, Bill Buckley, Lesley Judd, Lance Percival, Jean Rook, Norman Vaughan.
- 11 Oct. 1985: Bella Emberg, Pete Murray, Linda Nolan, Bill Pertwee, Fiona Richmond, Frankie Vaughan.
- 18 Oct. 1985: Charlie Daze, Peter Goodwright, Polly James, Eddie Kidd, Bertice Reading, Anneka Rice.
- 25 Oct. 1985: Janet Brown, Gary Davies, Lynsey de Paul, Cyril Fletcher, Nerys Hughes, Tommy Trinder.
- 1 Nov. 1985: Stacy Dorning, Aiden J. Harvey, Sally James, Nicholas Parsons, Claire Rayner, Bernie Winters.
- 8 Nov. 1985: Floella Benjamin, Katie Boyle, Susan Hanson, Alfred Marks, Duncan Norvelle, Peter Stringfellow.
- 15 Nov. 1985: Lionel Blair, Sharron Davies, Don Estelle, Jill Gascoigne, Paul Shane, June Whitfield.
- 22 Nov. 1985: Arthur English, Shirley Anne Field, Liz Fraser, Rolf Harris, Sue Lloyd.

• 29 Nov. 1985: Johnny Ball, Simon Bates, Samantha Fox, Marian Montgomery, Mike Newman, Anna Raeburn.

• 6 Dec. 1985: Anna Dawson, Clive Dunn, Clement Freud, Thora Hird, Karen Kay, Kenny Lynch.

• 13 Dec. 1985: Karen Barber, Geoff Capes, David Hamilton, Mary Parkinson, Ted Rogers, Helen Shapiro.

• 20 Dec. 1985: Ken Dodd, Cherry Gillespie, Anita Harris, Roland Rat Superstar, Wendy Richard, Freddie Trueman.

• 27 Dec. 1985: Debbie Greenwood, John Inman, Aimi MacDonald, Tom O'Connor, Mollie Sugden, Gary Wilmot.

• 3 Jan. 1986: Cheryl Baker, Sandra Dickinson, Diana Moran, Michael Parkinson, Danny La Rue, Dave Wolfe.

• 10 Jan. 1986: Leslie Ash, Lynda Baron, Tracey Childs, Bernie Clifton, Jack Douglas, John Dunn.

• 24 Jan. 1986: Barry Cryer, Georgia Brown, Bobby Knutt, Sandra Payne, Keith Harris, Dinah Sheridan.

• 7 Feb. 1986: Peter Alliss, Debbie Arnold, Roy Barraclough, Janice Long, Mike Reid, Bertice Reading.

• 21 Mar. 1986: Rory Bremner, Harry Carpenter, Vince Hill, Liz Rtson, Marti Webb, Barbara Windsor.
Directors: Tony Newman, Bruce Millar.
Producer: Stanley Appel.

Series 9: BBC1, 5 September 1986–3 April 1987 – 21 × 35 minutes; Fridays, mostly 19.35 (26 Sept., 31 Oct. 1986, 16 Jan., 30 Jan., 3 Apr. 1987, 19.40; 24 Dec., 17.05). L.D. hosts. Taking part:

• 5 Sept. 1986: Lionel Blair, Felix Bowness, Samantha Fox, Roy Kinnear, Maggie Moone, Bertice Reading.

• 12 Sept. 1986: Bruno Brookes, Eve Ferret, Sara Hollamby, Nerys Hughes, Derek Jameson, Freddie Trueman.

• 19 Sept. 1986: Henry Cooper, Dana, Les Dennis, Ruth Madoc, Fiona Richmond, Bernie Winters.

• 26 Sept. 1986: Janet Brown, Dave Lee Travis, Sabina Franklyn, Alfred Marks, Diana Moran, David Wilkie.

• 03 Oct. 1986: Lynn Faulds Wood, Lynda Lee-Potter, Linda Lusardi, Peter Powell, Barry Sheene, Gary Wilmot.

• 10 Oct. 1986: Moyra Bremner, Fenella Fielding, Sarah Greene, Roy Hudd, John Junkin, Mike Smith.

• 17 Oct. 1986: Cheryl Baker, Lynda Baron, Joe Brown, Norman Collier, Belinda Lang, Chris Serle.

• 24 Oct. 1986: Lennie Bennett, Bella Emberg, Rolf Harris, Lesley Judd, Karen Kay, Dixie Peach.

• 31 Oct. 1986: Gary Davies, William Gaunt, Madhur Jaffrey, Mary Parkinson, Mandy Shires, Nicholas Smith.

• 7 Nov. 1986: Roy Barraclough, Rustie Lee, Jan Leeming, Linda Nolan, Paul Shane, Jeff Stevenson.

• 14 Nov. 1986: Floella Benjamin, Barry Cryer, Jenny Hanley, Tom O'Connor, Greg Rogers, Dinah Sheridan.

• 28 Nov. 1986: Peter Dean, Leslie Grantham, Paul Medford, Sandy Ratcliff, Wendy Richard, Gillian Taylforth.

• 26 Dec. 1986: Lynda Baron, Frank Carson, Samantha Fox, Syd Little, Eddie Large, Wendy Richard.

• 16 Jan. 1987: Jeffrey Holland, David Griffin, Ruth Madoc, Su Pollard, Linda Regan, Paul Shane.

• 23 Jan. 1987: Frank Carson, Suzanne Dando, Emlyn Hughes, Janice Long, Mike Nolan, Claire Rayner.

• 30 Jan. 1987: Peter Goodwright, Thora Hird, Sneh Gupta, Ian Krankie, Jeanette Krankie, Tom Pepper.

• 6 Feb. 1987: Duncan Norvelle, Carmen Silvera, Alan Titchmarsh, Linda Hayden, Keith Chegwin, Sally Brampton.

• 13 Feb. 1987: Deryck Guyler, Charlie Williams, Cherry Gillespie, Aimi MacDonald, Peter Stringfellow, Jean Rook.

• 20 Feb. 1987: Michael Fish, John Kettley, Ian

McCaskill, the Beverley Sisters.
- 27 Feb. 1987: Mike Newman, Arlene Phillips, Simon Bates, Tessa Sanderson, Les Dennis, Hazell Dean.
- 3 Apr. 1987: Lionel Blair, Aimi MacDonald, Joe Brown, Suzanne Dando, Mary Parkinson, Gary Davies, Peter Powell, Janice Long, Bertice Reading, Linda Lusardi, Bernie Winters.

Directors: Bruce Millar, Tony Newman.
Producer: Stanley Appel.

Series 10: BBC1, 18 September 1987–26 February 1988 – 21 × 35 minutes, 1 × 40 minutes; Fridays, mostly 19.40 (20 Nov., 19.35; 26 Dec. 1987, 17.20; 1 Jan. 1988, 17.40). L.D. hosts. Taking part:
- 18 Sept. 1987: Lynda Baron, Roy Castle, John Conteh, Linda Nolan, Mike Reid, Lena Zavaroni.
- 25 Sept. 1987: Frank Bough, Bill Buckley, Ann Gregg, John Pitman, Gillian Reynolds, Kathy Tayler.
- 2 Oct. 1987: Jim Bowen, Linda Davison, John Junkin, Rustie Lee, Linda Lusardi, Paul Shane.
- 9 Oct. 1987: Joe Brown, Dana, Paul Heiney, Janice Long, Claire Rayner, Frankie Vaughan.
- 16 Oct. 1987: Beverly Adams, Frank Carson, Barry Cryer, Christian Dion, Su Ingle, Nina Myskow.
- 23 Oct. 1987: Bernie Clifton, Doc Cox, Gloria Gaynor, Maggie Moone, Gillian Taylforth, Dave Lee Travis.
- 30 Oct. 1987: Geoff Capes, Norman Collier, Bella Emberg, Rula Lenska, Dinah Sheridan, Dennis Waterman.
- 06 Nov. 1987: Cherry Gillespie, Debbie McGee, Duncan Norvelle, Wendy Richard, David Wilkie, Charlie Williams.
- 13 Nov. 1987: Cheryl Baker, Bernard Cribbins, Mark Curry, Jean Ferguson, Roy Walker, Barbara Windsor.
- 20 Nov. 1987: Thora Hird, Terry Marsh, Mo Moreland, Cynthia Payne, Bernie Winters, Steve Wright.
- 04 Dec. 1987: Joe Brown, Charlie Daze, Nerys Hughes, Victor Kiam, Ellie Lame, Angela Rippon.
- 11 Dec. 1987: Pat Coombs, Henry Cooper, Barry Cryer, Debbie Greenwood, Jenny Hanley, Tom Pepper.
- 18 Dec. 1987: Emlyn Hughes, Jan Leeming, Jessica Martin, Tom O'Connor, Ted Robbins, Sally Thomsett.
- 26 Dec. 1987: Lynda Brown, Joe Brown, Geoff Capes, Lorraine Chase, Roy Hudd, Wendy Richard.
- 1 Jan. 1988: Ken Bruce, Bernie Clifton, Bonnie Langford, Ian McCaskill, Aimi MacDonald, Kathy Staff.
- 8 Jan. 1988: Harry Carpenter, Claire Rayner, Phillip Schofield, Suzy Aitchison, Frank Carson, Liz Robertson.
- 15 Jan. 1988: Les Dennis, Peter Goodwright, Lisa Maxwell, Mary Parkinson, Karen Barber, Peter Powell.
- 22 Jan. 1988: Norman Collier, Vince Hill, Joe Longthorne, Wendy Richard, Anne Robinson, Tessa Sanderson.
- 29 Jan. 1988: Floella Benjamin, Suzanne Dando, Wayne Dobson, Arthur English, Aimi MacDonald, Fred Trueman.
- 12 Feb. 1988: Karen Kay, Ian Krankie, Jeanette Krankie, Bill Owen, Anna Raeburn, Alvin Stardust.
- 19 Feb. 1988: Pamela Armstrong, June Brown, Gary Davies, Samantha Fox, Henry Kelly, Kenny Lynch.
- 26 Feb. 1988: Lionel Blair, Debbie Greenwood, Danny La Rue, Aimi MacDonald, Duncan Norvelle, Bertice Reading.
- Directors: Geoff Miles, Tony Newman.
Producer: Stanley Appel.

Series 11: BBC1, 9 September–16 December 1988 – 12 × 35 minutes; Fridays, 19.40. L.D. hosts. Taking part:
- 9 Sept. 1988: John Dunn, Henry Kelly, Vicki Michelle, Hilary O'Neil, Wendy Richard, Freddie Trueman.
- 16 Sept. 1988: Lynda Baron, Joe Brown,

Eddie Edwards, Bonnie Langford, Rose Marie, Greg Rogers.

• 7 Oct. 1988: Floella Benjamin, Nerys Hughes, Ellie Lame, Chris Serle, Paul Shane, Roy Walker.

• 14 Oct. 1988: Christopher Biggins, Gavin Campbell, Su Ingle, Sandy Ratcliff, Claire Rayner, Steve Wright.

• 21 Oct. 1988: Simon Dee, Linda Nolan, Bill Oddie, Judi Spiers, Kathy Staff, Mark Walker.

• 28 Oct. 1988: Rachel Bell, Frank Carson, Suzanne Dando, Bill Gaunt, Tom Pepper, Sheila Steafel.

• 4 Nov. 1988: Henry Cooper, Debbie Greenwood, Jan Leeming, Phillip Schofield, Dave Lee Travis, June Whitfield.

• 11 Nov. 1988: Brian Blessed, Paul Coia, Doc Cox, Louise Jameson, Rustie Lee, Carmen Silvera.

• 25 Nov. 1988: Vince Hill, Caron Keating, Linda Lusardi, Claire Rayner, Mike Reid, Bill Wiggins.

• 2 Dec. 1988: Geoff Capes, Bernie Clifton, Barry Cryer, Bella Emberg, Debbie McGee, Adrienne Posta.

• 9 Dec. 1988: Lionel Blair, Mark Curry, Lisa Maxwell, Mollie Sugden, Gillian Taylforth, Frankie Vaughan.

• 16 Dec. 1988: Stan Boardman, Jean Boht, John Craven, Peter Goodwright, Aimi MacDonald, Jane Marie Osborne.
Director: Tony Dow. Producer: Stanley Appel.

Series 12: BBC1, 7 September 1989– 12 March 1990 – 21 × 35 minutes; Thursdays, 20.00 until 21 December; then Wednesday 27 December 19.10; then Mondays, 20.00. L.D. hosts. Taking part:

• 7 Sept. 1989: Terence Alexander, Cheryl Baker, Gary Davies, Frances Edmonds, Vicki Michelle, Duncan Norvelle.

• 14 Sept. 1989: Rachel Bell, Gyles Brandreth, Rose-Marie, Buster Merryfield, Maggie Moone, Steve Wright.

• 21 Sept. 1989: Trevor Brooking, Joe Brown, Dana, Jimmy Hill, Rustie Lee, Judi Spiers.

• 28 Sept. 1989: Pamela Armstrong, Colin Berry, Rodney Bewes, Paul Shane, Joan Sims, Gillian Taylforth.

• 5 Oct. 1989: Bill Buckley, Tom O'Connor, Jilly Goolden, Henry Kelly, Bertice Reading, Kathy Tayler.

• 12 Oct. 1989: Stan Boardman, Bella Emberg, Diana Moran, Linda Nolan, Dave Lee Travis, John Virgo.

• 30 Nov. 1989: Jill Gascoigne, Anne Gregg, Roy Hudd, Ted Robbins, Barbara Shelley, Gary Wilmot.

• 7 Dec. 1989: Jean Alexander, Roy Barraclough, John Conteh, Andy Crane, Louise Jameson, Tessa Sanderson.

• 14 Dec. 1989: Christopher Biggins, Lorraine Chase, Bernard Cribbins, Phillip Schofield, Vivien Stuart, Barbara Windsor.

• 21 Dec. 1989: Ray Clemence, Pat Coombs, Barry Cryer, Derek Hatton, Lisa Maxwell.

• 27 Dec. 1989: Floella Benjamin, Anne Charleston, Linda Lusardi, Danny La Rue, Ian Smith, Peter Woods.

• 1 Jan. 1990: Lynda Baron, William Gaunt, Bonnie Langford, Adrian Mills, Mike Reid, Carmen Silvera.

• 8 Jan. 1990: Frank Carson, Doc Cox, Sharron Davies, Jenny Hanley, Mo Moreland, Kevin Woodford.

• 15 Jan. 1990: Joe Brown, Bernie Clifton, Ian Krankie, Janette Krankie, Janice Long, Anthea Turner.

• 22 Jan. 1990: Tina Baker, Bruno Brookes, Pamela Power, Wendy Richard, Frankie Vaughan, Bernie Winters.

• 29 Jan. 1990: Floella Benjamin, Michael Groth, Vince Hill, Sue Lloyd, Gail McKenna, Charlie Williams.

• 5 Feb. 1990: Henry Cooper, Caron Keating, Ellie Laine, Dave Lee Travis, Jeff Stevenson, Mollie Sugden.

• 12 Feb. 1990: Aiden J. Harvey, Nerys Hughes, Debbie McGee, Vicki Michelle, Billy Pearce, Roy Walker.

• 26 Feb. 1990: Lynsey de Paul, Karen Kay, Patrick McNee, Barry McGuigan, Mick

Miller, Linda Thorson.
- 5 Mar. 1990: Gavin Campbell, Julian Clary, Polly James, Danny La Rue, Rose Marie, Jane Marie Osborne.
- 12 Mar. 1990: John Craven, Mark Curry, Thora Hird, Matthew Kelly, Linda Lewis, Cleo Rocos.
Directors: Sylvie Boden, John Burrowes.
Producer: Stanley Appel.

Opportunity Knocks
BBC1, 31 March– 2 June 1990 –
8 × 50 minutes, 1 × 60 minutes (live final), 1 × 30 minutes (live final results). Les Dawson hosts a revived version of the talent contest that launched his career.
Producer: Stewart Morris.

Fast Friends
BBC1, 30 March–28 June 1991 –
14 × 30 minutes; until 11 May (except 30 Mar., 19.00; 6 Apr., 13 Apr., 19.10; 4 May, 11 May, 19.30), then Fridays from 17 May, mostly 20.00 (28 June, 19.45).
Director: Sylvie Boden.
Producer: Stanley Appel.

BIBLIOGRAPHY

Barfe, Louis, *Turned Out Nice Again: the story of British light entertainment* (Atlantic Books, London, 2008)

Chapman, Graham, *A Liar's Autobiography: Volume VI* (Methuen, London, 1980 – paperback edition, Magnum, London, 1981)

Clare, Anthony, *In the Psychiatrist's Chair II* (William Heinemann, London, 1995)

Cook, William, *The Comedy Store: The club that changed British comedy* (Little, Brown, London, 2001)

Corbett, Ronnie, with David Nobbs, *And It's Goodnight From Him* (Michael Joseph, London, 2006)

Coward, Simon, and Christopher Perry (eds.), *Bob's Full House: A peek into the personal archive of Bob Monkhouse* (Kaleidoscope Publishing, Dudley, 2009)

Coward, Simon, Christopher Perry and Richard Down (eds.) *British Independent Television Drama Guide 1955–2010* (electronic edition – Kaleidoscope Publishing, Dudley, 2010)

Coward, Simon, Christopher Perry and Richard Down (eds.) BBC Television Drama Guide 1936-2011 (electronic edition – Kaleidoscope Publishing, Dudley, 2011)

Coward, Simon, Christopher Perry and Richard Down (eds.) *British Television Comedy Research Guide 1936–2011* (electronic edition – Kaleidoscope Publishing, Dudley, 2011)

Craig, Mike, *Look Back With Laughter*, Volume 1 (Mike Craig, Altrincham, 1996)

Craig, Mike, *Look Back With Laughter*, Volume 2 (Mike Craig, Altrincham, 2001)

Davies, Russell (ed.), *The Kenneth Williams Diaries* (HarperCollins, London, 1994)

Dawson, Les, *A Card for the Clubs* (Sphere Books, London, 1974)

Dawson, Les, *A Clown Too Many* (Elm Tree Books, London, 1985)

Dawson, Les, *A Time Before Genesis* (Elm Tree Books, London, 1985)

Dawson, Les, *Come Back With the Wind* (Robson Books, London, 1990)

Dawson, Les, *Hitler Was My Mother-in-Law* (Arrow Books, London, 1985)

Dawson, Les, *Les Dawson Gives Up* (Papermac, London, 1989)

Dawson, Les, *Les Dawson's Lancashire* (Elm Tree Books, London, 1983)

Dawson, Les, *No Tears for the Clown* (Robson Books, London, 1992)

Dawson, Les, *The Blade and the Passion* (Robson Books, London, 1993)

Bibliography

Dawson, Les, *The Cosmo Smallpiece Guide to Male Liberation* (Star Books, London, 1979)

Dawson, Les, *The Les Dawson Joke Book* (Arrow Books, London, 1979)

Dawson, Les, *The Malady Lingers On* (Arrow Books, London, 1982)

Dawson, Les, *The Spy Who Came...* (Star Books, London, 1976)

Dawson, Les, *Well Fared My Lovely* (Robson Books, London, 1991)

Dawson, Tracy (ed.), *Les Dawson's Secret Notebooks* (JR Books, London, 2007)

Fisher, John, *Funny Way to Be a Hero* (Paladin, St Albans, 1976)

Frayn, Michael (ed.), *The Best of Beachcomber* (William Heinemann, London, 1963)

Hudd, Roy, with Philip Hindin, *Roy Hudd's Cavalcade of Variety Acts* (Robson Books, London, 1997)

Lewis, Mark, *The Roly Polys: Fit, Fat and Fruity* (W.H. Allen, London, 1986)

Lewisohn, Mark, *Radio Times Guide to TV Comedy* (BBC Worldwide, London, 1998)

Margolis, Jonathan, *Bernard Manning* (Orion, London, 1996)

Meades, Jonathan, *This Is Their Life* (Salamander, London, 1979)

Middles, Mick, *When You're Smiling: the illustrated biography of Les Dawson* (André Deutsch, London, 1999)

Monkhouse, Bob, *Over the Limit: My Secret Diaries 1993–1998* (Century, London, 1998)

Perry, Christopher, and Richard Down (eds.), *The British Television Music and Variety Research Guide* (Kaleidoscope Publishing, Dudley, 1997)

Pixley, Andrew, *The Goodies: Super Chaps Three* (Kaleidoscope Publishing, Dudley, 2010)

Plater, Alan, *Doggin' Around* (Northway Publications, London, 2006)

Ravenscroft, Terry, *Les Dawson's Cissie and Ada* (Kindle eBook – Razzamatazz Publications, 2011)

Singleton, Steve (ed.), *The Dawson Slant* (The Gazette, Blackpool, 2008)

Tracy, Sheila, *Talking Swing: The British Big Bands* (Mainstream, Edinburgh, 1997)

Wilmut, Roger, *Didn't You Kill My Mother-in-Law?* (Methuen, London, 1989)

Wilmut, Roger, *From Fringe to Flying Circus* (Methuen, London, 1980)

Wilmut, Roger, *Kindly Leave the Stage* (Methuen, London, 1985)

ACKNOWLEDGEMENTS

First and foremost, I must thank the colleagues and friends of Les Dawson who spared their valuable time to talk, always warmly, about him: John Ammonds, Stanley Appel, James Casey, Con and Dec Cluskey, Barry Cryer, John Duncan, Ray Galton and Alan Simpson, Danny Greenstone, Andy Hamilton, Gary Husband, Vernon Lawrence, Peter Lee-Wright, David Mallet, Ernest Maxin, Fergie Maynard, Royston Mayoh, Stewart Morris, David Nobbs, Dan Patterson, Peter Pilbeam, Alan Plater, Johnny Roadhouse, Terry Ravenscroft, Lyn Took and Lydia Vine. Meanwhile, honourable mentions must go to Terence Blacker, Barry Bonner, John Fisher, Bernie Newnham, Peter Neill, Graham Pass, Keith Salmon and Tony Hayes for professional insights, pointers and introductions; to Stan Tracey and Jimmy Mulville for responding so swiftly to my communications, if only to apologize for being unable to remember anything; to Andrea Corti, partner of the late Robin Nash, for his help; to Ronnie Taylor's daughter Sue for help and support from her father's files; to Helen Kenworthy, who pointed me in the direction of the journalistic nostalgia site Gentlemen Ranters, and to Ranter-in-chief Revel Barker for asking his readers and contributors to contact me with any stories pertaining to Les, which put me in touch with Rob Ainsley, Alan Hart and Christine Hodgson; and to jazzman, wit and all-round credit to humanity Alan Barnes for furnishing me with an introduction to the aforementioned Alan Plater, whose understanding of comedy in general and Les Dawson in particular was second to none. Despite already being seriously ill, Plater, aided by his wife, Shirley Rubinstein, talked with me for two precious hours, an experience I will treasure always.

An enormous debt of gratitude is also owed to Martin Fenton and Gavin Sutherland, who made me this way when we were near-neighbours in east London over a decade ago. I had always been interested in archive TV and, in particular, light entertainment, but those pleasantly plastered evenings in front of tapes of dubious origin were formative experiences. Thanks also to Janine Fenton for tolerating three fat men in glasses squinting through timecode and several generations of VHS dubbing, trying to work out who was playing in the Sooty Braden Showband.

I couldn't have completed this book satisfactorily without the material lent or given to me by fellow archive television enthusiasts/researchers. In particular,

Acknowledgements

Steve Arnold, Ben Baker, Rory Clark, Ian Greaves, Simon Harries, Justin Lewis and Gary Mills have been responsible for mileage, not footage, of commercially unavailable Dawson TV and radio appearances coming my way, while Steve Williams contributed perfect recollections of *Fast Friends* at a time when it looked like locating a sample show would be impossible. Phil and Suzy Norman's hospitality and knowledge made research visits to London a joy. Walty Dunlop and Ian Tomkinson deserve serious respect for pulling together and making navigable every available TV and radio listing from 1955 to 1985. Friends like Graham Barnard, Ian Beard, Steve Berry, Shaun Butcher, George Grimwood, Robin Halstead, Andy Henderson, Neil Kennedy, Gareth Randall, Steve Rogers, Matthew Rudd, Jonathan Sloman, Alex Thomas and John Williams supplied discs, tapes and comments, often on licensed premises. Others, like Iain Jarvis, Jack Seale, Lee James Turnock, Rob Williams and Cameron Yarde Jr, I have yet to meet, but their help was vital. Also, the written work of Mark Lewisohn and Andrew Pixley has been an inspiration, added to which, they're smashing chaps.

The archive TV research institution Kaleidoscope has been endlessly kind and helpful to me, particularly Simon Coward and Alan Hayes. The Bob Monkhouse collection is in very safe hands with them. Long before I ever thought about writing a book on Les Dawson, my friend Peter Gordon wrote a critical but sympathetic essay on Dawson's literary works for his now defunct 'magazine of elderly British comedy', *Kettering*. Re-reading it alongside the books themselves helped me a great deal. Thanks also to Jo Cummins and Mark Van Landuyt, two of the funniest people I know and also two of the most perceptive on the subject of comedy, and to Roger Lewis for all of the hilarious, disgraceful, encouraging emails.

More general kindness, fellowship and guidance came from friends like: Richard Abram, Paul Barnes, Nick Bardsley, Ralph Baxter, Michael Bee, Rodney Burbeck, Ruby Cowling, Adam Cumiskey, Alastair Doughty, Professor Barry Fantoni, Ruth Ferris-Price, Gavin Gaughan, Alex George, Stephen Gilchrist, John Grindrod, Katy Guest, Terry Henebery and Valerie Silson, Geoff Hiscott, Roy Holliday, Patrick Humphries and Sue Parr, Ali Jackson, Amy Jackson, Terry James, Tanya Jones and John Hoare, Bill and Beth Kibby-Johnson, Charles Kennedy, George Langley, Don Lawson, Richard Lewis, Emily Lomax, Maria McHale, Adam Macqueen, James Masterton, the late Hugh Mendl, Alex Newton, David Oppenheim, Matt Owen, Paul Putner, Rachel and Richard Roberts, Hazel Simpson, Jerry Sutton, Kerry Swash and Allen Painter, Roger Tagholm, Ste Tansey, Ben Tisdall, Alan Wood, Clair Woodward and Francis Wheen.

In the general direction of Manchester, I send special thanks to Shaun Hutchinson, as serious a Dawson fan as has ever trod the earth. When I started this project, having seen Shaun's passionate, informed writing about Les on various websites, I wondered whether he wasn't planning a book of his own and worried about treading on his toes. Thankfully for me, he wasn't and I wasn't, and his kindness, generosity and good humour have been limitless. It was Shaun who introduced me, late in the day, to Les's eldest daughter, Julie, and her husband, Jon, who have been very helpful with background, important corrections and photographs.

In the BBC's Written Archive Centre at Caversham, Erin O'Neill found me as much Dawsonian paperwork as she possibly could, which was particularly valuable in providing vital information about the comedian's early performing years. I also spent a lot of very worthwhile hours in the British Library – both at St Pancras and Colindale – and the BFI Library, so thanks go to their excellent staff.

Thanks, obviously, to gentleman agent Euan Thorneycroft at AM Heath for doing the tricky negotiations that got this book commissioned. Over at Atlantic Books, Hull's very own Sarah Norman deserves full recognition for having the sense and taste to commission this book, and for editing it sensitively and granting me a much-needed deadline extension when I fractured my elbow. Thanks also to copy-editor Lucy Ridout and indexer David Atkinson, who has undertaken this vital task on all of my books so far. Thanks also to Richard Milbank and Toby Mundy, without whom . . .

Even when I was a stroppy teen favouring alternative comedy over the old school, I never lost my love for Les Dawson. Whenever he was on, we watched as a family, united. In particular, my late maternal grandmother, Jean Murray, a superb pianist, thought he was the bee's knees. Thanks to her, my grandfather and my mother for everything.

Finally, love and gratitude to my wife, Susannah. In some senses, a biographer's subject becomes an invisible house guest, and Susannah never made me feel that Les was unwelcome, not even when he and I were monopolizing the living room TV for hours on end with editions of *Jokers Wild*. Any errors are the fault of my dog Lyttelton and my daughter Primrose.

Lowestoft
September 2011

INDEX

Index

I found a masseur with sufficient skill to straighten out my spine and spare me the continuous pain. In all other medical regards we were encouraged never to self-medicate, and to be constantly aware of whether or not we were fit to fly. Any number of minor complaints, such as flu or even just cold, could upset the balance system enough to render a pilot a danger to himself and to others. Thus it was that I found myself at the airfield sick bay one morning complaining of a little constipation. I was ushered into the office of a brand new doctor who had qualified only a few weeks earlier. On completion of the examination I offered my prescription to the medic at the dispensary window. 'Are you pregnant, sir?' he politely enquired. On receiving the response that it was pretty unlikely he excused himself to check the prescription with the young doctor. Back he came a moment later with the observation that my prescription was an unusual way of treating constipation but who was he, a lowly petty officer, to argue with an officer? I wasn't to find out until the next day that I had been prescribed Maxalon, a drug designed to cure morning sickness during pregnancy, and had been allocated ten times the normal dose. The junior doctor's theory was that if it relaxed the stomach then it might cure constipation. I thanked the PO and set off to the squadron in good time for our midday duty start.

As luck would have it we had a couple of shouts almost immediately and so it was supper time before I remembered that I was supposed to take a pill with every meal. It was a fine and still summer's evening but had turned a little cold and we could be pretty confident that there would be no more flying trade for us in the hour remaining before darkness. The tourists would all be safely tucked up in the pub by now. We settled down to a final hour of watching the TV and I was more than entertained to see pink alligators climbing up the curtains next to the small black and white set. I did mention to Scouse that I wasn't feeling very well but by that time there were only a few minutes of duty time left so I braved it out.

The drive home was a trip in more ways than one. By the time I pulled into the driveway I had to honk the horn to get my wife to come and help me out of the car. I curled up in bed while she phoned the sick bay only to receive the classic naval medical advice: 'Take two aspirins, go to bed, and come and see me in the morning.' An hour later and I was in a pretty bad way. All my muscles were trying to contract at the same time with the result that I was curled up in a foetal position. Another call to the sick bay thankfully reached one of the regular and very senior doctors who normally ran the place. On hearing the odd symptoms the doctor suggested that my wife drove me back to the station for a proper examination. It was no small task to get me back into the car but only a five-minute drive to the base. The regular doctor took one look at me in the car and immediately ordered an ambulance to take me to Treliske, the main Cornish hospital that I was more used to visiting by air. (Had it been daylight, that's exactly how he would have had me transported.) Instead you have to imagine what it would be like to take a hair-raising 30-minute ride in an ambulance with lights and sirens going, while taking a bad trip on LSD. Each turn of the blue light reflected eerily into the back of the vehicle and apparently I found each lurch around a tight corner hysterically funny.

At Treliske they pumped my stomach and kept me in for observation overnight. By the morning I was fine again and I was able to return to flying just a couple of days later. From that day forward I never bought my own drink again if the junior doctor was in the Culdrose Wardroom, and I retain a lifelong mistrust of taking any form of pill. When asked to fill out forms asking about whether I have a known allergic reaction to any drugs I of course write 'Maxalon'. The inevitable response from doctors and nurses is: 'How on earth do you even know that?' and so it's a story I've had to tell many times.

The great summer event for us at Culdrose was the Air Day. Most operational airbases love to put on a show to the public: it sharpens up all the aviators, gives the public the opportunity to see the expensive hardware they're funding and generates income for deserving local charities. The event at Culdrose was particularly worth seeing for several reasons: we had more helicopters than at any other base in Europe, the Navy at that time had a good selection of fast, powerful and noisy jets, and there were never any noise complaints as the local populace recognised the value of having the base nearby. In fact, the majority were serving in the Navy, married to someone who was, or earned their living from the airbase.

Each different type of helicopter would perform a display that was suitable for their size and role but a highlight was the 'flutterby', when every helicopter that could possibly be made to fly would stream overhead in the biggest formation you were ever likely to see. Flying in formation is a demanding task in a helicopter. In a fixed-wing aircraft, regardless of the speed it flies at, a light touch on the airframe next to you could often be survived as there's very little relative movement; it would be like touching door handles on two fast cars running in the same direction. But the tips of the rotor blades on a helicopter are rotating at something close to the speed of sound, and the returning rotors on the helicopter next to you are travelling in the opposite direction, so a touch of two rotor blades would be catastrophic. The rule was therefore to space ourselves at two and a half rotor spans from each other.

Each squadron would first gather together in their own formation consisting of around a dozen helicopters. Leading the group was relatively easy as you just had to fly smoothly, at accurate speed and make any turn a wide and gentle event. At the back of the formation it was a tougher task as you had to match the movements of all the ones in front. The second and third rows in their many corrections to keep in formation would be inducing successively increasing movements up and down until it became like a roller coaster at the back. If, additionally, you were on the outside of the formation,

it was necessary to greatly reduce the speed on the inside of a turn and accelerate to high speeds on the outside of a turn. Once the CO at the front levelled out from the turn you needed to decelerate fast before you ran into the guy in front of you. Another difficult place to be was in the middle of a diamond formation with helicopters on every side of you. Of course, any squadron consisted of varying levels of pilotage skills and you would always check out who was scheduled to be alongside. The leader was the only one who had an easy time of it.

Each squadron practised independently in the preceding weeks and as it was something we didn't do very often most of us were rusty at the outset. By the time Air Day arrived we were doing it with less terror in our hearts and were looking pretty good. The dress rehearsal on the day before the event was the first time that all squadrons that year joined up together. This occupied a great deal of airspace as each independent formation lumbered around into a position where it could slot in behind the formation in front. The join-up point was about five miles on the extended centre line of the runway and it would take all of those five miles to get everybody organised into a pretty pattern. As we arrived overhead, everybody would simultaneously let off smoke. It was an impressive sight from the ground and made for great photographs – in which one could readily spot anybody who was incapable of judging two and a half rotor spans accurately.

Flutterbys all passed without incident during my time at Culdrose, but the day of the fleet review by Her Majesty the Queen on the occasion of her silver jubilee in 1977 produced a rather different result. An even bigger formation of machines from throughout all the navy bases had gathered for the big day and a mass practice for the day before was scheduled. The join-up point was over southern Hampshire, from where we would run up the Solent past the Needles lighthouse, along the impressive line-up of anchored warships and eventually over the top of the Royal Yacht *Britannia*. It was a tradition that went back to the days of Henry VIII (albeit without helicopters) and timing was everything. The plan had been made such that the huge stream of helicopters would arrive over *Britannia* at exactly the same time as the fast jets screamed overhead, about 500 feet higher. This would all have been fine if it were not for the vagaries of the English summer which produced un-forecast low cloud over the Solent just as we all arrived. Each squadron formation stuck it out for as long as they dared but flying in formation in cloud is not an activity to be recommended. One by one the COs cried chicken and peeled away out of the scudding clouds with little more than a prayer and an acute ear to the radio to prevent one squadron from running into the side of another. There was no single airfield capable of taking everybody on such a mass diversion from the plan and it took all of the next 24 hours to gather everybody back to their assigned departure points for the big day. The day itself still brought a pall of drizzle but passed without incident and it was a pleasure and a privilege to be a part of such a huge event.

Back at Culdrose the Air Days could also be relied upon to bring unpredictable weather, but it was a royal marine and not the weather that nearly caused my early demise. When the SAR and training outfit 771 Squadron upgraded from the single-engined Wessex Mark 1 to the powerful twin-engined Wessex Mark 5, we inherited the airframes from the 'Junglies', as we referred to the Commando Squadrons whose responsibility it was to deliver fighting forces into remote locations. It would be several months before all the airframes were repainted from their drab olive camouflage into the dark blue and dayglo orange that signified SAR. Thus it came about that I was flying a green Junglie Wessex on Air Day and had to take part in a mock assault scenario.

Many of the compatriots I had joined the Navy with had gone to Junglie training, but I had studied anti-submarine flying instead. Junglies had more fun and were a hardy bunch, often assigned to living and operating out of tents in the Arctic while the rest of us had nice warm cabins on aircraft carriers. HRH Prince Charles was a Junglie at around the same time and was highly regarded both as a pilot and a crewmate on the squadrons on which he served. Although I didn't have Junglie training, the basic techniques were pretty obvious and the task required flying with flare and gusto... all fine by me. The flutterby would be the culmination to the Air Day and so we all had smoke canisters fitted to our wheel struts, but first came the mock assault. My cabin was filled with fully kitted-out marines and my job was to deliver them in front of the crowd as part of a group of Junglies, just as the jets were dive-bombing the airfield and giving the armourers the opportunity to set off huge black explosions and frighten the kids.

We ran in as a formation, fast and low. As we crossed the airfield boundary we opened out the gap between each helicopter, then executed a massive flare to bring each machine to a shuddering halt in the sky. The trick was to execute the flare in such a way as to kiss the ground with the tail wheel, then rotate the rest of the helicopter around the tail wheel to bring the main wheels firmly into contact with the ground. At that point the crewman, in this case Detlef Wodak, would give a thumbs-up to the marines, who would smartly exit the aircraft cabin and throw themselves to the grass looking generally mean and war-like. The brief was to remain on the ground for no more than a few seconds, then pull to full power and climb away. Even in isolation it took some concentration but the act of doing it in a formation with a dozen other Junglies while attack jets were descending above us and explosions were going off beneath us added a bit of spice.

I was elated at the arrival and achieved a reasonable imitation of a Junglie landing in action. I called 'Go' to Detlef, the marines exited smartly and Detlef called 'Clear'. But as I hauled in full power and rotated the nose of the Wessex forwards to achieve maximum acceleration in formation with the others alongside us there was another cry from Detlef: 'Oh no!' The last marine out of the cabin had thought it a jolly good wheeze to pull the string that would ignite the smoke canister on our wheel. The act of pulling in the power had sent the airflow straight through the cabin and up into the cockpit, whereupon I went instantaneously blind. I don't mean I couldn't see ahead, I mean I couldn't see my instruments or windscreen, my whole world just went orange. It happened so fast and so unexpectedly that there was little I could do beyond continuing muscle actions that would take us along the pre-assigned flight path. If I slowed I would be run into by the guy behind. If I climbed I would be run into by the jets, and if I descended I would be taken out by the demonstration explosives going off beneath us. All I could do to help the situation was to lean my head as far out of the door as I could, not easy when you're firmly strapped into the seat, and try to peer through the thick and acrid orange smoke that was streaming past my helmet. Of course it felt like a lifetime but after about ten seconds the increased airspeed changed the flow of the smoke and it cleared from my cockpit as fast as it had appeared, enabling us to continue the climb in formation to join the next display.

The subsequent photos of the big formation fly-past are not quite as symmetrical as usual as just one Wessex is not streaming smoke. Detlef was still apoplectic when eventually we landed and re-grouped at the squadron and he went off to find the marine in question. I didn't like to ask how he had 'explained' to the marine the error of his ways, I was just happy to have survived another Air Day.

10

A PLEASANT SURPRISE

ONE DAY AN ADMIRAL CAME to Culdrose. I dusted off my dark blue suit, marched smartly towards him, saluted and shook his proffered hand. With his other he handed me a neatly rolled piece of paper in a bow. It read:

COMMENDATION
Lieutenant J. Grayson, Royal Navy
771 Naval Air Squadron

On 31 July, 1978 the duty Wessex 1 SAR crew from Royal Naval Air Station Culdrose was scrambled to the area of Trevose Head, North Cornwall to rescue four men trapped at the base of a 100 foot cliff.

The weather was poor with a 20 knot northerly wind, heavy rain and a cloud base level with the clifftop. On arrival at the scene the four men were found to be on a ledge just above the heavy surf, inside a small cove opening to the West.

Hovering the helicopter close to the cliff was extremely difficult as the downdraughts were severe and the cliff face vertical. Two attempts were made and, on the first occasion, the pilot, Lieutenant GRAYSON, had to initiate overshoot action, pulling full power to avoid being thrown against the cliffs. A successful hover was achieved with a reasonable power margin on the second attempt.

The diver, Leading Aircrewman GIBBS, was lowered and immediately began to spin at a fast rate due to strong air currents; this was only controlled when the winchman, Leading Aircrewman HARRIS quickly lowered the diver into the water. Leading Aircrewman GIBBS then swam through 10 foot high waves and heavy surf to reach the ledge. As he swam to the ledge the helicopter wash inched close to the cliff to lessen the bight on the inch wire.

After climbing on to the ledge, Leading Aircrewman GIBBS released the winch hook and a stretcher was lowered from the helicopter. Leading Aircrewman GIBBS then assessed the injuries and, after much difficulty, one injured man was stretcher-lifted to the helicopter and three shocked but uninjured men were double-lifted to the clifftop. The injured man was flown, in visibility of 1,000 metres and a cloud base of 150 feet to Truro Hospital.

I commend Lieutenant GRAYSON for the courage and professional skill which he displayed during this rescue.

Knight Commander of the Most Honourable Order of the Bath,
Vice-Admiral in Her Majesty's Fleet and
Flag Officer Naval Air Command

14 September 1978

So now I had something to stick into the section in my logbook marked 'Awards and Commendations', and this was something I had never expected to be able to do. I had always assumed it was a page for other people. There was no associated medal or ribbon to be worn but the real significance to me lay in the fact that (as I only then found out) 'H' Harris had landed from that sortie and gone to see the CO with the SAR report clutched in his hand and the suggestion that I ought to receive some form of recognition for the flight I'd just flown. The CO had listened to the story, submitted a recommendation and, hey presto, I was now the recipient of an Admiral's Commendation. That one of these hard-bitten matelots from a team that prided itself on nonchalance had seen fit to do this affected me greatly. It was high praise, and I was quietly very proud indeed.

11

A BAD DECISION

NOT ALL OF OUR SCRAMBLES HAD fortunate endings and some would stay with me for years afterwards. I very clearly remember my first 'stiff' – a Frenchman on holiday with his family. Too much wine for lunch, got a bit out of his depth and spent a good half hour on the bottom of the bay before anybody thought to call us. I don't think I'd ever seen a dead body up close before, but I happened to glance down as the diver came up on the winch with his sad cargo and, just for a moment, I looked straight into the lifeless eyes.

Nothing much was said between us on the way to Treliske hospital. The boys in the back weren't qualified to certify a man dead so they had to continue with resuscitation techniques on even the most unlikely victims. I was often in a hurry to get to the hospital to avoid putting my team through any more pain. As we bumped on to the grass playing fields there would inevitably be a doctor waiting for us and a nurse with defibrillation paddles primed and ready to go, in case something could be done.

The pilot is lucky. He's separated from most of the traumatic aspects of a rescue while the diver and the crewman have to go through experiences that must haunt them for a long time afterwards. In extreme cases they would remove their intercom microphones to separate me further from their activities down in the cabin.

On our return from the Frenchman job I was unsure how to play it with the boys. They didn't say anything all the way back from Truro to Culdrose and I wasn't going to be the first to break the silence. These guys had been there and seen it all many times before and there was obviously an etiquette to be observed, I just wasn't sure yet what it was. We secured the aircraft in silence and as we walked back to the crewroom together the meal wagon arrived. As usual we set about supper like wolves. Still nobody had said anything until suddenly, just as I was raising the second mouthful of steak and chips, the diver blurted out to the crewman some particularly unpleasant detail of the rescue. I slowly lowered the fork and pushed the plate away before excusing myself to do some paperwork in the other office. 'Oh, not eating, boss? Can I have your chips?'

I soon learned to harden up. There was to be no sparing of the pilot's sensibilities once we were on the ground. We either did things as a team or we didn't do them at all.

The divers had all trained as crewmen and then gone on to learn their particular specialisation. It was a tough course and they were as fit as athletes. Pete Gibbs, one of our favourite divers, and several of the others had served on the Field Gun Crew in the annual display of teamwork at Earl's Court. They trained together for months before the opening of the Royal Tournament. It was a gruelling job and many of them severely damaged limbs while hauling the iron barrels of ancient field guns across the wall, through the gap and over 'the ravine'. It was a matter of extreme pride each year as to which of the three teams won the tournament: Plymouth Naval

Base, Portsmouth Naval Base and the Fleet Air Arm crew. I have it in mind that we usually won but I can't be certain.

It was the diver who would have to put his life on the line time and time again. They never complained about danger; they would only rant if somebody had been particularly stupid. In the middle of 1979 they had good cause to complain and we all joined in with them. Word had come down from somewhere way on high that we were no longer going to have divers at all. I've no idea where this came from and I'm not about to start blaming the RAF, though it's true to say that the idea originated from the fact that we had divers and they didn't. This wasn't surprising; we operated from ships and around coastlines, while they operated from airfields that were often inland. We had each developed slightly different techniques to suit our field of operations. The RAF were, for example, unsurpassed in mountain rescue. Their Search and Rescue crews at Brawdy, Valley, Leuchars and Kinloss were regularly tasked into the Brecon Beacons, Snowdonia, the Cairngorms and the Isle of Skye. They were hot cookies at finding their way up a mountain pass in a zero-visibility blizzard, picking up a party of lost hikers and finding their way back down again. I wouldn't have liked to do it. We were good around the cliffs but I always had the luxury of a relatively flat seascape to descend to and find my way home from.

A yellow RAF machine arriving in a snowstorm with a diver dressed in a wetsuit would, I assume, have been less prepared than had they arrived with a trained and suitably attired mountaineer. On the other hand, it would not be sensible for a blue-and-dayglo Navy machine to arrive at the scene of a ditched aircraft with a mountaineer all dressed and ready to go. This seemed to us to be a pretty straightforward argument at the time, but sometimes the logic flies out of the window when funding cuts are sought. Decades of incompetent procurement had lead to the extraordinary set of circumstances where a pencil that could be bought from WHSmith

for something under a pound would cost the armed services over £70 by the time it had gone through the system. Cuts had to be made and we were an obvious target when our crews cost more to train than an RAF crew.

It's not generally appreciated that the Navy and the RAF never set out to provide a service to civilians. We each stationed helicopters at our airbases purely and simply to recover fixed-wing aircrew who got into difficulties and had to abandon their aircraft. Over a period of time the airbases would receive requests for assistance and, of course, they would do everything they could to help. As military air crashes came less and less frequently, so the civilian tasking increased. It was good practice for the crews, good PR for the local airbase and an efficient use of humanitarian resources. But it was a long time before the changing roles were recognised and the Department of Trade and Industry allocated extra funding to the military to help with this growing responsibility.

Inevitably much of our work in Cornwall was along beaches, up the sides of cliffs and sometimes even inland, but we were still a naval unit and our divers were invaluable. An RAF crewman was not allowed to disconnect himself from the winch and swim around in the water. He had to swing past the survivor and try to grab him from the safety of his harness. This was assuming that the victim was on the surface. The Navy's experience had taught us otherwise in our particular theatre of operations. In the early days of the big aircraft carriers we had regularly lost fixed-wing aircraft over the edge. They would try to overshoot from a poor approach, the engine would fail to spool up quickly enough and they'd wallow off the front of the ship into the water. We had therefore devised a system whereby the crewman stayed in the helicopter while the diver jumped from the open door with his breathing equipment and set off alone to find the survivors. Once he had brought them to the surface, attached them to his harness and was ready to go, he would give us the thumbs-up, we'd move over the top, he'd clip himself on together with his survivor and up they both would come. We'd been doing it that way for a very long time and our divers were the best in the world.

All of this seemed to go right over the heads of our lords and masters in the ministry who refused to be swayed by increasingly vociferous complaints from us that this decision could only lead to tragedy. In the last few days before the divers left the squadron we became more and more agitated. Letters were written to the captain saying things like: 'People will die as a direct result of this decision. It's not a question of whether, it's only a question of when.' We were met by a wall of silence. On 29 July 1979 the last of our divers left the squadron; on 30 July two people died.

It was a really fine day, bright blue skies, fluffy white clouds and a warm summer breeze. It would be a perfect day for the start of the Tall Ships race from Fowey on the south coast. Dozens of beautiful old ships, many of them crewed by under-privileged or handicapped children, glided majestically out of the harbour. It's a fabulous spot and a perfect harbour. Surrounded on all sides by a steep-sided and wooded valley, the water is calm, protected and deep. It has, for centuries, been the spot where coastal ships tie up to receive their cargo of china clay from the massive and ancient workings that extend for miles around. The tall white artificial mountains form a unique landscape that's often used by film companies to represent the surface of another planet. The rivers and streams that wind through the area carry a milky-white cocktail that flows out into St Austell bay. It has the effect of turning the water a stunning shade of light blue.

As their crews climbed into the rigging and unfurled enormous billowing sails, the ships slowly made their way past the castle and out to the start line off Gribben Head. They were accompanied by a large flotilla of local boats and some from much further afield. It was a prestigious event; the schools were on holiday and Cornwall

was already full of holiday-makers taking advantage of the warmest climate in the UK.

Back at Culdrose it was a very quiet day, although we had already been airborne twice on routine tasks. As the duty SAR crew we were pretty autonomous. It was up to us to practise the things we hadn't done for a while and on this occasion we took ourselves down the Helford River and out into Falmouth Bay to practise with the grappling hook, a four-pronged, anchor-like affair that was attached to the end of the winch line and used to capture the various items of detritus we'd often find around the coast. Sometimes we'd find an old life raft and need to haul it up to try to identify its origin. At other times we behaved more like jackdaws, picking at shiny things that took our fancy. Our collection of escaped marker buoys was among the finest in the land. On special occasions we'd find something really useful. Our best day was when one of the crews stumbled upon an entire container floating just beneath the surface. The doors were open and a steady stream of brand new parka jackets floated to the surface. Half of Cornwall were wearing parkas by the end of the week; our squadron children's charity benefited handsomely and we'd all become world experts in rapid recovery techniques. The Cornish salvage tradition in a modern guise.

It had become obvious to us that we'd be needing the grapple hook even more these days. Without a diver we were going to have to forget many of the techniques we'd learned over the years and try to compensate for them in some way. Leading Aircrewmen Steve Wooley and John Boulton repeatedly hauled the hook in with our practice buoy attached, threw it out and tried again as I circled back to the start position. It was quite a fun exercise but our collective heart wasn't really in it. Being without a diver was like losing a limb and we were very, very nervous.

At 10.50 we were scrambled to Gribben Head. Polruan Coastguard had reported a light aircraft ditched half a mile out to sea. We always used the expression 'scrambled', although on this occasion we were simply diverted from the activity we were on. They still played the scramble tones over the tannoy back at Culdrose, in order to alert doctors, fire crews and any other specialists who might be required along the way. As chance would have it my old diver Jamie Bauld had come into the air station that morning and was standing in line at the pay office to sort out his final paperwork before leaving to go to some mind-numbing desk job. Like everybody else on the air station he heard the scramble tones and subsequent announcement but, unlike everybody else, he understood the significance. The duty SAR didn't have a diver on board. An aircraft was in the water; a diver would be required. It was as simple as that.

Jamie flew out of the pay office, jumped into his car and hurtled back to 771 where Andy Halliday, the senior SAR pilot and a Canadian of few words, was wringing his hands at the futility of the situation. The place lit up as Jamie arrived and both Andy and his crewman Gordon Rae leapt for the standby aircraft while Jamie threw his wetsuit and diving gear into the rear cabin door. No sooner had his feet left the ground than Andy hauled the machine into the air and set off in pursuit of us. They'd moved at lightning speed but they were already fifteen minutes behind us.

A small boat waved frantically to us as we scanned the scene on arrival. We could see they had a young boy on deck and were trying to resuscitate him. Just off to one side of the boat we could see the outline of the light aircraft lying just beneath the surface. One day earlier and I would have despatched the diver straight into the water from a hover height of around 20 feet. Today I didn't have a diver. If there were other survivors left in the aircraft there was absolutely nothing I could do about it. I called the situation to another old mate, Jerry English, who had arrived in an anti-submarine Sea King which had been practising near us in Falmouth Bay and had come with us to the scene. While Steve, John and I went into the hover over the small

boat and collected the young boy, Jerry's crew spotted two adults as they burst to the surface and quickly went in to pick them up.

The young lad we now had on board was clearly not in a good state. He was only semi-conscious and the boys had started to administer oxygen from the tanks we carried in the cabin. Happy that Jerry English was dealing with the other survivors, I set off to Treliske Hospital. We would learn later that Jerry had collected the light aircraft pilot and a Dutch photographer who had been hired to photograph the start of the race. The young boy I had aboard was one of two brothers, the sons of an executive from Lancia Cars who had sponsored one of the race boats. We didn't know it at the time but his brother was still trapped in the cockpit breathing stale air from a small trapped bubble. Even if we'd known we would have been powerless to help him.

Five minutes after we had departed to the hospital Andy Halliday arrived at the scene with Jamie sitting ready in the back door. He'd changed out of his civvies and was booted and spurred. As Andy hauled the nose up to bring the big Wessex to a shuddering halt, Jamie leapt from the door. The divers always went in feet first, holding their mask, then surfaced briefly to give us a thumbs-up before disappearing again. It was a pretty powerful impact they suffered each time they hit the water and we needed to know they were in control of the situation. Jamie quickly found the aircraft in about 60 feet of water. It must have been slowly sinking and rolling ever since the others had made their escape as, by now, it was inverted and had reached the bottom. In the back of the aircraft he found the other boy trapped by a seat belt that had caught one of his legs as the aircraft sank. It was clear that he'd been able to sustain himself by forcing his head into a small pocket of air that had remained in the cockpit. By the time Jamie reached him the air had all gone and Jamie still had to get him up though 60 feet of ocean.

The two men survived but, three hours after Jamie's brave efforts, the young boy lost his battle for life. His brother was transferred to Papworth Hospital in Cambridge where sadly, three weeks later, he also died.

Every one of us was livid by the time we landed back at Culdrose. I can't remember the precise sequence of events because it was all seen through a red mist at the time. By eight o'clock the next morning our divers, every single one of them, had been returned to the squadron. Nobody ever said sorry. Nobody ever resigned or took the blame for such a truly awful piece of resource management. I just hope that the boys' family could take solace from the fact that their deaths were truly not in vain. I always intended to tell them myself but just a few days later (as we would shortly discover) we were in a major battle for our own lives and, somehow, I never quite got around to it. I wouldn't like to begin to count the number of lives that have since been saved as a direct result of the Navy keeping SAR divers; it will be many hundreds.

12

A COW CALLED JERRY

AMID THE INEVITABLE TRAGIC EVENTS of Search and Rescue there was also a great deal of laughter. We rarely allowed the morbid aspects of the job to get to us and there was much to keep us distracted.

As in a football or rugby team, as sailors we would rarely address one another by our real names. A sailor is called 'Jack', short for Jolly Jack Tar, by every other sailor, right up until he learns his real name. To attract the attention of another sailor you simply shout, 'Oi, Jack.' And when you did learn the 'real' name it was inevitably replaced by a nickname. We had 'Topsy' Turner, 'Shep' Woolley, 'Smiler' Grinney, 'Wally' Wallace and so on. The real name wasn't relevant, but once in a while you might discover it by accident while filling out an official form or something.

'Oi, Scouse, what initial shall I put on this wanky form?'

'It's L.'

'L? Nobody's got an initial L, that's a nancy sort of initial. What's it stand for then?'

'Nothin'.'

'It can't be nothin, that'd be an N, you dimwit.'

'It's Lawrence.'

At this point the whole crewroom erupted into gales of laughter. It was inconceivable that this lean mean scouse diver with a face like a boxer could possibly have been christened 'Lawrence'. He was ribbed mercilessly and continuously until the scramble tones went off or until something even funnier happened. Twenty-four hours later we'd all have forgotten, so that when it came up again it was just as funny as the first time.

If it was the real Navy then I, as an officer, would have addressed my crewman as Leading Aircrewman Woolley. He would salute smartly and address me as Sir. But it wasn't the real Navy, thank God. The thought of having that sort of exchange with Shep Woolley makes me giggle just to think of it. But one of us had to sign for the aircraft and one of us had to take the flack when we'd screwed up, so the pilot was always known as 'Boss'. The advantage of short sharp nicknames was that you didn't waste valuable time on the intercom pronouncing double-barrelled mouthfuls. Use a man's full title in the middle of a rescue and, by the time you'd got it all out, somebody would probably be dead.

We were visited one morning by the First Sea Lord Admiral Sir Henry Leach GCB, Commander in Chief of the Fleet. He'd requested to come flying and to experience an average morning with us, entirely without ceremony. This was just as difficult a request to fulfil as it would have been if the Queen had asked to drop by one day and help with the ironing. Sure enough he turned up at dawn in a goon suit marked 'CinC Fleet'. He joined us for scrambled eggs and rind-less rashers which Scouse had prepared in our tiny kitchen, until it was time for the morning SAR test.

He really enjoyed the flight and wanted to try his hand at the controls which, despite not being an aviator, he handled rather well. Afterwards he took the trouble to write a very charming thank-you letter and his visit had clearly been a great success. However, mid-flight I made a mistake that would haunt me for the weeks that followed. Relieved and overcome with the perfect weather conditions, and for want of conversation suitable for an admiral, I had muttered something like, 'It's mornings like this that make you glad to be alive, isn't it, sir?' I heard some strangling noises from down in the cabin before Shep and Scouse pulled their intercoms out of their sockets in order to avoid embarrassment with their laughter. It would be several weeks before I could walk past anybody in the corridor without having a brief burst of poetry quoted at me.

Sometimes even the rescues themselves offered opportunities for enjoyment, if they were simple and offered no danger to life or limb. We might have hoped for bikini-clad damsels in mild distress but they were few and far between, however. It's usually the male of the species who gets himself into a tight spot through bravado. One typical afternoon we were called to pick up two teenage boys who had managed to get themselves stuck halfway up a 200-foot cliff face. Most of the cliff faces in Cornwall are sheer. This one was unusual in that it was at a slight angle and had vegetation growing up it.

We had only just finished picking up a fifty-year-old gentleman from the upturned hull of his dinghy and were in the process of landing him on the beach. Normally this would be an opportunity for the diver to swagger around the beach for a couple of minutes chatting up the local talent and looking serious and macho, while the crewman and I stayed airborne to avoid chopping up enthusiastic children with our tail rotor. However, this time we touched our wheels briefly on the sand at Prussia Cove, unceremoniously left the survivor and headed off at top speed to Lantic Bay. The coastguards had been to the incident and decided that a helicopter would be the

safest bet to rescue the two boys. It's worth noting at this point that the coastguards would deal with dozens of incidents a day during the summer months and we often worked together with great mutual respect. The boys' exploration had led them to a peculiar position under an overhang of cliff and they were tiring rapidly. It was a long way to the bottom if they let go.

I brought the aircraft into a hover, settled into my seat and started to move slowly in to the cliff face under the guidance of Gordon Rae. My regular crew were taking a well-earned rest after a continuous three-day rescue operation (which I will describe shortly) so Ritchie Burnett was the diver. Our biggest concern was to get Ritchie into a position from where he could get to the boys without our downwash blowing all three of them on to the rocks below. A Wessex at full power has no remorse for anything that lies beneath. We realised we were going to have to put Ritchie out on a very long line, and this would mean hovering with the tips of our rotor blades no more than eighteen inches from the rock face. This wouldn't be a problem for a well worked-up crew but I'd only been with Gordon for 48 hours and we hadn't yet had time to discover each other's limitations. It was therefore with some trepidation that I hovered slowly sideways under his voice commands.

We were in place. I locked my head into a completely static position looking out to the right of the aircraft. Provided I didn't set the ear canals moving and that I visually lined up a piece of the window with a piece of the rock face I could be reasonably confident of keeping the aircraft in a decent hover while Gordon shifted his attention to lowering Ritchie down to the terrified boys. As Ritchie swung back and forth in an attempt to get under the overhang I caught sight of something very peculiar at the edge of my peripheral vision. On the left-hand side of the aircraft I caught a fleeting impression of something red. I knew that in that direction lay only the sea and the sky, and usually these are both blue. There was no way I could have turned my head to get a better look, however, or we'd have joined Ritchie on the rocks beneath us and the coroner would be filling out forms for five of us.

Gordon was doing a great job with his continuous patter of information and I was making tiny muscle movements to adjust our position one inch that way and then two inches the other. Up came one of the boys clasped firmly between Ritchie's thighs in the double-lift harness. No sooner did we have him on board than Gordon was lowering Ritchie back down on the winch again. Ninety-nine per cent of my brain was concentrating on the job in hand, it had to be, but that last one per cent was working overtime trying to decode what it was I'd seen. I was hovering a long way up a cliff face, right side towards the cliff, left side out to sea. Anything on my left side therefore had to be airborne. If it was an aircraft then I didn't have a problem but I was certain that it had been much closer than that. My little one per cent went through a list of possibilities until I had narrowed it down to only two candidates: either I'd blown a piece of debris from the cliff face or something had worked loose and departed from my aircraft. The debris gave me more concern than the possibility of losing a bit of the aircraft. One piece of debris meant the possibility of more and it only takes a small plastic bag lodged in the wrong place to bring millions of pounds worth of helicopter out of the sky. If anything important had fallen off the aircraft, however, I would have known about it straight away through my hands.

Whatever it was, at this point I could do absolutely nothing about it. Gordon brought Ritchie and the second of his survivors away from the cliff face and up towards the door. As soon as he'd hauled them both inside he returned his full attention to our proximity to the cliffs and began to give me instructions to manoeuvre our way clear. There's a wonderful sensation that goes through every muscle in your body as you allow them to relax a little, one at a time. I've often thought that the street entertainers who mimic statues would make great rescue pilots. As sensation came back into my fingers, toes and middle spine I looked down through my open window for a clue as to what the red flash might possibly have been. I didn't need the eyes of a hawk to spot the culprit. At the bottom of the cliff, impaled on the sharp rocks, was a very flat red car. Gordon and Ritchie were busy checking out our survivors in the cabin when I interrupted them with: 'Umm, chaps, sorry to bother you, but does anyone know where that car came from?'

We landed the boys on the clifftop, handed them into the care of the coastguards, their parents and the small crowd that had gathered. It would take a few phone calls and a read of the newspapers the next day before we would learn the full story. I'll quote straight from the *Sunday Express*:

> *There was no hesitation for Stephen Rescorie when a call went out for help in saving two boys stranded on a cliff. Stephen, a 24 year old building worker, of Pelynt, Cornwall was visiting his girlfriend Mary Rose Taylor at her home in Polruan. Mary's father Basil is a local coastguard. Stephen said 'It was the natural thing to do to offer to take two coastguards up to the clifftop when the alarm was raised. I ran down the cliff towards the edge with them and I thought I'd put the handbrake on but maybe I didn't. On Tuesday insurance assessors will examine the car, which was comprehensively covered. The National Trust have asked that it be removed. Stephen said the Marina 1.8, which had cost him £1,700 four years ago had been doing about 60 miles an hour when it overtook him and plunged over the edge, narrowly missing a helicopter.*

Even at 60 mph the car must have only just achieved enough momentum to clear our rotor blades. I don't like to dwell too long on the consequences if it hadn't.

Above Ten months old. Mum wrote, 'Admiral of the Fleet in his sailor suit'. I have obviously under-achieved!

Below left On the steps of the caravan I was born in.

Below right In front of one of the training Whirlwind 7s, 705 Squadron, with a very proud Mum after the ceremony of receiving our wings.

Above On HMS *Ark Royal* we thought we were a big
ship, with around 2,500 men and 38 aircraft, but alongside the nuclear-powered USS *Nimitz* in Norfolk Naval
Base, Virginia, we were dwarfed during our annual visits.
(Photo: US Navy)

Above Hovering alongside the mighty *Ark* as we all wait for fixed-wing flying operations to begin for the day. (Photo: US Navy)

Below left When big green waves started breaking over the bows of an aircraft carrier you knew you were in for a rough night, but it was nothing compared to the day of Fastnet '79.

Below right I had hovered next to that helicopter for several hours as she fought to stay afloat, but in the end the battle was lost. To catch fire on the crane was the final ignominy.

Above At the height of the Cold War, flying the Wessex 1. F4 Phantoms parked on the deck of *Ark Royal* in the foreground, and a Russian warship, a Kresta II Class Cruiser called the *Admiral Makarov*, shadowed our every move just off to our stern.

Below With smoke still pouring from the cockpit I am flying completely blind during an air display joke that went dangerously wrong.

Above My diver, in his orange wetsuit, and crewman sitting with their feet out of the cabin door as we fly a coastal patrol, imprinting every inch of the towering Cornish cliffs into our memory banks.

Below Every new pilot had to earn the trust of his crew by balancing both wheels on the wall of a disused tin mine. It was the pinnacle of teamwork and required all three of us to be at the very top of our game.

Above 'Smiler' Grinney plays to camera while waiting on the slippery deck of a nuclear submarine. Down below 'Doc' Morgan is in a hurry to collect a very sick American sailor before the sub is obliged to dive.

Below Balancing one wheel on the 'Camel's Head'.

Above Fastnet 1979. After four straight hours in the saddle it's time for a 'hot' refuel and crew change. No time for posing and the adrenalin is still on overload.

Below left Serving breakfast to the real Admiral of the Fleet, Admiral Sir Henry Leach GCB, both in our goon suits, before going flying together.

Below right Checking out of the beaches on our way home from six rescues in one day.

Above left On the steps of Buckingham Palace in March 1981 with Mum an[d] my (then) wife Charlotte, who had put up with my long months away at sea. [...] and an alarm clock that went off at 3.30 most mornings when I was at home[.]

Above right My Air Force Cross. A confusing name when awarded in the Royal Navy, but it has applied across all military aviators since the Second World War.

Below I am in two minds as to whether death in a scrapyard or life in a paintball venue is best for an old friend who was heroic in her own right. I gue[ss] the latter since I can one day go back and see her. This one served on Fastnet. (Photo: Gunsmoke Paintball)

And from the *Western Morning News* that week:

One of the rescued boys, Matthew Pickering said, 'We thought we'd had it but that pilot was an ace.'

Now you would think that gaining the nickname 'Ace' Grayson would be pretty cool. Not a chance. Ten days later a local farmer found one of his cows at the bottom of a small cliff. The animal had fallen over the edge and there was no way up. We took a vet, lowered a net, lowered the vet, watched him walk the cow on to the net, stun the cow, then we moved in and picked them all up. We landed our confused cargo on the grass and it went on to live a happy and presumably fulfilling life. The farmer and his wife were so grateful that they felt it necessary to express their gratitude to the local television station by announcing that, henceforth, the cow would be known in the herd as 'Jerry Ace Grayson'.

13

'WHAT RACE?'

MY ALTERCATION WITH A FLYING Morris Marina had come only three days after the end of the most significant rescue exercise ever carried out at Culdrose. The media at the time called it the 'most intensive rescue operation in maritime history'. The lessons learned during these three intensive days would lead to a complete rethink in the design of all ocean-going yachts, and the name of a tiny rocky outcrop off southern Ireland would cement itself in the history books. The name was Fastnet.

It was the middle of summer. The Royal Naval Air Station at Culdrose was effectively closed as the Navy tried to acknowledge that their employees had wives, children and a life beyond wearing a blue suit. You accept, when you join, that leave is a privilege, not a right. The Navy trains you, the Navy pays you, the Navy owns you, but at some point in the past they had realised that if married men were to be sent to sea for months at a time they had to be given the chance to spend time with their families when they were ashore. Culdrose is the biggest helicopter base in Europe and, as such, it's home to many different squadrons. There are initial training squadrons, operational training squadrons, 'second line' squadrons conducting various trials, and front-line squadrons who go to sea. Then there are all the support departments to administer the domestic side of running such a large organisation. There was no hope of ever coordinating the holidays of three thousand men and women when they all wanted to take time off during the school summer holidays so the place just shut down for three weeks and left the bare essentials running, including us. We used to joke that if you wanted to invade the UK it would be a good idea to do it on a Wednesday afternoon in August: the Navy were on holiday and the RAF had their mid-week sports afternoon.

We loved this time on the SAR team. We kept up our usual routine and we had the whole airfield to ourselves. When we were on the ground we didn't have to pretend we were also naval officers with reports to write and training exercises to run, we just lounged around – and we were pretty good at that. The duty crew could often be found asleep in the sunshine or, if we felt particularly energetic, we'd all wash our cars until it was either time to eat or to watch the TV news. Little did we know that Kate Adie would soon be filing her hourly news reports from our own tiny crewroom. But we always knew the quickest route to the helicopter and we were regularly pushing our scramble times below the 90-second base mark.

Of course, an English summer is never quite as fine as it ought to be and, although it was warm, the holidaymakers weren't having much fun on 9 August 1979 as a small tropical storm with 70 mph winds scythed a path of havoc across the country. We scrambled to a cabin cruiser named the *Zanadu*, which began taking on water when three portholes were smashed, 12 miles off Plymouth. We accompanied the boat all the way into harbour but our winch stayed firmly in its housing and the family on board suffered only a big fright and a little discomfort. Elsewhere various people were picked up by lifeboats around the coast and no lives were lost. The storm abated as quickly as it had arrived, just in time for me and my crew to enjoy our scheduled three days off.

Although we worked a regular routine, it was a schedule the body's natural clock didn't like at all. We'd start at dawn for three mornings and work till midday, then work four afternoons till dusk, then have three days off. Next we'd have four mornings, three afternoons and four days off before starting the routine again. It was a good way of coping with summer days that started at 3am and finished at 10.30pm, but the constant change over three years would eventually give me a massive stomach ulcer.

We came back to work on the morning of the thirteenth but it turned out to be a quiet day. We launched at about nine for a quick check of the airfield and surrounding area but the visibility was beginning to deteriorate and we didn't feel like stretching ourselves when everyone else was on holiday. Even the standby crew would stay at home in August. We would prepare their aircraft for them and they would stay near a phone. Whenever we went a long way from base our resident coastguard would phone around the boys, who could be in and dressed within a few minutes. We lounged professionally for the remainder of the morning and were ultimately surprised not to get any call-outs. By lunchtime we were home but the clouds were turning very dark.

As we came into work at 03.30 on the morning of Tuesday the fourteenth it was as if winter had arrived four months early. Trees were down across the road and dustbins were lying on their side. Dawn would arrive in an hour but the rain was horizontal and it would be a while before we really saw any daylight. Unusually I was first in through the swing doors on the ground level of the squadron office block, but I could hear that the coastguard telephone was already ringing upstairs. I took the stairs three at a time and found myself speaking to the Culdrose Air Officer of the Day. He was starting to receive calls from the rescue control centres at both Plymouth and Lands End. He had a very unclear picture so far but there were a number of reports of yachts aground on the Scilly Isles, about 40 minutes' flying time to the west of Culdrose. He asked that we get airborne as quickly as we could while he started to ring around to find some extra crews. He suspected that the overnight storm had caught out a number of yachts in the race and that we were going to have our work cut out. I innocently asked, 'What race?' and was met with disdain. I had no idea that the most prestigious event in the yachting calendar had departed from the Isle of Wight the previous Saturday afternoon.

The best yachtsmen in the world had gathered for Cowes Week and the Fastnet Race was the culmination of a week of racing. By the Monday they had cleared the south-west tip of Cornwall and made their way up towards Ireland. By around noon the leaders had rounded the Fastnet Rock and headed back towards Cornwall. The Radio 4 shipping forecast was giving 'South-westerly 4 or 5, increasing 6 or 7 for a time, veering westerly later'. Four hours later this was amended to include a warning of Gale Force 8 for the Fastnet area but most of the skippers had missed that broadcast. A further amendment, warning of an imminent severe force 9 gale, never made it to the BBC studio in time for the evening shipping forecast. Thus most of the fleet of 303 racing yachts had sailed on through Monday night believing that the weather was on their side. By halfway through the night it had reached storm force 10.

I leapt back down the stairs to tell the engineers to hurry their preparations, nearly knocking over our very experienced coastguard officer, Dick Harvey. Coming in the doors at the bottom of the stairway were my diver 'Smiler' Grinney and a new crewman, John Charnley. I refer to him as new because I'd never flown with him before but he was actually a superb instructor who was just filling in for one of the regulars. By the end of the day I would be eternally grateful that he was on our crew.

Very little was said as we each concentrated hard on ticking off our individual responsibilities. Getting airborne quickly is a good thing, getting airborne under-prepared is unforgivable and the only fear we knew well was that of letting down the rest of the crew. By 04.35 we were airborne and on our way to the Scillies. It was certainly a rough and bumpy ride but the visibility wasn't too bad and the cloud-base was nearly 1,000 feet. We still had no idea of the size of the racing fleet, nor of the scale of the storm that was raging about 80 miles north of us. As far as we were concerned, we were on our way to find either one or two abandoned yachts on the coast of the Scillies and maybe their crews huddled on the beach. We arrived at the little cluster of islands and began our visual search, far too low to pick up radio calls from Culdrose. We couldn't find anything and had only been there a short time when the local coastguard called us on the radio to say that the crew from the only definite incident had been found alive and well having breakfast in the local guest house. He ended the transmission with a request from Culdrose that we climb higher on our way home and establish early communications with them.

As we passed through 700 feet and our radio reception improved it seemed that the whole world had gone stark staring mad. Bearing in mind that it was still only 05.40 in the morning and that Culdrose was all on leave, I simply could not believe the sheer volume of radio chatter going on. It seemed that one helicopter after another was coming hurtling out of Culdrose, every one of them trying to speak at the same time, either to receive a briefing or to send new information. Meanwhile, on our coastguard emergency frequency there was complete bedlam as one yacht after another put out a Mayday call asking for immediate assistance. We had only been gone just over an hour and the weather didn't seem to be as severe as all that. Where, indeed, had the Air Officer of the Day found so many aircrew at that time of the morning? The more I listened the more I realised that there were only three other aircraft, they were just all talking at once and I was listening to two separate frequencies simultaneously. I quite literally couldn't believe my ears as all three of us in my aircraft strained to put a picture together. At 05.43 Culdrose issued a situation report, known universally as a SITREP. It consisted of:

Yacht MAGIC rudderless and shipping heavy seas.
Yacht GRIMALKIN 30 miles north west of Lands End, capsized.
Yacht TARANTULA sinking over 100 miles beyond the Scillies.
Yacht MULLIGATAWNY dismasted and in distress even further out.
Red flares sighted by yacht MORNING TOWN.
Four men sighted in a life raft by unknown yacht, and then lost to view.
Three yachts ashore on the Scillies, updated ten minutes later to five yachts.

I faced a serious dilemma. There was still another 20 minutes before I could make it back to Culdrose for fuel. Should I continue and top up my tanks or should I turn around and do what I could with the fuel remaining? We rarely flew with full tanks; it was simply too much weight to carry when we might find ourselves wanting to hover near the cliffs and needing enough power to do it. The Wessex Mark 5 is a very powerful helicopter but with a severe downdraught curling over the cliff edge it could still leave you short of lift. We measured power in terms of percentage; at 100 per cent you were about to run out. You could use a little extra for a few seconds but you were running the risk of blowing up the two big Rolls Royce jets that turned the rotors. It was usually only in the hover that you'd ever find yourself short of power; a helicopter loves to fly forwards and uses much less power to do that – maybe only 40 or 50 per cent of the power available. If we were going to be hovering out at sea in such a strong wind I knew I'd be able to take a full fuel load on board. We'd be hovering stationary over the water but in a 60 or 70 mph wind the helicopter would think it was flying forwards and therefore use a fraction of the power. My mind was made up as I was passed by a Sea King and then the standby Wessex flown by Albie Fox, both going in the opposite direction. The Sea King would head out to the very long-distance Maydays while Albie would start to deal with the more immediate problems closer to shore. There were over 20,000 square miles of ocean for us to deal with and I could hear on my radio that the RAF had launched a Nimrod from St Mawgan to coordinate and prioritise the various requirements. I would be far more useful with a full tank of fuel so I pressed on to Culdrose.

The ground crew, as ever, were superb. The big hose was already uncoiled and lying across the tarmac. All I had to do was accurately land on the spot and within seconds they would be pumping many gallons of Avtur aboard my aircraft. John Charnley supervised the refuelling while Smiler ran inside to try and get a better picture of what the hell was going on. Within minutes we were airborne again. There were now two Sea Kings attacking the problem and two Wessex. Broadly speaking, the Sea Kings were dealing with the area to the west of the Scillies while Albie and I headed north. The controller on the Nimrod was reeling off the names of yacht after yacht in difficulties: *Charioteer, Magic, Tarantula, Grimalkin, Bonaventure II, Trophy, Camargue, Hestrul II, Skidbladner, Ariadne, Gunslinger, Callirhoe III, Polar Bear, Anatomy* and so it went on. As we crossed the north Cornish coast I just kept shaking my head. I couldn't believe what was happening. In the little town of Helston the crews who hadn't gone away on holiday were waking up and hearing the BBC news. Anybody who'd stayed in Cornwall rushed straight into the airbase.

The seas to the north were incredible. I could only guess at what they must have looked like from the deck of a yacht; from where I was sitting in my relatively cosy cockpit it seemed that every wave was bigger than the last. We were all muttering expletives as giant rollers curled in from the Atlantic. My guess was that some were over 40 feet from crest to trough and the powerful wind was throwing a horizontal jet of spray from the top of every one. We stayed at a height of about 200 feet: if we went too high we'd suffer a reduction in speed as the wind increased; if we went too low we might pass a yacht and never spot it. Frankly we were having trouble putting a scale to the waves and thereby knowing what a yacht would actually look like. Your eyes are much more efficient if they know what to expect. Smiler was leaning out into the gale and wiping the salt from his eyes as he scanned the trough of every wave we passed. Even at 200 feet the rain had salt in it. John was carefully plotting our every move on his chart, noting our speed, noting any changes in our direction of travel and simultaneously trying to build up a picture of where the yachts in trouble might be in relation to our position.

On the emergency channel we heard a call; it seemed to be louder and clearer than the other calls. A plaintive voice was calling the unknown helicopter that had just passed over his position. The call sign of the yacht was *Magic*. I circled back and three pairs of eyes strained nearly out of their sockets to see if there was a yacht behind us. The wind had caught us and we were being blown back far too quickly to do a meaningful search. We called the *Magic* on the radio and asked if the helicopter he'd just seen had turned back. He confirmed it had. It must be us. As I retraced our route we simply couldn't find him but I knew he couldn't be far away. I turned back into wind and asked the *Magic* whether he had any flares or smoke left. A few moments later we were rewarded with the sight of a small patch of sea spray turning red – the yacht had to be in the trough beyond. We spotted her. She was in a hell of a state and was taking each wave side-on. Instead of riding smoothly up the wall of water each time, she was being knocked completely flat and then rolling all the way through over 100 degrees until her mast nearly touched the water on the other side. I turned sharply to the right, trying to stay visual with the yacht, then brought the aircraft once again around into wind. The torrential rain was making it almost impossible to see out of the cockpit windscreen and I was having to move my head around a great deal to stay in contact with the boat. As I brought the big Wessex lower and lower the waves grew to mythic proportions.

Two problems: first, there was no way we were going to be able to pick up the crew from the deck of the yacht; the mast and tattered rigging would have swatted Smiler like a fly. Second, the waves were indeed over 40 feet high. Our normal hover height was 15 feet. If I was to have any chance of doing something useful I was going to have to get well down below the crests and ride up each one. There's no way you can lower a man accurately from above 40 feet. There are just not enough visual references and he would have been swinging like a pendulum by the time he hit the water. It was quickly decided between us that Smiler would have to stay attached to the winch wire throughout; if he disengaged himself we might never get him back.

The next task was to brief the crew of the *Magic* on how we were going to try and get them. The only option was to ask them to jump into the water. I don't ever remember hesitating during a rescue before but I did just at that moment. There were five people on the boat beneath me, none of them were injured and they were aboard a boat which, although very battered, was still afloat. I was going to ask them, one by one, to separate themselves from that boat and jump into the water. The moment they did that it would be up to me whether they lived or died. If the aircraft suffered a malfunction or if I'd simply over-estimated my capabilities and found that I couldn't put Smiler into the water accurately enough for him to be able to join hands, then I would have personally signed a man's death warrant.

I asked John and Smiler to wait just a moment while I practised hovering down in the troughs, I had to be at least reasonably certain in my own mind that I was going to be able to hack it. John had abandoned his mapping equipment and taken up station in the open cabin doorway. As I lowered the aircraft down into the waves he kept up his patter of information. I wasn't too bothered about position, the yacht was a couple of hundred yards off to one side of us and it didn't matter if I drifted around a bit to start with. My major concern was to discover if the Wessex would respond quickly enough to ride the waves up and down. I tried experimenting with rhythm. As the crest of a wave passed beneath me I thought about lowering my left hand on the collective lever (height control); this would reduce the power and we'd descend. I watched for the trough and tried to anticipate the moment at which I would then raise the collective lever and start the climb to the crest. Once a couple of waves had passed I was pretty sure I'd got the rhythm sorted out in my head and we began our vertical descent.

We reached the height of 15 feet and things were going pretty well. I was getting into the rhythm and the aircraft was following beautifully. I'd kept my head looking out to the right as not only did this allow me to see through the open door but it also gave me the best chance of gauging my height visually. Then I chanced a look round to the front and nearly had a heart attack. Through the rain-splattered cockpit windscreen the wave in front of us seemed to tower impossibly high and be rushing at us too quickly. I was mesmerised and pulled the lever up a little too quickly. It wasn't any bigger than any of the other waves, I just hadn't ever seen a wave of that size rushing towards me like an express train. I decided to return to looking out of the side.

John called the *Magic* and asked them to prepare their first man. We wanted him with a fully inflated lifejacket and we wanted him to wait until he got a thumbs-up from Smiler before jumping into the water. John made absolutely certain that they understood our instructions – particularly that we only wanted one man in the water at any one time. The last thing I wanted to see was five men in the water; the chances of getting all of them would be too slim.

We hovered over towards the *Magic*, although 'hover' conjures up a rather more stable environment than we were in. Both the yacht and the helicopter were going up 40 feet and then down 40 feet; the trick was to keep the helicopter doing this dance in time with the yacht. We wanted to get fairly close to the *Magic*, first in order to be able to keep each survivor in sight, and secondly so that they didn't have to spend too long in the water between jumping from the yacht and making contact with Smiler. The closer we hovered the easier the flying became as I used the movement of the yacht to give me a visual height reference. We could see the first man gripping a rail on the windward side and struggling to keep his footing. The three of us took a deep breath and I asked, 'Are we ready?'

'Ready, boss,' called John.

'Ready, boss,' called Smiler, with the enthusiasm that went so well with his nickname. He sounded well pumped up.

'OK, give him the thumbs-up.'

Smiler gave the yachtsman the signal while John also called the yacht on the radio. We weren't sure which had the effect but, sure enough, the first man went over the side. With amazing speed the yacht was blown away from him giving us the chance to move in. John raised Smiler on the winch until he was clear of the door and then quickly set him on his way down, calling out my relative position all the time. Although I couldn't see it happening, the stream of information into my earpiece told me that John had dropped Smiler into a nearly perfect position, right next to the survivor. With a practised movement Smiler grabbed the man with one arm while the other moved the double-lift strop around his body, under his arms, and clipped the loose end back on to the winch hook.

He threw both arms out sideways in a thumbs-up gesture and John brought them out of the water together like a cork out of a bottle. The wind set them spinning quite violently, a common problem that was severely disorienting for the diver. All Smiler could do at this point was cling tightly to his man as John brought the winch to a halt just below the aircraft step; if he brought them up too quickly they would break limbs against the aircraft side. He waited a few moments for the spin to die down, then quickly raised the winch, twisted them both around and hauled them on to the cabin decking. Well, that was easier than we thought. We went for it again. One after another we brought four men into the relative safety of the aircraft. They were tired and soaked to the skin but the smiles on their faces were of pure relief.

Smiler himself was beginning to tire. He was expending huge amounts of energy with each lift. We gave him a few moments in the doorway to get his breath back while I hovered away a little in order to relax some muscles. Only one man remained on the *Magic* and I could see that he was not looking forward to the jump into the maelstrom. He was now alone on the boat and was holding on very tightly in the cockpit. Bizarrely he seemed to be wearing glasses and I couldn't imagine how he'd managed to keep them intact against all the violence the sea was throwing at him. Smiler had got his breath back and he indicated to John that he was ready for his last lift. Up went the thumbs and… nothing happened. Our last survivor was either frozen in fear, unable to see us through his salty glasses or not looking the right way. Smiler tried again and again as we willed him to follow his crewmates and jump into the water. Together we were softly calling out to him, as if he could hear us, when suddenly it all came together and he climbed out of the cockpit of the yacht, paused for one short moment, then threw himself into the water – on the *wrong* side.

I guess he must have been manning the radio and hadn't seen the way the others had departed but, whatever the cause, we lost him.

All three of us had shouted 'No' as he went over the leeward side of the boat and, sure enough, the broken yacht just blew right over the top of him. It was leaning over at such an angle that we could see the keel coming up to the surface with each roll, but there was no sign of our man. He had been wearing a lifejacket when we last saw him but the power of the sea must have taken him down beneath the hull and maybe caught him on a part of the ruined rigging that was hanging off the boat in all directions. We desperately looked around for some sign of life. It would be easy to miss him in the churning water if he surfaced away from the boat so our eyes scanned an increasing radius around the abandoned *Magic*. It seemed like a lifetime; it was definitely more than a minute before he suddenly bobbed to the surface at the end of the keel. The boat had driven right over him before releasing him back to the sea and we moved quickly to reclaim him. As he came up on the winch for the last time Smiler had a grin from ear to ear. No longer did I need to stay down in the waves and so, keeping with the rhythm, I pulled in a little extra power and started to climb out of the turmoil. I couldn't begin to move very much until John had them both safely inside but I could afford to relax a little and glance downwards at the winch wire. Not only had our man survived a last look at the underside of his vessel, but he still had his glasses on.

Smiler made our guests as comfortable as possible but the Wessex is little more than a truck in the cabin area and there wasn't much he could do beyond handing out blankets from our stretcher kit. John, meanwhile, had a big task on his hands. We wanted to get our survivors on to terra firma as quickly as we could and I had set off in the approximate direction of Cornwall, but the navigation equipment consisted of little more than a compass. I would have to rely entirely on John's skill in knowing where we'd been and consequently where we now were. We'd been twisting and turning during the search, plus the wind would have been blowing us backwards at an unknown rate during the hover. One small miscalculation and you could be way off track. We later learned that one of our other aircraft had re-crossed the coast nearly 40 miles out from where he expected to be. It was therefore with no small relief, and frankly my amazement, that John guided us back to the north coastal painters' village of St Ives. We were no more than 100 yards away from the exact point we'd departed land over an hour earlier.

The radio chatter was intense but it seemed that there was more discipline now as each aircraft crew understood more about their own part in the overall picture. It was still only 09.00 in the morning but Dick Harvey's logbook back at Culdrose was filling up rapidly:

> 0615 Rescue 01 (Nimrod) and Dutch Frigate OVERIJSSEL investigating four men in a liferaft.
> 0620 Mayday from TARANTULA, no assistance available at this time.
> 0625 MULLIGATAWNY dismasted, Rescue 97 (Sea King) tasked to assist.
> GRIMALKIN capsized 30 miles North West of Lands End, Rescue 21 (Wessex) tasked to assist.
> 0746 Three survivors sighted in position 50.50N 06.50W. Rescue 21 will transit this position enroute to GRIMALKIN.
> 0750 Rescue 77 reports he has lifted one casualty from TARANTULA, remainder of Tarantula's crew are remaining onboard.
> 0755 Further Sea King crew becoming available shortly.
> 0835 Rescue 20 returning to Culdrose with five survivors from MAGIC, all crewmembers accounted for.
> Rescues 77, 79 and 21 all refuelled and returning to the scene of search.
> 0915 Rescue 97 has picked up two survivors from GRIMALKIN.
> 0939 Rescue 97 has picked up a further 3 survivors from TROPHY. There are an additional 3, plus one dead, in a liferaft. They have agreed this will be dealt with by the Dutch Frigate.

At 09.50 we landed back at Culdrose. Rescue 97 had beaten us by two minutes with her five survivors and we each had an ambulance to meet us. We'd been airborne for a total of four hours, so we handed our aircraft over to another crew and collared a vehicle to take us to the airfield operations room. Within five minutes our Wessex had been refuelled, taken a good freshwater hosing down the engine intakes and the oncoming crew were ready to go. As we drove off around the perimeter track she overtook us, heading back out into the teeth of the storm.

The radio calls were being written down by our veteran coastguard officer Dick Harvey, while the radar 'plot' was being run by Dave Roue, a great personal friend and a superbly professional observer. (He would later die when his Sea King flew into the water at 120 knots one night.) Dave was one of those who'd responded to the news, found the ops room empty and simply decided to start recording everything he heard on to a map. He had quickly become the prime source of information for all crews, both when returning and prior to launch. Even with the number of aircraft now available it was clear that this was going to be a mammoth job. It wasn't as simple as being tasked, finding your target and picking up the survivors. Along the way you'd spot something in the water, maybe a life raft with men in it or a yacht firing distress flares, and if you didn't record it or deal with it there and then, there was a good chance it would never be seen again. While you were dealing with this new task, somebody else would stumble upon your original target and begin to sort it out and, all the time, aircraft were asking other aircraft for help.

The RAF Nimrod was a great asset. She could move at over 400 knots and therefore quickly take over responsibility for watching over a group in a life raft while the helicopter dealt with another group twenty miles further on. She was also the only aircraft that could simultaneously communicate with all the helicopters hovering down low in the troughs of the waves, and with Culdrose, the

coastguards, her own base at St Mawgan and the multiple yachts transmitting their Maydays. It must have been bedlam for her radio operators and in many cases quite painful to listen to the stories unfolding beneath.

We reported all we knew to Dave, whose plot was a patchwork of multi-coloured markings, and headed back to the squadron for a quick bite of breakfast. Or we would have done so if we could have got into the crewroom. The whole squadron was by now streaming in to help and each new arrival was asking what on earth was going on. In the meantime the world's media had been quick off the mark and at least four separate camera crews were filming in a room no bigger than a large domestic sitting room. Household TV names were filing their reports and, of course, a crew returning from 'the front' were fresh meat to talk to. While they were a bit of a shock to us they didn't get in our way at all. There was plenty for them to film and although hard at work themselves they would always stop to hold a door open for the next crew hurtling out. Before long many of them moved off to interview the survivors who, by now, were starting to stretch the capacity of the sick bay.

Our third flight of the day is recorded starkly in my logbook as: 'Fastnet, *Golden Apple*, 4 hours 35 minutes'. At 12.20 John, Smiler and I took over Rescue 21 from the incoming crew who had just picked up all eight yachtsmen from *Camargue*. Our tasking was to join two other helicopters searching for a survivor who'd been seen in the water from the yacht *Festinia Tertia*. This part of the operation is a bit hazy in my memory and even on the day each event had begun to blend seamlessly into the next. The report shows that our mates in Rescue 30 landed Culdrose at 15.23 with a hypothermia case from *Festinia*, so presumably we were successful between us.

The next sequence I remember vividly. We'd been for a fuel top-up on the Scilly Isles and were tasked to pick up the crew of *Golden Apple of the Sun* some 35 miles further out into the Atlantic.

We asked the coastguard how many to expect and were knocked sideways when the answer came back: 'Ten.'

The rain had pretty much stopped around the Scilly Isles and there was even the odd ray of sunshine now and again through the scudding clouds. Even the seas seemed calmer but everything is relative and it was still blowing a force 8 to severe gale 9. *Golden Apple* had lost her rudder completely; this was something that would feature heavily in the post-race analysis by the yachting fraternity as she was one of six yachts carrying new carbon-fibre rudders. We would later learn that this was a 43-foot Irish contender and that her young New Zealand designer Ron Holland was aboard, along with principal helmsman Rodney Pattisson MBE, an Olympic gold and silver medallist in sailing. He was the first Scot ever to win an Olympic medal in sailing and was Great Britain's most successful Olympic sailor right up until 2008.

Even from above, the whole crew looked completely exhausted, albeit clearly a professional team at the very top of the Admiral's Cup rankings. Even without a rudder they had been trying to make it back to safe haven, but forecasts of another big blow that night had persuaded them that discretion was the better part of valour. We established a good radio link and began to consider how to get these ten guys off their disabled boat. Asking them to repeat the process of jumping into the water one by one wasn't appetising. We all felt we'd rolled that dice once too often. Lifting them straight off the deck was again out of the question with the mast swaying drunkenly from side to side.

In the end we settled on a life raft solution. *Golden Apple* had only one inflatable life raft on board. We asked them to inflate it, get into it and let it drift away from the yacht until it was clear enough of the mast for Smiler to descend and pick them up one by one. This would have been a perfect plan if only the life raft would drift away from the yacht, but some peculiar force of nature kept dragging it back alongside. It didn't matter what anybody tried, the thing just kept returning. The only solution we could come up with was to lower Smiler into the water as close as we dared and then let him swim, still attached to our winch line, to the life raft. We hoped we'd then be able to tow Smiler and the life raft far enough away from *Golden Apple* to hover vertically above and pick up the survivors one by one.

This was a lot to ask of Smiler. We'd been up since around 03.00 that morning and it was now getting into late afternoon. He'd already been swimming five times in a force 10 storm with a set of breathing apparatus on his back and we were all starting to feel the cold and the tiredness. But navy divers are cut from a tough cloth and their training includes daily crawls up to their armpits through endless mud flats with the equipment on their back. When you see the Fleet Air Arm crew doing the field gun race at the Royal Tournament, the team is almost always composed of divers.

With the positive and chirpy attitude that we all loved about him, Smiler called 'Ready, boss,' unplugged his intercom and swung out over the water as John and I worked together to drop him as close to the yacht as we could without swatting him with the mast. Once again I had to rely on John's continuous patter on the intercom to guide me.

'He's in the water, I've got a thumbs-up, I'm giving him some slack, he's starting to swim, come up two feet and back two feet, position is good, Smiler's taking a breather, he's setting off again, come forward one, up one, back two, he's got another twenty yards to swim, height's good, position good, ten yards to go, the survivors are trying to paddle towards him, they're leaning over, they've got him, come up two and left two, Smiler's got hold of the dinghy and the survivors have got hold of him, he's taking off his mask, we'll give him a moment to brief them, you're beginning to drift, come back four, he's putting his mask back on, I've got a thumbs-up, we're going to try and tow them, come up two and begin drifting slowly left, that's good, keep coming, keep coming, keep coming, you OK, boss?'

'Yup, how much further?'

'We'll go another twenty feet just to be sure, come down two and keep drifting as you are, fifteen feet, come up one, keep coming, keep coming, ten feet, slow down a little, Smiler is OK but he's struggling to hold on, five feet, two, one, hold your hover, I'm raising Smiler out of the water, he's putting the strop around the first man, come left two, survivor is in the strop, come left another two, you're drifting right, raising the winch, at the door, turning them around, pulling them in, releasing the survivor, strapping him into a seat, he's in the seat, returning to the winch, raising the winch, thumbs-up, lowering the winch, Smiler's going down, come left four feet to re-establish position over the life raft...' and so on, for a total of ten lifts.

The lifting was a relatively straightforward exercise for us so I settled down to learn a poem. This might seem a strange thing to do while flying a rescue chopper but the poem was written on the large flat transom at the stern of the *Golden Apple* and fixating on it was a good technique in maintaining a precise distance from the gradually abandoned yacht.

Every so often, without moving my head, my eyes would glance inside the cockpit at the fuel and the engine instruments. Fuel was fine, although we'd need to take more from the Scilly Isles before returning home, but the engines were starting to clog. The constant sea spray borne on the gale was being sucked down the intakes and the salt coating was clearly growing. We were using a fairly constant power setting but the intake temperature was slowly rising. We'd seen this happening all day and it wasn't yet cause for alarm but it did need monitoring.

By the time the last of the ten-man crew was safely on his way up to the cabin door I was word-perfect on the poem.

Though I am old with wandering
Through hollow lands and hilly lands
I will find out where she has gone

And kiss her lips and take her hands
And walk among long dappled grass
And pluck till time and times are gone
The silver apples of the moon
The golden apples of the sun

We all exhaled loudly as the last man took the last spot on the cabin floor and I'd never been so glad to hear Smiler plug back into the intercom.

'Nice one, boss.'

'You OK?'

'Bit tired, can we go home now?'

'On our way.'

A quick suck of fuel on the Scillies and we really were on our way. Just another forty minutes and we'd be back at base.

At 16.55 our wheels touched down for the last time that day and our ten passengers were helped to the waiting ambulances. We'd been on the go for a good fourteen hours and spent more than eight and a half of them airborne, but it was nothing compared to what the yachtsmen had been through. Never the less it was time for John, Smiler and me to hand over to a fresher crew, get some food, get some sleep and be back for the following dawn. Our squadron total for that day would be 29 hours 35 minutes of flying by nightfall, using only four helicopters. The longer-range Sea Kings could fly on into the night and would end up with a total of 49 hours by midnight, using five airframes.

Fastnet '79 is the largest and most effective maritime rescue operation ever mounted in peacetime in the UK. I'm proud to have been a part of it and proud to have been the first helicopter airborne on the first morning. But in an age of GPS, instantaneous mapping systems, infrared thermal search cameras and automated tracking devices, it's hard to convey the sheer scale of the chaos of this event.

The second and third days of rescue operations were a mopping-up exercise. Abandoned yachts were checked, deflated life rafts were pulled from the sea and exhausted yacht crews were monitored as they made their way back to safe haven, but no additional lives were saved.

I don't remember any point at which it felt as though we, or any of the other crews, had made a bad decision, but who can ever possibly know? I do know that as aviators we deal in a lot of 'what-if?' scenarios. What if an engine fails, what will be my actions? What if my fuel state gets to the point where I can only go to Ireland, not back to Cornwall? One particular question haunted me: What if I see a flare when I'm en route to another assigned target? I never properly resolved all the combinations of possibilities. Thankfully my own crew were never put to the test with a conflict of interest but these things lurked in the back of my mind throughout the task on day one. We were all in the same frame of mind. Get out there as fast as possible, pluck as many people from the water as possible, and get them back on to dry land.

I recently read the extraordinary book *Left For Dead* by Nick Ward, the last man to be picked up alive after having been left in the cockpit of *Grimalkin* with a dead compatriot for most of the night of the thirteenth and all day of the fourteenth. According to his introduction, it took Nick thirty years to get to the point where he could write the story. Having witnessed at first hand the seas he writes about, I couldn't put the book down until I'd finished it. I went back to my own records of that day and found the notes of Dick Harvey, our coastguard liaison officer, who so diligently tried to keep track of events alongside Dave Roue in the operations room at Culdrose: assimilate the information, put it on a map, retask the airborne crews, disseminate the information, do it all again. I've already listed some of the entries from Dick's log but I repeat the remainder of his notes from just that first day below, in the hope

that it conveys some sense of the sheer scale of the task and the extraordinary lengths that everybody went to in sorting logic and fact out of chaos and confusion. (SK = Sea King, WX = Wessex.)

R97 (SK) landed on Culdrose 0946Z with five survivors who were admitted to Culdrose Sick Bay, and at 0948Z R20 (WX) landed on, her five survivors were also admitted to Sick Bay.

From R21 (WX) at 1020Z returning with 8 survivors from CAMARGUE: All yacht's crew accounted for.

R98 (SK) reports returning Culdrose at 1037Z with one survivor on board in a bad way, picked up in position 50.54N 07.25W. R98 (SK) instructed to proceed direct to Treliske Hospital Truro.

Backup Sea King 304 arriving from Prestwick ETA 1220Z.

1137Z R97 (SK) tasked with R20 (WX) to make pick up in position 50.45N 06.42W where five persons reported in a dinghy. R20 (WX) Double lifted five survivors at 1155Z from SKIDBLADNER in position 50.46N 06.42W returning to Culdrose.

R97 (SK) reports proceeding to one person in the water in position 50.55N 07.50W.

R98 (SK) returned Culdrose from Treliske, landed on 1200Z.

Report from R77 (SK) double lifted twelve survivors at 1213Z. Six from GAN in position 50.41N 07.38W and six from HELSTRUL in position 50.43N 07.35W. R77 (SK) landed on 1217Z survivors admitted to Culdrose Sick Bay, aircraft refuelled. At 1225Z R20 (WX) returned with her survivors and refuelled.

R98 (SK) returned to scene of search 1225Z.

R77 (SK) and R30 (WX) returned search area 1250Z, and R25 (WX) at 1310Z.

1301Z From Lands End MRSC. Report received from Bishops Rock Lighthouse. Yacht observed 5 miles SSW of rock, no longer visible, request helo investigates.

R97 (SK) have double lifted seven survivors from GRINGO in position 50.56N 07.30W, one of the survivors has a broken rib. GRINGO's crew all accounted for. Only 30 minutes endurance left, returning Culdrose.

1407Z R97 (SK) and R20 (WX) land on to refuel. Two Lynx helicopters from Yeovilton to assist.

1439Z R96 (SK) returned to scene of search, and R463 (LYNX) at 1515Z.

1502Z From R25 (WX) returning to Culdrose to refuel, landed on 1507Z.

R77 (SK) and R21 (WX) airborne to position 295 Round Island 30 miles, to search for survivor in the water, believed to be from FESTINIA.

1512Z R30 (WX) reports returning with hypothermia case from FESTINIA. Landed on 1523Z.

R21 (WX) tasked to position 50.16N 07.18W to pick up ten crew members from GOLDEN APPLE.

R25 (WX) airborne and tasked to work with R77 (SK) 1529Z.

R90 (SK) tasked by SRCC at 1550Z to search area on the south and west of Scillies.

R98 (SK) returning to Culdrose with two survivors on board, one from GUNSLINGER in position 51.23N 07.22W and one from FLASHLIGHT in position 50.23N 07.07W at 1618Z, ETA 7/8 minutes. Landed Culdrose 1628Z. Casualties admitted to Sick Bay.

From R21 (WX) returning with ten survivors, complete crew of GOLDEN APPLE in position 50.16N 07.18W. ETA 55 minutes.

R25 (WX) have double lifted four survivors at 1647Z from FLASHLIGHT in position 50.23N 07.03W. All crew of FLASHLIGHT now accounted for.

R77 (SK) returning Culdrose 1716Z, no survivors on board. Land on 1735Z.

R21 (WX) returning scene of search at 1722Z, tasked to work with Nimrod, search area 50.20N 06.20W – 51.00N 07.30W.

1735Z Warship BROADSWORD to assume duties as CSS.

1630Z R463 (LYNX) returned Culdrose to refuel.

R96 (SK) returning Culdrose with eleven survivors on board 1755Z. Five from ALLAMANDA in position 50.30N 07.30W and six from BILLY BONES in position 50.40N 07.30W. Crews of both yachts accounted for.

WEATHER IN THE SEARCH AREA SOUTHWESTERLY GALE 8 TO SEVERE GALE 9, SHOWERS, GOOD VISIBILITY.

1755Z From SRCC via R90 (SK) 7/8 yachts in difficulties in position 50.40N 07.40W. Warship BROADSWORD's position 7 miles NW Scillies, searching the area.

R96 (SK) landed on, survivors admitted to Sick Bay. R96 (SK) returned scene of search 1842Z. R463 (LYNX) to scene of search 1915Z.

R21 (WX) returning one survivor and one body on board 1925Z from GRIMALKIN.

1930Z R747 (LYNX) to scene of search.

1930Z R90 (SK) returned to refuel and rejoined search at 1955Z. Sitrep at 1955Z.

R96 (SK) tasked to work with Dutch Frigate OVERIJSSEL.

R463 (LYNX) tasked to position 50.17N 07.15W to investigate life rafts, yachts and life-jackets.

1957Z R25 (WX) reports the following yachts sighted in positions:-
FLASHLIGHT 50.20N 07.10W. Helm secured, sea anchor streamed, Abandoned.

GOLDEN PRINCESS 50.18N 07.08W. OK.

GOLDEN APPLE OF THE SUN 50.19N 07.15W Abandoned.

R25 (WX) returning to base.

2030Z R20 (WX) sighted 17 yachts, visibility too bad to continue.

2035Z R463 (LYNX) and R747 (LYNX) returning Culdrose.

2230Z R96 (SK) returned Culdrose.
0030Z R90 (SK) returned to Culdrose.
AIRFIELD NOW CLOSED UNTIL FIRST LIGHT. SEA
KINGS PLACED AT 15 MINUTES NOTICE.

It's a truism in the Navy that however serious anything has become there will always be a moment of light relief. And the more serious the circumstances perhaps the greater the release that humour provides. Sure enough, on the fourth day, two Germans appeared in the crewroom just before breakfast time. They came from *Stern*, a glossy German news magazine that specialised in great pictures and minimal text. Their story of finding us was something of a survival story of its own. In halting English it seemed to consist of cancelled airliner flights, sunken ferry boats, broken charter planes, incompetent taxi drivers and on through a plethora of mishaps which had led to them spending three full days and nights on the road towards capturing one of the biggest news stories of the year. By the time they had reached our crewroom they were exhausted themselves.

All the other news crews had gone home by now and the morning was turning into a bright summer's day. It was the turn of Jamie Bauld to fry the breakfast. He was the archetypical Scotsman, so broad in his language that no Englishman, let alone a German, could fully understand everything he said, and exhibiting the sort of tight-fisted approach for which the Scots are famed. In fact, he revelled in it and turned it into an art form. Never the less he took pity on the Germans and included them in the breakfast arrangements. Jamie duly produced a classic SAR fry-up with all the works, which our new friends wolfed down with enthusiasm. At the end of the meal as Jamie was doing the washing-up, the reporter sidled up to him and pressed two crisp fifty-pound notes into his hand, muttering something about a contribution to the coffee fund.

'Good grief, man,' exclaimed Jamie. 'If I'd known you were going to do that, I'd have given you two eggs.' I defy anyone to find a tougher, more professional or funnier bunch of guys than I had the privilege to serve with on the Fastnet, or any of our other rescue escapades.

Survivors and bodies picked up by helicopter, in chronological order.

Day One – 13 August

TARANTULA	1		Sea King
MAGIC	5	Complete crew	**My Team**
GRIMALKIN	2		Sea King
TROPHY	3		Sea King
CAMARGUE	8	Complete crew	Wessex
ARIADNE	1		Sea King
SKIDBLADNER	5		Wessex
GAN	6		Sea King
HELSTRUL	6		Sea King
GRINGO	7	Complete crew	Sea King
FESTINIA TERTIA	1		Wessex
GUNSLINGER	1		Sea King
FLASHLIGHT	1		Sea King
GOLDEN APPLE	10	Complete crew	**My Team**
FLASHLIGHT	4	Crew now complete	Wessex
ALLAMANDA	5		Sea King
BILLY BONES	6		Sea King
GRIMALKIN	2	One dead	Wessex

Day Two – 14 August
None

Day Three – 15 August

HELSTRUL	1	Dead	Sea King

Day Four – 16 August

BON ADVENTURE	1	Broken arm	Sea King

Statistics

Yachts started	303
Yachts finished	85
Yachts retired	189
Yachts abandoned	24
Yachts lost believed sunk	5
Lives saved	136
Lives lost	15

14

FASTNET REVISITED

RECENTLY I HAPPENED TO STUMBLE upon a news item about a memorial that had been dedicated at the twenty-fifth anniversary of the Fastnet event in 2004. A ceremony had been held at the Cape Clear Island Museum and Archive, just four miles away from the Fastnet Rock in County Cork, Ireland, at which the names of the deceased were read out as wreaths were cast on the waters. Over 400 people attended, Ted Turner donated a painting of his yacht *Tenacious* winning the '79 event, and two of the crew who had survived the disaster established the 'Fastnet Race Remembrance Collection'. By an extraordinary coincidence, they were both members of *Magic* and *Golden Apple* crews, which my own team had rescued.

Not really expecting an answer, I sent an email off to the originator of the project and the website, Dr Eamon Lankford. Within 24 hours he had not only replied but had put me in touch with the two crew members, Peter Whipp (skipper of *Magic*) and

Neil Kenefick (trimmer and offshore driver of *Golden Apple*), giving
me the opportunity to ask them about their perspective of the brief
moment our lives had come together.

Peter Whipp, of *Magic*, responded:

*We were one of the earlier boats to get into trouble; the rudder
snapped clean away at about half past midnight. We were lucky
because I sensed trouble in the previous afternoon on seeing a
huge halo around the sun. It was quite uncanny and I saw that
all our loose things were lashed down and used a little portable
generator which we had to charge up our battery; we had no
engine on* Magic. *We were probably the smallest boat in the fleet
and I believe that we were doing quite well in the race.*

*The charged battery gave us VHF right up to the time you
pulled us out which enabled us to know what was going on and
to relay messages back to the rescue team. Just before you arrived,
we saw a Nimrod and we spoke to the pilot and he verified that it
was us who was speaking to him by banking left and then right.
We told him that we were in no immediate danger and settled in
to wait for the storm to abate. We were OK but with two crew
members suffering from panic.*

*I remember when you came by I protested that we would be
OK but you had more sense and told us that it would be a waste if
you returned empty just to get some more fuel. That sealed it. Our
crew was myself and four others. I think one of the stronger two
went first to show the nervous two the way. As tradition dictates,
I came last. I can't remember getting off the wrong side but the
boat did spin around regularly. I swam away from the boat and
your diver came down for me. Then something went wrong, I
only had one arm in the loop and the diver didn't have a proper
hold of me and so he let me back into the water. You explained
back in Culdrose that you had to fly around a little to regain*

your concentration which, of course, I fully understand, but the memory of seeing you fly away without me and my boat a few very big waves upwind of me will remain with me forever.

I then remember getting into the helicopter to find that it was full of water and so the diver and, I think, your navigator tried to push it out of the door with his flippers. I wanted to be back on my boat despite the fact that we knew that she had sustained some structural damage; she was built of wood.

I have never wanted to read any of the books about the race although I did help a Canadian journalist write one because we met up with a Canadian boat called Evergreen as she was making her way back to Cornwall and we met up with their crew again after the race in Plymouth.

I can never thank you enough for rescuing us. It was an experience I never want to repeat but I did force myself back on to the sea and I do still sail. I went back to do the Fastnet Race in 1981, 1983 and then won it overall in 1985.

I was thrilled to get this response and amazed at Peter's two recollections. First, I had no memory at all of talking him into being airlifted but I do remember a certain fear associated with what might happen if we left a yacht that had been so hard to find.

John Charnley, my crewman, was constantly dividing his time between being an essential pair of eyes and a 'dead reckoning' navigator, scribbling times, tracks and positions on to a paper map with a pencil. Remember there was no GPS, no sophisticated moving maps; we could only have knowledge of our position by virtue of passing over a known point such as a lighthouse. To that we could sometimes add a radio bearing that told us we were in such and such a direction from RAF St Mawgan, but usually we were at such low level that they were of no use to us.

All the while we would be straining to assimilate aural information from several radio sources and from each other. This formed into a 3D virtual world in our heads and through years of practice it was a surprisingly accurate world, but the moment you returned to base for fuel or to drop off survivors you would have to 'reboot' the 3D world in your head and start again as circumstances had changed so much in the short time you were off-task. Perhaps that was partly why we were reluctant to leave Peter and his crew aboard *Magic*.

Peter's second comment about the effect it had on him of me 'flying away' was sobering indeed. He's referring to how difficult it was for Smiler to catch him in the waves and how we had therefore backed off to start a fresh run at collecting Peter. To us it was all part of the normal routine. After several unsuccessful attempts at threading a needle in bad light we all know how a pause, a deep breath and a fresh start will often yield a perfect conclusion right at the start of the second attempt. That's how it was for us that day as we hovered sideways: it gave Smiler a chance to catch his breath in the water and me a chance to flex my finger muscles. We probably moved no further than 30 metres away from Peter's position and took no longer than 30 seconds to reconvene for the fresh attempt, but to Peter we were no longer directly over his head and were probably hidden behind each wave as it came tumbling through our field of play. To him it was as if we had flown away and left him.

From Neil Kenefick of *Golden Apple* I also received an interesting fresh perspective but one that matched my own memory:

We had one life raft manufactured in the USA, very lightweight!!
I recall sending out the Pan Pan. Suddenly you were there. We
put Rodney Pattisson (MBE) on the radio. We then launched the
raft and the rope broke, Rodney dived into the raft and I threw a
rope to him. The raft was very shoddy. We then boarded and we
were underwater with 10 aboard, with the roof collapsed. The raft

would not separate from Golden Apple. *I recall looking up at you in the sky and throwing her on her side to get the down draft to blow* Golden Apple *away so you could then hover and take us 1 by 1.*

Neil also forwarded my email to Ron Holland, the designer of *Golden Apple*, who also kindly replied:

Neil sent me your chapter and preceding communication. I think you can understand reading this brought back memories. (Like when I read Left For Dead).

My recollections:

– Aware of good communications with the heli.

– Feeling guilty about leaving a mostly good yacht. After hearing the weather was to deteriorate again, evening coming on and with the Scillies to leeward, we all agreed to go.

– Inflating a raft (we only had one raft) in 40+ knots of wind on the deck of a small yacht was a challenge. (The height of the storm was over.) The umbilical cord tore away from the raft and we kept it close to the leeward side with difficulty.

– The raft did not fully inflate and I felt very claustrophobic jammed chest deep in water with my crew mates.

– The raft was pinned under the lee side of Golden Apple of the Sun, *drifting quickly downwind on top of the raft.*

– We had the impression the heli downdraft helped separate the yacht from the raft?

– Hugh Coveney, the owner and I, were the last two to be saved. Before he left me in the arms of the wireman: 'For God's sake, Holland, who would have thought it would end like this?'

– In the chopper we first learnt of the devastation the Fastnet Race fleet had experienced. That was shocking.

The final postscript must come from one of the smallest boats in the fleet which survived the storm and crept into Plymouth late on Friday 17 August, having sat out a second storm on the Thursday night. The skipper signed his declaration: 'Retired due to inclement weather.'

15

CIVVY STREET

ALL GOOD THINGS MUST COME TO AN END. When I'd first donned a uniform in 1972, the prospect of eight years in a blue suit seemed to stretch into infinity but as the aftermath of Fastnet continued into the end of 1979 I began to realise that next year would be my last in the Fleet Air Arm. I say 'aftermath' because the event had not only attracted huge attention at the time of the stricken race but also continued to do so for the months that followed as various organisations questioned their rules, their structure and their roles. The Royal Yachting Association and the Royal Ocean Racing Association set about generating the official report and enquiry, which was eagerly awaited by the yachting fraternity around the world. Yacht design had been changing rapidly as technologies developed and components made from new materials such as carbon fibre were introduced. Questions had to be asked about whether some of the ancient wisdom of vessel design had been forgotten in the headlong rush towards speed at all cost.

At the same time there was immense public interest in the multitude of personal stories of bravery, tragedy and human strength in the face of adversity. Although our little crewroom was no longer bursting at the seams with television cameras and our routine had returned to relative normality, there was still a steady stream of reporters from both national and international publications interviewing the duty crew in an attempt to cement all the final pieces of the jigsaw into place.

Our regular presentations to local organisations had become particularly popular and there's no doubt that the attention of these audiences had significantly increased, along with their sizes. We also ventured much further afield in order to say thank you to those who had played their own part in providing manpower, skills or hardware. The CO tried to divide up the responsibilities fairly among us, woven in between the day-to-day SAR operations that inexorably continued. My own highlight was a flight to Farnsworth, near Manchester, to visit the Rolls Royce factory where our engines had been assembled. It was a rare opportunity to fly outside the usual confines of our patch and entailed the study of air-traffic structures in regions that were unfamiliar to us in order to arrive safely at the appointed hour. We landed in the car park and were ushered on to the podium in a cavernous workspace full of over 1,500 enthusiastic individuals who were keen to hear stories of how their product had helped to save lives.

The Royal Western Yacht Club, being the hosts at the finish line of the Fastnet race, were also generous in inviting all of our aircrew to a black tie prize-giving dinner in late November. It was inevitably an event tinged with sadness and introspection for those for whom the race had been their last but we were honoured to be a part of it. The invitation letter had specifically said that the vice commodore would do no more than simply welcome us as guests. Thus we were able to relax and enjoy the company of our hosts in the unfamiliar civilian environment.

Three months later an unexpected letter arrived from FONAC, the admiral in command of the Fleet Air Arm:

3 March 1980

Dear Grayson

I am delighted to inform you that Her Majesty the Queen has approved the award of Her Commendation for Valuable Service in the Air to you in recognition of your outstanding contribution to the rescue of participants in last year's Fastnet Race. Please accept my heartiest congratulations.

Until the publication of the award in the *London Gazette* on 4 March you should keep this news to your immediate family. You will be informed of the arrangements for the presentation of your award in due course.

Your sincerely
Rear Admiral Edward Anson
Flag Officer Naval Air Command

At the subsequent ceremony my crew, Albie's crew and two of the Culdrose Sea King crews were formally presented with the oak leaves to be worn on the chest of our uniform.

By that time I was studying hard. I was still only 24 but the date of my discharge was rapidly approaching and I needed the licence that would allow me to fly as a civilian. The Navy was very aware of its responsibilities and gave every leaver the opportunity to study for and apply for a new career. The correspondence course for the Airline Transport Pilot's Licence (ATPL) was just about the hardest studying I ever had to undertake. Initial flying training for the Navy had been an ordeal but at least I was doing it in the company of others. Burning the midnight oil alone took some getting used to.

Bizarrely the Civil Aviation Authority made very little distinction between the exam requirements for a commercial helicopter pilot and those required to qualify as an airline captain. Learning about navigation equipment that is only used when flying trans-oceanic seemed like a pointless exercise when your fuel was unlikely to last beyond the furthermost lighthouse, but there was no argument to be had so I just knuckled down to it. By June of 1980 the hard work had paid off and I was the proud holder of an ATPL (Helicopters).

It was all very well working towards a licence but the landscape of opportunity was then almost too wide. The extra gratuity to stay in the Navy and the addition of a pension (at 29) was certainly tempting, but deep down inside I knew that if I took the easy route it would be something I'd regret. It would be back to sea and another four years of 'Yes, sir, no, sir'. So I firmly resolved to take the eight-year break point that I'd been working towards.

At that time the accepted career path was to apply for a job on the North Sea. The oil industry was booming and most of my contemporaries had found that the jobs on offer were well paid and not dissimilar to the Navy life to which they had become accustomed. The cold and wet climate around Aberdeen didn't seem to bother them and the long and dull hours carrying a helicopter full of oil-rig workers across a grey ocean to a huge structure looming out of the fog seemed to suit those who had stayed operational on Sea Kings. The Sikorsky S61 was simply a stretched civilian version of the Sea King, so that brought another familiar aspect to the job, but the idea of piloting an airframe I had been used to in a military context as a kind of a taxi didn't sit well with me.

Quite out of the blue I got it into my head that I would like to start a helicopter company. I don't have any recollection of arriving at that decision by a logical path, it was just suddenly there as an absolute certainty in the forefront of my plans. In many ways it was an unrealistic aspiration; I had no business training whatsoever and the price of a good second-hand helicopter was many hundreds of thousands of pounds. I also arrived at the arrogant and self-limiting decision that I was going to do this in the county of Cornwall and in collaboration with an old friend, Keith Thompson. Keith and I had shared a cabin on the *Ark* and he was due to come out of the Navy just a couple of months before me. He was still away at sea at the time so I pressed on in the assumption that he'd be up for this new adventure.

Very short letters of proposal were despatched to just about every successful company in the south-west, and very short letters of rejection soon came flooding back. However, the letter I composed to a local car dealer was written rather more carefully. Rumour had it that he owned the only private helicopter in the county and that he had achieved local notoriety by buying it in order to get round the loss of his driving licence for speeding. The response came by phone the next day and Keith (recently returned from sea) and I were soon on the way to Liskeard, at the other end of the county from Culdrose, to meet the famed Mr Roy Flood. The helicopter, which he kept in a neat hangar next to his country home, was beautiful. Having spent the best part of my career to date in the Wessex, this Longranger seemed to be little more than a flimsy toy. It was immaculately kept, had smooth leather seats and there was not a drop of oil to be seen on the aircraft or the hangar floor. This was all new to me.

Before the day was over we'd sketched out a plan. Following on from my proposal we agreed that Roy would continue to use G-LRII for his private pursuits but that Keith and I would form a company with him to operate it on commercial activities. We went on to talk about how we might structure the arrangement and about how it might be better to build another hangar next to Castle Motors, Roy's company which would fund the start-up. Roy had also phoned his flying instructor to book me in for a conversion course and I began to grasp the first understanding of how some parts of the commercial world didn't hold committee meetings and insist on piles

of paperwork. This would be the style of operation for the next ten years in what was immediately named Castle Air Charters.

There were still some months to go before my official naval flying duties would come to an end. Commercial charters and company preparations had therefore to be squeezed in between my regular SAR duties. I completed the flying conversion course to the new Longranger and began to make a few trips around the country with Roy as he went from auction to auction in the pursuit of good value cars to sell from his forecourt. On SAR duty days I no longer had the luxury of watching television in the squadron crewroom as there were operations manuals to be written and all the paraphernalia of a new company to be sorted out. I now had a desk of my own in Liskeard and the ninety-minute drive from one job to the other was made at every spare opportunity. By June of 1980 we had gained the licence from the Civil Aviation Authority to begin commercial operations, and Keith and I alternated our time between the Navy and Castle Air. We began to fly short pleasure trips at various events around the country, an activity that didn't stretch the aviator in me but opened my eyes to the connection between flying hours, company income and an eventual salary.

On 2 July a small conflict arose in the calendar. I had the morning SAR duty but also a commitment at Castle Air to fly some Euro MPs on a tour around Cornwall, beginning from Falmouth. The timings would work out OK if I took the Longranger home with me, finished SAR at the usual time of midday, then jumped into my civilian role to fly off to Falmouth. But a helicopter isn't something you can just park in the driveway of a semi-detached house in a small town. The only option was to ask the CO if he minded me keeping the Longranger on the squadron apron overnight, prior to the afternoon flight to Falmouth. Permission was sought from the captain of the airbase and happily given. I positioned up from Liskeard to Culdrose late on the evening of the first, came into work at dawn on the second, flew a couple of sorties and then gave the boys a few minutes of prodding my strange but beautiful new toy before climbing out of one uniform and into another, leaving the afternoon SAR crew to take over my Wessex. The juxtaposition of one career with another and the almost seamless transition between the two felt strange but exciting.

On 2 September 1980 I flew my last flight in a Wessex. It was an unremarkable flight that went down in the logbook as 'Coastal patrol'. In fact, it was a flight of pure self-indulgence, visiting all the places around the coast of Cornwall that had played such a big part in my formative years. We went and bounced our wheels on the Camel's Head for the last time, took some pictures and generally enjoyed the last hour in the flying machine that had shared so much of the drama. The next day I packed up my small locker, shook hands and exchanged insults with the boys and drove across the airfield to return my flying helmet.

There was to be one last typical naval moment when I went for my leaving medical. The procedure is more intense than the joining examination: designed to ensure that you can't come back in a few years' time and claim that the Navy caused your bad back or your pathological aversion to bacon rolls. My old friend Rick Jolly, a fantastic surgeon commander who later ran the field hospital in San Carlos Bay in the Falklands (see his book *The Red and Green Life Machine*), conducted the examination. We went through all the usual rituals including stripping down to briefs and performing various balancing and coordination tasks. Knowing that this would be a more strenuous medical than usual I complied without question when Rick told me to take off my Y fronts, put both hands out in front of me, close my eyes, stand on one leg and balance there for as long as possible. I was just priding myself on my ability to remain in that position when he told me to relax and open my eyes. There before me stood a very cute nurse holding up

a score-card while Rick doubled over with tears of mirth running down his face. I was going to miss much of the fun and irreverence of Navy life.

But my involvement with the Navy didn't entirely end at that point. There would be one last involvement in an SAR story from a civilian perspective, which I will tell later.

During our first year at Castle Air it became clear that the commercial operation was hindering Roy's ability to fly around the country purchasing cars, so the Castle Motors cash-flow funded the purchase of a second helicopter: a brand new Jetranger. The British pound bought a lot of dollars back in 1981 so it was only a few months later that a third helicopter joined the stable.

At Castle Air the assumption was that if you needed something doing, you did it yourself. We needed a bigger hangar so we just built one. I learned how to drive a JCB backhoe to prepare the ground, we laid concrete during the day, then polished it all night until you could play billiards on the surface. Massive trucks turned up with long and heavy RSJs but it wasn't in Roy's nature to buy pre-prepared steel so I learned to cut with oxy-acetylene and to join by arc-welding. It was a jigsaw puzzle where you had to make all the pieces yourself and then put them together with a crane.

On New Year's Day 1982 (no days off when there's business to be done). I was way up at the top of a scaffolding tower carefully welding together two extremely large RSJs when somebody shouted from ground level that my wife was on the phone.

'Tell her I'll call her back later,' I hollered to the floor below.

'No, she says you'll want to hear this and you have to come now.'

I clambered my way down the four flights of wooden ladder we'd lashed together, in direct opposition to any concept of health and safety, and took the phone.

'Are you sitting down?' my wife asked.

'No, I'm standing holding a telephone cord through the office window with a welding mask on my head.'

'I think you should sit down.'

'Look, I'm really busy at the moment,' I grumbled. 'Why are you calling me at work?'

'You're in the New Year's Honours List. You've been awarded the Air Force Cross.'

I sat down.

To this day I have no idea how this happened, who submitted the recommendation nor who judged it but, sure enough, I was named in both the local and national papers that were lying around in the showroom as being the only recipient of the Air Force Cross that year. Suddenly I had letters after my name. I climbed back up the scaffolding, picked up the welding torch and welded 'Jerry AFC' in very big letters to the side of the RSJ.

Apparently you would normally know of the award in advance, as indicated by the letter post-marked Buckingham Palace that eventually turned up saying, 'Please keep this to yourself and your immediate family until…' It also contained advice that 'the investiture by Her Majesty the Queen will take place at Buckingham Palace on a date to be advised'.

It was long before the days of Google and our little library in Liskeard didn't have the sort of reference section I needed in order to discover exactly what it was that I'd been awarded, so I took myself off to the big county library in the seafaring city of Plymouth to work it out.

Instituted in 1918, the Air Force Cross (AFC) was issued for acts of gallantry while flying on non-active operations to warrant officers and officers of the Royal Air Force. It was later made available to equivalent ranks in the Royal Navy and Army for acts of gallantry in the air.

Simply put, it was the highest gallantry award for flying that could be awarded in peace time. I was totally bowled over.

Over the course of time more letters followed from the palace to secure the arrangement. I dug out my uniform, my wife and mother bought new hats, and off we went to see the Queen. Dad had died a couple of years earlier and had left me the considerable sum (for the time) of £6,000. In his last two years he had risen to become the managing director of Ferrari in the UK so, in his honour and memory, I had blown the whole lot on a Ferrari 308 with the appropriate number 'RU 27' (my age that year). Thus came the spring morning when I drove my Ferrari through the gates of Buckingham Palace and parked it in the central courtyard.

The day passed in a blur. A lady who bore more than a passing resemblance to Queen Elizabeth II shook my hand, said a few kind words and handed me a box containing an unfeasibly large silver cross. By six o'clock I was being interviewed in the studios of the BBC National News programme *Nationwide*, which had run a documentary series two years earlier about our day-to-day life on 771 squadron. I have no idea what I said nor where we went to celebrate, but it was still a day to remember for ever.

In due course the bigger twin-engined Agusta 109 was added to the fleet at Castle Air and about that time a rather grey man in an equally grey suit arrived at our offices in a grey Ford, unannounced. Our initial impression was entirely unfair and he turned out over the course of around three years to be an interesting guy with an interesting job. He came from the Admiralty Underwater Weapons Establishment (AUWE) and his job was to test new torpedoes. His problem lay in the fact that he needed a rather large swathe of sea-space in which to set these monsters running and that space had of course to be entirely clear of civilian boats before he could start the day's work. Despite promulgating the activities, the odd sailor inevitably failed to read the warnings and strays like this were frequently bringing his tests to a premature halt. He needed a helicopter with a loudspeaker attached that could patrol the weapons range and shout at errant yachtsmen who looked like they were about to wander into danger.

We fitted a loudspeaker arrangement into the side of one of our Jetrangers and began the task. It was an extremely good commercial activity for us and not a particularly demanding job for the pilot. We knew the protocols to adopt when talking to submariners on the radio and the task of patrolling the ocean was entirely familiar. For the AUWE, who could never get hold of a Navy helicopter on the days they needed one, our relative cost was as nothing when compared to the savings they were making in trial days that would otherwise have been lost.

In most cases the yachties would take our 'advice' in good grace, give us a cheery wave and reverse their direction. We only once lost a couple of hours to a small green sailing boat that simply refused to deviate from the course he was on. My calls to him over the loudspeaker were entirely ignored, to the extent that I began to wonder if he was deaf. But he couldn't be blind as well, as he proved when I hovered in front of him and he obliged me with the internationally recognized maritime signal of raising his middle finger. The submarine was loitering in the area at periscope depth but for some reason I couldn't raise him on the radio and I could see from the periscope wake that he was in a turn that would bring him right underneath the sailing boat.

The level of my voice over the loudspeaker went up a couple of octaves as I shouted, 'There is a submarine behind you. If you do not alter ninety degrees to starboard NOW you are in SERIOUS danger.' The bearded yachtie glanced casually over his shoulder but was suddenly galvanised into action and threw his tiller hard to starboard. The submarine was completely unaware of the yacht and from the direction that its periscope was looking it seemed to me that he was studying something on the shore to the north. I descended to the hover in front of the periscope lens and frantically waved and pointed in the direction of the yacht. The periscope whipped around and almost appeared to bulge like a cartoon eye. Only seconds later I could see the huge black shadow roll quite violently as the captain must have shouted, 'Hard to port'. I could only imagine the sound of breaking tea cups in the tin tube as submariners scrabbled for support. From my lofty point of view I could see the prominent sonar bulge at the very bows of the submarine pass less than 10 feet behind the yacht as the sub went one way and the yacht went the other. One very lucky sailor lived to sail another day.

Once we were entirely sure that the weapons range was clear, we would authorise the warship or submarine to carry out a live run and release the torpedo. The 'fish' would do its thing and, at the end of its run, it would inflate a little lifejacket collar and pop to the surface for recovery. At this point a small fishing-boat-like vessel would take our guidance to the floating torpedo and begin the process of trying to recover it using their on-board crane.

The process of recovery took a long time and the light was often fading too quickly to allow us to carry out a second firing, so I asked why they had never attempted torpedo recovery using a helicopter. It had apparently been tried in the past but the recovery contraption beneath the helicopter was over-complicated and failed more often than not. I was intrigued by this problem and that night I retired to the bathroom with a half-used can of hairspray (it floated nicely in the vertical position of an expended torpedo), a small fishing net, some lengths of string and some bent paperclips. By the time I'd finished my hands were wrinkly but I had successfully and repeatedly recovered my 'torpedo'. The recovery net looked like an inverted shuttlecock and was suspended from the helicopter by two ropes. When the release button for the cargo hook was pressed, the relative lengths of the two ropes changed and thus closed the bottom of the net, allowing the helicopter to smoothly lift the torpedo out of the water in the upright position.

Over the coming months my bathroom experimentation was actioned, the real-sized thing was manufactured by AUWE, and we went on to use it successfully. It was a classic win/win whereby we were able to use the more expensive Agusta 109 – the Jetranger and Longranger helicopters didn't have the external lifting capacity for a torpedo – and would often be asked to position to other weapon ranges as far north as the Isle of Skye. The AUWE, meanwhile, achieved many more trial runs each day and thus saved hundreds of thousands of pounds in manpower and vessels. I later learned that every warship in the Royal Navy had been issued with one of my nets but it was a long time before I understood the concept of intellectual property rights so I have nothing to show for it beyond great pride.

It was good still to have a naval connection but the 109 was not really designed for long periods of hovering and lifting. The sleek helicopter was better suited to the fast cruise. Over time the torpedo recovery task took its toll on our helicopters and, as I was to find out later, very nearly took its toll on me.

16

TRANSPLANT

A WONDERFUL ORGANISATION CALLED UK Transplant matches organ donors with needy recipients. In the London area most helicopter operators are registered with UK Transplant, who call on them when they need one of the transplant teams to be moved around the country quickly. Two of the best-known hospitals specialising in transplants are Papworth in Cambridgeshire, and Harefield, which lies just inside the M25 on the north-west corner of London. Harefield is one of the largest and most experienced centres in the world for heart and lung transplants but at the time of my story in 1986 it was still a relatively new procedure. Christiaan Barnard was the first surgeon to perform a successful heart transplant in Cape Town, South Africa, in 1967; it was not until 1981 that a combined operation was carried out successfully to transplant both heart and lung. Two years later Harefield hospital performed their own first double transplant.

The advantage of a helicopter, of course, is that it can go door to door, whereas a fixed wing, albeit usually faster, has to use a runway and therefore involves at least two other forms of ground transport to achieve delivery. UK Transplant favoured the Agusta 109 because it was one of the fastest helicopters of its time in the world and would confidently sit in the cruise at up to 140 knots. With two engines it was also good for night flying and the cockpit had all the instrumentation and autopilot facilities needed for full certification under IFR (Instrument Flight Rules): the art of flying through cloud. (Having been a total dunce at flying on instruments at the start of my flying career, I had been determined to rectify the situation. By the time I left the Navy I had become an instructor in the subject.) I enjoyed the extra capability that the 109 gave us. Even on a fine day it was fun to plug in the autopilot with a deft flick of the fingers and then administer the flight by gentle adjustments to various knobs and switches instead of physically wrestling the machine along. It felt like being a grown-up aviator. The workload was actually higher but it kept the mind alert on otherwise long and laborious transit flights.

The previous day at Brands Hatch had been long but by no means dull. At that time the Grand Prix alternated each year between Silverstone and Brands. We preferred Silverstone because of the wide-open spaces and the old wartime airfield in the middle of the track; Brands Hatch was a different kettle of fish. The track itself lies in a steep-sided valley bowl so the helicopter 'airport', which for one day each year becomes statistically the busiest airport in the world, had to be located in a field at the top of the hill. The airborne shuttle to and from the Grand Prix was a heart-stopping exercise at the best of times but Brands raised the pucker factor by having a very tall row of electricity pylons across the end of the runway. This became yet another obstacle on a day when you were vying for the same tiny piece of airspace with 150 other helicopters. I seriously frightened myself there one year when I was departing to collect my next load of passengers from Battersea Heliport in central London. At about 200 feet I became aware of the sound of another helicopter. I can assure you that if you can actually hear another helicopter, he has to be very close. My head jerked from left to right and then above me and beneath me to try to find where the noise was coming from, but I dared not move a muscle to avoid the other machine for fear of going in the wrong direction and colliding with him. After what can only have been seconds, but which felt a hell of a lot longer than that, the culprit appeared in the Perspex panel beneath my feet, climbing much too fast and far too steeply. Once I knew where he was it was relatively easy to reduce my speed and increase my rate of climb, thus avoiding collision. I was positioned above and behind him, which meant there was no way that he'd seen me at all. He never knew how close he'd come to riding a rotor-less helicopter to the ground, and I went on to fly the rest of the day with all my senses dialled into self-preservation mode. But on Grand Prix day there's little time to dwell on incidents like this. The pressure of getting everybody in before race start and out before darkness descends lays claim to your full attention.

In 1986 the race at Brands was won by Nigel Mansell with five British drivers in the top five including Martin Brundell and Jonathon Palmer, whom I knew quite well as a fellow helicopter pilot. The big drama in that year was a first lap pile-up in which the French driver Jacques Lafitte broke both his legs. It was with quiet pride that I'd watched him being whisked away to hospital by my old Wessex 5 from 771 Squadron, there as the air ambulance in a Navy tradition I'd instigated seven years earlier.

The operational problem with Grand Prix Sunday is that all the pilots use up their legal 'duty hours' so that it's virtually impossible to find a pilot that can legally fly the day after. Thus it was that none of the London operators had a pilot available when the call came from UK Transplant on the Monday evening. Having spent the majority of Monday recovering from the 'Thank God we survived another

Grand Prix day' party at Fairoaks airfield in Surrey, I was planning to fly back home to Cornwall on the Tuesday morning. Events conspired to crown me as the only available pilot/helicopter combo available for work on Monday evening. My helicopter was already on the tarmac at Fairoaks so it didn't take long to flash her up and high-tail it over to Harefield, a short hop across the top of Heathrow.

I hadn't been to Harefield before but the regular flights by others meant that their landing pad was well marked and easy to find. The light was fading as I touched down just after 8pm but it was clear that it was going to be a still night with good visibility, just the sort of weather I like for night flying, which can be stressful at the best of times. I had been briefed to wait at the helipad until the eminent surgeon and his assistant arrived and then to take them to Taunton hospital in Somerset, a matter of about an hour's flying away, where they would extract the heart and lungs from a highly valued female donor who had lost her life in a road accident.

In chatting to the nurse who waited patiently at the helipad with me for the arrival of the surgeon, I learned two things. First, despite this transplant business being a relatively new craft, they were already performing over 800 operations a year. I was astonished at this since it still felt to me like something I'd only recently seen being heralded on television as a breakthrough. But what floored me was the fact that my two passengers, both surgeons, one female, had already performed two such operations since they had come on duty. Just to put that into perspective: it was a requirement that the removal and the insertion of the organs be performed by the same team. Without knowing anything about the subject I could see why this would be a good idea but staff shortages meant that this team had, so far, in the working 'day' done the following:

Driven to an airport.
Flown by fixed wing to Belgium.

Extracted a heart.

Flown back to London.

Driven to the hospital.

Inserted a heart.

Driven back to another airfield.

Flown chartered fixed wing to Scotland.

Extracted a heart.

Flown back to London.

Driven to the hospital.

Inserted their second heart.

So it was little surprise that having loaded their chilly-bins of special instruments into the rear of the helicopter, strapped themselves in and wolfed down the sandwiches that the operations department had laid on, they were both curled up on the seats and fast asleep by the time I'd started and lifted from Harefield.

It was a beautiful night flight down to Taunton. Two ambulances had been sensibly positioned with the beams of their headlights crossing at the 'H' where they wanted me to land. It was 10.30pm as our wheels touched down and my two passengers poured themselves a coffee from the thermos as I slowed the engines and rotors. I removed the two chilly-bins from the baggage compartment and began to carry them across the grass to the deserted hospital entrance, at which point the surgeon, who had obviously been here before, said, 'Look, it's pretty quiet here in the evenings. There's a television room with a coffee machine but I'm afraid it's in the sterile area'. I found myself scrubbing up and helping the surgeon on with his gown, just like you see in the movies. I naively tagged along behind him, carrying their bins of instruments, as he strode down the corridor and pushed through a double swing door into the well-lit operating room. I hadn't really been thinking ahead and was a bit surprised to find myself right next to an operating table with the donor laid out and 'prepared'.

'You're very welcome to stay and watch if you like but we could be anything up to four hours.'

I declined the offer (something I've often regretted as one of life's opportunities missed) and excused myself to find the coffee and television room. Apart from the activity in the operating room, the small country hospital was as quiet as the grave, and the irony of that expression was not lost on me at the time. I switched on the TV for the late news and was not altogether surprised to note that the BBC weather forecast was talking of overnight fog. There had been no mention of fog in the pre-flight forecast but the still winds on a summer night had increased the possibility soon after we'd departed from Harefield.

Normally I'd have grabbed a bit of shut-eye at this point but I was acutely aware of the need to get going as soon as the organ removal was complete and I would have been highly embarrassed to have been found asleep by two people who had clearly had a much longer day than me. So I made a couple of phone calls to forecasters I trusted and although there were pockets of fog beginning to appear around the south-west of the country it didn't look like big trouble brewing. I settled in to watch a few hours of dreadful TV programming well past the witching hour. At one point I idly glanced out of the window towards where the helicopter was parked and was horrified to note it had disappeared. A thick blanket had descended on Taunton.

Perhaps surprisingly, fog is not an absolute deterrent to take-off in a suitably equipped helicopter. It takes a bit of nerve but you can ascend vertically, albeit blind, until you pop out of the top and can begin to transition to forward flight. A fog layer, however dense, rarely rises more than a couple of hundred feet above the ground when it forms in the valleys on a still evening. The problem arises on landing, where a helicopter simply doesn't have the sophisticated equipment to permit a fully automated descent into a fog bank. So my attention, and another couple of phone calls, focused on the destination at Harefield rather than the departure from Taunton and the conditions en route.

I let myself back into the operating room and waited quietly until the surgeon noticed I was there. I wanted to ask where his parameters lay since the possibility of not being able to fly him, and of course the organs, back to Harefield had begun to rear its head. I wasn't sure whether that had any bearing on how he now viewed the operation. With his elbows deep inside a chest cavity he reassured me that they would press on towards conclusion regardless, and if I had to throw away the flight they would get a flashing-blue-light escort by road. The longer journey back would reduce the chances of a successful transplant but he kindly recognised that when it comes to weather it is what it is. (I say 'kindly' because I've had many passengers who do not acknowledge this simple fact and think that it's the fault of the pilot.)

About an hour later the operation was complete and we were ready to depart. I made one more quick phone call to ensure that the fog hadn't yet settled in to Harefield and that I had a couple of alternative destinations to aim for if it did. With that done we loaded up.

'Do you mind strapping this chilly-bin into the co-pilot's seat this time?' asked the surgeon.

'Sure I can. Why's that?' I responded.

'Because it contains the organs.' Ah.

With everything running and ready to go I took a deep breath, checked the instruments, reminded myself of what I was going to do in the event of various possible problems and then pulled smoothly up to full power. Taunton hospital just disappeared... one... two... three... and the night sky appeared as we came up out of the fog like a cork out of a bottle. It was as if Taunton had never existed. The sudden change in visual landscape was quite unsettling. I pushed the nose gently forward and we began to accelerate and climb to our cruise altitude. I levelled out at a comfortable 5,000 feet, which feels like space travel in a helicopter, and turned around to check that my passengers were happy. They were both fast asleep again in the faint warm glow from the overhead reading lights.

I settled into my seat for a solo flight. Except that it wasn't really solo for beside me in the co-pilot's seat was a human heart. It had finished its role with one life and was on its way to a role with another, propelled by me. It was an eerie feeling, not a bad one at all, just a little challenging, and it felt somehow momentous. One of those snapshot moments you carry with you for ever after.

As the heart and I continued on our journey towards London, the landscape beneath us became one of the most beautiful night tableaus I have ever seen before or since. If the masters of film illusions had created it, you would think it too unreal. Above us the full moon and insanely bright stars cast silver light downwards. Below us about sixty per cent of the land was crisply seen in the moonlight with hedges and fields clearly visible. But in the valleys the fog stood out in thick patches, again illuminated by the moon. Within most of those patches lay a hamlet, a town or, in the case of Salisbury, an entire city, blanketed, invisible and asleep. Sodium street lights illuminated the fog bank from within, giving the only clue to the life that lay under the blanket. I felt a distinct link between what I was seeing outside the aircraft and the human heart that sat patiently beside me as my co-pilot. It was a seminal moment in my flying career.

We landed safely, the team disembarked and disappeared inside the hospital only an hour or two before the sun was due to rise. As with so many of the rescues I'd performed in the Navy I never did find out the result of the operation, nor where 'my' heart was destined for. I took off back to Fairoaks feeling good but humbled.

17

BREAKING THINGS

AEROPLANE PILOTS REGARD THEIR flying machines as elegant doves that soar effortlessly on a warm breeze and gilded wings. By and large an aeroplane will glide, often some considerable distance, when the engine fails, and there are very few failures catastrophic enough to wrench them from the sky. A helicopter pilot, on the other hand, accepts that his machine is an intricate intermeshing of mechanical components, any number of which can cause heart-stopping moments.

The rotors are no more than thin and flexible wings but they must be constantly propelled in a circle by at least one, often two, and sometimes as many as three engines. It's pretty rare to get a failure of a rotor blade although the slightest change in shape, just a thin layer of ice for example, can dramatically change the way the blade travels through the air, causing violent vibrations through the airframe. Ice is a notorious enemy of the helicopter since it can build up on the blades so insidiously. When flying through cold and damp air it's likely that ice builds up evenly across all the blades and you only become aware of trouble when a small piece breaks away and puts one blade out of balance. We've all experienced ice to some extent and we learn to give it a wide berth and plenty of respect. My own experience was pretty benign. On a routine training flight in the rescue Wessex I descended from an area of relatively cold, dry air into very wet and slightly warmer air. As the warmer air hit the cold airframe it turned instantly to ice and the windscreen became opaque. This wasn't a huge problem in itself since I was able to slow down and lean my head out of the combined door/window, albeit catching icicles on my face. But the fact that ice was forming quickly on the windscreen was a good indication that it was surely doing the same on the blades, so I put out a Pan call and gingerly landed in the nearest field to wait for the airframe to warm up just a degree or two and be able to continue without gaining more ice. It made the local newspaper that week but didn't really qualify as a big problem as it had been such an obvious problem and solution.

Before we go any further, let me put to rest one of the most common misconceptions about a helicopter. When the engine or engines fail it does not fall out of the sky. The Sycamore tree sheds its seeds to the ground, each attached to a single 'rotor blade'. As the seed falls, the rush of air coming up at it spins the rotor blade and it floats gently towards the earth. So it is with a helicopter. Normally the engines are using brute force to turn the rotor blades, which in turn generates lift. But sometimes the engines stop providing the service, when the fuel runs out or through some kind of mechanical failure. When that happens the pilot encourages the helicopter to descend and it becomes a huge Sycamore seed. The air rushes upwards as the helicopter drops and the blades keep turning as a result. When the ground is getting close there is enough momentum in the blades for the pilot to convert it to lift and use it to safely alight on the surface.

The catch is that you only get one go at it before all the momentum is exhausted from the blades, so it's a good idea to time it right. It's not good to make your 'landing' 20 feet above the ground because the blades then have no energy left in them and you know the last 19 feet will be spent in a plummet. Every six months or so all helicopter pilots go flying with an instructor and practise the technique of 'autorotation', or 'autos', until an engine failure is no longer a thing to fear.

I've had three engine failures in my flying career so far. Two of these were in single-engined helicopters, but with the first there was no time for an auto. It was three years after I'd left the Navy. I had been working in the London area and popped into the old Brooklands motor-racing track at Weybridge, which served as the base for Air Hanson, probably the most prominent helicopter operator in the UK at the time. This visit was partly to see a few old mates for a coffee and partly to collect some fuel for my return trip to Cornwall, a trip of only a couple of hours. While I took a look at the weather details en route, one of the ever enthusiastic and efficient Air Hanson ground crew fuelled my Longranger helicopter. All start-up checks completed, I lifted into a hover of around 10 feet and air-taxied away from the fuel pumps. As I did so I was glancing at the instrument panel to check that all were in good shape before accelerating and climbing away to the west. But one instrument, designed to indicate the internal running temperature of the small jet engine, didn't seem to be in good shape at all. Instead of showing something around 700°C TOT (Turbine Outlet Temperature), it was suggesting that it was operating at around half that figure. This would be impossible, since there wouldn't be enough power coming out of the engine to continue to drive the rotors at full speed, and therefore was probably why the 10 feet between me and the ground had diminished to half that height and why the helicopter's next move was to very politely and gently settle on to the tarmac.

Just as I was thinking that that was a very strange thing, the engine stopped completely. It transpired that the chap who'd refuelled me had diligently carried out all the usual checks that morning, including draining some fuel into a glass jar from the bottom of the airfield storage tank and checking that it was clear. This was to ensure that no water was present in the fuel. It certainly had been clear but he'd missed doing the additional chemical check that would have told him it was clear because it was *all* water. The ground crewman was mortified to discover that about forty gallons of the stuff had found its way into the tank overnight and most of it had been transferred to my Longranger. So, on reflection, my poor helicopter had done rather well to get us airborne at all. It would be another 24 hours before the engineers could be confident that they'd flushed every drop of water out of the system and I could continue on my way. Every time I returned to Brooklands thereafter I always asked for the same guy to refuel me. I knew that at the sight of me approaching he would always double-check every last potential for a slip-up and, after all, no harm had been done.

My other engine failure in a single-engined helicopter was a less gentle affair but was also in a civilian helicopter, about ten years later, in a slightly smaller Jetranger. We had spent about six months stripping down and rebuilding a low-time (the air equivalent of low mileage) import from the USA. We'd christened her with the registration G-HELE and she gleamed like new in every detail. (All British flying machines start with a G, followed by four letters. You can have any combination of letters provided it's never been used before and isn't offensive. The only time I've heard of an application being rejected was when Prince William of Gloucester wanted a registration that went with his initials.) G-HELI had been taken many years earlier, so G-HELE it was.

Mick Wright was an engineer from Air Hanson I'd taken on as chief engineer at Castle Air. When I'd left to start another company,

Helifilms, he stayed with me and we've been together ever since. When Mick gives up engineering, I'm giving up flying. He is the most diligent engineer you could ever come across but with an entirely balanced and pragmatic judgement on whether a given sign of trouble is safe or not to go flying with. He's been watching my six o'clock for nearly thirty years now and as we've grown older together we've hopefully both grown a little wiser.

The day in question was the very first day we'd used G-HELE commercially since the rebuild, and I was airborne over a power station at Didcot in Oxfordshire, filming the extent of the huge cooling towers and other assets there on behalf of an advertising agency. Thankfully only the cameraman and myself were on location for the very simple shoot when I decided it might look nice if we flew straight across the top of the only brick chimney that didn't have smoke or steam billowing from it. The shot did indeed look great as we flew low across the lip of the giant and cavernous chimney, but just before we reached the other lip there was a very loud pop and the engine simply shut itself down. There was just enough forward momentum for me to convert speed into height and we hopped over the outer lip with only a few feet to spare.

G-HELE, despite no longer having an engine to run the rotors, responded beautifully to my request for autorotation and everything was going well. But of course a power station is completely surrounded by power lines, many of which criss-crossed the short 300-foot gap between me and the ground. Over one set, under another, over a third and within less than ten seconds I was pulling up the collective lever to cushion our landing on the grass. As the rotors ran down the cameraman and I looked at each other in astonishment that a) we'd survived the wires and b) that the engine had failed at all. Opening the doors we looked back towards 'our' cooling tower and could clearly see from our new position on the ground that there may not have been visible smoke or steam emanating from it but something was

making the air shimmer. Whatever that something was, it obviously didn't have enough oxygen in it to feed a hungry jet engine, and I knew the 'pop' I'd heard was entirely in keeping with a compressor stall, exactly what you get if you starve an engine of oxygen.

Feeling chastened and hugely embarrassed at my own stupidity, I restarted the engine, checked it out for a few minutes on the ground and then gingerly tried a hover. As suspected, the engine was running beautifully, and we were able to finish the task and return Mick's pride and joy to him without a scratch. Only my pride was dented.

In the thirty years I've just mentioned there has only been one occasion on which Mick has made the slightest error. Thankfully it was funny enough to report here, and in due course Mick will forgive me for doing so. Another filming task in G-HELE had taken us to London Docklands. That morning Mick had completed some work on the hydraulic system at our base, while being pressurised by me to be ready in time for the allotted task. Almost all helicopters no longer have direct mechanical linkages from pilot to rotors; the control is effected via a series of hydraulic jacks that take the physical load away from the pilot and turn what would otherwise be a strenuous exercise into a light and precise form of flying controls. In broad terms these consist of a collective lever in your left hand that lifts the helicopter up and down, a cyclic control in your right hand that tips the rotors in the direction you want to travel, and two yaw pedals that control which way the nose of the helicopter is pointing. A failure of the hydraulic system is another thing we practise by simply switching it off, at which point all the controls become extremely heavy. This sort of failure would normally be caused by a leak from the hydraulic fluid system, but there's a good amount of fluid in reserve and you have to lose enormous amounts of it to affect the control system.

I met the film director in the Docklands at the appointed hour, strapped him securely into the rear cabin of G-HELE and began work with the cameraman, who was sitting beside me in the front cockpit. We stuck to the line of the River Thames, as all single-engined helicopters are required to do. In this way they can be sure of having somewhere to go in the event of an emergency without fear of injuring third parties on the ground in the busy city. The shot the director requested was a simple forward-looking progression along the Thames that said 'This is London', a shot we had done many times before (and since). The director had a TV monitor in the back and declared himself happy with our work after only the second run along the river. It was only a short five-minute trip back to the east where we would drop the director in the Docklands and continue home to our base. But as I made all the usual radio calls and turned over Albert Bridge to return to the Docklands I had the distinct impression that the controls were becoming heavier.

After a few tentative experiments I confirmed that the hydraulic system was indeed failing. I put out a Pan call. Our Docklands landing site (long before they built London City Airport there) was still the closest point to land and I started to make my way gingerly there. The controls were becoming heavier by the minute but regular practice meant it wasn't something to be feared, it would just make the final touchdown – always a bit tricky in a helicopter – much harder to achieve gently. But gentle it was and once on the ground I slowed the engine to the idle setting to allow the usual two-minute cool-down period before stopping the engine and rotors completely. This gave me a moment to turn around in my seat to apologise to the director for frightening him.

'Oh my God!' I exclaimed. The poor chap patiently sat there with his hair slicked down over his face by gallons of hot red sticky hydraulic fluid that was then dripping off his chin into a large puddle in which his feet and ruined shoes were resting.

'I am *so* sorry,' I stuttered. 'How long has it been doing *that*?'

'Oh, pretty much since we took off,' he politely responded.

'But why didn't you say something?'

'I thought it must always be like this in the back of a helicopter.'

I couldn't think of a suitable response to that one.

It only took a quick glance to see that I'd pressurised Mick just a little too hard to finish the work on time and that the final tightening of one of the hydraulic pipe connections had been missed. As I said, we're a bit older and a bit wiser now.

The only mechanical failure I suffered in a naval aircraft happened over Malta. We were on a tour of the Mediterranean in HMS *Hermes* and I was flying as co-pilot to Bob Barton, one of those pilots who is not only a great aviator but backs it up with detailed technical knowledge. He later went on to become the harbour master in Guernsey, which I thought was a loss to aviation.

Hermes was tied up alongside the wharf in Valletta harbour and most of the squadron were ashore getting some R&R, but we'd been assigned to a test flight before we could join them in the sunshine. There were few facilities on board for opening up a helicopter engine in the event of a problem so the standard procedure was to change the entire engine and let the workshops back in the UK solve the problem. The test flight following an engine change generally took about an hour and a half and, to me, was a remarkably boring exercise involving flying the helicopter through various flight parameters and carefully noting down the temperatures, pressures and power readings. We were accompanied by the squadron engineering officer who was standing behind the pilots' seats when the brand new engine blew up.

The engines on a Sea King, as with most helicopters other than the Wessex, are just above and behind the pilot's head. A tiny metal fracture had caused a small turbine blade, no bigger than a thumbnail, to depart the engine. Since a turbine (or jet) is rotating at about 96,000 rpm, you can imagine that a departing blade is travelling at something not far below supersonic and certainly behaves like a bullet. As we later discovered it had exited straight down and only narrowly avoided drilling down through the top of the engineer's head by virtue of hitting a solid control box about the size of two cigarette packets and bouncing back up.

The noise alone was enough to cause Bob to shut down the engine but the instruments were already showing that this engine had no interest in continuing its participation in this flight. Of course, we didn't know the cause of the problem at that moment, but the air traffic controller at Luqa, the international airport, did call us to ask if we knew we had smoke and flames trailing behind us into the clear blue sky over Malta. We declared an emergency and headed to the airport while I pulled the big red handle that would inject fire retardant into the engine bay. If a fire stays confined to within the engine then there's not too much of a problem, but once it spreads towards the second engine and various other essential items it does get more interesting. The fire extinguisher evidently did its job as the control tower could no longer see flames, only smoke, trailing out behind us.

A nice long runway is a good idea when only running on one engine. In some circumstances you can come to a hover on one engine if the helicopter is very light but there's no point in putting more strain on the good engine than absolutely necessary and a helicopter flying forwards uses considerably less power than one in the hover. The runway was a huge expanse of concrete, the fire trucks had all lined up to meet us and Bob knew exactly what he was doing so, apart from calling out a few power parameters in order that he could continue to concentrate on the flying task, I had time to enjoy the drama of the moment. Bob landed the helicopter beautifully and having successfully restrained the Maltese fire fighters from covering us in foam we were able to abandon the Sea King to the care of the engineering officer and hurry off to regale our compatriots in the bar with increasingly lurid details of how we'd battled the forces of darkness and come out on top.

The worst card a helicopter ever dealt me was a tail rotor failure, which neatly and directly joined together the experience learned in the Navy with survival in civilian flying. The job of the tail rotor is to stop the aircraft from spinning on its own axis. Any sort of problem involving the tail rotor sends a shiver down the spine of every helicopter pilot. You can't practise it in the real world so the best you can do is to talk about it a lot, listen carefully to anybody who has suffered the problem, and read all the post-accident reports you can lay your hands on.

When two powerful engines and a gearbox are constantly working to push heavy rotor blades through the air, the blades are resisting and trying to turn the helicopter in the opposite direction. This is known as torque and is why the tail rotor is more correctly referred to as the 'anti-torque' rotor. Without one, the main rotor blades would still turn but the body of the helicopter would end up spinning the other way. The results of failure of the tail rotor while a helicopter is in a high hover will almost always be fatal unless the pilot has the presence of mind to shut down the engines within one or two seconds. If it happens to you in forward flight, however, you're in with a chance as the big shark's fin at the back of the tail helps to work against the air and keep you from spinning. It won't keep the nose of the aircraft pointing in the way you're travelling but it will stop it from beginning the spin. The catch is that once you slow down your forward speed (in order to land), the air over the tail reduces, it becomes less effective and eventually the spin begins.

So, if the tail rotor itself breaks up, or if the long and slender driveshaft that powers it should break, there are only two options. You can immediately shut down your engines and give yourself about twenty seconds to learn to fly a new sort of flying machine before it meets the earth, or you can buy yourself some thinking time by keeping up your forward speed and letting the big tail fin compensate. But eventually you're going to have to make a landing, by which time you'd better have a good plan in place.

I'd only once met a crew who'd experienced the problem. While still flying Sea Kings on anti-submarine work the squadron had been flying from HMS *Hermes* to the south of Portland. The crew in question had suffered a fracture in the tail rotor driveshaft and had gone for the option of continuing to fly forward. The Sea King had wheels so you could make your fast approach to a runway until eventually, just before touch down, you had to stop the engines to allow the nose of the helicopter to point along the runway just at the moment the wheels touched the ground. If you didn't do that then you'd hit the runway going fast and partially sideways. This would result in rolling the helicopter at high speed, a manoeuvre unlikely to be survivable.

When we eventually met up again with the crew in the bar that evening we crowded around them asking question after question. What was the first indication? What did it feel like? How far round did the nose come when the failure happened? How slowly could you go before feeling she would spin? How low were you when you cut the engines? Would you do the same again next time? And so on and so on. All this information contributed to saving my life over a decade later.

I was flying our Agusta 109, a beautiful sleek Ferrari of a helicopter that could carry seven passengers faster than most others. I loved flying the 109, not least because it – unusually – had a very comfortable pilot's seat. You could spend eight hours flying and still get out of the cockpit unaided and without the need for an immediate visit to a chiropractor. I had been working for about eight weeks on a documentary called *Landshapes* about the geology of the British Isles. It was an innovative programme in so far as being almost continuously shot from the air. For most of the shoot I'd used a single-engined Jetranger. It was lighter, cheaper to

operate and better for low-level filming work, but the last part of the documentary related the story of the mountains on the Isle of Skye. The need to travel over the sea and the need to work in the high mountains dictated that the two engines in a 109 would be the sensible choice.

After a full day of filming I was on my way back down to southern England. If we hurried we could just about make it back before darkness, not essential but a good idea when we were all pretty tired and the weather was unpredictable. The cameraman, Chris Cox, was fast asleep in the rear cabin surrounded by the tools of his trade. He'd spent most of the day hanging out of the open door operating a Tyler mount, a wonderful contraption of heavy metal that we used to help stabilise the camera before the days of the sophisticated gyro-stabilised Cineflex mounts that we use now. It was a physical and tiring job for him at the best of times but he'd additionally been out in the freezing cold airstream and rotor downwash for a lot of the day so he was curled up in his ski suit and sleeping the sleep of the just. The producer/director was Tim Fell who had devised the documentary series and had put full trust in me to organise all the logistics and permissions we needed to achieve the shoot. Thank heaven he had chosen to fly back sitting next to me in the co-pilot's seat, as I was shortly going to need his help.

We were at about 5,000 feet over the bleak Pennine Hills of Yorkshire when there was an almighty bang and the nose of the helicopter slewed around to the right by about 30 or 40 degrees. I instantly knew in my heart what the problem was and the first question was: 'Are we still capable of flying?' It was uncomfortable, it was scary, and it was an unnatural way to be flying, but she seemed to be coping. We were rolled over on one side to the extent that I was looking down at Tim on my left but things weren't getting any worse than they had been in that first violent manoeuvre at the moment the tail rotor driveshaft had sheared.

Two quite extraordinary things happened, both of which will live with me for ever. They used to say about Ayrton Senna, the great racing driver, that his brain worked much faster than the rest of us. Most other drivers returned to the pits and simply reported that the car had behaved well through a particular corner, but Ayrton was renowned for being able to give a step-by-step description in great detail of how the tyres, the suspension and the aerodynamics had worked through each section of the corner. When you consider the speeds he was doing and that it only took a second or two to negotiate a corner you can begin to understand the amount of information his brain was assimilating, then processing and committing to memory. When my driveshaft sheared I experienced the same phenomenon. If you'd asked me only seconds earlier to relate everything I knew about tail rotors I would have stumbled and stuttered and mumbled a few disconnected facts, but at the instant of failure my brain speeded up to a flash of lightning that I have never experienced before or since. I very meticulously remembered everything I'd ever read, heard or talked about relating to tail rotors. I instantly recalled every nuance of that bar conversation with my Navy pals over a decade earlier. I discarded any information that was peripheral or inappropriate to my own circumstances, then sorted the remaining items into priority order and made a plan. It's hard to know exactly how long that took but in discussing it among ourselves some time later I reckon it took something under two seconds. As Tim put it, 'I couldn't believe how instinctively you knew what to do and began to do it.'

No, Tim, nor could I.

The second extraordinary phenomenon was how long it took me to shake the belief that I'd caused the problem. There were few ways that I could have done. About the only thing I could think of was if I'd left one of the cowlings unlatched during my pre-flight inspection and it had blown off and taken the tail rotor with it. This thought kept

coming back to the forefront of my mind, accompanied by a very real fear of peer ridicule at the subsequent enquiry. This far outweighed any fear of injury or death and I had to take a firm decision to put it out of my mind as whatever had caused the thing didn't now matter and I had to use all available brain power to deal with the consequences and aftermath. (Eventually I would learn that it was a pure metallurgical fracture that had been latent since manufacture, so my fears were unfounded.)

Having established that we were still airborne and capable of remaining that way, my next move was to put out a Mayday call and declare my intention to make my way towards Teesside airport. Not only was this the nearest civilian airfield with a tarmac runway but it was well equipped with fire and emergency services in the event that I turned this flying machine into a small bonfire. But it was still a good twenty minutes' flying away so I had good time available to put the rest of the plan in place. Chris was, of course, now wide awake and I asked him to spend the time ensuring that everything in the rear cabin – cameras, camera mount and any other loose articles, however small – was very firmly strapped down. The last thing we wanted at the critical moment was to have a lot of loose metal flying around our ears. Next I asked the air traffic controller to put in a phone call to base and advise Mick, my engineering partner, of the predicament I was in. I've no idea why I did this other than some half-formed thought that he would soon have to drive up to Teesside, whatever the outcome. He still raises his eyes to the heavens when reminded that I put him through the next twenty terrifying minutes, despite there being nothing whatsoever he could do about it to help me from 250 miles away.

I received two offers of help, first from a big Sikorsky 76 helicopter that was inbound to his base on the Yorkshire coast from an oil rig out in the North Sea. I gladly accepted his offer to fly towards me and he appeared about halfway through the journey to Teesside. There's no way you can see your own tail from the cockpit and I was keen to learn what it looked like back there as it would, to a certain extent, dictate what I could expect to experience in the latter stages of the approach to the runway. If I'd left a cowling open and the tail rotor had been ripped away entirely, which I still believed was a possibility, then the effect could be marginally different to that if the driveshaft had simply sheared and left the static tail rotor assembly attached. But most importantly I was anxious to learn whether there had been any damage to the big fin. If that too was about to fail then I would need to be ready for an instantaneous engine shutdown and autorotation to earth. Thankfully everything looked intact to the Sikorsky pilot as he manoeuvred around the rear of my helicopter in close formation and took a good squint at all the detail. He kindly offered to stay with me until the end and I was frankly glad of his moral support. There was nothing he could do to help and he didn't bother me with any unnecessary radio calls, but I was very glad he was there.

The second offer of help came from Tim Fell sitting next to me.

At first glance this was a somewhat ludicrous offer made out of a feeling of helplessness at a time when I was clearly well loaded up with tasks. However, I took the opportunity to brief both Tim and Chris quite thoroughly on the sequence of events they could expect from here on. I didn't pull any punches about the scale of the problem but I did avoid mentioning that my accelerated sifting of available knowledge had reminded me that the last 109 crew to suffer the same problem, in Germany earlier that year, had rolled the helicopter down the runway at high speed and had all perished.

As I was working my way through describing the critical actions I'd be taking during the final approach I realised that I was going to run out of hands at exactly the wrong moment. The engine throttles, and shutdown valves, were positioned in the overhead panel just above my left ear, but at the very instant I was going to be needing to shut down the engines I would be only 10 feet above the runway and would need my left hand on the collective lever to time the moment of 'kissing' the tarmac precisely. I therefore spent the next few minutes briefing Tim on how to operate the throttles and shut down the engines. He listened intently and we ran through it a second time to confirm the commands I would give and when he could expect them. So his offer of help was not in vain after all.

The last part of the journey down from the hills towards the airport were used to experiment with the flight envelope of this new and strange flying machine without a tail rotor. I had to plant my feet firmly and consciously on the floor to avoid automatically trying to use the now useless yaw pedals. I needed to select the speed at which I would make my final approach. Too fast and the potential for drama increased, too slow and we ran the risk of beginning to spin or at least the risk of flying so unnaturally sideways that a survivable landing would be extremely difficult to achieve. I eventually settled on around 60 knots.

By this time the light was beginning to fade and we could easily see the terminal lights of the airport in the middle distance. We were not yet lined up with the runway so the view of the airport was not yet dominated by the runway lights. Instead our eyes were inevitably drawn to the blue flashing lights of a good dozen emergency vehicles lined up beside the runway threshold, ready to follow us down the runway and deal with the aftermath. I had talked with the air traffic controller about the option for laying a foam runway, a procedure used when fire is highly likely to break out, such as when an airliner is landing with its wheels up. We'd decided between us to dispense with that option since it had the potential to introduce new problems if the runway was wet and there was foam flying around in the turbulence from the rotors.

As the runway lights began to line up in the gathering gloom I eased the nose around to the left on to my final approach. The speed was nicely holding to the allocated 60 knots, we were fully briefed and all knew what we were about to do. I made the standard 'finals' call on the radio, perhaps a little superfluous as all other traffic had been cleared away from the airport and all airport eyes were already looking in our direction. The Sikorsky pilot peeled away from the station he'd been holding alongside me and simply called 'Good luck' on the radio.

I felt suddenly very alone, as if I were drowning and somebody had just let go of my hand.

It didn't happen quickly, it happened slowly. The runway lights gradually grew bigger in the windscreen and I had too much time to wonder if there was anything I'd forgotten, if there was something I should be doing differently. And then we were over the threshold, the blue flashing lights had passed behind our left-hand window and there was only the ground left to meet.

I didn't try to arrest the shallow descent I'd initiated. I didn't want to change any of the characteristics that had served well up to that point. I'd briefed that we would chop the engines at 10 feet above the runway but as we passed through 10 feet something held me back until half that height. Our nose was still a good 30 degrees off runway heading but I left it until about 5 feet before calling, 'SHUTDOWN.' Tim neatly, quietly and efficiently brought both engine controls back to idle, released the gate that was designed to prevent inadvertent engine shutdown, and pulled the levers fully aft. As the engines disconnected their drive to the rotors the nose of the helicopter swung violently and rapidly to the left. I was glad I'd left it until later as there was only just enough time to descend through the last 5 feet and get the wheels on to the ground before the nose would otherwise have swung past the runway heading and we would have been lost.

The wheels touched firmly but not heavily and every nerve ending in my body was straining to feel the slightest nuance of what the aircraft was doing. In horror I could feel the right wheel come up into

the air again as the other two wheels struggled against the spinning momentum and screeched against the tarmac. The rotors were still turning but would not have much effect as they slowed; never the less I held the cyclic control over to full right and just held my breath. As the speed fell below 50 knots the right wheel decided it would rejoin the tarmac after all and we were finally down. I gently applied the foot brakes, she slowed to a stop and I applied the rotor brake to induce silence in everything. In unison the three of us exhaled very slowly and very deeply.

As the big airfield fire trucks arrived alongside us, together with an ambulance and some extra fire appliances that had been called in from the city fire brigade, we firmly shook hands with each other and looked one another in the eye and nodded. There wasn't really anything to be said for the moment – that would come later in the bar as we talked and talked into the night (and into a bottle of scotch) to exorcise the demons. We just opened the doors and took a deep lungful of Yorkshire seaside air. It was an immense surprise that I couldn't make it all the way from the cockpit door to the rear of the helicopter to take a look at the tail. I wasn't shaking and my legs didn't give way or anything so dramatic, I just needed desperately to sit for a moment on the tarmac. I looked up at the chief fireman and said, 'Look, I know we're in the middle of an airport runway and everything, but I'm going to light up a cigarette, OK?'

'You go right ahead, mate,' he kindly responded.

18

EMMA

WHEN FLYING RESCUE WORK professionally it's possible and necessary to remain detached from the human drama unfolding beneath the aircraft. People are injured, people die, people are saved and the overriding concern is whether we exercised full professionalism throughout the operation. Occasionally you might react passionately to an event, such as when the young boys were lost in the aircraft ditching on the day that our divers had been withdrawn. If any technique could be improved, even slightly, then it might save just one more life in the years that followed and so we were hard on ourselves and hard on our team mates if we ever felt there was room for improvement. But in terms of the people we lifted we only recorded their names for the sake of the paperwork and our lives only touched theirs for just a few minutes, albeit probably their most significant few minutes ever. It was therefore more than ironic, and perhaps a closing of the circle, that the last

time I ever took part in a Search and Rescue operation was the first time I ever had a pre-existing relationship with the victim.

When we started Castle Air we were happy to employ our helicopters on just about any revenue-earning task and in the course of first looking for work we were introduced to the warden and manager of Lundy Island, a rocky outcrop and the largest island in the Bristol Channel. Lundy was and still is a rather eccentric British institution with a chequered past. It lies just twelve miles off the Devon coast, measures three miles by three-quarters of a mile and gives its name to one of the British sea areas used in the shipping forecast. In fact, it's the sea area that adjoins Fastnet.

The name Lundy is said to mean Puffin Island in old Norse; highly appropriate in view of the number of birds of the same name who used to alight and breed there and which are just beginning to make a comeback. Inscriptions on stones in the island's cemetery date back to the 5th century AD. Island history includes lurid tales of piracy, disputed ownership and dramatic shipwrecks throughout the centuries. In 1969 the island was put up for sale and caused apoplexy among traditionalists when it was rumoured that it might become an offshore tax and gambling haven. In the end a British millionaire named Jack Hayward bought the island and gave it to the National Trust in the interests of the nation. But the catch is that the National Trust are unable to take on projects that are not financially self-supporting so it was duly leased to the Landmark Trust.

The Landmark Trust set about making the island a fully functioning and self-supporting tourist destination and soon succeeded in this tremendous task by virtue of good management and the sensitive restoration of the eleven properties on the island, all of which can be stayed in as holiday rents. During the summer months the island's own ship carries visitors from the ports of Bideford and Ilfracombe, but the problem in the winter months was that the high seas usually precluded landings at a time when birdwatching enthusiasts and those seeking an isolated break still wanted to visit. Our first major commission at Castle Air was to ferry visitors back and forth to the island from the nearest point of land at Hartland Point. We set up a little helipad on top of the windswept clifftop and positioned an old caravan there to sleep in on a Saturday night.

The Landmark Trust is a private trust set up by Sir John and Lady Smith, a remarkable couple with great vision who found a way to buy and restore buildings or locations with historical or architectural merit and then offer them for holiday rental. Founded in 1965, the trust has around 190 properties. Sir John, now deceased, came from a banking dynasty and was a director of, among other things, Coutts private bank for over forty years. He also numbered many other accomplishments such as being a director of Rolls Royce, a Member of Parliament and the Lord-Lieutenant of Berkshire. But he was one of my personal heroes as a result of having been an observer in the Royal Navy, flying in Swordfish, Barracudas and Avengers. His was one of three aircraft that attacked the German battleship *Tirpitz* in 1944.

Soon after we started the shuttle flights to Lundy I was pleased to meet Sir John's son Barty, who was also an aviation enthusiast and a very good helicopter pilot himself. We went on to become firm friends over the years, sharing a love of helicopters and motor racing. (Barty was also to become something of a patron to me in subsequent aviation projects and for many years we shared a helicopter between us. He provided the capital and I provided the ongoing operational costs until my emigration to Australia in 2002.)

At the time in question Barty had been tasked with overseeing the growth of Lundy Island as a destination and took an enormous personal interest in every detail. The Smith family had five children but it was Barty and his youngest sister Emma who particularly felt a deep personal connection with the island and would often fly over with us. On occasions they would remain for a few days longer than

expected and we would be asked to come and pick them up when they were ready to return.

So it was that on Wednesday 9 November in 1983 I rang Barty at 9.30am to ask if he and Emma still wanted picking up and bringing back to the mainland that morning. His response that they had 'lost' Emma sent a shiver down my spine. Emma had set out for a walk around the island the previous evening but by 6pm had failed to return. Being dark by then the level of concern rapidly rose and the RAF were asked to begin a search for her using their well-equipped yellow Sea King out of the nearby base at Chivenor. All the islanders had set out to search in lines, calling out to Emma. By the time I rang Barty on the Wednesday morning the RAF had also been airborne all night and failed to find her. I told Barty I would be there right away and alerted Roy Flood, who I knew would be equally concerned and would want to come.

Roy and I set off in great trepidation knowing that the fact that the RAF had failed to locate Emma during an all-night operation meant that this situation was unlikely to have a happy outcome. From our base to the island was a flight of about 30 minutes. I took the time to brief Roy on how we would set about the search, how we would divide up the cockpit responsibilities and what we would do in any number of possible outcomes. Roy visibly paled and it was the only time in ten years of working together that I ever saw him in any way unsure of himself.

We landed at our usual spot, next to the windswept church on the highest point of the island, and Barty immediately climbed into the rear of the Jetranger. We were using G-SPEY, a really beautiful helicopter in dark green with two gold stripes. It had been originally owned by the proprietor of the Spey whiskey distillery in Scotland and he had stylishly fitted it out to match his Rolls Royce. The seats were thus in beautiful soft tan leather and it actually featured a small drinks cabinet. This was all a far cry from the helicopters I had been used to using on SAR work and, of course, there was no rescue winch fitted, but the real issue was that all the fancy interior rendered it a very heavy machine for any hovering work close to the cliffs.

We took a two-minute brief from Barty in which we learned that the RAF crew had been airborne again at first light but were currently breakfasting at their base while their Sea King was refuelled. Barty described Emma's intentions and the likely route that she would have taken on her walk. We knew that the powerful lights of the Sea King had covered all the surface area of the island quite thoroughly through the night and so I decided to begin our own search by covering the rocky 300-foot cliffs that surrounded the island. I took a moment to brief Roy and Barty on how a casualty always looks much smaller than your eyes expect it to appear.

These cliffs were almost sheer at every point around the island. A good deal of turbulence was created as the westerly winds encountered the enormous rock walls for the first time since departing the eastern shores of America, over 3,000 miles away. But this day was almost unique in being perfectly still. I climbed up from the island and then curved to the right and down to descend below island height and begin our search of the cliffs.

Within what seemed like only seconds but was certainly less than five minutes, suddenly there was Emma. She was sitting very peacefully, just above sea level, with her back to the cliffs looking out across the ocean, or so it seemed at first. As I circled around in order to be able to hover closer there was no sign of a response from Emma, no wave to us, nor even a sign of movement. I banished terrible thoughts of how she might have got there and concentrated on putting the helicopter into a position whereby either Barty and/or Roy could exit the helicopter and go to Emma on foot. There was really only one place where I had any chance of doing this and that would involve employing the technique I had practised for so many years on the Camel's Head. I would have to continue to hover but place the corner of one of the skids in a position where it was touching a small rock just above the water. If I took it gently I figured Roy would just about be able to climb out of the front seat, stand on the skid and then transfer his weight to the rock. I say 'transfer his weight' rather than 'jump' because the weight of a person leaving a helicopter as small as a Jetranger has an immediate and quite dramatic effect on the way it flies. I would have to correct for that change and I wanted it to be as smooth as possible so that the helicopter didn't lurch.

I was also aware that we were all deeply shocked by what we had seen and what we were potentially about to encounter, so I took a little longer than usual to brief both of the guys on what was about to happen and in what order. Neither Roy nor Barty had spent any military time and so the civilian tendency to rush at the prime objective without full consideration of all the peripheral issues had to be gently curtailed. Once I was certain that Roy knew exactly what to do and I was confident that Barty wasn't going to try and leave the aircraft at the same time I began my approach to the tiny rock.

The helicopter performed smoothly and I was once again thankful for the strange stillness in the island air. In the latter stages of the approach I would lose sight of the target rock completely but had absolute faith in Roy's ability to perform like a professional crewman and talk me into the spot with a continuous patter of commentary. (Only the year before we had flown to Annecy in France for the European helicopter championships and had won the civilian class by virtue of our team precision work.) G-SPEY moved cautiously towards a position just above the touch-down point. To describe the next move as a descent would be an exaggeration. When moving a helicopter around in the hover with tight precision any control input is more of a thought than a movement. It's almost a Zen thing that you will the machine to a new position and the tiniest of muscle movements in the pilot's fingers make it happen. In his early flying days a pilot will execute an actual movement, the aircraft will move too quickly, he will over-respond and suddenly both pilot and flying machine are in all sorts of problems.

I felt the left skid kiss the top of the rock and could begin to use it as a pivot point about which I could control the hover. Roy waited until I gave him the positive confirmation that he could begin to extricate himself and he then very gingerly began the process. The Jetranger does not have a sliding door like the big old Wessex, it has a small and very lightweight door that hinges at the front like one on a car.

Roy's weight transfer on to the skid went smoothly and, as briefed, he carefully closed and latched the door before making the next move. As he stepped on to the rock I had to simultaneously reduce the power, once again just a thought, in order that the helicopter didn't try to jump into the air from the sudden lightness it would feel. Roy then felt his way along the side of the half-flying helicopter until he could help Barty down from the rear cabin on to a more treacherous few inches of rock. In order not to increase the gale-force wind that a helicopter generates, I remained in the same spot until Roy and Barty were well clear of the airframe and had crouched down and given me the thumbs-up. Lifting up and away from his position was then a straightforward movement.

I hovered 50 metres out to sea and watched Barty's slow and tortuous progress from the drop-off point to where Emma was sitting. Roy followed at a respectful distance. I was willing Barty on and willing him to give me a thumbs-up when he reached her position, but it was not to be. As we would later confirm, poor Emma had gone just one step too close to the cliff edge, which had crumbled away beneath her feet and sent her on the 300-foot slide to the bottom.

The next half hour exists only in snapshots in my memory. I could no longer have the luxury of remaining detached from events. I remember climbing to 1,000 feet to call out the RAF and to brief them on the circumstances. At some point Roy got back into the Jetranger, respectfully leaving Barty to spend time with Emma before the Sea King came over the horizon. I remember being irritated at how long it took them to arrive. Despite knowing that they would be moving as fast as possible I was painfully aware of how every extra second that Barty had to stay with Emma would remain with him for the rest of his life.

I got angry when the Sea King made a huge meal of getting itself into position to recover the body. All the old prejudices of Navy versus RAF came bubbling to the surface as they flew a dummy approach, then dropped a smoke pot into the water to judge the wind, then dropped another just to be sure. My anger was undoubtedly unfair and I knew they had their own procedures to follow, but it wasn't the way I would have done it and I was suffering serious levels of frustration at not having a Wessex strapped to my back.

It still astonishes me today that I can remember just about every detail of the other 115 SAR incidents I was involved in but that whole chunks of Emma's day have disappeared. It used to be dull to always finish a flight by meticulously writing down the details in the pilot's flying logbook but I've latterly learned to be grateful for those details. It's therefore only my log that confirms that by 12.30 I was on my way back to our fuel supply at Hartland Point and from there on to Berkshire. Roy shared the front cockpit and Barty sat quietly in the back. Some of the aviation details served to distract us (all three of us being pilots) from the hard task ahead of Barty.

I do very clearly remember landing on the lawn at Shottesbrooke House to collect Sir John (Lady Smith happened already to be in Devon on business and was to meet us at the hospital). Sir John's dignity in distress was extraordinary. His prime concern was for me and for Roy and his thanks for our efforts were overwhelming. I could only guess at the terrible inner grief he was suffering. We flew back to Barnstaple, a flight lasting an interminable hour and a quarter. As we landed on the lawn of the hospital, Barty and his father thanked us once again and I remember a very new feeling of being connected with the events that were *about* to happen in the hospital, as opposed to the usual feeling of having completed my part of the task and having the luxury of leaving it all behind. The following day G-SPEY and I were back at the hospital in order to take the family across to Lundy Island where they would spend some quiet time together at the spot of Emma's accident.

Emma was buried in the family chapel at Shottesbrooke House in a ceremony attended by literally hundreds of people, as is so often the case with those who die young. It wasn't the first time I'd been to a funeral but it was certainly the first time I'd been to the funeral of somebody with whose demise I had been intimately associated in the helicopter role. It gave me pause to think.

Some weeks later the Smith family presented us with the most beautiful gift, a solid silver hand-crafted model of G-SPEY. It took pride of place on the cabinet in Roy's office, became a symbol of times shared and a constant reminder of Emma and the day she took just one step too far.

19

FILM PILOT

IT'S SAID THAT AN EX-MILITARY MAN has spent the first part of his life feeling like a civilian in uniform and goes on to feel for the rest of his life that he's a military man in civvies. So it has proved to be the case for me. Not so long ago it was a requirement that all young men should serve three years in the military, as is still the case in some countries today. There are arguments both for and against that system and there is no doubt that anyone's opinion on the subject will be heavily coloured by their own experience. I count myself very lucky to have never gone to war. My time in uniform was spent learning the ropes, learning to fly and then putting those skills to work in a role that felt worthwhile in the saving, rather than the taking, of lives. I'm sure that if I'd been to the Falklands, Iraq, Afghanistan, or any one of the other conflicts around the world in the last thirty years I'd feel very differently about it all, but the fact remains that I had a wonderful eight years serving before the mast and wouldn't change any of it. It gave me a trade that I still practise

today, instilled confidence in a spotty teenager, taught me strength in the face of adversity and gave me the ability to work through a problem, however frightening, with logic and methodology until a successful conclusion can been reached. In short, it was the making of the man.

Once out, there's a serious danger of retreating into past glories and boring everybody to death with long stories to which they cannot relate. Thankfully, as I drew my last month's salary from the public purse, I was about to embark on a new career that would lead me into circumstances that were just as demanding and full of equally entertaining adventures, but it did feel like agoraphobia at the time. For eight years my every waking hour had been defined and dictated by others. Suddenly I had to begin thinking and planning for myself, and it felt very alien at first. The big hurdle came in 1982 when most of the people I had spent so many happy years with got into their helicopters, flew them on to ships and sailed south to the conflict in the Falklands. It felt strange not to be going with them and somehow dirty to be conducting a commercial life while they headed south, some of them never to return.

I soon settled into the new job and every day brought new experiences as I learned how to use a helicopter in the civilian commercial role. I'd occasionally get pangs of nostalgia when the media reported the successful completion of a particularly challenging rescue flight out of the old base at Culdrose or when one of the old team dropped by our new hangar to chew the fat and gossip about old mates. It sometimes felt like they had come to look at a strange new animal in the zoo but since they all concluded the visit with a request for a job when they came out of the Navy I guess the syndrome of the other man's grass always being greener was coming into play.

In early 1982 Cornwall was hit by a freakish ice storm that just about wrecked the infrastructure of the electricity lines throughout the county. This resulted in a two-month contract to fly along the lines and report the faults. We employed Ted Webber to be the observer; a man who had only recently retired from doing the job full-time and therefore knew the role back to front. For 300 flying hours I flew no more than 100 feet above the ground and concentrated on which direction Ted was looking, rather than which way the aircraft was pointing. Without knowing it at the time these were the skills required of a film pilot whose task it is to concentrate on which way the camera is pointing and simply use the helicopter as a means of moving the camera position. As an increasing number of film companies began to use us for work in the glorious landscapes of South-West England I gradually found myself forging a career path that I don't think I'd previously known existed, but it was one into which I jumped with relish. I was becoming a film pilot.

In many ways film flying contained elements of life that I was already comfortable with. I'd pack a bag, sometimes knowing that I'd be away for a long stretch, sometimes just for a few days. Once on the job there would be a large number of people working together as a team to achieve a common objective, all of whom were there because they were at the top of their profession and could be relied upon to get the job done without causing stress to the rest of the team. The organisation was generally impeccable and the catering was outstanding.

Initially the film work was principally confined to Cornwall and the south-west, an environment I knew so well from the air that I could easily come up with suggested locations to fulfil any given set of requirements. Tasks varied from filming a local documentary about a shepherd who had walked his sheep the length of the country to major car commercials for the likes of Ford and BMW. Commercials for the television were my first introduction into the excesses of advertising. The producers of a commercial for insurance came to our patch to shoot a script about a guy who had left the handbrake off and allowed his car to roll over the edge of a clifftop – which brought back a few memories. In order to leave room for error they'd brought along five identical yellow cars. While waiting for my turn to get airborne and shoot the long drop I took a glance inside one of the cars expecting to see an empty shell. But no, it was a complete car straight out of the factory, ready for the forecourt, with engine, leather seats and stereo system. Three of the five cars plummeted to an early end before the director declared himself happy with the visual effect.

As time went by the various production teams who had come to Cornwall and enjoyed using us would ask us to go further and further afield. Even if the cost of having us fly hundreds of miles to the location was high, it was as nothing compared to the cost of hiring a local helicopter pilot who was used to flying from A to B and would thus cost the production tens of thousands of pounds in lost time while they struggled with the film task. The great fear of all producers was being on location and being unable to complete the film script as envisaged by the director. In this regard the helicopter shot was always a big risk for them so they paid for us to fly the long distances as a form of insurance for themselves, knowing that we'd get the job done. I'd frequently find myself flying the length of the country to shoot just one small sequence that would end up as no more than a couple of seconds in the final cut.

My first feature film experience took me straight to the top with a week of work on the James Bond movie *A View to a Kill*. If you've seen the film then you'll remember the sequence of the Zorin Industries airship flying over the Golden Gate Bridge in San Francisco. I'm sorry to tell you that although I shot that sequence I never went to California. The airship was filmed over the waters of the English Channel just south of Chichester and superimposed in the editing process.

In 1984 I made the huge helicopter flight to Sarajevo, in what was then Yugoslavia, in order to take part in the world broadcast of the Winter Olympics. The experience would stand me in good stead twenty years later when Helifilms, the new company I formed in 1989, won the contract to supply ten helicopters for the Athens Summer Olympics. As with much of my film work one thing led to another and in the last decade we have supplied all of the broadcast helicopters for the Asian Games in Qatar, the Commonwealth Games in Melbourne and the Soccer World Cup in South Africa.

At the end of the 1980s I flew my last passenger trip and concentrated entirely on film work. I'd been subcontracted by another helicopter company to fly an executive from London to Paris for the day, in order that he could have lunch with his daughter. He had requested the fast, sleek, twin-engined (and expensive) Agusta 109 for the trip. When we met at Battersea Heliport I warned him that the weather over Northern France was not looking good and it would be fifty-fifty whether we could complete the journey. Never the less he wanted to give it a try and so we set off into the gloom and the drizzle. The weather over the Channel turned out to be better than I expected but soon after Calais the forecasters were proved correct as the cloud base came down and the rain increased. The weather reports out of Paris precluded the choice of climbing higher and making an approach into the capital on instruments so I was forced to grope my way along at lower and lower levels. When I'd got to the stage of following a line of electricity pylons I suddenly woke up and asked myself what on earth I thought I was doing. I wasn't a rescue pilot any more and there were no lives at stake other than mine and my passenger's, so I took the right decision, albeit about thirty minutes later than I should have, and diverted to a French airfield for fuel and a reassessment of the weather.

The resultant tirade of abuse from the passenger left me dumbfounded. Had it not been for my loyalty to the other company that had given me the job I would have left him right there and then to find his own way to wherever he wanted to go. As it was I confined

myself to telling him that our survival somewhat outweighed the need for him to increase his fat arse with a lunch in Paris and that I was off back to London if he wanted to join me. From that day forwards I have enjoyed a life of film flying, largely in beautiful weather.

One of the contracts that provided the backbone to the film work during my ten years at Castle Air was for a 'cult' light entertainment show for television called *Treasure Hunt*, presented for many years by the lovely Anneka Rice, and then the former tennis player Annabel Croft, who stepped in to present the last series when Annie fell pregnant with her first child. Each year we would supply two helicopters for up to two months, hurtling around the country chasing clues for the contestants back in the studio. It was an early lesson in the difficulties associated with getting a broadcast signal back to the ground from a helicopter although in those days we only sent the voice signal and cut it together with the 'live' pictures later. On the final broadcast of the series I met Sara Hine, an incredibly switched-on researcher who made my organisational task a dream. By 1989 we had formed our company, Helifilms, and in 1994 she became my second wife. To this day we work together on all projects with Sara acting as producer and thus relieving me of commercial and organisational pressures so that I can concentrate on the aviation and the film content.

Sara claims that I stated in very early days that I wanted to direct productions, which is not an aspiration I can remember voicing but was certainly a natural progression. Apart from running the big sports gigs I mentioned, we've made many films over the years together and it's taken us to some extraordinary locations across the globe. The one that surpasses all others was filming from the top of launch pad 39B at Kennedy Space Centre just after Shuttle Atlantis had launched. On the day that we finished filming she returned to a perfect landing as I stood on the very edge of the runway. It was an emotional moment where a whole career in aviation and film seemed to come together at the same spot and I remember thinking, 'Hmm, this is fun. Not bad for a little ole' country boy born in a caravan.'

In 2011 we won the contract to supply all of the aerial filming for the twenty Formula One races around the world, another closing of the circle. In 2013 I wrote, directed and flew the helicopter on Australia's first IMAX film to be made in over 10 years, *The Earth Wins*, which Sara produced through our company Helifilms. I'd promised myself that this would be my last hurrah but then the news broke that the Commonwealth Games of 2018 would take place on the Gold Coast of Australia. Who knows if I shall be there with a helicopter strapped to my back? As with so many of the extraordinary experiences life has thrown at me, it would seem such a shame to miss it.

ACKNOWLEDGEMENTS

When my daughter Tiffany was still a small child her favourite pastime was to be read a good story. When 'Tips' reached 25 she picked up the first chapter of what would eventually become this book and exhorted me to write down the rest of the stories. I was reluctant at first; I wasn't sure how much of my time in the Search and Rescue role would be of interest to a party girl in her mid-twenties, but when your daughter flutters her eyelids can any of us resist? My son and best mate Sam, on the other hand, prides himself on rarely reading a book. If Sam reads this one, and if Tips one day uses it to tell some stories to her own children, then my job is done.

Three women have shared parts of my life. Ruth, my mum, taught me a love of words and gave me an open and enquiring mind. Charlotte, the mother of Sam and Tips, had to spend many years sharing me with helicopters. In the middle of it all she did a great job of raising two children I'm very proud of. Sara became stepmother to my kids over twenty years ago and has been the rock throughout my second career as a film pilot and director. Without her tenacity and good sense I couldn't possibly have achieved all the things that lead one good friend to remark, 'You guys just have the longest bucket list of anybody I know, and you seem to be getting through it.'

My special thanks go to:

- Janet Murphy and Jonathan Eyers for believing in the project and for fast-tracking the decision process. Also to all the team at Bloomsbury in the UK, Australia and the USA.
- My copy editor Mari Roberts for her meticulous attention to detail, her good advice and her endless sense of humour. She withheld the fact that she is the daughter of an RAF officer until the final hours of work together.
- Belinda and Wendy in the UK, to Aussie pals Adrian, Eleanor, Ross, Sarah, Martin and Jane for giving me the confidence to keep going, and for pointing out the words that meant nothing to an Australian reader, such as "tannoy"... who would have guessed?
- Paul Chaplin, an accomplished stovie, for teaching me to incorporate good common sense into aviation, to Nick Ross (who later achieved fame when he gave Kerry Packer one of his kidneys) for getting me into helicopters and to Phil Shaw for getting an impossible student through both Sea King and instrument flying training.
- Roy Flood for giving me the opportunity to slowly morph into a civvy at his expense, for teaching me the ethics of work, and for ultimately being the impetus to me in following a new path.
- Barty Smith for the many productive and fun years together in G-HELE. Also for his kindness in sharing his own memories of Emma with me.
- Mike (Mick) Wright for keeping me safe and alive for several decades by means of his consummate engineering skills.
- To Tim Fell for an all-year filming job which taught me that a film pilot needs more than a couple of basic moves in his toolbox, and for his extraordinary control of two jet engines under duress.

Most of all my thanks go to the wonderful men and women of the Fleet Air Arm with whom it was my privilege to serve for eight short years. Many of them are mentioned in the body of the book but there wasn't room for everybody. You know who you are. It was a good and special time together wasn't it?

Finally I am indebted to HRH The Duke of York, Prince Andrew, for his kindness in agreeing to write the Foreword. Notwithstanding my aversion to conflict I have great respect for the many individual helicopter pilots around the world, including His Royal Highness, who have taken their machines to war, which I thankfully never had to do.

For more information please visit my website: http://www.rescuepilot.net